Information Communication Technologies and Human Development:
Opportunities and Challenges

Mila Gascó-Hernández, International Institute on Governance of Catalonia, Spain

Fran Equiza-López, Intermón Oxfam, Spain

Manuel Acevedo-Ruiz, Independent Consultant

T0321697

IDEA GROUP PUBLISHING

Hershey • London • Melbourne • Singapore

Acquisition Editor:	Kristin Klinger
Senior Managing Editor:	Jennifer Neidig
Managing Editor:	Sara Reed
Assistant Manging Editor:	Sharon Berger
Development Editor:	Kristin Roth
Copy Editor:	Shanelle Ramelb
Typesetter:	Sharon Berger and Jamie Snavely
Cover Design:	Lisa Tosheff
Printed at:	Yurchak Printing Inc.

Published in the United States of America by
    Idea Group Publishing (an imprint of Idea Group Inc.)
    701 E. Chocolate Avenue
    Hershey PA 17033
    Tel: 717-533-8845
    Fax: 717-533-8661
    E-mail: cust@idea-group.com
    Web site: http://www.idea-group.com

and in the United Kingdom by
    Idea Group Publishing (an imprint of Idea Group Inc.)
    3 Henrietta Street
    Covent Garden
    London WC2E 8LU
    Tel: 44 20 7240 0856
    Fax: 44 20 7379 0609
    Web site: http://www.eurospanonline.com

Library of Congress Cataloging-in-Publication Data

Information communication technologies and human development:
    opportunities and challenges / Mila Gasco-Hernandez, Fran Equiza-
    Lopez and Manuel Acevedo-Ruiz, editors.
        p. cm.
    Summary: "This book aspires to describe the link between ICTs and
    human development (which includes economic, social and political
    development), to identify the potential applications of ICTs in several
    areas, and to provide insightful analysis about those factors (also
    contextual and institutional ones) that affect ICTs for development
    initiatives success or failure"--Provided by publisher.
    Includes bibliographical references and index.
    ISBN 1-59904-057-3 (hardcover) -- ISBN 1-59904-058-1 (softcover)
-- ISBN 1-59904-059-X (ebook)
    1. Information technology--Social aspects. 2. Information technology
--Economic aspects. 3. Information technology--Political aspects.
I. Gascó Hernández, Mila. II. Equiza-Lopez, Fran, 1970-   .
III. Acevedo-Ruiz, Manuel, 1963-   .
    HM851.I5314 2007
    303.48'33091724--dc22
                            2006027722
British Cataloguing in Publication Data
A Cataloguing in Publication record for this book is available from the British Library.

Information Communication Technologies and Human Development:

Opportunities and Challenges

Table of Contents

Section I:
Digital Dividends and Digital Divides around the World

Foreword

Many of those involved in considering what knowledge societies are, or will become, seem to believe that the very existence of technology will create the conditions for equitable human development. They hold fast to this belief even in the face of accumulating evidence demonstrating that the presence of information and communication technologies is not a sufficient condition to make a difference in poverty reduction. As we said in our 1998 Knowledge Societies report prepared for the United Nations Commission on Science and Technology for Development, "assembling the tools is only part of the task." We also need to assemble human capabilities that enable people to decide for themselves how they wish to take advantage of these technologies.

The dilemma is always that the innovation process with respect to both technological and human capacity has negative and positive features. For example, one of my doctoral student's research works highlights the experiences of carpentry microentrepreneurs in a small town south of Santiago, Chile. They have received training in ICT use and their business applications, and regional funding to help them acquire the necessary tools, and they have access to a regional e-procurement system. The medium- and large-sized firms in the region have taken advantage of the e-procurement system to build their businesses. But, not a single one of the microentrepreneurs has accessed the online system. The microentrepreneurs explain that they are busy working and they do not have the time to access the system or to keep up to date with its complexities. Furthermore, their profit margins have been cut dramatically because the larger firms have reduced their production costs thanks to efficiencies associated with the use of the e-procurement system. This ICT system is creating a foundation for substantial economic benefit for some, but it is having a profoundly negative impact on others. When we consider the potential role of ICTs in human development, it is essential to take account of the potential for disempowerment as well as for positive achievements.

Information and Communication Technologies and Human Development: Opportunities and Challenges provides numerous examples of why it is crucial to shift the focus from technology to information and even to communication itself. The reasons for the unsustainability of ICT investment time and again can be shown to be attributable to problems of communication, to organisational issues and poor coordination, and to a lack of financial resources as well as to failures to enable local ownership of ICT-related projects. The contributors to this volume advocate the improved mainstreaming of ICT strategies within poverty-reduction programmes, but they caution that mainstreaming will not improve the dividends associated with ICTs unless lessons about the innovation process and effective, practical application are heeded.

The first section of this book is organised around the many facets of "digital divides." The central messages are clear. There is a requirement for needs assessment, training and awareness building at the local level, and continuing opportunities for practice. National or regional e-strategies often amount to long lists of wishes unless they can be soundly embedded in broader poverty-reduction strategies—backed up by financial resources and political will. When top-down effort is disconnected from the efforts of local actors and their intermediaries, inappropriate choices about ICTs are also likely, and long-term efforts to sustain new applications, whatever the sector, will not materialise.

As Cecchini argues:

Key to the success of ICT projects for development are 'soft' issues such as local ownership and participation of the community, implementation by grassroots-based intermediaries that have the appropriate incentives to work with marginalized groups, and provision of access to locally contextualized information and pro-poor services.

This observation is echoed in Rezaian's analysis of national ICT policies in Africa. Morolong and Lekoko emphasise the need to value local knowledge and to resist "expert-led ICTs." In the case of a telecentre initiative in Indonesia, Robinson emphasises that the involvement of local partners must amount to more than a façade constructed to match the rhetoric of participation. Failure in this respect simply "accentuated differences and reconfirmed preexisting relations of power."

The second section of the book is concerned with lessons that might be drawn for future action. There is now a track record of efforts to use ICTs to better enable the poor to improve their livelihoods. The huge potential of microcredit and microfinance schemes is discussed by Amin with the caution that such initiatives remain in their infancy 30 years after they were first introduced. Lannon and Halpin show that the use of the Internet in support of the human rights movement is growing through the use of e-mail and blogs, but that information-management skills and respect of confidentiality and privacy are crucial. Similarly, in Africa the role of ICTs in education, while increasing, is subject to Northern-led discourses with insufficient resources being devoted to support local curricula development and teacher training. And in the health sector, Ibrahim, Bellows, Bhandari, and Sandhu argue that efforts to integrate ICTs must "approach the process holistically, addressing human factors, with respect to organizations, cultural context, and end users." Raghavendra and Sahay make the same point with respect to ICT support in the health sector in India in Andra Pradesh, a state that has considerable experience with promoting ICTs for development, but still experiences many failures.

Much can be learned from systematic research on the experiences of others, but as Burtseva, Cojocaru, Gaindric, Magariu, and Verlan state, "One should not automatically transfer the methods of the solution of the digital-divide problem from one country to another." Borge's work on a model for understanding how ICTs might be used to support various forms of political communication shows the large number of interdependent variables that influence choices about ICT implementations.

With the follow-up to the World Summit on the Information Society creating renewed expectations for real change, this volume must be essential reading for all those involved in making choices about how best to deploy ICTs. If the contribution of ICTs to human development is to be amplified in a way that enables people to make effective changes in areas that they value, it needs to be acknowledged that equitable societies do not develop spontaneously and that the greater speed with which information circulates in networks does not eradicate poverty. Progress depends on investment in human capacities through interventions that are realistic, ethical, and cooperative, and where strategies are responsive to needs. As Morolong and Lekoko put it, it is essential to listen.

Professor Robin Mansell

Department of Media and Communications

London School of Economics and Political Science, UK

July 2006

Robin Mansell *holds a PhD in communication. She holds the Dixons Chair in new media and the Internet in the Department of Media and Communications (London School of Economics and Political Science). She is internationally known for her work on the social, economic, and technical issues arising from new technologies, especially in the computer and telecommunication industries. Her research examines the integration of new technologies into society, the interaction between engineering design and the structure of markets, and the sources of regulatory effectiveness and failure. Her most recent book publication is* Trust and Crime in Information Societies *(Edward Elgar Publishing, 2005). She was also lead editor and contributor for* Knowledge Societies: Information Technology for Sustainable Development *(Oxford University Press, 1998).*

Preface

Technology has always played a decisive role in humanity's progress. Many international organizations have already stated that there is no doubt about the interrelationship that takes place between the adoption of information and communication technologies and economic development.

Throughout history, technology has not only strengthened economic development, but it has become a powerful tool for human development from a Senian point of view. There are many examples that endorse this thesis. Since the late '30s, and for a period of three decades, antibiotics and new vaccines gave rise to an important mortality reduction in Asia, Africa, and Latin America (a process that took about 100 years in Europe alone). In the same way, famine and undernourishment levels dropped in South Asia from 40% in 1970 to 23% in 1997 as a result of the application of technologies to crops and to the use of fertilizers and pesticides that tripled rice and wheat production levels. Finally, it is also true that, in this age of globalization, nongovernmental organizations and other civil-society movements and coalitions have become vastly diverse and influential thanks to more fluent and fast flows of information allowed by the emergence of new technologies. Due to these changes, knowledge has been widely spread.

The set of new available tools also imposes challenges to human development. New technologies establish what and how things can be done because they create new capacities to be developed by people so that they can achieve the objectives that make sense to their lives. Also, new technologies allow a better management and redistribution of resources to achieve these goals. Therefore, technology is key to human development because it improves how well resources are allocated and expands the possibilities of capacities fulfillment.

However, the positive impacts technology may have on human development may become tainted by the risks it entails. Left adrift, the technological tools may become a dangerous and wicked instrument. Their use may give rise to social exclusion, economic inequality, tension, and violence growth. That is why it is so important to design human-development policies in the context of the information and knowledge society that promote the use of new technologies in the widening of the basic structure of rights and opportunities. These should allow individuals to exercise their freedom to develop those capacities and to fulfill those achievements that make sense in their lives.

It is not easy. Today, many initiatives are still in their early stages. There is not a solid background to learn from, and many projects have been designed on a trial–and-error basis.

It is therefore the intention of this book to compile some international experiences from which to draw some lessons that could be of use to those interested in how ICT can make a difference in human development.

Human Development

The idea of development is a complex one. When the subject began in the 1940s, it was primarily driven by the progress in economic-growth theory that had occurred during the preceding period. It was dominated by the basic vision that poor countries are just low-income countries and therefore it was focused on transcending the problems of underdevelopment through economic growth. This perspective proved to be an insufficient way of thinking about development, and since the early 1990s, a new approach, pioneered by Mahbub ul-Haq, Amartya Sen, and the United Nations Development Program (UNDP), among others, began to take shape.

The human-development approach, as it was called, is the development paradigm that conceptually frames this book. It is understood as the process of expanding people's choices, that is, the range of things that a person could do and be in life, or the functioning and capabilities to function such as to be healthy and well nourished, to be knowledgeable, or to participate in the life of a community (Sen, 1989). The idea behind the concept is that development is about improving human lives and, therefore, about removing the obstacles to the things that a person can do in life.

This way of conceptualizing development has two main connotations (Sen, 1999). On one hand, development is understood as a process of expanding the real freedoms that people enjoy. If that is the case, there is a major argument for concentrating on the ends that make development important rather than merely on the means that, inter alia, play a prominent part in the process. As a result, enhancing the development process goes beyond pursuing the growth of gross national product. It requires the removal of any major sources of unfreedom such as "poverty as well as tyranny, poor economic opportunities as well as systematic social deprivation, neglect of public facilities as well as intolerance or overactivity of repressive states" (p. 3). That is why Sen distinguishes five different types of freedom: political freedoms (in the form of free speech and elections), economic facilities (in the form of opportunities for participation in trade and production), social opportunities (in the form of education and health facilities), transparency guarantees, and protective security.

On the other hand, the achievement of development is thoroughly dependent on the free agency of people. What's more, not only is free agency itself a constitutive part of development, it also contributes to the strengthening of free agencies of other kinds. As Sen wisely puts it:

what people can positively achieve is influenced by economic opportunities, political liberties, social powers, and the enabling conditions of good health, basic education, and the encouragement and cultivation of initiatives. The institutional arrangements for these opportunities are also influenced by the exercise of people's freedoms, through the liberty to participate in social choice and in the making of public decisions that impel the progress of these opportunities. (pp. 4-5)

Seeing freedom as the principal ends of development but also as its primary means is the conceptual perspective this book has adopted. As a result, the chapters included not only approach the impact of new technologies on economic development, but on the process of expanding different types of freedom. Human rights, political participation, health, and education are, therefore, some of the issues that have been sensibly tackled by our authors.

Information and Communication Technologies and Human Development: Digital Opportunities for the World

The conceptualization of the digital divide is moving beyond that of a lack of ICT infrastructure. It reflects the differences in opportunities presented to individuals, communities, or organizations by ICT and the digital revolution, mainly as a consequence of deficits in access to the technologies, capacity to use them, and relevant contents and applications. It is a consequence of other developmental divides at the same time that contributes to them. Just as ICTs are horizontal tools that span applications from agriculture to zoology, so does informational poverty have a pervasive tendency to spread to all areas of human development. It is a classic example of vicious cycles of poverty: Insufficient access to the proper resources (in this case, ICTs as information tools) results in a decreasing ability to successfully overcome development challenges and improve the quality of life, which in turn diminishes the possibilities of accessing the proper resources, and so on.

The main question is whether ICT can help reduce poverty, or as brilliantly put by Nobel laureate Nadine Gordimer, "the sum of all hungers." The answer may ultimately reside in the value of information for confronting those hungers. What is the value of information about food prices to a farmer? Or information about legal rights to someone in the "wrong" ethnic minority? Or that about pedagogic materials to a teacher in a village? In collective terms, we could also consider the aggregate value of information to an entire community. In addition, it should be noted that the "last mile of connectivity" does not need to be the last mile of information. Often the true value of ICT for poor people will reside in how their intermediaries—local government, public-service institutions like schools or clinics, nongovernmental organizations, community radio stations, and so forth—can use ICT to better address their individual needs.

It is only after assessing the value (and thus the need) of information that informed choices can be made about whether and how to use particular ICTs in specific settings. This is why, for example, there are cases of poor and marginalized women who have taken enthusiastically to the Internet for the chance to expand their horizons and communicate with others (e.g., other marginalized women) or, in other words, to expand their freedoms (in Senian terms). Thus, one way of assessing the utility of ICT in a particular context is by directly relating it to the value of information (and communication) to the people in it.

There are parallels with education worth considering. Today, education is considered a basic human right and universally accepted as fundamental for ending poverty. Yet basic education, or even just simple literacy, is at the very core of being able to access and process information, and to enable us to communicate properly, for which ICTs are practical tools.

However, only 100 years ago (and in some countries like Afghanistan, much more recently for girls) education was not a right. It was more important to have the skills for a job, and indeed many illiterate people managed to live adequately by older standards. This implies that access to ICT may in time be considered very important for individuals and a necessity for human-development processes. In fact, the very concept of literacy increasingly incorporates basic ICT skills.

In some development circles, even more importance is assigned to knowledge than to information as a critical resource. Knowledge can be described in many ways. One is through the flow from information to knowledge, where information becomes knowledge as it is interpreted and made concrete in light of personal or organizational understanding of a particular context and previous experience. Fukuda-Parr, Lopes, and Malik (2002) offer a succinct development approach to knowledge management: "scan globally, reinvent locally" (p. 18). Knowledge is increasingly perceived as one of the principal drivers of economic growth and development, whether in the north or south, as expressed in international fora like ECOSOC (Economic and Social Council), or by organizations like the World Bank, UNDP, or OECD (Organization for Economic Cooperation and Development). Most development organizations have more to provide in terms of knowledge resources than of financial resources.

The application of ICT modifies how resources are used to produce outputs, particularly when this is mediated by knowledge. Hence, gaps in the means to generate knowledge (like those resulting from the digital divide) add to the disparities in resource availability. Stiglitz (2002) claims that it is the compounded gap of resources, knowledge, and organization that really separates developed from developing countries today. Taking a cue from advanced resource-constrained countries (like Japan, Singapore, South Korea, Ireland, and now Estonia), we could propose the notion that knowledge generation is the critical link for socioeconomic development. If this is correct, modern cooperation strategies must be aimed at supporting and enabling local knowledge generation and in its wider access and sharing. In this regard, ivory towers should give way to adobe lighthouses, and ICTs are key tools for this purpose.

The issue is not so much whether ICT causes further exclusion or not, but whether it is appropriately utilized for development purposes. ICT in itself is not the cause of exclusion. This is not unlike considering whether public libraries in developing countries contribute to the exacerbation of differences because illiterate people cannot benefit from them. ICTs are tools that can be used in practical, beneficial ways, and there are myriad examples around the world to prove it; some of these uses are analyzed in this book. The problem is that the inability to apply important resources for development (and ICT is among them) will constrain the advance of human development, causing some people and communities to fall further behind. For all the concerns of the techno-skeptics, the reality is that ICT is the fabric that weaves the nervous system of the network society. Hence, the need to accelerate the developmental appropriation of ICT so that it is put to use to meet people's needs is indicated in the millennium development goals (MDGs).

Developing countries have little option but to integrate into the global network society described by Castells (1996, 1998). If the costs of these efforts are substantial (for infrastructure, capacity, and contents), they should be compared with the price of inaction, which is likely sky-high. Castells' notion of a fourth world, lacking the ability to connect or disconnect from the network society and not marked by traditional geopolitical boundaries, symbolizes collective and extreme exclusion. No wonder there are more critics of ICT for development in the north than in the south, for it is in the south that people better understand the effects and impacts of being in that fourth world.

The digital divide is the "dark side" of ICT for development. On the brighter side, however, there is an array of digital dividends, demonstrating the opportunities and resulting benefits from the developmental appropriation of technology. The problem is that they most often come in the form of small pilot projects, and pilots, in development jargon, amount to little more than anecdotes that with luck may be significantly replicated for real human impact. As Jeffrey Sachs put it in the address to the UN ICT Task Force in June 2002, speaking as special advisor to the UN secretary general on the millennium development goals and director of the UN Millennium Project, "you can't put out a forest fire with one fireman." Pilots cannot end poverty.

Pilots (and also larger projects) do, however, offer more-than-sufficient evidence to demonstrate that there are practical and valuable applications of these technologies in just about every development area. The list of applications is as wide as there are development problems. The following give just a flavor:

- Posting coastal weather information accessed through the Internet to warn fishermen of threatening conditions
- Awareness of real market prices for agricultural produce, positioning farmers in a better bargaining condition, and contributing to increase their income
- Access to legal information for human rights organizations
- Electronic networks to support the work of HIV/AIDS workers
- E-tenders in government to diminish corruption and increase efficiencies
- Telemedicine to improve medical care for people in isolated areas
- Electronic communications for coordination and real-time information during natural disasters
- Geo-referenced information systems to facilitate water-basin management
- Remote information processing as a means of job generation (sometimes for people with disabilities)
- Telecenters that become local development centers with access to information and ICT

The targeted, widespread, and innovative harnessing of ICT will make an important contribution to reaching the MDGs, which serve as a kind of present global blueprint for development. The UN ICT Task Force, a multistakeholder group under UN auspices active from 2001 to 2005, created resources to guide the use of ICT for the achievement of the MDGs in timely conjunction with the World Summit for the Information Society process. However, in the larger picture of digital dividends, we just need to return to the concept of human development: The best digital dividends come through increased choices and freedoms for increasing the quality and dignity of human life.

So do we invest in health or ICT? Even if it is a little oversimplified, that is the type of dilemma that decision makers ponder while weighing the need to shorten a particular digital divide. And when someone as well known and informed as Bill Gates publicly discusses this dilemma and questions the rationale of ICT for development, as he did during the Digital Dividends Conference in Seattle (October 18, 2000), the debate is served. There is, however, a starting problem with the way the question is formulated. Health is a human need while ICTs are tools, and therefore they cannot be compared. A similar question regarding health vs. X-ray machines more clearly illustrates the dissonance of this false dilemma. Key development objectives, such as those contained in the MDGs, should be articulated first at the national and local level. Then, in the case of health, the ICT-for-development question would be better posed as "Can ICT tools help to achieve a given health objective, and, if so, what are its costs and benefits?"

For decisions on the use of ICT for human-development processes, one perspective comes, for example, from the field of a given project or activity. Objective and methodical analysis about the use of ICT in a specific context is needed to make informed decisions on whether to use it for a defined objective, what type of ICT should be used, how much should be spent, and how those technologies should be integrated in the specific development activity. This type of analytical capacity will be practical for development actors and stakeholders, particularly during the formulation phase of projects and programs.

From the macro perspective, deciding over priorities and choices is the essence of management and at the core of public policy. Can we really say that ICTs can and should be applied for all areas of development? The short answer might be yes if and only if they are cost effective in advancing development policies. The UN ICT Task Force (2003, p. 7), referring to ICT and policy making, claims that "their potential contribution to the achievement of development objectives reinforces the need to place ICT in the mainstream of development strategies and thinking, both nationally and internationally." Moreover, UNDP (2001) and the UN Millennium Project (2003) indicate that technology is a tool for development and economic growth, and not simple reward or consequence of them. Mansell and Wehn (1998), in one of the early groundbreaking works on ICT and development, wrote the following about ICT and development priorities:

investment in ICT competes with other investments necessary for addressing development goals. This competition has sometimes suggested that there is an "either/or" question to be resolved before substantial investments in ICT or related capabilities can de decided upon. A key message of this report is that combining existing social and technological capabilities is likely to produce spin-offs in terms of social and economic value. The tensions created by competing investment priorities will not disappear. However, it is more productive to view the use of ICT as an enabler of development and a source of skills and capabilities that can make contributions in many different development contexts, than as an isolated sector for investment. This is a strong argument for establishing an effective ICT strategy. (p. 257)

If evidence and analysis (admittedly together with a bit of instinct and risk taking) lead one to accept the notion that ICT has important potential for advancing human development and empowering people, the challenge that resides is how to properly (and rapidly) harness that potential. In particular, it is how to use these technological tools for socioeconomic inclusion instead of further exclusion. The risks of the gap widening between the information "haves" and "have-nots" in a political economy characterized by globalization and competition are unacceptably high, to the point that the gap may become insurmountable, at least for many decades.

In this context, two key messages emerge from our book. First, without extensive and deliberate emphasis on building human and institutional capacity to apply ICT to development processes, any investments in infrastructure will miss the mark (and no digital divides will be bridged). Second, development stakeholders in both the south and north cannot afford to sit idle and ignore ICT in development policies and actions because of the value of information and knowledge as development resources and the emerging context of the network society (or knowledge societies). Applied to human-development concepts, ICTs become tools to address needs (or curtail unfreedoms) as well as to access opportunities (thus increasing choices). They do so across the thematic spectrum of development as the horizontal tools they are.

So what are we to make of ICT? The authors in this book provide a diverse range of approaches—some geographic, some thematic—all providing useful knowledge for policy makers. A shorthand recommendation might be to make the best of it, and to make the best with it. The key is to be realistic, objective, and practical. Leaving the hype out of the ICT-for-development equation will help: ICT is surely no development panacea. While ICTs provide access to information and stimulate the creation of knowledge, they are only part of the development puzzle. They do not provide direct benefits like food, medicine, shelter, or credits. Whoever expects development miracles needs to look elsewhere. However, ICT can be one of the pieces of the development puzzle. We do not eat information, but we can use information to grow more food and learn better nutrition habits. And in some circumstances, like natural disasters, the AIDS epidemic, or simply being in the face of rough seas (for fishermen), information simply saves lives. Most importantly, let us listen intently to stakeholders from the south as they are in the best position to understand what is best to address their own development needs.

International cooperation agencies can have significant influence on the introduction of ICT into development processes through their catalyst role as funders of pilot (experimental) projects and the support of human and institutional capacity building in developing countries. The catch is that ICT mainstreaming in cooperation agencies is in its infancy in most agencies. They integrate ICT in their operations and fieldwork to a lesser extent that what they themselves recommend to the countries they support. Data from an OECD/Development Assistance Committee (DAC) study (available at http://www.oecd.org/document/55/0,2340,en_2649_34835_34906999_1_1_1_1,00.html), which includes data up to December 2003, indicated that less than half of the 23 main donor countries represented in the DAC has an appreciable level of ICT integration in their cooperation practices; additionally, they do not explicitly contemplate it in their policies. Insufficient human capacity in ICT for development is the probable main factor to explain this, as staff from the agencies do not have sufficient understanding about the uses and possibilities of ICT for the work they do, nor do they have specialists (in most cases) to support them. A report from the UN Millennium Project (2004) goes further when it indicates that "the general attitude in a number of international agencies towards technology is skeptical or even hostile" (p. 133).

Moreover, ICT mainstreaming into development agencies will feed change processes that go far beyond instrumental changes. In many respects, development cooperation practices remain much the same as in pre-Internet days. The process of informational and technological updating should be inserted in a more comprehensive renovation in the modus operandi of these agencies. This is not that much different from what has been occurring in companies, governments, and universities, where ICT has allowed renewed models related to e-business, e-government, and virtual and online universities, respectively. To better adapt to the context

xvi

of globalization and the emergence of the information society, the international cooperation sector would do well to restructure along some type of e-cooperation or network-cooperation models, where the agencies (and their projects) would function much more as networks and through networks than is the case today.

About this Book

Information Communication Technologies and Human Development: Opportunities and Challenges is a book aimed at enlightening the above concepts and therefore at understanding how ICT can contribute to human development in several areas. In particular, its overall objectives are as follows:

1. To describe the link between ICT and human development (which includes economic, social, and political development)

2. To identify the potential applications of ICT in several areas

3. To provide insightful analysis about those factors (also contextual and institutional ones) that affect ICT for development initiatives' success or failure

4. To propose strategies to move forward and to address future challenges

The book presents insights gained by leading professionals from the practice, research, academic, and consulting side of the ICT-for-development field. This is why it should be useful to a variety of constituencies who are interested in the interrelationships between information and communication technologies and human development, including the following:

1. Politicians and public-sector officials (civil servants) who need a convenient source of information on what ICT can do for the development of their communities

2. Development professionals and practitioners who want to further explore the potential of ICT for development. This target includes headquarters and field-offices staff of large development organizations (such as the World Bank or the United Nations Development Program), staff and volunteers of nongovernmental organizations, or bilateral development agencies' staff (such as USAID, AECI, or CIDA).

3. Academicians, researchers, and students interested in the field of ICT for development

The book is presented in two sections. The first, **Section I**, "Digital Dividends and Digital Divides around the World," is a wide-ranging section that contains six chapters focused on the use of information and communication technologies in poverty-reduction initiatives as well as on the problem of the digital divide and the challenges to overcome it at regional, national, and local levels.

In particular, **Chapter I** examines the digital divide that exists within Latin American countries. It argues that ICTs are creating new opportunities that can be seized to support human development and poverty-reduction strategies. However, it also clarifies that ICT on its own cannot leapfrog the old institutional and organizational weaknesses of Latin American economies and societies.

Chapter II reviews the role of ICTs in socioeconomic development and poverty-reduction programs in sub-Saharan countries, providing an overview of the status of ICT and national ICT strategies in sub-Saharan Africa, and analyzing three major policy documents that provide the framework for economic growth and poverty-reduction efforts in most developing countries: national poverty-reduction strategies, country assistance strategies of the World Bank, and poverty-reduction support credits.

Chapters III and **IV** state shortly the basic components and the manifestations of the problem of the digital divide, as well as the ways of its solution in a specific country with its specific regional, social, historical, and political features: Moldova.

Chapter V invites readers to rethink basic questions of what the benefits of community-compatible ICT for the poor are in the context of Botswana and other African countries.

Chapter VI presents a case study of an ICT-based attempt to reduce poverty in a rural Indonesian community. Differences between the theoretical approaches adopted by the implementing agencies and the difficulties inherent in achieving these aims in practice are outlined, emphasizing, particularly, how issues relating to implementation impact on efforts to move toward greater beneficiary inclusion in socioeconomic networks.

Section II, "How ICT Promote Development? Lessons from Different Fields," reviews several initiatives that have taken place all over the world and that illustrate the use of ICT to enhance the different dimensions of the human-development concept.

Therefore, **Chapter VII** focuses on microcredit-microfinance and ICT as synergistic coagents and powerful poverty intervention tools to reach the poorest people and narrow the digital divide, thereby reducing poverty significantly in developing countries and contributing to achieving the MDGs.

Chapter VIII looks at the impact of the Internet on the worldwide human rights movement, and examines the opportunities and pitfalls of the technology and its applications for human rights organizations.

Chapter IX discusses Africa's experiences with ICT for education initiatives in current schooling systems, analyzing examples of the successful application of ICT in African schools and their actual and potential developmental spin-offs with caution. It warns of the disconnection with glaring social, infrastructural, economic, and political realities that mitigate against further system-wide success.

Chapter X approaches ICT for health applications in developing countries and argues that these projects require a deep understanding of various contextual factors, such as health and ICT infrastructure, disease burden, and sociocultural issues.

Chapter XI presents an empirical investigation of the introduction of health information systems in the primary health-care sector in India (India Health Care Project, Family Health Information Management System, and Integrated Health Information Management Systems).

Finally, **Chapter XII** seeks to build the basis for an explanatory model that establishes which factors affect and condition different political uses of ICT and which principles underlie that behavior both in developed and developing countries.

References

Castells, M. (1996). *The information age: Economy, society, culture: Vol. 1. The rise of the network society.* Oxford, UK: Blackwell Publishers.

Castells, M. (1998). *The information age: Economy, society, culture: Vol. 3. End of millennium.* Oxford, UK: Blackwell Publishers.

Fukuda-Parr, S., Lopes, C., & Malik, K. (Eds.). (2002). *Capacity for development: New solutions to old problems.* New York: Earthscan Publications.

Mansell, R., & Wehn, U. (Eds.). (1998). *Knowledge societies: Information technology for sustainable development.* New York: Oxford University Press for the United Nations Commission on Science and Technology for Development.

Sen, A. (1984). *Resources, values and development.* Cambridge, MA: Harvard University Press.

Sen, A. (1985). *The standard of living.* Cambridge, UK: Cambridge University Press.

Sen, A. (1989). Development as capabilities expansion. *Journal of Development Planning, 19,* 41-58.

Sen, A. (1999). *Development as freedom.* New York: Anchor Books.

Stiglitz, J. (2002). Knowledge of technology and the technology of knowledge: New strategies for development. In S. Fukuda-Sarr, C. Lopes, & K. Malik (Eds.), *Capacity for development: New solutions to old problems* (pp. 271-280). New York: Earthscan Publications.

United Nations Development Program. (2001). *Human development report 2001: Making new technologies work for human development.* New York: Oxford University Press.

United Nations ICT Task Force. (2003). *Tools for development: Using information and communications technology to achieve the millennium development goals.* New York: Author.

United Nations Millennium Project. (2004). *Interim report of Task Force 10 on science, technology and innovation.* Retrieved January 13, 2006, from http://www.unmillenniumproject.org/documents/tf10interim.pdf

Acknowledgments

The editors would like to acknowledge the help of all involved in the collation and review process of the book, without whose support the project could not have been satisfactorily completed.

Deep appreciation and gratitude is due to Kristin Roth, our development editor, and, most important, our friend. Her editorial support, her encouragement, and her good advice during this year have turned this project into a worthwhile book. Special thanks also go to all the staff at Idea Group Inc., whose contributions throughout the whole process from inception of the initial idea to final publication have been invaluable. In particular, thanks go to Mehdi Khosrow-Pour, whose enthusiasm motivated us to initially accept his invitation for taking on this project.

We also want to sincerely thank all those who offered constructive and comprehensive input for the different chapters. Some of these colleagues should actually be mentioned as their reviews set the benchmark. Those who provided the most comprehensive, critical, and constructive comments include Ben Bellows, Ana Sofía Cardenal, Scott D'Urso, Anatol Gremalschi, Eddie Halpin, Mahad Ibrahim, Seth Kahan, David Keogh, James Lawson, Rebecca Lekoko, Shirin Madon, Firoze Manji, Bolanle Olaniran, Stephanie Petrasch, Bruno Piotti, Steve Rains, Josep Mª Reniu, Melissa Rogers, Jean-François Tardiff, Erik Timmerman, Antony Trowbridge, and Yanina Welp.

In closing, we wish to thank all the authors for their insights and excellent contributions to this book. They have shared with us their priceless expertise, carrying out an outstanding work. Thank you to all of you for helping us spread your knowledge in the field of ICTs for development.

Finally, we want to thank our loved ones for their understanding and support throughout this project.

To Marcos, our dear "big boy," who pretended to be Tarzan, Captain Hook, Mowgli, Mr. Incredible, and many others while we were working on this book (Mila and Fran's special thanks). To Hawa, our Ethiopian princess, who elightened our lives with her arrival when this books was already finished.

To Sandra, my wife, for being an objective and sympathetic sounding board for my projects and ideas. To Mila Gascó for inviting me to take part in this particular one and her helpful guidance for some years now. To Douglas Evangelista for our long conversations about ICT and changes in the international cooperation system, and his companionship in some risky projects. And finally to the late Sharon Capeling-Alakija (formerly executive coordinator of UN Volunteers) who allowed me to dream up big projects and get them off the ground (Manuel's special thanks).

Mila Gascó-Hernández, Fran Equiza-López, and Manuel Acevedo Ruiz
Barcelona-Madrid, Spain
July 2006

Section I:

Digital Dividends and Digital Divides around the World

Chapter I

Digital Opportunities, Equity, and Poverty in Latin America

Simone Cecchini, United Nations Economic Commission
for Latin America and the Caribbean (ECLAC), Chile

Abstract

This chapter examines the digital divide that exists within Latin American countries. It argues that information and communication technology is creating new opportunities that can be seized to support human development and poverty-reduction strategies. However, it also clarifies that ICT on its own cannot leapfrog the old institutional and organizational weaknesses of Latin American economies and societies. The author hopes that understanding the deep-rooted inequalities that underlie ICT access in Latin America will not only inform researchers on the challenges for the development of the information society in the region, but also assist policy makers in the preparation and implementation of appropriate public policies.

Realizing the Human-Development Potential of ICT is not an Automatic Process

Poverty and inequality represent two enormous challenges for the countries of Latin America. In 2004, about 220 million people—43% of Latin Americans—were poor, and the average incomes of the richest 20% of the population were between 10 (Uruguay) and 44 times (Bolivia) higher than the average incomes of the poorest 20% (Economic Commission for Latin America and the Caribbean [ECLAC], 2005b). The region is considered the least equitable in the world, with vast disparities not only between rich and poor, but also between urban and rural areas, men and women, African descendants, and indigenous and nonindigenous people (ECLAC, 2005a).[1]

In an age where information and communication technology[2] is bringing about profound changes to societies in the developed world—where it is becoming essential for economic success and personal advancement, entry into good career and educational opportunities, full access to social networks, and opportunities for civic engagement (Norris, 2001)—it is thus relevant to analyze whether these technologies can contribute to human development and poverty reduction in the Latin American region, and what the impact on inequality may be.

Consensus exists that the primary task for the countries of Latin America is the transformation of their productive structures in a context of progressively greater social equity. Such a process should make it possible to achieve some of the objectives inherent to development: growth, improvement of income distribution, consolidation of the democratization process, greater autonomy, establishment of conditions that will halt the deterioration of the environment, and improvement of the quality of life of citizens (ECLAC, 1990).

It is also apparent that ICT can be utilized to support human development and poverty-reduction strategies in at least two areas: developing poor people's capacity, mainly by enhancing their access to education, health, and government services, and increasing their opportunities by improving their access to markets and the labor force (Cecchini & Scott, 2003; World Bank, 2000). However, as highlighted by Kirkman (1999, p. 1), translating the potential of ICT into reality is not simple:

> In practice, whether or not a developing country can build an ICT-based economic or social sector depends on overcoming many of the same macroeconomic and microeconomic barriers that have long contributed to its underdevelopment—What is the state of its educational system? How are telecommunications costs regulated? Is there a reliable transportation network? Are there limits on direct foreign investment? What sources of investment capital are there for small or medium sized businesses? ...The list goes on and on.

Indeed, while ICT such as the Internet and mobile phones is growing significantly in Latin America (Table 1), its increased penetration goes hand in hand with the persistent structural heterogeneity of the region's economies, characterized by the presence of a great number of low-productivity firms and workers in the informal sector, as well as with high levels of social inequality. It is thus clear that ICT on its own cannot leapfrog the old institutional and organizational weaknesses of Latin American societies and economies. Digital technologies can be used as a tool to execute solutions to poverty, but cannot root out poverty on their own; the risk that ICT actually ends up contributing to higher inequality is thus very much real (Cimoli & Correa, 2003).

Drawing on micro- and macroeconomic theory and empirical data, this chapter argues that realizing the pro-poor potential of ICT requires attentive public-policy formulation and careful policy design. Insufficient information and communication infrastructure, high access costs, and low levels of education have so far bestowed the benefits of ICT on the better off, urban segments of the population rather than on the poor and rural areas. In order to reach the poor, policies that foster the supply of low-cost and accessible telecommunications and information-technology infrastructure are needed. This chapter maintains, however, that the success of ICT projects and programs for development also depends on policies that promote the demand of ICT. These policies include the provision of locally contextualized information and pro-poor services, as well as investment in ICT training and awareness-raising campaigns. Furthermore, it suggests that successful projects are led by grassroots-based organizations that have the appropriate incentives to work with marginalized groups, and are characterized by the use of appropriate technology, local ownership and participation of the community, financial sustainability, and the use of monitoring and evaluation (M&E) techniques.

Literature on the Internal Digital Divide

In this chapter we will focus on the gaps that exist between different socioeconomic groups within the countries of the region—the "internal" digital divide—rather than on the divergence in ICT access between Latin American and developed countries—the "international divide." Accordingly, we present at this point a very brief review of some of the literature related to the internal divide.

Rogers' (1995) diffusion theory provides an important interpretation of social stratification in technological adaptation, showing that early adopters of new innovations are characteristically drawn from groups with higher socioeconomic status. Rogers also suggests that the adoption of successful new technologies often reinforces economic advantages so that the rich get richer and the poor fall farther behind. This pattern, however, is not inevitable since the conditions under which an innovation is implemented determine, in part, their social consequences. These conditions include the existence of initiatives to broaden technological access by the state and nonprofit sectors, the degree of inequality in the society, and the financial resources and educational skills required to access technology. Without state intervention, for instance, a relatively costly ICT requiring high educational skills such as the Internet is expected to exacerbate existing social divisions (Norris, 2001).

Cecchini and Scott (2003) come to similar conclusions by using a microeconomic model showing why the rich and the poor use different communication techniques and how the nature of technological change has until now been biased toward the rich, widening the digital divide. Since the value of time is lower for the poor, due to underemployment, and the cost of ICT capital is high,[3] when ICT consists of communications techniques such as oral (person to person), written word, and fixed-line telephony, the poor tend to communicate orally. The rich, who face the opposite constraints, choose to communicate via fixed-line telephony, which is relatively capital intensive. When the Internet, requiring more capital per unit of information communicated than any other existing technique, becomes available, the rich switch from fixed telephony to Internet usage,[4] while the poor continue to communicate orally. Therefore, the model has two implications for a pro-poor ICT policy. First, the relative price of capital for communications purposes should be reduced for the poor. Second, the focus of research and development in ICT has to favor user-friendly hardware and software for the poor.

Indeed, mobile phones, which unlike the Internet can be easily used even by illiterates and do not need a permanent electricity supply, are now seen by some observers as potentially the most effective response to the digital divide ("Technology and Development: The Real Digital Divide," 2005).

Using macroeconomic evidence, Forestier, Grace, and Kenny (2002) show that historically telecommunications rollout has benefited the wealthy, with a positive and significant impact on increasing income inequality within countries. The authors' regressions illustrate that countries with high initial teledensity (allowing for income) and countries that have high growth in teledensity (allowing for growth in income) see significantly higher growth in income inequality. The diffusion of the Internet in developing countries is said to be following a similar pattern, suggesting that it is a force for growing income inequality. Without intervention, ICT might be even more strongly "sub-pro-poor" than has been true for the telephone. The Internet, in fact, requires not only more ICT capital, but also a higher level of education and skill to operate than the telephone (Forestier et al.).

As Heeks and Kenny (2002) point out, the diverging effects of ICT may be a consequence of the fact that ICT was almost entirely developed within the context of high-income countries. ICT was thought of for a capital-rich setting and embodies significant quantities of technical, human, and institutional capital. Since rich countries already have a large stock of personal computers (PCs) and telephone lines, Internet access represents a small marginal investment compared to the existing fixed stock of ICT capital. They also have more educated, highly skilled employees to install, operate, and maintain ICT. In developing countries, with few PCs, limited telephone networks, and lower levels of human capital, the same is not true. Furthermore, ICT embodies within it rich countries' assumptions about ICT-friendly institutional strategies at the organizational level and ICT-friendly laws and regulations at the national level. For developing countries, where such institutional arrangements are less likely to exist, ICT warrants a range of investments in institutional reform.

Access to ICT within Latin American Countries[5]

During the 1990s, access to ICT grew at exponential rates, and today Latin America and the Caribbean is one of the developing regions with the highest penetration rates of fixed and mobile phones, the Internet, and PCs. ICT access rates, however, are still much lower than those in the developed world (the international digital divide) and testify that countries

Table 1. Percentage of ICT in Latin America and in the world, 1990 and 2003 (Source: United Nations Statistics Division [UNSD], 2006)

Region	Fixed & mobile phones		Internet users		PCs	
	1990	*2003*	*1990*	*2003*	*1990*	*2003*
Latin America and the Caribbean	6.4	40.4	0.0	9.0	0.6	6.8
Transition countries of Southeastern Europe	13.8	57.7	0.0	13.5	0.2	6.5
Eastern Asia	2.4	47.3	0.0	8.9	0.3	5.6
Western Asia	10.0	45.8	0.0	7.2	1.2	5.6
Commonwealth of Independent States	12.5	29.4	0.0	3.6	0.3	6.8
Northern Africa	2.9	21.0	0.0	3.4	0.1	3.4
Southeastern Asia	1.4	20.4	0.0	6.1	0.3	2.8
Oceania	3.4	10.1	0.0	3.8	0.0	6.1
Southern Asia	0.7	7.1	0.0	1.7	0.0	1.1
Sub-Saharan Africa	1.0	6.0	0.0	1.1	0.3	1.2
Developed countries	45.4	124.7	0.3	44.8	11.1	44.9

of the region are still far from reaching universal access (see Table 1). Here, we will thus again focus on how access is distributed within countries (the internal digital divide) using data from household surveys that support some of the ideas presented in the previous section on ICT literature.

The internal digital divide is a multidimensional phenomenon tapping many social divides (Norris, 2001) related to differences in incomes, education, and geographical area of residence. Starting with the income dimension, we can note that within Latin American countries, the poor have much worse access to ICT than rich citizens (Table 2). In Chile, in the year 2000, only 32% of the poorest 10% of households had a fixed or mobile phone; computer presence (1.9%) or Internet connection (0.8%) in the poorest households was even more infrequent. Among the richest 10% of Chilean households, contrarily, 60% had a computer and 38% an Internet connection; almost all (95%) had a fixed or mobile phone (SUBTEL, 2002). In Paraguay, in 2001, the percentage of people with access to ICT in the poorest quintile of the income distribution was close to zero, with the exception of mobile phones (6.1% of the poorest quintile declared possessing a cell phone). However, among the richest quintile, more than half of the people had a fixed or mobile phone in the household, 22% owned a PC, and 4.6% had Internet access. In Peru and in the urban areas of Ecuador, we can observe similar results. Table 2 also suggests that, with the exception of data on fixed phones in Paraguay, access to PCs and the Internet is worse distributed than access to telephones.

In a region characterized by the stratification and inequality of its educational systems, which over time have tended to become more elitist (Hopenhayn, 2002), more educated people have better access to, and make better use of, ICT. Data from household surveys show that in the countries of Latin America, between 19% (Nicaragua) and 68% (Brazil) of people with 15 years or more of education have a PC in the household. Ownership of a PC by those with less than 2 years of education ranges instead between 0.4% (Nicaragua) and 11% (Uruguay).

Table 2. Access to ICT by the poorest and richest quintile of the income distribution; selected countries, 2000-2002 (Source: Author; SUBTEL, 2002).

ICT	Country (year)	% of people with access to ICT in the household		
		Quintile 1	Quintile 5	Quintile 5/ Quintile 1
Fixed telephone	Chile (2000) a/	22.0	86.0	3.9
	Ecuador (2002) b/	33.0	81.0	2.5
	Paraguay (2001)	0.6	56.5	94.2
	Peru (2001)	7.8	46.4	5.9
Mobile phone	Chile (2000) a/	13.0	79.0	6.1
	Paraguay (2001)	6.1	55.6	9.1
	Peru (2001)	1.7	10.2	6.0
PC	Chile (2000) a/	1.9	59.7	31.4
	Paraguay (2001)	0.0	22.2	-
Internet	Chile (2000) a/	0.8	38.0	47.5
	Paraguay (2001)	0.0	4.6	-

Note: a/ deciles, b/ urban areas.

Similarly, Internet access rates of more educated citizens are between 6 (Uruguay) and 107 (Chile) times higher than those of less educated citizens.[6] As a consequence, in a country like Chile, about 89% of Internet users have had tertiary education (UNDP, 2001).

Urban areas are much better connected to ICT than rural areas. The case of Peru is illustrative: In Lima, the national capital, 45% of households have a fixed-line phone at home and 18% own a cellular phone, while only about 0.5% of rural households own a fixed-line telephone or a mobile phone. The divide is no better with respect to PCs and the Internet. In Lima, 14% of households have a computer and 44% use public Internet services, while in rural areas of Peru, these percentages are 0.1 and 3.6, respectively (see Table 3; INE Peru, 2003). In Chile in 2000, only 0.8% of rural households had access to the Internet, compared to 9.4% of urban households (SUBTEL, 2002).

Table 3. Percentage of urban and rural access to ICT in Peru, 2002 (Source: INE Peru, 2003).

	Lima	Other urban areas	Rural areas
Households with fixed telephone	44.7	21.6	0.4
Households with mobile phone	17.9	7.9	0.5
Households with computer	14.1	6.4	0.1
Households using public Internet service	44.2	30.2	3.6
Households with Internet	2.3	0.5	0.0

Table 4. Access to ICT in selected municipalities of Santiago, Chile, 2000 (Source: Raad, 2004, on the basis of the 2000 CASEN survey)

	Las Condes	La Florida	La Pintana
Monthly average household income (US$)	3,833	964	445
Poor (%)	0.2%	8.5%	31.1%
Average years of schooling	14.3	11.3	8.7
People with access to a PC (%)	85.4%	56.5%	11.3%
People with Internet access (%)	71.7%	20.1%	8.7%

Note: Exchange rate CH$/US$: 620.

It must be noted, however, that in Latin America a great heterogeneity of incomes and human development also exists within urban areas. This is reflected in different levels of access to ICT. In one of the richest municipalities (Las Condes) of the capital of Chile, Santiago, 85% of people have access to a PC, while in La Pintana, one of the poorest, access is only 20% (see Table 4; Raad, 2004).

The internal digital divide is not limited to income, education, and geographical area of residence, but also extends to gender, age, race, and ethnic inequalities. The percentage of female Web users in Latin America and the Caribbean has been estimated at around 38%, which is far from gender parity,[7] although the gender gap seems to be closing in many countries (Bonder, 2002; SUBTEL, 2002; UNDP, 2001). Older and indigenous people are also at a disadvantage. In Mexico in 2002, 36% of people aged 20 to 29 used the Internet, against 9% in the age group of 40 to 59. In the 60-and-above age group, Internet use was only 4%. In the year 2000 in Costa Rica, Mexico, and Panama, the probability of having a computer at home was 5 times higher for nonindigenous sectors of society than it was for indigenous people (ECLAC, 2003). Furthermore, data from the 2000 census show that in urban areas, household access to telephones and personal computers is lower for African descendants than for the rest of the population, especially in countries such as Brazil and Ecuador (see Table 5).

Table 5. Percentage of household ICT access by racial group in urban areas of Brazil, Costa Rica, Ecuador, and Honduras, 2000 census (Adaptation of Rangel, 2005).

Country (year)	Telephone lines		PCs	
	African descendants	*Others*	*African descendants*	*Others*
Brazil (2000)	8.1	16.1	1.3	5.1
Costa Rica (2000)	17.4	18.2	3.7	5.2
Ecuador (2001)	7.0	13.1	...	...
Honduras (2001)	6.3	6.6	...	...

Public Policies: ICT Supply

The careful formulation and design of national strategies to promote the information society is essential for countries to realize the potential of ICT for human development. Examples of such strategies in Latin America are the Digital Agenda in Chile, the Connectivity Agenda in Colombia, and e-Mexico (ECLAC, 2003). Specifically, an effective mix of public policies to foster both the supply and the demand of ICT is required to improve poor people's lives and to contribute to equitable development. Supply-side policies focus on increasing connectivity and lowering information infrastructure costs, and are a crucial prerequisite for poor people to be able to access ICT.

Universal Access to ICT

Low-cost access to information infrastructure is the basic necessary but insufficient condition to reach the poor, as inadequate or absent connectivity, expensive hardware and software, and unstable power supply reduce the economic viability of ICT projects (Kirkman, 1999). Given the budget constraints faced by Latin American governments, it is not realistic to provide telephone lines, computers, or Internet access to all households ("universal service"). Government and regulators in the region are thus concerned with policy instruments for achieving universal access, of which community telecenters[8] and public pay phones are the most common examples.

Countries such as Argentina, Brazil, Chile, Peru, and others have focused their universal-access policies on the extension of telephone lines to isolated rural areas and on the provision of free Internet access for low-income citizens through community telecenters. Indeed, in Latin America, telecenters represent one of the most common public-policy tools to provide universal access to ICT (Proenza, Bastidas-Buch, & Montero, 2001). In Argentina, the National Program for the Information Society focuses on universal access to the Internet through a countrywide network of 1,350 community technological centers that give free Internet access to lower income citizens (Finquelievich, 2003). In Chile, various governmental organizations have contributed to the creation of a network of more than 1,300 telecenters (Díaz, 2003).

Telecommunications:
Competition and Regulatory Mechanisms

During the 1990s, fixed-line teledensity and especially mobile-phone penetration grew greatly in the region. Indeed, data presented in Table 6 suggest stagnation in the growth of fixed-line phones given that in most countries mobile phones' penetration is now higher than fixed-line phones' penetration. The widespread diffusion of mobile phones in Latin America can be explained in part with the existence in several countries of forms of prepayment, which are particularly appealing for low-income citizens. The International Telecommunications Union (ITU, 2001) cites, together with competition and lower connection rates, the introduction of prepaid services in Bolivia in 1999 as one of the key factors for the rapid

Table 6. Telephone main lines and mobile telephones in Latin America, 1990-2003; per thousand people (Source: World Bank, 2005)

Country	Telephone main lines		Mobile phones	
	1990	*2003*	*1990*	*2003*
Argentina	93	219	17	178
Bolivia	28	72	4	152
Brazil	65	223	16	264
Chile	66	221	22	511
Colombia	69	179	13	141
Costa Rica	101	251	14	111
Dominican Republic	48	115	11	271
Ecuador	48	122	5	189
El Salvador	24	116	4	176
Guatemala	21	71	4	131
Honduras	17	48	0	49
Mexico	65	158	11	291
Nicaragua	13	37	1	85
Panama	93	122	3	268
Paraguay	27	46	7	299
Peru	26	67	8	106
Uruguay	134	280	25	193
Venezuela	76	111	26	273

growth of subscribers to mobile phones in the country. Before, many people did not have a credit rating sufficient to ensure post-payment mobile-phone services.

Prices of residential telephone and Internet connection remain high, both in absolute terms as well as in terms of percentages of per capita incomes, especially in the poorest countries of the region. While in developed countries such as the United States or France Internet access charges—about $15 per 20 off-peak hours—represent less than 1% of monthly per capita income, in Latin America, where charges go from $13 (Argentina) to $51 (Nicaragua), there are countries (Bolivia, Ecuador, El Salvador, Guatemala) where charges are more than 20%, 37% (Paraguay), 53% (Honduras), or even 139% (Nicaragua) of monthly per capita income (see Table 7).

One explanation for high costs is the existence of impediments to effective competition: During the 1990s, first entrants in the business after privatization often got generous exclusivity periods, as was the case of the Telefónica Group of Spain (Estache, Manacorda, & Valletti, 2002; Rozas Balbontín, 2003). Furthermore, the market by itself has not been able to provide a sufficient level of connectivity to the poorest and most isolated rural areas. Large telecommunications companies give priority to more lucrative urban markets and are reluctant to enter the smaller, less profitable rural markets. In Peru, the fixed-line telephony

Table 7. Telephone and Internet access costs in Latin America (Source: Estache et al., 2002; World Bank, 2005)

Country	Fixed monthly charges for residential phones (US$)		Average cost of a local call (US$ per 3 minutes)	Internet service provider (ISP) charges per 20 off-peak hours (US$)	ISP charges per 20 off-peak hours (% of monthly gross national product [GNP] per capita)
	1996	1999	2003	2003	2003
Argentina	11.1	13.2	0.02	13.3	3.9
Bolivia	5.5	1.7	0.09	22.3	29.8
Brazil	2.7	6.0	0.03	28.0	11.8
Chile	15.3	16.3	0.10	21.8	6.1
Colombia	2.9	3.8	0.03	18.6	12.2
Costa Rica	5.3	3.9	0.02	25.8	7.6
Dominican Rep.	6.6	6.6	0.06	33.1	17.1
Ecuador	1.0	1.7	0.03	31.8	26.3
El Salvador	...	7.1	0.07	48.1	27.8
Guatemala	0.7	0.0	0.08	31.2	21.4
Honduras	2.3	1.5	0.06	40.6	52.9
Mexico	...	14.5	0.16	22.6	4.6
Nicaragua	6.6	2.1	0.08	51.1	138.6
Panama	...	...	0.12	36.0	10.7
Paraguay	3.3	4.8	0.09	36.3	37.3
Peru	8.9	14.0	0.08	32.8	19.2
Uruguay	9.1	8.5	0.17	26.5	7.3
Venezuela	2.5	9.5	0.02	19.5	5.7
United States	...	19.9	0.00	15.0	0.5
France	...	...	0.15	14.2	0.8

market is officially liberalized, but the incumbent Telefónica del Perú offers the only wire-line service outside Lima. Many telecenter operators outside of the capital complain about bottlenecks, delivery at much lower speeds, and slow response to problems. Telecenters in Lima, where there are multiple service providers, are more likely to lease faster connections and pay lower rates (Best & Maclay, 2002).

The key to achieving connectivity for poor and rural areas is to determine how far market forces will carry the rollout of voice and data networks. The gaps left by the private sector can then be remedied by public intervention through regulatory mechanisms. One alternative is to invite private operators to bid for services in areas that are not commercially viable in return for a subsidy financed from a universal access fund. A concession contract is then awarded to the company requesting the smallest subsidy. In Chile, this mechanism was used by the telecommunications secretariat to leverage $40 million in private investment on the basis of just over $2 million of public subsidy. As a result, 1,000 public telephones have been installed in rural towns at around 10% of the costs of direct public provision. In Peru, since 1999, OSIPTEL (n.d.) has subsidized the provision of public pay phones and community telecenters to about 4,500 rural villages and 500 rural district capitals. Another alternative is represented by "microtelcos," small-scale telecom operators that combine local entrepreneurship, and municipal and community action to extend ICT services in areas that are unattractive to large private operators. The advantage of microtelcos lies in the mobilization of local resources, such as in-kind labor and private rights of way, as well as in the use of new low-cost technologies and innovative business models. In Latin America, a variety of microtelcos, ranging from telephone cooperatives in Argentina to small private operators in Colombia, are effectively servicing areas of little interest to traditional operators (Galperin & Girard, 2005).

Public Policies: ICT Demand

Even if information infrastructure becomes available at a very low cost, there is no guarantee that the poor will access ICT applications in a meaningful way. What are some of the public policies available to foster the demand for ICT?

Locally Contextualized Information and Pro-Poor Services

Content provided through ICT should not be limited to the knowledge that can be accessed from outside sources, but rather extended to ensure that the poor have the means to speak for themselves, as they know their needs, circumstances, worries, and aspirations best. In summary, the poor may demand access to locally contextualized information more than access to existing information from an alien context (Heeks, 1999). It is also advisable that ICT projects focus on a limited number of well-run pro-poor services and expand them incrementally rather than offer a great number of services that end up unutilized. Among the core services that telecenters can offer to attract clients and generate revenue, voice and text communication services are among the best candidates. Information systems that connect people to each other despite barriers of time, distance, literacy, and ownership of a telephone or PC are in fact in high demand among poor rural communities (Best & Maclay, 2002).

"Old" ICTs such as the telephone have demonstrated to be able to contribute in important manners to improve the economic opportunities of small farmers and entrepreneurs in isolated regions. An evaluation of the use of public telephones installed in poor rural areas of the Frontera Norte region of Peru in 1999 reveals that around 20% of the population use the telephone to conduct economic activities, and of that 20%, about 72% use the phone to get information on market prices. With respect to the economic impact of the project, people highlight improvements in agriculture, cattle raising, and trade. In particular, they emphasize improvements in the access to market information, which allows them to negotiate better prices and to sell more products, as well as in their contacts with clients and suppliers, in technical assistance for agriculture and cattle raising, and in the coordination of products transportation (see Table 8; OSIPTEL, 2002).

Innovative examples of the provision of content relevant for human development are Agronegocios in El Salvador and Viva Favela in Brazil. Agronegocios[9] is a project launched in 2000 by the Ministry of Agriculture that offers technical and entrepreneurial training to small farmers and fishermen through computer centers, videos, and a Web site with practical information. Ten Agronegocios centers throughout the country offer technical and commercial assistance as well as free access to a Web site with information on recommended crops, market prices, financial costs and benefits of agricultural activities, investment opportunities, and a virtual market where product supply and demand can be published (Op de Coul, 2003). Viva Favela[10] is a Web site offering information on job opportunities, credit sources, taxes, and other topics relevant for the informal sector.

In order to provide information and services that truly respond to the necessities of low-income communities, it is critical to make use of participatory surveys, such as the participatory rural appraisals (PRAs), which ensure community participation and ownership of development projects. In the rural and isolated Peruvian Alto Amazonas province, the Hispano-American Health Link program (EHAS) carried out a study on the information and communication needs of primary health-care personnel before launching a low-cost voice and e-mail communication system. The study identified poor infrastructure, time spent traveling to transmit administrative reports, lack of feedback information on epidemiological topics, and insufficient training as the main problems faced by health-care professionals. As a result, EHAS decided to center its services on remote access to health information and on distance training. Each week, an electronic health training publication is sent to health-care personnel, and courses on childhood and maternal health, childhood diarrhea, infectious diseases, nutrition, and other prevalent diseases of rural areas are sent through e-mail. These distance courses can be used off-line and have a system for self-examination and remote evaluation. Furthermore, health-care personnel can now use e-mail to receive information from health experts (A. Martínez, Pozo, Seoane, & Villaroel, 2002; F. A. Martínez, 2003).

Table 8. Economic impact of public telephones in rural areas of Frontera Norte, Peru (Source: Author, on the basis of OSIPTEL, 2002; survey in which 401 people were interviewed)

	Agriculture	Cattle raising	Commerce
Activities that have improved with the use of public phones (%)	83.3	40.9	39.9
Improved activities (% over the total in each activity):	100.0	100.0	100.0
Information on market prices	36.2	4.3	28.1
Contacts with clients and/or suppliers	33.3	5.5	54.4
Technical and/or veterinary assistance	10.2	18.9	0.6
Sales and/or prices	7.5	5.5	8.7
Products transport and/or communications needed to sell cattle	6.0	64.6	0.6
Other	6.8	1.2	7.6

Awareness Raising and Training

The presence of useful ICT applications does not guarantee that the poor will make use of them. Raising awareness among the poor about the potential of ICT (for instance, in the creation of new opportunities in the job market) is thus another key aspect of successful ICT projects and programs. Word of mouth is often a very powerful tool for publicity: Leaders of poor communities, as well as schoolchildren, could be brought to telecenters for a demonstration that shows what ICT can do for them. Furthermore, investment in customized training in information-technology skills represents one of the most important factors that may facilitate access to new ICT by low-income citizens (Norris, 2001). In particular, training for poor people with low levels of education should focus on innovative, interactive, and participatory training approaches as learning is more effective through practice.

In Brazil, the Committee for Democracy in Information Technology (CDI) has provided computer and civics training to young people living in urban slums, or favelas, since 1995. CDI emerged from the belief that computer literacy can maximize opportunities in the job market and promote democracy and social equity. Along with training in word processing, spreadsheets, accounting programs, and Web design, CDI teaches civic participation, nonviolence, human rights, environmental awareness, health, and literacy. There is growing anecdotal evidence of CDI's success on several fronts. After a 3- or 4-month course, graduates are said to find well-paid jobs, start microbusinesses, or become certified teachers within the organization. Some CDI graduates who had dropped out of public school have decided to go back and complete their formal education; many others put their computer skills to work in various community activities, including health education and AIDS awareness campaigns. A survey conducted in 2000 by Instituto de Estudos da Religião (ISER), a research institute, confirmed that the program is reaching the poor and that 87% of students consider that CDI courses have contributed to positive changes in their lives (see Table 9). The teaching environment, however, is a difficult one: Sometimes students cannot get to school because criminal gangs do not let them (CDI, n.d.; World Bank, n.d.).

At the national level, it is important to launch countrywide awareness campaigns to sensitize the population to the potential of ICT and to train poor people in the use of the new technologies. In 2003, the government of Chile trained about 100,000 people in the use of personal computers and the Internet through a national campaign of digital alphabetization. The campaign, which will continue up to 2005, is directed at workers and microentrepreneurs. These take 18-hour courses that help them learn word processing and Web surfing (Gobierno de Chile, 2003).

Public schools can also play an important role in the diffusion of knowledge about ICT through programs that provide computer and Internet access to students. These programs are currently under way in several countries of the region, such as Brazil, Chile, and Costa Rica (Hopenhayn, 2002, 2003). However, while it is important to train and sensitize students about the use of ICT, to expect PCs to be a source of deep changes in classrooms seems naïve and could lead away from a thorough analysis of what prevents institutional reforms of education. Research from the United States, where the average number of students (from kindergarten to grade 12) per PC in school went down dramatically from 125 in 1981 to only 5 in 2000, shows no evidence that computers can be credited with any student achievement gain at any level (Cuban, 2001).

Table 9. CDI student profile and impact of courses in Brazil (Source: Author, on the basis of the Information and Development Program, infoDev, 2003)

	%
Student profile:	
Aged between 10 and 18	65
Women	56
African descendants	65
Live in households with four or more members	77
Without income	63
With income between one and two minimum salaries	29
Impact of courses:	
Courses corresponded to expectations	90
Courses contributed to a positive change in the life of the student	87

Implementation of Public Policies

Appropriate Technology

Some prerequisites are needed to make the introduction of ICT in development projects and programs cost effective and sustainable, including not only a stable electric power supply and good connectivity, but also the human capacity to manage hardware and software. If these essential factors are not present, it may be better to look for low-tech but more appropriate solutions.

For instance, in Latin America, the use of electronic commerce on the part of micro and small businesses still faces enormous obstacles. Among the most important challenges to the financial sustainability of micro and small electronic-commerce activities, we should highlight the high costs of deliveries; the low levels of the quality of telecommunications infrastructure, especially in rural areas; the lack of human capital needed to fix equipment when problems arise (SustainIT, n.d.); and the low penetration of credit cards in several countries of the region. In Bolivia, for example, at the end of the last decade there were only 200,000 credit cards in circulation, corresponding to less than 2% of the population (ITU, 2001).

Clearly, no single technology constitutes a "magic bullet," and the type of ICT that will be appropriate depends on the circumstances (Organisation for Economic Cooperation and Development [OECD], 2005). In Peru, EHAS devotes special attention to the maintenance of its low-cost voice and e-mail communication system based on VHF (very high frequency) radio and solar power. The program has set up local security backups for all hard drives and a remote maintenance system to reach all the computers through radio links (A. Martinez et al., 2002; F. A. Martinez, 2003). In Bolivia, Prodem Private Financial Fund (Prodem FFP) employs smart cards,[11] voice-driven ATMs (automated teller machines), and fingerprint-recognition technology to provide financial services to low-income communities. Many of its 50,000 customers are illiterate, speak only the local Quechua or Aymara languages, have no familiarity with modern financial services, and often live in rural areas lacking a reliable telecommunications infrastructure. In order to serve this market, Prodem FFP offers secure access to ATMs with color-coded touch screens. When customers use an ATM, they can choose to receive audio instructions in Spanish, Quechua, or Aymara. Since the customers' account balances are stored in the smart card, it is not necessary for the ATM to connect to the Internet to complete a transaction. ATMs are assembled in Bolivia at half the cost of a traditional ATM with limited functionality (Hernandez & Mugica, 2003).

Radio programming, cheap enough to be produced locally and in a range of languages, can be used to inform farmers about agricultural techniques and commodities prices. In Latin America, most radio programming (as opposed to Internet content) is produced locally or nationally. In Peru alone, an estimated 180 radio stations offer programs in Quechua, a language spoken by around 10 million people and almost completely absent from the Internet (Kenny, 2002). Furthermore, in areas with poor connectivity, databases that can be accessed off line as well as the delivery of documents and certificates on floppy disks may be an alternative to Internet-based versions of e-government.

Community Participation and Ownership

The advantages of community ownership[12] have long been demonstrated in infrastructure projects in developing countries. Whether in irrigation or electricity projects, community ownership and participation means that the community is willing to invest in the projects, that the projects are well maintained, that the infrastructure can better address community needs, and that community resources can be leveraged (Girard & Ó Siochrú, 2005). Organizations planning ICT projects and programs should thus ensure that ICT applications respond to the priorities of the community as the ownership and development of ICT applications in collaboration with local staff foster the success and resilience of ICT projects. In Brazil, CDI schools are created through partnerships with community organizations, nongovernmental organizations (NGOs), and religious groups. Communities have complete ownership of the schools and are responsible for their staffing, management, and maintenance. To develop a CDI school, a community sets up a committee to assess local demand, identify future instructors and a suitable location, and establish security measures for the computers. CDI trains the instructors, works with the school to obtain a hardware donation from sponsors, helps the school install the computers, and once a school has been established, serves as a consultant. It is the community that is responsible for making the school self-sustainable (CDI, n.d.; World Bank, n.d.).

In contrast, outside control and top-down approaches waste resources in the initial periods of projects, endangering their future sustainability. A 2000 survey of Internet access centers set up by the government of Buenos Aires found that although the program was providing free Internet access, it did not provide training to users nor did it promote the participation of the local community in the decisions related to the project. Researchers that analyzed the survey observed that telecenters can have an impact on society when the members of a local community have a sense of ownership and take active participation in management activities, promoting the telecenter sustainability (Finquelievich, 2001). Menou, Poepsel, and Stoll (2004, p. 48) noted that governmentally initiated telecenters set up without adequate preparation on the part of the institutions hosting them (schools, public libraries, and others) have been characterized by a "continuing seesaw between emphatic promises, delayed and/or partial implementation, and occasional implementation especially in pre-election times" more than by sustainable development. Others in Latin America have observed that purely commercial telecenters have a particularly limited capacity to benefit low-income populations with little education (Proenza et al., 2001).

Grassroots ICT Intermediaries

In Latin America, direct ownership and use of ICT, for instance, through a PC with Internet access, applies only to a relatively small fraction of the population. Poor people have to rely on a human intermediary between them and ICT, in what is termed a "reintermediation model" (Heeks, 2001).

In Chile, for instance, the majority of Internet users belonging to middle and lower middle socioeconomic classes access the Web through a third person, while high-income citizens are usually direct Internet users (Instituto de Estudios Mediales UC, 2004).[13] The profile of the intermediaries who add human skills and knowledge to the presence of ICT is thus critical for projects that want to reach the poor (Heeks, 1999). Successful examples of ICT projects for poverty reduction are conducted by grassroots intermediaries that have the appropriate incentives and proven track record of working with poor people. A study on telecenter initiatives in Latin America noted that to achieve economic and social development, they need to "be run by someone that is personally committed to the project, willing to contribute his or her own capital and time, backed by the community in which the center operates, and willing to address the community's objectives and needs" (Proenza et al., 2001, viii). If these intermediaries are grassroots based, understand the potential of ICT for social change, and can be held accountable to the communities they serve, they can be tremendously effective in promoting local ownership of ICT projects. Given the right incentives and opportunities, these intermediaries are keen to make access to information easily available for everybody and are willing to train others in the community.

Financial Sustainability, Monitoring, and Evaluation

A major challenge for ICT projects is reaching financial sustainability, but, since most ICT projects are recent, experience in sustainability is limited. The spending capacity of the poor is low by definition and limits the chances to provide for operating costs, which are higher in rural than in urban areas. In rural areas, telecommunications cost much more, computer equipment maintenance is hard to find and expensive, and skilled operating and maintenance personnel are practically nonexistent. Deficiencies in the rural power supply make additional devices necessary, such as voltage stabilizers, surge suppressors, backup power supplies, shock protection, and grounding. Where no electricity is available, recourse must be made to solar or wind energy, which raises costs (Proenza et al., 2001).

How will we know whether the benefits derived from existing ICT projects outweigh the costs? In order to answer this question, rigorous monitoring and evaluation of the social and economic benefits of ICT projects are needed. M&E measure performance, identify and correct potential problems early on, and improve the understanding of the relationship between different poverty outcomes and ICT policies (Kenny, Navas-Sabater, & Quiang, 2001). M&E are especially needed to measure the success of many pilots currently under way. In fact, in the case of pilots, successful outcomes might be implicitly biased due to the choice of favorable places and conditions. Projects might not yield the same results in more challenging and realistic situations. Some (infoDev, 2005) even go as far as suggesting that while undertaking M&E during and after an ICT pilot project is a standard good practice to address the immediate purposes of a project, this is not sufficient; ICT pilot projects should thus be viewed as applied research, addressing specific hypotheses and generating appropriate ideas. In particular, ICT pilot projects should be assessed in terms of their contribution to core development priorities and as to whether they can be taken to scale.[14]

Conclusion

In Latin America, as in much of the developing world, reaching the poor and realizing the potential of ICT for human development and poverty reduction is a difficult endeavor. Low-cost and accessible telecommunications and information-technology infrastructure are necessary but insufficient conditions to reach the poor. Key to the success of ICT projects for development are "soft" issues such as local ownership and participation of the community, implementation by grassroots-based intermediaries that have the appropriate incentives to work with marginalized groups, and provision of access to locally contextualized information and pro-poor services. Attention must be also placed on training, awareness-raising campaigns, financial sustainability, and monitoring and evaluation.

References

Best, M. L., & Maclay, C. M. (2002). Community Internet access in rural areas: Solving the economic sustainability puzzle. In *The global information technology report 2001-2002: Readiness for the networked world* (pp. 76-88). Cambridge, MA: Oxford University Press.

Bonder, G. (2002). *From access to appropriation: Women and ICT policies in Latin America and the Caribbean.* Paper presented at the Expert Group Meeting on ICTs and their Impact on and Use as an Instrument for the Advancement and Empowerment of Women, Seoul, Republic of Korea.

Cecchini, S., & Scott, C. (2003). Can information and communications technology applications contribute to poverty reduction? Lessons from rural India. *Information Technology for Development, 10*(2), 73-84.

Cimoli, M., & Correa, N. (2003). Nuevas tecnologías y viejos problemas: ¿Pueden las TICs reducir la brecha tecnológica y la heterogeneidad estructural? In F. Boscherini, M. Novik, & G. Yoguel (Eds.), *Nuevas tecnologías de información y comunicación: Los límites en la economía del conocimiento* (pp. 55-72). Buenos Aires, Argentina: Miño y Davila.

Committee for Democracy in Information Technology (CDI). (n.d.). *Institutional profile.* Retrieved January 14, 2004, from http://www.cdi.org.br

Cuban, L. (2001). *Oversold and underused: Computers in classroom.* Cambridge, MA: Harvard University.

Díaz, A. (2003). *La agenda digital 2003-2005.* Chile: Ministerio de Economía del Gobierno de Chile.

Economic Commission for Latin America and the Caribbean (ECLAC). (1990, March). *Changing production patterns with social equity* (LC/G.1601-P/I, ECLAC Books No. 25). Santiago, Chile: Author.

Economic Commission for Latin America and the Caribbean (ECLAC). (2003). *Road maps towards an information society in Latin America and the Caribbean.* Santiago, Chile: Author.

Economic Commission for Latin America and the Caribbean (ECLAC). (2005a). *The millennium development goals: A Latin American and Caribbean perspective.* Santiago, Chile: Author.

Economic Commission for Latin America and the Caribbean (ECLAC). (2005b). *Panorama social de América Latina 2004.* Santiago, Chile: Author.

Estache, M., Manacorda, M., & Valletti, T. (2002). *Telecommunication reforms, access regulation, and Internet adoption in Latin America.* Washington, DC: World Bank.

Fink, C., & Kenny, C. (2003). *W(h)ither the digital divide?* Washington, DC: World Bank.

Finquelievich, S. (with Lago Martínez, S., Jara, A., Bauman, P., Pérez Casas, A., Zamalvide, M., Fressoli, M., & Turrubiates, R.). (2001). Los impactos sociales de la incorporación de las TICs en los gobiernos locales y en los servicios a los ciudadanos: Los casos de Buenos Aires y Montevideo. In M. Bonilla & G. Cliche (Eds.), *Impactos sociales de las tecnologías de información y comunicación (TIC) en Latinoamérica y el Caribe* (pp. 213-278). Quito, Ecuador: FLACSO-IDRC.

Finquelievich, S. (2003). *ICT and economic development in Latin America and the Caribbean.* Paper presented at the World Summit of Cities and Local Authorities on the Information Society, Lyon, France.

Forestier, E., Grace, J., & Kenny, C. (2002). Can information and communication technologies be pro-poor? *Telecommunications Policy, 26*, 623-646.

Galperin, H., & Girard, B. (2005). Microtelcos in Latin America and the Caribbean. In H. Galperin & J. Mariscal (Eds.), *Digital poverty: Latin American and Caribbean perspectives* (pp. 93-114). Lima, Perú: REDIS-DIRSI.

Girard, B., & Ó Siochrú, S. (2005). *Community-based networks and innovative technologies: New models to serve and empower the poor.*

Gobierno de Chile. (2003, May 13). Campaña de alfabetización digital beneficiará a medio millón de chilenos. *Economia.cl.* Retrieved June 30, 2003, from www.economia.cl

Godoy, S., & Herrera, S. (2004). Internet usage in Chile and the world: First results of the World Internet Project-Chile. In *Cuadernos de información* (No. 16, pp. 71-84). Santiago, Chile: Universidad Católica, Escuela de Comunicación.

Heeks, R. (1999). *Information and communication technologies, poverty and development* (Development Informatics Working Paper Series, Paper No. 5). Manchester, United Kingdom: University of Manchester, Institute for Development Policy and Management.

Heeks, R. (2001). *Understanding e-governance for development* (i-Government Working Paper Series, Paper No. 11). Manchester, UK: University of Manchester, Institute for Development Policy and Management.

Heeks, R., & Kenny, C. (2002). ICTs and development: Convergence or divergence for developing countries? In *Proceedings of the Seventh International Working Conference of IFIP WG 9.4, Information and Communication Technologies and Development: New Opportunities, Perspectives and Challenges* (pp. 29-44).

Hernandez, R., & Mugica, Y. (2003). *Prodem FFP's multilingual smart ATMs for microfinance: Innovative solutions for delivering financial services to rural Bolivia* (What Works Case Study). World Resource Institute.

Hopenhayn, M. (2002). Educar para la sociedad de la información y de la comunicación: Una perspectiva Latinoamericana. *Revista Iberoamericana de Educación, 30*, 187-217.

Hopenhayn, M. (2003). Educación, comunicación y cultura en la sociedad de la información: Una perspectiva Latinoamericana. *CEPAL Review, 81*, 175-193.

INE Peru (Instituto Nacional de Estadística, Peru). (2003). *System of indicators of information and communication technologies.* Presented at Monitoring the Information Society: Data, Measurement and Methods, Geneva, Switzerland.

Information and Development Program (infoDev). (2003). *ICT for development contributing to the millennium development goals: Lessons learned from seventeen infoDev projects.* Washington, DC: World Bank.

Information and Development Program (infoDev). (2005). *Framework for the assessment of ICT pilot projects: Beyond monitoring and evaluation to applied research.* Washington, DC: World Bank.

Instituto de Estudios Mediales UC (Universidad Católica). (2004). *Principales resultados WIP Chile.* Santiago, Chile: Instituto de Sociología UC-World Internet Project.

International Telecommunications Union (ITU). (2001). *Internet en los Andes: Estudio de caso sobre Bolivia.*

International Telecommunications Union (ITU). (2003, November 19). *ITU Digital Access Index: World's first global ICT ranking* [Press release]. Geneva, Switzerland: Author.

Kaufmann, D. (2002). *Governance, corruption and poverty: Analytical and empirical approaches.* Presented at *Attacking Poverty for APP Family*, Washington, DC.

Kenny, C. (2002). *The costs and benefits of ICTs for direct poverty alleviation*. Washington, DC: World Bank.

Kenny, C., Navas-Sabater, J., & Quiang, C. (2001). Information and communications technologies and poverty. In *World Bank poverty reduction strategies sourcebook*. Washington, DC: World Bank.

Kirkman, G. (1999). *It's more than just being connected: A discussion of some issues of information technology and international development*. Paper presented at the Development E-Commerce Workshop, MA.

Martínez, A., Pozo, F. del, Seoane, J., & Villaroel, V. (2002). EHAS program: Rural telemedicine systems for primary healthcare in developing countries. In *Proceedings of the 2002 International Symposium on Technology and Society (ISTAS '02), Social Implications of Information and Communication Technology* (pp. 31-36).

Martínez, F. A. (2003). *Evaluación de impacto del uso de tecnologías apropiadas de comunicación para el personal sanitario rural de países en desarrollo*. Unpublished doctoral dissertation, Escuela Técnica Superior de Ingenieros de Telecomunicación, Universidad Politécnica de Madrid, Madrid, Spain.

Menou, M., Poepsel, K., & Stoll, K. (2004). Latin American community telecenters: It's a long way to TICperary. *The Journal of Community Informatics, 1*(1), 39-57.

Norris, P. (2001). *Digital divide: Civic engagement, information poverty, and the Internet worldwide*. New York: Cambridge University Press.

Op de Coul, M. (2003). *ICT for development case studies: Central America*. Oneworld International/Building Digital Opportunities.

Organisation for Economic Cooperation and Development (OECD). (2005). Good practice paper on ICTs for economic growth and poverty reduction. *DAC Journal on Development, 6*(3), 27-96.

OSIPTEL (Oranismo Supervisor de Inversión Privada en Telecomunicaciones). (2002). *Estudio sobre las condiciones de uso y el impacto de la telefonía en los centros poblados rurales que forman parte del Proyecto Frontera Norte*. Fondo de Inversión en las Telecomunicaciones (FITEL).

OSIPTEL. (n.d.). *Rural telecommunications and universal access in Peru: Fund for Investment in Telecommunications (FITEL)*. Retrieved February 2, 2004, from *http://www.osiptel.gob.pe/Index.ASP?T=P&P=3295*

Proenza, F. J., Bastidas-Buch, R., & Montero, G. (2001). *Telecenters for socioeconomic and rural development in Latin America and the Caribbean*. Washington, DC: FAO, IADB, ITU.

Raad, A. M. (2004). Reflexiones sobre la participación en una cultura digital. In R. A. Dujisin & M. A. Porrúa (Eds.), *América Latina puntogob: Casos y tendencias en gobierno electrónico*. Santiago, Chile: FLACSO-Chile & Organization of American States (OAS).

Rangel, M. (2005). *La población afrodescendiente en América Latina y los Objetivos de Desarrollo del Milenio. Un examen exploratorio en países seleccionados utilizando información censal*. Presented at Seminario Pueblos Indígenas y Afrodescendientes en América Latina y El Caribe, Santiago, Chile.

Rogers, E. M. (1995). *Diffusion of innovations* (4th ed.). New York: Free Press.

Rozas Balbontín, P. (2003). Gestión pública, regulación e internacionalización de las telecomunicaciones: El caso de Telefónica S.A. *ECLAC, Serie Gestión Pública, 6*. Santiago, Chile: ECLAC.

SUBTEL (Subsecretaría de Telecomunicaciones). (2002). Caracterización socioeconómica de los servicios de telefonía y tecnologías de información y comunicación. *Serie Informes de Estadísticas del Sector de las Telecomunicaciones, 4*. Santiago, Chile: Gobierno de Chile.

SustainIT. (n.d.). *PEOPlink*. Retrieved January 10, 2004, from http://www.sustainit.org/cases/full_cases.htm

Technology and development: The real digital divide. (2005, March 10). *The Economist*, p. 9.

United Nations Development Program (UNDP). (2001). *Human development report 2001: Making new technologies work for human development*. New York: Oxford University Press.

United Nations Development Program (UNDP). (2002). *Human development report 2002: Deepening democracy in a fragmented world*. New York: Oxford University Press.

United Nation Statistics Division (UNSD). (2006). *World and regional trends: Data for years around 1990 and 2000*. Retrieved January 30, 2006, from http://millenniumindicators.un.org/unsd/mi/mi_worldregn.asp

World Bank. (2000). *World development report 2000/2001: Attacking poverty*. New York: Oxford University Press.

World Bank. (2002). *Information and communication technologies: A World Bank group strategy*. Washington, DC: Author.

World Bank. (2005). *World development indicators 2005*. Washington, DC: Author.

World Bank. (n.d.). Case study: Committee for the Democratization of Information Technology Brazil. In *School based telecentres training materials*. Retrieved January 14, 2004, from http://www.worldbank.org/worldlinks/telecentres/workshop/sbt-pdf/case-studies/allcasestudies_pdf.pdf

Endnotes

[1]   In Latin America, indigenous people (who account for more than 25% of the population in Bolivia, Ecuador, Guatemala, and Peru) and African descendants (who account for more than a quarter of the population in Brazil, Nicaragua, and Panama) are, to a large extent, the poorest in the region, have the worst socioeconomic indicators, and receive scant cultural recognition or access to decision-making levels (ECLAC, 2005a).

[2]   ICT can be defined as the set of activities that facilitates the capturing, storage, processing, transmission, and display of information by electronic means (World Bank, 2002).

³   In this model, ICT capital consists of hardware, software, and human capital.

⁴   Of course, in practice the rich are likely to use both mobile phones and the Internet, but each for different purposes. Furthermore, mobile phones can in certain circumstances provide access to the Internet.

⁵   As highlighted by Fink and Kenny (2003), the digital divide should not be measured only on the basis of access to ICT, but also on the basis of the impact of the use of the new technologies. However, the current availability of data substantially limits measurement possibilities and, therefore, we will have to focus on access to ICT.

⁶   Again, we are comparing persons with 15 years or more of education with persons with 2 or less years of education, and are referring to Internet access in the household.

⁷   Given that women have a life expectancy (75.2 years in Latin America) higher than men (68.8 years), and that the elderly have less access to ICT than other age groups, it would be advisable that gender parity indices on ICT access take into account the age structure of the population.

⁸   In Latin America, telecenters have fairly standard features. They consist of premises stocked with several PCs located on desks or tables and with chairs for users. The main service offered is access to the Internet and to software such as word processing and spreadsheets (Proenza et al., 2001).

⁹   See http://www.agronegocios.gob.sv

¹⁰   See http://www.vivafavela.com.br

¹¹   A smart card looks like a plastic credit card and has a microprocessor or memory chip embedded in it. The chip stores electronic data and programs that are protected by security measures enabling controlled access by appropriate users. Smart cards provide data portability, security, convenience, and transparency of financial records and transactions.

¹²   Community ownership can refer to three related concepts, often found in some combination: a process of internalisation of responsibility for a development process and its outcomes, a determining degree of decision-making power, and full or majority legal ownership of an initiative (Girard & Ó Siochrú, 2005).

¹³   The study excluded the poorest Chileans, those with household monthly incomes lower than $160, corresponding to 13.5% of the population (Godoy & Herrera, 2004). It is to be expected that the proportion of Internet users through intermediaries among the poorest is even higher than in other socioeconomic levels.

¹⁴   It must be noted, however, that the rapid pace of technological innovation and social adaptation often makes studies on the impact of ICT what Norris (2001, Chap. 2 p. 1) has called "blurred snapshots of a moving bullet."

Chapter II

Integrating ICTs in African Development:
Challenges and Opportunities in Sub-Saharan Africa

Bobak Rezaian, The World Bank, USA

Abstract

This chapter reviews the role of information and communication technologies in socio-economic development and poverty-reduction programs in sub-Saharan countries. To this end, the author first provides an overview of the status of ICTs and national ICT strategies in sub-Saharan Africa. He then analyzes the treatment of ICTs in three major policy documents that provide the framework for economic growth and poverty reduction efforts in most developing countries. These are (a) national poverty-reduction strategies, (b) country assistance strategies of the World Bank, and (c) poverty-reduction support credits. The analysis reveals that while a majority of national ICT policies strongly promote the use of ICTs for socioeconomic development, the poverty-reduction and country assistance strategies focus primarily on the use of ICTs in public-sector management. Hence, there is a persistent disconnection between the ICT policies and the poverty-reduction strategies. The author identifies some of the main challenges and the substantial opportunities that would arise from the mainstreaming of ICTs in national development initiatives.

Background

The contribution of information and communication technologies to economic growth in developed countries has been the subject of research, discussion, and debate since the early 1990s.[1] The Organization for Economic Cooperation and Development (OECD) has quantified the positive contribution of ICTs to gross domestic product (GDP) growth in several advanced economies.[2] Some of these countries have taken the necessary steps to create an information society by educating citizens and gradually organizing their economy around knowledge and information.

The potential impact of ICTs on socioeconomic development and the possible use of ICTs as effective tools for facilitating service delivery to the poor have led to a global debate on the role of ICTs as enablers of poverty reduction in developing countries. Based on a series of ICT success stories in developing countries, various researchers suggest that ICTs can help promote local economic growth, expand social and cultural opportunities, increase the efficiency of markets and institutions, facilitate public-service delivery, and provide the poor with a voice in decisions that affect their lives and communities.[3]

Developing countries and their development partners are investing considerable resources in harnessing the promise of ICTs for poverty reduction and economic growth.[4] Yet, most ICT success stories have remained anecdotal as scaling up pilot initiatives on a sustainable basis has proven difficult.[5] This trend has been more pronounced in sub-Saharan Africa (SSA), where the development efforts are often exacerbated by the complexity of challenges in adapting the global knowledge and technology to local conditions and needs.

Clearly there are major differences between the developed and developing countries in terms of requirements for the effective use of ICTs. These requirements include adequate information and communication infrastructure, affordable access to ICTs, well-trained human resources, and incentives for the use of appropriate technologies to improve productivity and efficiency in service delivery and production. These differences are bound to influence how ICTs can play an effective role in the socioeconomic development process.

In September 2000, the United Nations Millennium Summit adopted eight specific millennium development goals (MDGs) to measure the progress of global development efforts. These include the eradication of extreme poverty and hunger; universal primary education; gender equality and the empowerment of women; the reduction of child mortality; the improvement of maternal health; the combating of HIV/AIDS, malaria, and other diseases; the ensuring of environmental sustainability; and global partnerships to attain a more peaceful, just, and prosperous world.[6]

The MDGs are now a benchmark for measuring the success or failure of most poverty-reduction programs, and the more recent national poverty-reduction strategies have incorporated the MDG targets as an integral part of their goals and objectives.

In what follows, the national poverty-reduction strategies, country assistance strategies (CASs) of the World Bank, and the poverty-reduction support credits (PRSCs, which are often a multidonor basket fund for providing budget support to developing countries) are reviewed for their discussion of ICTs as development tools. Key categories for identifying the appropriate ICT discussions in poverty-reduction strategy papers (PRSPs), CASs, and PRSCs are selected from different aspects of the ICT sector, as well as the priority sectors in each country, for example, in health, education, agriculture, and the environment.

The broader categories selected for this review include telecommunications infrastructure; broadcasting; computer technology; local content and applications; human-resource development; public-sector applications; policy and regulatory environment; information generation, access, and dissemination; ICT applications in agriculture, health, and education; rural connectivity; service delivery to the poor; ICT-sector development; small- and medium-enterprise development, and poverty monitoring.

In this chapter, the author reviews the set of available policy documents (30 PRSPs, 25 CASs, and 21 active or closed PRSCs). He then normalizes the results within each category to allow for a more meaningful comparison. At the time of this review (mid-2005), there were only 11 countries in Africa that had prepared all three poverty-reduction strategy documents (PRSP, CAS, and PRSC). Therefore, the author makes a comparison between the results for the above group of 11 countries and the larger set to examine the consistency of his findings.

The majority of national ICT policies strongly promote the use of ICTs for economic growth, improved governance, public-service delivery, and private-sector development. However, these recommendations often have neither been integrated into the strategies and action plans for poverty reduction in their respective countries, nor have they strongly influenced them. Some of the contributing factors to this endemic disconnection are discussed, and a few practical steps are proposed for closing this gap.

It must be noted that the analyses in this chapter are qualitative in nature since the available data on the role and impact of the ICTs in developing countries are very limited. Quantifying and measuring the impact of the ICT activities proposed in PRSP, CAS, and PRSC documents also pose very significant challenges. In the absence of more reliable quantitative data, however, it is hoped that the qualitative assessments of this information will contribute to a better understanding of the challenges and opportunities, and will lead to a more effective integration of appropriate technologies in development efforts.

The Dialogue on ICT for Development

The past decade has witnessed a series of high-level international efforts to integrate information and communication technologies into development programs and poverty-reduction efforts. We define poverty to mean more than inadequate income or the inability to meet basic needs like nutrition, clothing, and shelter: It also incorporates disadvantages in access to land, credit, health, and education, and vulnerability to violence, external economic shocks, natural disasters, and social exclusion.[7]

In 1996, the United Nations Economic Commission for Africa (UNECA) initiated the African Information Society Initiative (AISI) as a common vision for Africa to create effective digital opportunities to speed up the continent's entry into the global information and knowledge economy.[8]

Several international initiatives have supported the use of ICT for development (ICT4D), the most prominent being the G-8's (group of eight major industrial democracies, namely, Canada, France, Germany, Great Britain, Italy, Japan, Russia, and the United States) Digital Opportunity Task Force, the United Nations' ICT Task Force, and the World Summit on the

Information Society (WSIS).[9] Encouraged by the support of various bilateral and multilateral development organizations, most African countries have begun developing policies and strategies for the use of ICTs in their broader national development programs.[10]

Accenture Consulting, the Markle Foundation, and the United Nations Development Programme (UNDP; 2001) reviewed the record and potential of ICTs in development and presented their findings in *Creating a Development Dynamic: Final Report of the Digital Opportunity Initiative*.[11] This report includes several case studies, including some from Africa. A key finding of the report is that when strategically deployed, ICTs can trigger a development dynamic that gains momentum as targeted steps are taken in key areas of policy, infrastructure, human capacity, entrepreneurship, and development of locally relevant content and applications.

MDGs have now become the global yardstick for measuring the success or failure of poverty-reduction efforts in many developing countries. In most developing countries, they have also become the framework for development policies in general, and ICT4D initiatives in particular.

At the regional level, the secretariat for the New Partnership for Africa's Development (NEPAD) has prepared an integrated socioeconomic-development framework for Africa. This framework includes proposals for various initiatives to bridge the digital divide in Africa (see Box 1).[12]

During the past decade, most African countries' initial focus on ICTs has been on (a) the computerization of public-sector operations, (b) the expansion of telecommunications infrastructure, (c) the liberalization of telecom value-added services, and (c) the introduction of ICTs in higher education institutions.

This trend is still evident in several ICT strategies, PRSPs, CASs, and PRSCs. In the public sector, for example, African governments are showing increasing interest in the computerization of their budget and expenditure management, payroll, customs, and other operations.

Various international agencies and bilateral and multilateral development organizations

Box 1. NEPAD and ICTs in Africa (NEPAD, 2002)

> "The problem of inadequate access to affordable telephones, broadcasting services, computers and the Internet in most African countries is due to the poor state of Africa's ICT infrastructure, the weak and disparate policy and regulatory frameworks and the limited human resource capacity in these countries. Although African countries, in recent years have made some efforts to facilitate the ICT infrastructure deployment, rollout and exploitation process in a number of areas, Africa still remains the continent with the least capability in ICT and least served by telecommunication and other communications facilities.
>
> The threat posed by the digital divide to the rapid development of African countries can on the whole be attributed to their inability to deploy, harness and exploit the developmental opportunities of ICTs to advance their socio-economic development. There is therefore an urgent need to put in place and implement ICT initiatives to bridge the digital divide at four levels namely: (i) bridging the divide between the rural and urban areas within a given country, (ii) bridging the gap between countries of a given sub-region, (iii) bridging the inter-regional gap and (iv) bridging the gap between Africa and the rest of the world."

support the computerization of public-sector operations in African countries. They find this approach consistent with their own public-sector capacity building and good governance objectives and initiatives. The governments' desire for modernization of the public sector, and the international organizations' advocacy of improved public-sector management and telecom-sector liberalization have been major factors in the framing of national ICT strategies in Africa.

ICTs in Africa

The growth of ICTs in SSA is a story of uneven development, with discernible general patterns dotted with exceptions. Three major trends emerge from the data: (a) Other factors being equal, the middle-income sub-Saharan countries are performing consistently better in the ICT sector compared to the lower income countries, (b) countries with smaller populations are generally doing better in terms of ICT competitiveness compared to more populous countries, and (c) sub-Saharan countries are generally far behind in terms of connectivity infrastructure and the use of new technologies compared with rest of the world.

Of the 48 sub-Saharan countries, 38 fall in the low-income category (based on the 2004 gross national income, or GNI, per capita of $825 or less).[13] The SSA countries that are performing well in the ICT sector are all middle-income countries. For example, the GNI per capita for Botswana, Mauritius, Namibia, and South Africa is $3,530, $4,100, $1,930, and $2,920, respectively (World Bank, 2005). These countries also have higher levels of per capita telecommunications infrastructure, personal computers (PCs), Internet hosts, telephone main lines, and mobile phones compared with other SSA countries. The economic performance of these countries has a direct bearing on their state of education, infrastructure, availability, and affordability of ICTs for public, business, and private applications.

Between 1 to 9% of the population of every middle-income SSA country uses the Internet. Among the smaller middle-income SSA countries (both in terms of size and population), Cape Verde and Seychelles stand out in terms of the number of telephone main lines and personal computers per capita.

With the exception of South Africa, all these middle-income countries have relatively small populations (see Table 1). As a result, South Africa's performance in any of the ICT categories has a significant impact on the overall performance of the subcontinent.

For example, in 2002, the number of personal computers in sub-Saharan Africa was 11.9 per 1,000 people. Excluding South Africa, this number would decrease to 7.02 computers per 1,000 people. Also, in 2000, the average number of Internet hosts for sub-Saharan Africa was 3.1 per 10,000 people (see Table 2). However, excluding South Africa, this number would decrease by an order of magnitude to 0.32 Internet hosts per 10,000 people. The impact of South Africa's performance on the overall performance of the region in the telecom sector is also very significant (see Table 3).

It is important to note that the official data from international sources do not fully reflect the fast pace of growth in the telecommunications sector in some SSA countries, particularly in the mobile segment (e.g., the Democratic Republic of Congo and Ethiopia). This

Table 1. ICTs in sub-Saharan Africa: Population, income, and literacy (Source: Compiled from Africa Development Indicators 2005)

	Population Mid-2003 (millions)	GNI Per Capita 2003 (Atlas dollars)	% Literacy Rate (2002) Population 15 Years and Above		
			Total	Male	Female
SSA	705.2	506	65	72	58
Excluding SA	659.4	342	62	71	54
Angola	13.5	760			
Benin	6.7	440	40	55	26
Botswana	1.7	3,530	79	76	82
Burkina Faso	12.1	300			
Burundi	7.2	90	50	58	44
Cameroon	16.1	650			
Cape Verde	0.5	1,440	76	85	68
Central African Rep.	3.9	270			
Chad	8.6	240	46	55	38
Comoros	0.6	430	56	63	49
Congo, D. R.	53.2	100			
Congo	3.8	650	83	89	77
Cote d'Ivoire	16.8	660			
Djibouti	0.7	910			
Equatorial Guinea	0.5	...			
Eritrea	4.4	190			
Ethiopia	68.7	90	42	49	34
Gabon	1.3	3,400			
Gambia, The	1.4	270			
Ghana	20.7	320	74	82	66
Guinea	7.9	430			
Guinea-Bissau	1.5	140			
Kenya	31.9	400	84	90	79
Lesotho	1.8	590			
Liberia	3.4	100	56	72	39
Madagascar	16.9	290			
Malawi	11	160	62	76	49
Mali	11.7	300			
Mauritania	2.8	400	41	51	31
Mauritius	1.2	4,100			
Mozambique	18.8	210	46	62	31
Namibia	2	1,930	83	84	83
Niger	11.8	200	17	25	9
Nigeria	136.5	350	67	74	59
Rwanda	8.4	190	69	75	63
Sao Tome & Principe	0.2	330			
Senegal	10.2	550	39	49	30
Seychelles	0.1	7,350			
Sierra Leone	5.3	160			
Somalia	9.6	...			
South Africa	45.8	2,920	86	87	85
Sudan	33.5	460	60	71	49
Swaziland	1.1	1,340	81	82	80
Tanzania	35.9	310	77	85	69
Togo	4.9	310	60	74	45
Uganda	25.3	250	69	79	59
Zambia	10.4	380	80	86	74
Zimbabwe	13.1	...	90	94	86

Table 2. ICTs in sub-Saharan Africa: PCs, Internet hosts, and users (Source: Compiled from Africa Development Indictors 2005)

	Personal Computers (per 1,000 people)	Internet Hosts (per 10,000 people)	Internet Users (thousands)		Internet Users (%)
	2002	*2000*	*2001*	*2003*	*2001*
SSA	11.90	3.10	4,491	2,957	0.64%
Excluding SA	7.02	0.32	1,601	2,957	0.24%
Angola	1.94	0.01	20	…	0.15%
Benin	2.21	0.04	25	70	0.37%
Botswana	40.70	13.99	50	…	2.94%
Burkina Faso	1.59	0.19	19	48	0.16%
Burundi	0.72	0	7	14	0.10%
Cameroon	5.69	0.01	45	…	0.28%
Cape Verde	79.73	0.05	12	20	2.40%
Central African Rep.	2.02	0.02	3	6	0.08%
Chad	1.65	0.01	4	…	0.05%
Comoros	5.51	0.72	3	5	0.50%
Congo, D. R.	…	0	6	…	0.01%
Congo	3.94	0.01	1	15	0.03%
Cote d'Ivoire	9.34	0.38	70	240	0.42%
Djibouti	15.24	0.62	3	7	0.43%
Equatorial Guinea	6.93	0	1	…	0.20%
Eritrea	2.51	0.02	6	30	0.14%
Ethiopia	1.48	0.01	25	75	0.04%
Gabon	19.25	0.21	17	35	1.31%
Gambia, The	13.85	0.11	18	…	1.29%
Ghana	3.78	0.06	40	…	0.19%
Guinea	5.48	0	15	40	0.19%
Guinea-Bissau	…	0.1	4	19	0.27%
Kenya	6.39	0.32	200	…	0.63%
Lesotho	…	0.49	5	30	0.28%
Liberia	…	…	1	…	0.03%
Madagascar	4.40	0.36	35	71	0.21%
Malawi	1.34	0	20	36	0.18%
Mali	1.41	0.05	20	…	0.17%
Mauritania	10.81	0.20	7	12	0.25%
Mauritius	116.48	27.68	106	150	8.83%
Mozambique	4.50	0.1	30	…	0.16%
Namibia	70.93	18.16	45	65	2.25%
Niger	0.60	0.12	12	…	0.10%
Nigeria	7.10	0.01	115	750	0.08%
Rwanda	…	0.47	20	…	0.24%
Sao Tome & Principe	…	45.00	9	15	4.50%
Senegal	19.85	0.51	100	225	0.98%
Seychelles	160.85	0.49	9	…	9.00%
Sierra Leone	…	0.16	7	…	0.13%
Somalia	…	0	1	…	0.01%
South Africa	72.60	41.94	2,890	…	6.31%
Sudan	6.15	0	56	300	0.17%
Swaziland	24.22	7.07	14	27	1.27%
Tanzania	4.18	0.16	60	250	0.17%
Togo	30.78	0.35	150	210	3.06%
Uganda	3.32	0.07	60	125	0.24%
Zambia	7.48	0.88	25	68	0.24%
Zimbabwe	51.57	2.5	100	…	0.76%

Table 3. ICTs in sub-Saharan Africa: telecom, radio, and TV (Source: Compiled from Africa Development Indictors 2005)

	Main Lines (per 1,000 people)	Mobile Phones (per 1,000 people)	Radios (per 1,000 people)	Television (per 1,000 people)
SSA	15	37	198	69
Excluding SA	8	18	188	62
Angola	6	9	78	52
Benin	9	32	445	12
Botswana	87	241	150	44
Burkina Faso	5	8	433	79
Burundi	3	7	220	31
Cameroon	7	43	161	75
Cape Verde	160	98	181	101
Central African Rep.	2	3	80	6
Chad	2	4	233	2
Comoros	13	0	174	4
Congo, D. R.	0	11	385	2
Congo	7	67	109	13
Cote d'Ivoire	20	62	185	61
Djibouti	15	23	83	78
Equatorial Guinea	17	63	425	116
Eritrea	9	0	464	50
Ethiopia	5	1	189	6
Gabon	25	215	488	308
Gambia, The	28	73	394	15
Ghana	13	21	695	53
Guinea	3	12	52	47
Guinea-Bissau	9	0	178	36
Kenya	10	42	221	26
Lesotho	13	42	61	35
Liberia	2	1	274	25
Madagascar	4	10	216	25
Malawi	7	8	499	4
Mali	5	5	180	33
Mauritania	12	92	148	99
Mauritius	270	289	379	299
Mozambique	5	14	44	14
Namibia	65	80	134	269
Niger	2	1	122	10
Nigeria	6	13	200	103
Rwanda	3	14	85	0
Sao Tome and Principe	41	13	318	93
Senegal	22	55	126	78
Seychelles	269	553	543	202
Sierra Leone	5	13	259	13
Somalia	10	3	60	14
South Africa	107	304	336	177
Sudan	21	6	461	386
Swaziland	34	61	162	34
Tanzania	5	19	406	45
Togo	10	35	263	123
Uganda	2	16	122	18
Zambia	8	13	179	51
Zimbabwe	25	30	362	56

fact notwithstanding, the overall teledensity in the sub-Sahara still remains far below other regions.

The Global Information Technology Report (Dutta, Lanvin, & Paua, 2004) provides the Networked Readiness Index (NRI) ranking for 102 countries, including 21 sub-Saharan African countries. The NRI is defined as the degree of preparation of a nation or community to participate in and benefit from ICT development. NRI is a composite measure of three components: the environment for ICTs offered by a country, the readiness of the countries' key stakeholders (individuals, businesses, and governments) to use ICTs, and the usage of ICTs among these stakeholders. The Networked Readiness Index is therefore a good indicator for evaluating a country's relative development and use of ICTs.

The Africa Competitiveness Report 2004 (Hernandez-Cata, Schwab, & Lopez-Claros, 2004) provides data on the Growth Competitiveness Index, reflecting the combined effects of public institutions, macroeconomic environment, and technology indices. This report also provides a Technology Index for the same group of African countries. The Technology Index is a measure of innovation, technology transfer, and ICTs in the country. These data confirm that the performance of countries like Botswana, Mauritius, Namibia, and South Africa is in fact consistently better than the rest of the SSA countries in all these assessment categories, while still lagging considerably behind the rest of the world (see the rankings in Table 4).

The same data show that compared to rest of the world, even the best performing SSA countries are barely keeping up with other regions as demonstrated by their global ranking among the 102 countries considered. It appears that the higher GNI per capita and the lower population of most middle-income SSA countries are making it easier for them to deal with the questions of infrastructure development, investment in information technology, and human-resource development.

However, a closer examination of the in-country variations in terms of per capita income, telecom access, and other factors demonstrates that while the overall national statistics may appear impressive, there is a high level of disparity among the larger and smaller urban centers, and between urban and rural populations in terms of income, connectivity, access to resources, literacy, and related factors that make the use of ICTs possible.

The prevalent lack of adequate connectivity infrastructure, human resources, an enabling policy environment, and local content in most sub-Saharan countries require more in-depth assessment. The disparities within and across countries in the access to and use of ICTs also require more serious attention by government policy makers, regional organizations, and development partners.

At the regional level, it is also important to point out that the existence of connectivity infrastructure does not necessarily translate into affordable access to communications for consumers. For example, the SAT-3/WASC (South African Telecommunications/West African Submarine Cable) project connects several West African countries to international networks. However, the price of local access to this infrastructure has been high, and its development impact has therefore remained low so far.

More recent initiatives like NEPAD's backbone infrastructure development in Southern and Eastern Africa and the Regional Communications Infrastructure Program (RCIP), which is a multipartner initiative to overcome the major bottlenecks to growth and competitiveness in the region, are initiatives that require strong support. RCIP's key difference with SAT-3 is that RCIP plans to ensure that access to its infrastructure will be priced competitively so that it can bring benefits to users. These programs could to a large extent address the lack of adequate regional ICT infrastructure in Eastern and Southern Africa, and could facilitate access to affordable ICT services. The RCIP initiative is proposed as the lead instrument for a broader NEPAD regional connectivity program supported by many development partners.[14]

Table 4. Networked readiness and growth competitiveness indices for 21 SSA countries (Source: Adoted from The Global Information Technology Report 2004, & The Africa Competitiveness Report 2004).

Country	Networked Readiness Index		Technology Index		Growth Competitiveness Index	
	Score	Rank	Score	Rank	Score	Rank
South Africa	3.72	37	4.35	40	4.37	42
Mauritius	3.62	43	4.10	49	4.12	46
Botswana	3.34	55	3.78	59	4.56	36
Namibia	3.28	59	3.72	62	3.99	52
Tanzania	3.09	71	3.22	81	3.77	61
Ghana	3.06	74	3.10	86	3.49	69
Nigeria	2.92	79	3.16	82	3.21	83
Uganda	2.90	80	3.25	77	3.34	79
Senegal	2.90	81	3.04	89	3.34	79
Gambia, The	2.85	82	3.22	80	3.93	55
Cameroon	2.82	83	2.80	93	2.98	91
Kenya	2.81	84	3.36	74	3.21	83
Zambia	2.80	85	2.96	90	3.1	88
Malawi	2.71	88	2.79	94	3.36	76
Madagascar	2.60	92	2.47	97	2.85	96
Zimbabwe	2.53	95	3.34	75	2.85	96
Mali	2.52	96	2.36	99	2.84	97
Mozambique	2.51	97	2.84	92	2.91	93
Angola	2.32	99	2.43	98	2.6	100
Ethiopia	2.13	101	2.17	100	2.92	92
Chad	2.09	102	2.06	102	2.31	101

National ICT Policies and Poverty Reduction

Since the 1990s, a few middle-income sub-Saharan countries such as Mauritius have completed several cycles of e-strategies as part of their broader development programs. Most other SSA countries, however, have started looking seriously at the potential role of ICTs in their development efforts since the beginning of the new millennium.

By mid-2005, close to 30 African countries had already developed national ICT policies and/or e-strategies, and 15 more were in the process of doing so.[15] At this pace, all major African economies will have the first generation of their national ICT policies in place before long.

Various bilateral and multilateral development organizations (e.g., UNECA[16], UNDP, the International Development Research Center [IDRC; Canada], and others) have supported the development of national ICT policies in sub-Saharan Africa with some variation in their approach to the process of policy development.[17] By and large, however, the countries' national development priorities are proposed as the framework within which the role of ICTs as enablers of change and growth are defined.

In reviewing the national ICT policies and e-strategies of sub-Saharan countries, the first challenge is accessing the existing documents. Several of the 30 or so sub-Saharan ICT policy documents are not publicly available. Others are available in draft form, often in multiple versions, making it difficult to verify their official standing. During the preparation of this chapter, the author had access to 18 of these documents. Therefore, to ensure that any other available information on these ICT policies was taken into account, several review papers were consulted, the most significant of which are listed below.

UNECA has published several reports on national, sectoral, and regional ICT policies, plans, and strategies in Africa (see, for example, UNECA 2003a, 2003b, 2004a, 2004b, 2004c). These documents provide an overview of ICT policy-development efforts in Africa, UNECA's framework for policy development, and its role in that process.

Tipson and Frittelli (2003) summarize the experience from various national strategies and initiatives on ICT for development, including some examples from Africa. Their basic conclusion is that despite major opportunities to take advantage of the development potential of ICTs, the results of most national strategy efforts to date have been disappointing. The authors believe that national strategies frequently flounder or fail by becoming focused on particular technologies or applications in isolation from broader policy, resource, and training initiatives necessary to exploit their capabilities in specific settings.

Wild (2003) reviews the evolution of ICT strategies in various regions, and analyzes the connection between e-strategies and poverty-reduction strategies. She finds that many e-strategies recognize a social dimension but do not systematically address poverty and achievement of the millennium development goals. Among her conclusions, Wild suggests that the international community has now clearly recognized the importance of developing a stronger poverty focus in e-strategy work, and makes a number of recommendations on the steps that can be taken to help countries incorporate an MDG dimension into their national ICT planning process.

Adam (2004) critically discusses the implications of e-strategies for civil-society organizations in Africa by drawing on lessons from the ICT policy-making experience during the past decade in the region. He asserts that:

> [i]n practice, although the number of countries aiming to benefit from ICTs by developing their e-strategies is increasing and some of the ICT policies were useful in mobilizing resources and attracting collaborators, by and large, the result of broad-based ICT policy implementation has been inadequate. (p. 3)

He further concludes that:

> [c]onsequently, the formulation and implementation of e-strategies has been sluggish in Africa—mired by faulty assumptions about the role of ICTs in development in the region, overestimation of the capacities and underestimation of structural obstacles in the countries and by occasionally cumbersome processes under which policies are promoted, developed and implemented.

As part of the explanation for this, Adam suggests that:

> [f]or the most part the debate on e-strategies does not involve countries and institutions who need the ICTs the most. It takes place amongst ICT professionals, donor agencies and a few policy experts independent of the mainstream development professionals and empirical research. Limited involvement of development professionals means that beyond a list of [sic] menu of opportunities there is less substance on the actual impact of ICTs in key development sectors like health, education and agriculture. (p. 10)

He further suggests that civil-society organizations can play a key role in influencing local policy development and promoting broad participation and representation, among other activities.

Adamali, Coffey, and Safdar (2005) provide an overview of how countries are formulating national e-strategies and what they are focusing on. They examine the trends in the national e-strategies of 40 countries, including 8 from sub-Saharan Africa, and evaluate the strength, scope, and direction of these countries' ICT programs based on the goals stated in these countries' e-strategy documents. Adamali et al. identify four themes that appear in over 85% of the e-strategies. These are e-government, infrastructure expansion, e-education, and an enabling legal and regulatory environment. They also identify five additional themes that appear in at least 40% of e-strategies. These are the creation or expansion of the domestic ICT industry, the development of human resources with ICT skills to support the domestic ICT industry, e-business, the creation of locally relevant content, and ICTs to support more effective provision of health services. Based on these reviews and lessons learned, they then offer recommendations for formulating effective e-strategies.

The author's own field experience and his review of the available ICT policies are consistent with most of the above assessments. Several ICT policies consider poverty reduction as a major objective or a key driver of the policy (e.g., Cameroon, Ghana, Mozambique, Nigeria, and Tanzania). Zambia's second-draft ICT policy defines ICTs as tools for poverty reduction and development[18] (see Box 2). Other national policies and strategies discuss the

Box 2. Poverty reduction and ICTs in Zambia (Republic of Zambia, 2004)

"1.3   POVERTY REDUCTION & ICTs IN NATIONAL DEVELOPMENT

The need to integrate ICTs as part of the holistic national development agenda means taking ICTs as part of the tools and services in Poverty Reduction Strategy Programmes (PRSP) as well as in developing National Development Plans (NDP). Therefore, it is expected that each sector will mainstream ICTs in their action plans to address the PRSP and the NDPs. The communications sector has registered significant progress and contribution to the GDP1 over the past ten years (1994-2004). This signifies that with further positive policy direction, integration of ICTs in poverty reduction programmes and restructuring of the ICT sector; greater achievements can be recorded. Therefore, this policy framework is by design integrating ICT implementation in all key economic and social sectors with a view of making the ICT sector one of the positive contributors to job creation and other empowerment opportunities."

role of ICTs in poverty reduction either explicitly or in the context of ICTs as tools for the achievement of MDGs through the mainstreaming of ICTs in business and trade, education, health, tourism, agriculture, public-sector services, community centers, and other types of service delivery to the poor.

While the process of ICT policy preparation may vary across countries, the general objectives and areas of priority are similar in most policy documents. These priorities include improvements in the broader ICT-sector policy and regulation, infrastructure, human capacity, content and applications, and an enabling environment for active private-sector participation.

The national ICT policies often include a framework for the use of ICTs as enablers of service delivery to the poor, improved governance, and economic growth. The policies generally encompass a subset of the following topics: (a) expanding the telecommunications infrastructure; (b) using new technologies in public administration, service delivery, and e-government; (c) fostering the use of ICTs in academic, educational, and research institutions; (d) creating a conducive policy, legal, and regulatory environment for the growth of ICTs; (e) creating opportunities for private-sector development and the growth of the ICT sector; (f) developing human resources in the ICT sector; (g) producing local-language content and applications; (h) providing rural connectivity and universal access; (i) facilitating e-commerce; (j) supporting access to ICTs by civil society and NGOs (nongovernmental organizations); and (k) facilitating applications of ICTs as enablers in health, education, agriculture, mining, environment, trade, art and culture, tourism, and other sectors. Malawi's proposed ICT policy is typical of some of the focus areas that are normally found in African ICT policies with an emphasis on certain national priorities (see Box 3).

To establish a clear link between ICT policies and poverty-reduction efforts, a few countries have also developed implementation strategies or action plans for their ICT policies that are aligned with their broader poverty-reduction strategies. Mozambique, for example, has developed an implementation strategy that proposes specific projects and activities for each focus area of the national ICT policy, with corresponding implementation schedules and budgets. Other countries have engaged in large-scale rollouts of connectivity or ICT-enabled applications for development. Ethiopia's national secondary school network initiative is one example of such initiatives.

Box 3. Specific goals of the Draft Malawi ICT policy (Republic of Malawi, 2003)

- To facilitate the creation of the necessary enabling environment to support the deployment, utilization, and exploitation of ICTs within the economy and society
- To promote the development of a globally competitive local ICT industry
- To support the development of the nation's human-resource capacity
- To facilitate the deployment and exploitation of ICTs within the educational system to improve on educational access and delivery
- To aid the process of improving Malawi's scientific and industrial research capacity as well as its research and development (R&D) capabilities to support economic development
- To promote and support the development of the nation's information and communications infrastructure as well as the physical infrastructure
- To facilitate the modernization of civil and public service through the deployment and exploitation of ICTs to improve on the effectiveness and efficiency of its operations and service delivery
- To promote and facilitate the development and implementation of the necessary legal, institutional, and regulatory framework and structures required for supporting the development, deployment, and exploitation of ICTs in the country
- To support and encourage the development and promotion of the necessary standards, good practices, and guidelines to guide the deployment and exploitation of ICTs within the society and economy

Evaluating the impact of such programs in poverty reduction and economic growth in sub-Saharan countries, however, requires careful monitoring of various initiatives over longer periods, and detailed impact assessment at various levels. These are tasks that require more attention by all parties involved in the promotion of ICTs for development.

Despite some promising progress, in most SSA countries, the development of an ICT policy has not led to the flourishing of the ICT sector or the large-scale use of ICTs as effective tools for development. A major contributing factor is the starting point (initial conditions) of each country with respect to the main prerequisites for the growth of ICTs, including the communications infrastructure, human resources, the policy and regulatory environment, affordable access, entrepreneurship, and relevant applications (see Tables 1, 2, and 3). This is particularly more visible in lower income countries, where the level of readiness in various areas of ICT development (e.g., infrastructure, human resources, etc.) lags considerably behind those of middle-income countries. For example, countries like South Africa, Mauritius, Botswana, and Namibia are in a better position to deliver on the promises of their respective ICT programs compared with lower income SSA countries.

Size also matters. Countries like Mauritius and Botswana, with smaller geographic areas and populations, can be more agile and effective in the expansion of their ICT infrastructures across their countries and the mainstreaming of ICTs compared to, say, South Africa.

Disparity between urban and rural areas also matters. For example, Namibia is a middle-income country with a well-developed communications infrastructure that connects the major urban areas. However, the majority of the population lives in the rural areas, and there is a marked difference between the urban and rural communities in terms of income, access to affordable communications infrastructure, and ICT tools and services. This could make it more difficult for Namibia to attain its ICT policy goals in an equitable manner across the country.

Other impediments to the growth of ICTs in many African countries include (a) the inadequacy of the infrastructure, human resources, local-language applications, and funding for large-scale rollouts of ICTs in government, education, and other public-service areas, (b) an overestimation of the existing implementation capacity on the ground, (c) the affordability of the ICT tools and services for the general population, (d) the lag between the fast rate of technology introduction (automation factors) and the slow rate of adaptation to change (human factors), and (e) the "brain drain" due to inadequate local incentives.

A reliable and continuous supply of electricity as a basic requirement is still a problem even in major urban areas across the continent. While countries like South Africa are trying to develop the required power and telecommunication infrastructure for effective use of ICTs, most SSA countries are trailing behind.

For example, South Africa's annual average power consumption per capita is 3,739.9 kWh (World Bank, 2005). The same indicator for SSA countries excluding South Africa is 116.4 kWh, which is only about 3% of South Africa's corresponding power usage per capita. Nigeria and Ethiopia's average power consumption per capita are 73.1 and 22.4 kWh, respectively, reflecting the fact that most rural areas are yet to have access to electricity. In the absence of these prerequisites for the growth of ICTs, the scope of some ICT policy documents appears rather unrealistic.

Despite these obstacles and challenges, the introduction and mainstreaming of appropriate technologies in development programs, when and where possible, are necessary for the growth of ICTs in Africa. This is an effort that will require considerable coordination among the various local and global stakeholders and partners involved.

ICTs in Poverty-Reduction Strategy Papers

PRSPs are documents prepared by countries as the frameworks for their development programs. Since 1999, the preparation of a PRSP has become a standard requirement for countries that wish to benefit from the concessional credits, grants, and debt relief offered by the International Monetary Fund and the World Bank Group. The development of PRSPs (or their equivalents under different names) has become prevalent among developing countries, particularly in Africa. By mid-2005, there were a total of 58 countries with PRSPs, of which 30 are in Africa.[19]

The approach to preparing PRSPs has evolved over the past few years, moving steadily toward a more participatory and consultative process. As a result, while the earlier PRSPs are mainly focused on government priorities, recent ones are more representative of the needs of diverse communities and stakeholders.

Like the PRSPs themselves, the discussion of ICTs in PRSPs is a new phenomenon, gradually starting in late 2000 (e.g., in Mauritania) and becoming a fairly common topic in PRSPs by 2002 and beyond (e.g., in Benin, Malawi, and Senegal).

The OECD (2003, 2004) is among the few international organizations that has studied the discussion of ICTs in PRSPs. In these studies, OECD reviews whether the PRSPs define or position ICT as a strategic component for poverty reduction and discuss it as an independent item. The OECD studies found that worldwide, over 40% of the PRSPs (12 out of 29, including 8 sub-Saharan countries) meet these criteria (OECD, 2003). The rest mention telecommunications-sector development as an important factor for rural and agricultural development, or as one of the components of the infrastructure for economic growth.

The current study reviewed the 30 sub-Saharan African PRSPs that were available in mid-2005. The results indicate that 16 PRSPs and 1 interim PRSP refer to ICTs as a component of their poverty-reduction efforts or as a means for facilitating economic growth. Some define a more specific role for ICTs as tools for improved communication, public-sector modernization, improved service delivery, and applications in health, education, and rural development.

About half of the PRSPs make references to information and communication technologies as a significant tool for development. These documents also emphasize the telecom sector as an important part of their infrastructure development needs and significant for economic growth. Over 20% of the PRSPs discuss one or more of the broadcast media (radio and television) and Internet as relevant tools for information dissemination and communication on development issues.

Box 4. New ICTs in Ghana's PRSP ("Ghana Poverty Reduction Strategy", 2003)

"Utilising information and communication technology to further enhance our development efforts.

6.1.11 Information and Communication Technology (ICT). The creation of awareness in information access is recognized as being of prime importance. With respect to ICT usage and application, an information technology policy framework is currently being developed which recognizes that the dynamics of global economic growth are changing at a very fast pace. The role of the Internet as a pervasive phenomenon and its implications for the traditional factors of production is taken into account. Economic potential is recognized as being increasingly linked to the ability to control and manipulate information. Within this policy context also, the need for an effective legal and regulatory framework is identified. A National Communication Authority is operational and a National Information Technology Agency is to be established as part of the regulatory and licensing environment. Also to be established is a national communications backbone facility to provide access throughout the country.

In the medium term, the intention is to support the development of electronic commerce to enhance production, productivity and to facilitate business transactions. Government intends to establish Information Technology (IT) parks and incubator areas equipped with the necessary infrastructure for ICT related businesses and to develop human resources that support the deployment and rehabilitation of modern ICT. Government will re-negotiate the existing telecommunications agreements to introduce more competition and accelerate access to telephones, Internet and information technology in the country."

The majority of PRSPs (70%) emphasize the important role of information technology in improving public-sector management and service delivery. These PRSPs include a discussion of improved governance through the appropriate use of ICTs in budget tax, customs, payroll and personnel management, and the establishment or improvement of integrated financial-management information systems (IFMISs).

Over 50% of the PRSPs include fairly extensive references to the potential role of new information and communication technologies in diversifying the economy for accelerated growth, job creation, improved performance in the productive sectors and government services, better access to regional and global markets, and other benefits. An example from the Ghana PRSP is given in Box 4.

In the area of government service delivery, 67% of PRSPs discuss one or more services that focus on streamlining and/or computerizing the corresponding activities. These include developing national health information systems and HIV/AIDS monitoring, legal issues, water and sanitation, social security, and other services. In the education sector, over 30% of the documents refer to one or more of the following actions to improve the efficiency and effectiveness of the corresponding activities: creating or improving higher education networks, strengthening institutional administrative capabilities, establishing computer labs and access to the Internet in secondary schools, introducing computer-based instruction, establishing sector-wide computerized performance-tracking systems, and strengthening distance education programs.

An interesting finding is that only 17% of the PRSPs propose ICT activities that will directly benefit civil society and the private sector, such as the development of streamlined and computerized business registration and market information systems.

On rural-development issues, about 20% of the documents propose plans for the extension and/or expansion of rural connectivity through the establishment of community telecenters, wireless phones, and some use of ICTs for agricultural development.

Regarding information technology (computer technology, hardware, software, networks, applications), almost every document has some discussion on computerization, networking, information systems, and related topics as shown in Figures 1 and 2.

About one third (33%) of PRSPs include some reference to content development and information dissemination. These include the promotion of rural and community radios, expansion of radio-programs development, production of farmer newsletters, translation and distribution of training materials in local languages, provisions for citizens' access to

Figure 1. ICT Subsectors in PRSPs.

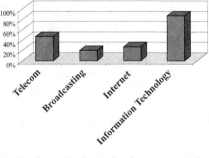

Figure 2. ICTs in PRSPs

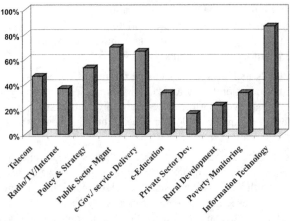

government information, delivery of meteorological information to farmers and fishermen, and dissemination of information on health and agricultural market information.

The coverage of ICTs in PRSPs is encouraging. However, the PRSP documents often reflect the generic global discourse on the potential of ICTs for poverty reduction. There is very little detail in terms of whether the necessary conditions exist on the ground to make the ICT4D interventions successful and effective in a sustainable manner. It is therefore not surprising to see that there is a visible disconnection between most PRSPs and the corresponding national ICT policies and e-strategies. Only a few PRSPs (Benin, Cameroon, Ghana, and Rwanda) discuss or refer to the existing national ICT policies or e-strategies and their relevance to poverty-reduction efforts. Most other PRSPs and the ICT discussions therein are not informed by the ICT policy documents or the ongoing ICT efforts and initiatives that are already under way in the country.

Several factors contribute to this situation. The process of ICT policy development is often led by national organizations and ICT professionals who are well familiar with the global discourse on the role of ICTs in development. The international partners who support the ICT policy-development efforts are also eager to introduce ICT policy frameworks that are driven by the broader poverty-reduction MDGs and economic-growth objectives. Therefore, most national ICT policies (particularly those supported by international partners) have an ICT4D orientation. However, these ICT advocacy groups are not necessarily involved in the national poverty-reduction strategy planning, and therefore have little influence on such policy formulations.

The local stakeholders involved in poverty reduction and economic-development planning, on the other hand, are mainly focused on identifying and prioritizing the specific national development objectives in traditionally well-established sectors such as health, education, agriculture, water and sanitation, roads, and so forth. In this process, the potential role of ICTs as crosscutting tools for development is often treated as a side issue and not a priority. Consequently, the preparation of existing ICT policies and PRSPs has often taken place on two independent parallel tracks with limited influence on each other.

As the global discourse on the role of ICTs in development continues (e.g., WSIS and NEPAD), it is expected that the integration of ICTs into poverty-reduction strategies will continue to grow in a more substantive manner.

The international development organizations are often consulted during the preparation of PRSPs. Therefore, they may be in a position to point out the need for a more holistic articulation of the potential of ICTs for development in line with the specific development objectives of the PRSPs.

These international partners could also coordinate their technical advice and financial contributions in such a way that the multisectoral and crosscutting nature of ICTs as enablers of socioeconomic development is more clearly understood, assimilated, and articulated by all stakeholders, including the donor community and the bilateral and multilateral development organizations. Box 5 provides some additional examples of ICT discussions in PRSPs.

Box 5. Examples of ICTs in PRSPs (Republic of Benin, 2002; Republic of Cameroon, 2003)

Benin: New ICTs

"96. New Information and Communication Technologies (NTIC). The Government also intends to promote the development of new information and communications technologies to benefit from their economic and social potential. These technologies will spur economic growth by better integrating the Beninese economy within the global economic and trade systems, as well as by creating new economic activities and jobs. The development of NTIC and their use in the health and education sectors will lead to a noticeable improvement in quality and a greater range of services offered to poor people and thereby contribute to poverty reduction. The planned actions involve the drafting of a national development strategy for NTIC, support for the dissemination of NTICs and their introduction in the health and education sectors, arrangements to exempt imports of computer equipment from duties and taxes, of these measures to consumers."

Cameroon: Economic Potential of ICTs

"242. During the participatory consultation, the difficulty of accessing, and the lack of information were mentioned as a determinant of poverty. Moreover, the United Nations considers access to information, this is, access to the knowledge required for basic life functions, to be a major human development indicator. Given the requirements of the New Economy, which is heavily reliant on information, communications, and artificial intelligence, the government will take measures to greatly improve citizens' access to information. 243. The government intends to: (i) open multimedia community centers in each of the 10 provinces to provide the landlocked population with Internet access to important health, education, agricultural, livestock, and environmental information; and (ii) install, with support from the UNDP and UNESCO [United Nations Educational, Scientific, and Cultural Organization], new rural radio stations in addition to the 15 already operational stations. The authorities also intend, through the Ministry of Communication, to support the national HIV/AIDS strategy through the implementation of a sector communication plan.

244. The government understands the economic potential of information and communications technologies (ICT) and is committed to promoting the development of this sector. In addition to reducing or eliminating some import duties and taxes for computer equipment, it created a National Information and Communication Technologies Agency (ANTIC) in April 2002. Within its missions, the agency must promote broader access to ICT as well as activities related to these new technologies, which are becoming increasingly popular among the population."

ICTs in Country Assistance Strategies

The multilateral and bilateral development agencies provide their country assistance to developing countries based on development frameworks that highlight the focus areas of mutual interest. Examples include UNDP's country program outline and country cooperation framework (CCF) documents, DFID's (Department for International Development) country assistance plan (CAP), and the World Bank's country assistance strategy.

The CAS is a document that describes the World Bank Group's framework for working with a country based on an assessment of priorities in the country as reflected in its PRSP or equivalent documents.[20] It also delineates the bank's intended level of assistance based on its comparative advantage and the country's portfolio performance.

The CAS normally outlines the sector-specific and/or programmatic operations that are planned in support of achieving the PRSP objectives. It also specifies whether there is a mutual agreement with the government to provide multisectoral budget support to the government through a PRSC. PRSPs generally provide the framework for the CAS, which in turn will inform the formulation of the PRSC for achieving the midterm goals of the poverty-reduction strategy. There is, therefore, a sequential yet iterative process that is normally followed in formulating these three documents.

A review of the 25 current CAS documents for African countries reveals that by far the most significant discussion of ICT issues is focused on telecommunications infrastructure and telecom reform. Over 84% of the CAS documents discuss one or more of the following aspects of the telecom sector in the country: (a) challenges in terms of the existing short-comings and the required investments to improve and expand the telecom infrastructure, (b) plans for the introduction or expansion of privatization, liberalization, or competition, and (c) the necessary reforms to improve access and connectivity through the licensing of new or additional mobile operators. Despite the high frequency of these discussions, the

Box 6. Telecom examples from CAS documents ("Uganda Country Assistance Strategy", 2000; "Senegal Country Assistance Strategy", 2003)

Uganda

"A recent noteworthy success was the privatization of the telecommunications utility in the spring of 2000 and the accompanying sector reform which have brought in a second national operator and a second cellular licensee, expanding service options and lowering prices."

Senegal

"The advent of private participation in infrastructure, notably telecommunications and water, has accelerated economic growth, and extended service access.* New information technologies are widely available in Dakar and in the larger secondary cities. Rapid growth in coverage is now common."

---

* The bank estimates that the privatization of the national telephone company, SONATEL, and the related introduction of two cellular phone licenses has added 1% each year to GDP growth since 1997.

Figure 3. ICT subsectors in CASs and PRSPs

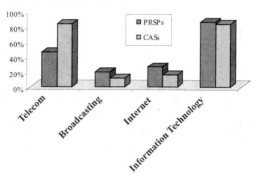

references are very brief. Two examples from the Uganda and Senegal CAS documents are given in Box 6.

Figure 3 compares the relative frequency of CAS discussions on different aspects of ICT subsectors with those in the PRSPs. The graph shows very clearly that telecom reform and infrastructure expansion are much more strongly emphasized in the CAS documents compared with PRSPs.

The graph also shows that while there is a high level of emphasis on information-technology applications in CASs, there is limited discussion on the potential role of radio in education and service-delivery efforts, and less emphasis on the Internet. The use of radio and the Internet are areas that could be more effectively explored and discussed during the PRSP and CAS consultations. These options could be of particular interest to the local private-sector and civil-society organizations that are more akin to the use of these tools for information dissemination and service delivery.

On the broader ICT applications, the CAS documents put more emphasis on the public-sector management applications. The development of management information systems and the computerization of budget, expenditure, tax, and customs operations are regularly discussed. IFMISs are often mentioned (43%) either as existing operations in need of improvement, or as new initiatives to improve public-sector management.

The provision of access to government information is an emerging area of policy reform in sub-Saharan Africa. A few countries (e.g., Ghana and Uganda) have taken the necessary steps in developing the policies and laws that will provide their citizens access to various government information. An example from the Ghana CAS highlighting this new trend is presented in Box 7.

Box 7. Ghana CAS: Freedom of Information Bill. (Ghana Country Assistance Strategy, 2004)

> "The draft Freedom of Information Bill is intended to bring about fundamental improvements in political and bureaucratic culture as regard access to information on government business."

Figure 4. ICT in PRSPs and CASs

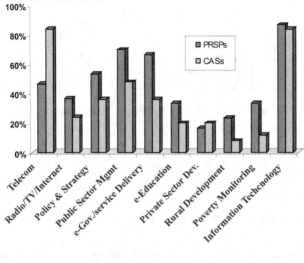

Figure 4 provides an overview of the various ICT topics discussed in CAS documents as compared with the discussion of the same topics in PRSPs. The graph shows that with the exception of the treatment of telecom-sector reform and private-sector development, almost all other aspects of ICTs are treated more emphatically and fully in PRSPs as compared to the CAS documents. This implies that the priorities of the actual development investment plans in the ICT area differ somewhat from those proposed in the broader poverty-reduction strategies, with a stronger emphasis on telecom liberalization and infrastructure expansion, and a somewhat weaker emphasis on public-sector investment in ICT-sector development and ICT applications in sectors.

The graph shows that there is a high level of demand from the countries for information-technology solutions, and the CAS documents also reflect a strong response. In financial terms, however, this response is much more limited in scope compared to the requirements of the demand. This aspect is treated in more detail in the PRSC section below. The results also reflect the strong support of the World Bank's country programs for the use of ICTs in public-sector management. This is not surprising since the findings of the bank's core fiduciary analyses of each country's capabilities in this area also confirm the need for different levels of computerization and other ICT-enabled interventions in the public sector.

About one fourth of the CAS documents mention local content development and information dissemination in various forms. Some CASs propose support for market information systems for small and medium enterprises, and the development of independent media, community, and commercial FM radio stations and private television stations.

The anecdotal examples sited in Box 8 offer a flavor of the evolving nature of ICT discussions in CAS documents between 2000 and 2004. These examples show that the ICT discussions in CAS documents have shifted from focusing on the development of ICT policies in 2000 to articulating the role of ICTs as enablers of development and growth in 2004. This is also partly a reflection of the fact that the level of awareness of the bank teams, as well as the governments and their domestic or external partners on the role of ICTs in development, has also changed considerably during this period.

Box 8. Examples of ICTs in CASs from various years ("Uganda Country Assistance Strategy", 2000; "Mauritius Country Assistance Strategy", 2002; "Ghana Country Assistance Strategy", 2004)

Uganda (2000)

"Information and communication strategy and policy: It is recognized that the use of information and communication technologies (ICTs) and modern information management systems can increase the credibility and effectiveness of efforts to improve access to information, transparency in public sector decision-making and build private and public sector capabilities. To promote the use of ICTs in Uganda, the Bank will support the Government's efforts to (i) develop a National Information and Communication Strategy to establish a national ICT policy framework to promote the use of information and communication technologies for development; (ii) implement an integrated Public Sector Management Information System to promote fiscal oversight, transparency and accountability; and (iii) provide support for the establishment of the Uganda Country Gateway web-site."

Mauritius (2002)

"38. To support the move to a more service based economy, the regulatory framework for the information and communications technology (ICT) and financial sectors has been overhauled. The Government is actively seeking foreign investments in the ICT sector by developing a package of incentives and through the creation of a Cyber City that is expected to be completed by September 2003."

Ghana (2004)

"26. Information and communication technology (ICT), tourism, and manufacturing: other non-traditional sectors with potential. The potential crosscutting impact from a well-functioning ICT environment on growth and employment, improved government services, and accountability and empowerment, is high. For example, a dynamic ICT sector in Ghana has the potential to bring greater efficiencies to day-to-day operations of both government and private sector, as well as a platform for value-added services, such as outsourced data and call center services for overseas corporations. Strengthening the policy environment and regulatory capacity, and improving ICT infrastructure and access in both urban and rural communities, including resolving an investment dispute between the government and a shareholder of Ghana Telecom, are necessary preconditions to realizing this potential. Ghana's ICT policy, developed in June 2003 following extensive consultation with stakeholders countrywide, seeks to engineer an ICT-led socio-economic development process with the potential of transforming Ghana into an infrastructure-rich, knowledge-based and technology-driven economy and society."

ICTs in Poverty-Reduction Support Credits

The PRSC is a CAS-based development-assistance instrument that is often a multidonor basket fund to support the policy and institutional reform programs intended to help implement the country's poverty-reduction strategy as described in the PRSP. This type of lending does not finance specific investments, but instead finances overall country budget execution. It is expected that the PRSP/PRSC framework will allow donors to combine their efforts behind a single program with consistent and harmonized monitoring and evaluation focusing on results at the project, program, and country levels within a short to midterm execution period.

As of mid-2005, 11 sub-Saharan countries had active (ongoing) PRSCs. Six of these countries (Benin, Cape Verde, Madagascar, Mozambique, Rwanda, and Senegal) had their first PRSC in 2004 to 2005, while the other five countries (Burkina Faso, Ethiopia, Ghana, Tanzania, and Uganda) were in the second, third, or fourth cycle of their PRSCs. The rather limited number of countries with PRSCs poses a challenge in terms of any comparative analysis of the PRSC, CAS, and PRSP documents.

To address this challenge, the following approach was adopted for the purposes of this analysis. First, since PRSCs are instruments for the implementation of PRSPs, and each country has only one PRSP, the 21 PRSCs were grouped together by country, leading to 11 groups of PRSCs, and each group was then treated as a single integrated PRSC per country. Next, the ICT-related discussions in each country's one or more PRSCs were tabulated per category and topic, and for each category and topic, all redundancies across a single country's PRSCs were removed so that there would be no double counting of any category or topic per country. The results were then normalized with respect to the total number of countries that have PRSCs. This allowed for each country's total number of PRSCs to be treated as a single document for a single operation in support of the corresponding PRSP.

This approach may have skewed the PRSC results to some extent in favor of the countries with multiple PRSCs. Nevertheless, it does provide a means for the qualitative comparison of PRSCs with the corresponding CAS and PRSPs, as well as an overall comparison among all PRSP, CAS, and PRSC documents.

An overall comparison of the key categories of proposed ICT interventions in PRSCs and their corresponding treatment in CAS and PRSPs are presented in Figure 5. Since PRSCs provide the necessary funding for the implementation of any mutually agreed-upon proposed activities, it is reasonable to assume that the statements in these documents offer a more realistic picture of the actual priorities of the governments and donors.

The results in Figure 5 indicate that with respect to telecom reform and the extension and expansion of communications infrastructure and services, the PRSPs (reflecting the countries' priorities) and the PRSCs (reflecting the agreed-upon course of action and the corresponding financing by the donors for its implementation) treat these issues with a fairly high level of priority (47% and 45%, respectively). The CAS documents, however, show

Figure 5. ICTs in PRSPs, CASs, CASs, and PRSCs.

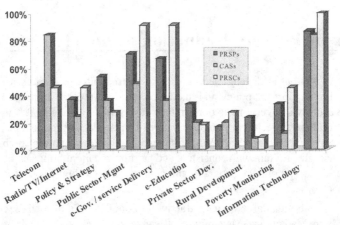

Box 9. ICTs in poverty-reduction support credits ("Benin Poverty Reduction Support Credit", 2004; "Burkina Faso Fourth Poverty Reduction Support Credit", 2004; "Rwanda Poverty Reduction Support Credit and Grant", 2004; "Senegal Poverty Reduction Support Credit", 2004; "Uganda Third Poverty Reduction Support Credit", 2004)

Benin: Government Accounting System. "Improvement of the reliability of government accounts is expected from the completion of full-fledge IFMIS [Integrated Financial Management Information System], in particular with; (i) the strengthening and comprehensiveness of the SIGFIP [integrated expenditure management system]; (ii) the installation of the computerized government accounting system (ASTER); and (iii) the development of a functional interface between SIGFIP and ASTER."

Burkina Faso: Computerization of Customs. "...(iv) modernizing customs administration by strengthening customs offices 9 by the end of April 2004)."

Rwanda: Environmental management information system. "Enhance capacity of REMA to conduct environmental public awareness campaign. Design and installation of information and ICT systems in REMA. Training of staff to use, update and maintain these systems."

Senegal: Computerization of the Courts. "49. The private sector operating in Senegal is demanding a better-functioning judicial system. This is also one o f the Government's major objectives, which will be supported by the World Bank Support Credit. Having developed a new sectorial strategy in collaboration with the community as a whole, the Government is now committed to allocating greater budgetary resources to this sector, to launching a human resource development program, and to proceeding with the computerization of courts in order to enhance the efficiency of Senegal's judicial apparatus."

Uganda: Integrated Financial Management System. "Completed a detailed study of the Government's Fiscal Management Systems providing a detailed Information Technology Architecture and Plan, a common Chart of Accounts and User Requirements for an Integrated Financial Management System (IFMS); Contracted consultants to deliver and install an Integrated Financial Management System. The implementation is to be phased through selected Pilot Sites in the 2003/04 fiscal year with further rollout to selected sites commencing in the 2004/05 fiscal year; Established a financial management team of accounting professionals appointed to support the reforms to (a) strengthen the legal and regulatory framework for financial management; (b) enhance the capacity building activities amongst the accounting and auditing cadre in government; and (c) strengthen the budgeting and accounting systems in government (the IFMS); Twenty recent graduates were recruited to assist in the IFMS implementation; MOPS has authorized the recruitment of an additional 16 graduate accountants to strengthen the compliment of accounting staff. The recruitment has been completed and posting to the various ministries is being arranged; ..."

---

a much higher level of emphasis on telecom issues (84%). This may reflect the fact that CASs often emphasize the telecom reforms that are considered as important requirements to facilitate economic growth.

The establishment of community radios and the use of radio, television, and the Internet as tools for awareness raising on development issues (e.g., in public-awareness campaigns on HIV/AIDS, community programs, etc.) is emphasized more strongly in PRSCs than the other documents.

The policy and strategy indicator used here reflects the cumulative references in the relevant documents to the national ICT policies, e-strategies, or specific policy discussions around the use of the new information and communication technologies for development.

It is worth noting that the discussion of ICT policy and e-strategies continues to decline from action planning (PRSPs) to financing envelopes and programs (CASs) to implementation plans (PRSCs).

An interesting overall finding is that by far the strongest focus of the PRSCs is on the implementation of ICT-based solutions to improve public-sector management and public service delivery. This is significant because it demonstrates a strong consensus among donors and governments alike that ICTs do have a major role to play in improving the governments' fiscal management, accountability, and transparency. At the same time, this focus on ICTs is purely in the context of their use as appropriate tools to improve the efficiency of public-sector management activities only. There is very little emphasis on the significance of sharing information with the general population through the use of appropriate technologies, or the impact of such applications on the broader objectives of poverty reduction and economic growth.

PRSC support for the introduction of new technologies in education is mostly focused on the introduction of education-management information systems, and in some cases on the introduction of new technologies in the higher education institutions. This does not necessarily imply that one of the broader objectives of PRSPs to mainstream ICTs in the education system is put on the back burner. Rather, it could mean that the sector reform activities and large-scale introduction of ICTs into the education system may require a different implementation support and funding mechanism such as a sector-focused project.

PRSCs also show a moderately strong trend toward increased support for small and medium enterprises; incubation programs; automation; new service-based, ICT-assisted businesses (e.g., call centers, etc.); and similar initiatives. This is encouraging since the trend could be further strengthened in the subsequent PRSCs. Compared to other priorities, the level of implementation support under PRSCs remains rather low.

The use of ICTs for rural development is an area that seems to need special attention. The indicators used in this category are for rural connectivity, the use of appropriate ICTs for rural development, agricultural information systems for farmers, and management information systems at various levels. Overall, this is the least discussed category in the reviewed documents with respect to the role of ICTs as enablers of development. Certainly, the endemic lack of reliable infrastructure and human resources, particularly in rural areas, may partly explain why this is not a priority area. However, successful examples of these types of initiatives could inform future policy discussions.

Another significant finding is that 45% of the PRSCs give high priority to the use of ICTs for poverty monitoring in the form of statistical capacity building, specific poverty indicator monitoring across sectors, environmental monitoring, and similar systems. This is a much stronger emphasis compared to CAS documents (12%) and PRSPs (37%), and indicates a growing shift toward focusing on results. References to local content development and information dissemination appear in four PRSCs.

Figure 6 provides an overview of the ICT discussions in the same set of documents for the 11 sub-Saharan countries that by mid-2005 had poverty-reduction support credits. The Figure shows that the salient features of the above comparison among the ICT discussions in all

Figure 6. ICTs in PRSPs, CASs, and PRSCs of the 11 PRSC countries

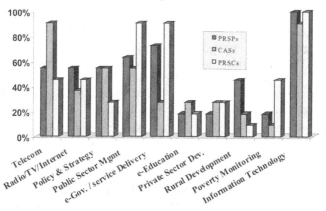

the PRSP, CAS, and PRSC documents for sub-Saharan Africa are also broadly applicable to the subset of documents for the 11 PRSC countries. See, for example, the emphasis on telecom in CASs, and the public-sector-management and service-delivery emphasis in PRSPs and PRSCs. The other trends are also generally consistent with the above findings, with minor variations.

In comparing the overall results among countries, it is interesting to note that Benin, Mozambique, Rwanda, and Senegal (from the group of countries with one PRSC each) all have fairly extensive discussions on the significance of ICTs for poverty reduction and economic development in their PRSPs. However, their respective PRSCs are almost exclusively focused on computerized applications in public-sector management, tax, and customs, and a variety of monitoring or management information systems in different sectors. In other words, major aspects of the role of ICTs in development have been left out of these PRSCs, probably with the expectation that such activities could be funded through other sources. This finding also suggests that the development organizations and donor agencies who are interested in the mainstreaming of ICTs in other aspects of the economy and service delivery to the poor, or as a sector, need to devise or utilize appropriate funding mechanisms beyond PRSCs.

Box 10. Uganda's Access to Government Information Law. ("Uganda Third Poverty Reduction Support Credit", 2004)

> "48. Government plans to improve the right of access to public information, as one of the measures to improving accountability. First, we plan to revise the Official Secrets Acts, and replace it with a modern access to government information law. Consultations with stakeholders on access to government information have already started and in the next fiscal year, the plan is to assemble reccomendations for enactment of the law."

Challenges and Opportunities

The poverty-reduction strategy documents and MDGs provide the framework for country assistance strategies and poverty-reduction support credits in sub-Saharan Africa. The preparation of ICT policies is often carried out based on methodologies that incorporate the framing of the ICT policy in the context of the country's development priorities, the PRSP, and the MDGs. As a result, there is an increasing emphasis on the role of ICTs for economic growth and poverty reduction in the ICT policy documents.

Nevertheless, there is a persistent disconnection between the poverty-reduction strategy-development efforts and the ICT policy-development process. While many PRSPs refer to the role of ICTs in development, they are generally not informed by the ICT policy documents (where they exist), or by the discussions and the partnerships formed around their preparation. Consequently, the ICT policy papers often have little (if any) impact on the ICT priorities set forth in the PRSPs, CASs, or PRSCs. This has led to a strong focus on ICTs as tools for improved efficiency in public-sector operations rather than service delivery to the poor.

Reviewing the national ICT policies, PRSPs, CASs, and PRSCs, six trends stand out among the results.

1.   Telecom reform, competition, and the expansion of infrastructure are much more strongly emphasized in country assistance strategies compared to PRSPs and PRSCs. This partly reflects the direction of the ongoing policy dialogue, and the significance that the World Bank Group ascribes to the implementation of telecom reform and the introduction of competition in the sector for economic growth and poverty reduction. The above finding not withstanding, it is important to note that these issues are all prominently present in PRSPs and PRSCs as well, indicating at least a high level of ongoing dialogue on these themes.

2.   Public-sector-management information systems in general and integrated financial-management information systems in particular are much more strongly emphasized in PRSCs than in CAS or PRSP documents. This is indicative of the fact that when it comes to improved public-service delivery, fiscal accountability, and transparency, both governments and the World Bank and donor community agree on the importance of these systems, hence the high level of emphasis on the actual implementation of these systems, and the corresponding appropriation of funds in PRSCs for that purpose.

3.   Applications of information and communication technologies for development, particularly in education, the private sector, and rural development, are given low to moderate prominence in these documents. Since the private sector is expected to make most of the investments in the ICT-sector development initiatives, the references in these policy documents to ICT-sector development do not mean much if the private sector does not have the right enabling environment (whether for business at large or for the ICT sector in particular) to play an active role.

4.   With very few exceptions, the actual support proposed in PRSCs is mostly focused on the monitoring and/or dissemination of information only rather than on the production and dissemination of relevant content based on local knowledge and/or the adaptation of relevant global experience. These and other areas could potentially benefit from

more focused attention in future policy discussions, development strategies, and implementation-support programs.

5. The consultations and discussions during the ICT policy preparations are useful for awareness raising and sensitizing the policy makers and the public toward the potential of ICTs for development. However, there is a noticeable disconnection in most countries between the ICT policy-development process on the one hand, and the poverty-reduction strategy development and the corresponding poverty-reduction efforts on the other hand.

6. Although the national ICT policies and e-strategies articulate many of the potential benefits of ICTs for development and propose potential applications, these documents also appear to be driven by, and follow, the proposed frameworks of the development agencies, donor organizations, and their local partners that have funded the process. Therefore, some of the policies seem more like a wish list rather than a road map for the use of ICTs in the development process consistent with the realities on the ground. This may partially explain the limited influence of the national ICT policies on the actual poverty-reduction strategies and programs developed by most African countries.

These findings confirm that for ICTs to become effective tools for economic development and poverty reduction, they need to be fully mainstreamed in the national development programs. This is to ensure that the necessary policy decisions as well as the required resources could be put in place for the holistic integration of ICTs in development efforts. The role of the private sector in all aspects of ICT-sector development also needs further emphasis both in poverty-reduction efforts as well as in the use of ICTs for development.

Applications of ICTs in development efforts need to have a clear focus on the use of appropriate technologies for targeted interventions aimed at improving the well-being of the citizens. Such applications of ICTs must be driven by the underlying development objectives and not by technologies. ICTs could play an important role in poverty reduction only if they are properly adapted to the existing circumstances and used as tools that can help facilitate the achievement of development objectives in specific settings.

Additional work is needed in analyzing the effectiveness of the ICT investments that have been made by the public and private sectors alike in sub-Saharan countries and the impact of these investments on the ground. It is also necessary to assess whether the discussion of various ICT initiatives such as rural connectivity and other ICT programs in PRSP or CAS documents have actually translated into higher public-sector investments in these areas.

The integration of ICTs in development strategies is a necessary, but not sufficient, condition for ICTs to play an important role in the socioeconomic development of sub-Saharan countries. The current realities on the ground in terms of low levels of infrastructure, human resources, policy environment, local-language content, and competitiveness are among the major factors that will define the scope of success in the use of ICTs for development in Africa. Therefore, the development of the appropriate ICT infrastructure, human resources, private enterprises, and institutional capacity to respond to these needs must become an integral part of the broader development strategies. In this context, many challenges as well as opportunities lay ahead for sub-Saharan Africa, requiring multifaceted and coordinated efforts to deal with them effectively.

Note

The findings, interpretations, and conclusions expressed in this chapter are entirely those of the author and do not necessarily represent the views of the World Bank Group, its executive directors, or the countries they represent, and should not be attributed to them.

References

Accenture, the Markle Foundation, & the United Nations Development Programme (UNDP). (2001). *Creating a development dynamic: Final report of the Digital Opportunity Initiative.*

Adam, L. (2004). *National ICT policies making in Africa: Implications for CSOs.* Retrieved January 15, 2006, from http://www.ssrc.org/programs/itic/publications/knowledge_report/memos/adammemo4.pdf

Adamali, A., Coffey, J. O., & Safdar, Z. (2005). *Trends in national e-strategies: A review of forty countries* [Draft paper]. World Bank GICT Department.

Bedi, A. (1999). *The role of information and communication technologies in economic development: A partial survey.* Bonn, Germany: ZEF.

Benin poverty reduction support credit. (2004). *Document of the World Bank. Report No. 26272,* pp. 31-32.

Burkina Faso fourth poverty reduction support credit. (2004). *Document fo the World Bank. Report No. 28293-BUR,* p. 61.

Dutta, A., Lanvin, B., & Paua, F. (Eds.). (2004). *The global information technology report 2003-2004.* New York: Oxford University Press.

Gerster, R., & Zimmermann, S. (2003). *Information and communication technologies (ICTs) for poverty reduction* [Discussion paper]? Swiss Agency for Development and Cooperation (SDC).

Ghana Country Assistance Strategy. (2004). *Document of the World Bank. Report 27838-GH,* pp. 12-13.

Ghana poverty reduction strategy: 2003-2004 An agenda for growth and prosperity. (2003). *Vol. I: Analysis and Policy Statement,* 75-76.

Hernandez-Cata, E., Schwab, K., & Lopez-Claros, A. (Eds.). (2004). *The Africa competitiveness report 2004.* World Economic Forum.

Lallana, E. (2004). *An overview of ICT policies and e-strategies of select Asian economies.* UNDP Asia-Pacific Development Information Programme.

Marker, P., McNamara, K., & Wallace, L. (2002). *The significance of information and communication technologies for poverty reduction.* London: DFID.

Mauritius Country Assistance Strategy. (2002). *Document of the World Bank. Report No. 23904 MAS,* p. 12.

McNamara, K. S. (2003). *Information and communication technologies, poverty and development: Learning from experience.* Washington, DC: World Bank.

New Partnership for Africa's Development (NEPAD). (2002). *Short-term action plan: infrastructur*, p.8

Organization for Economic Cooperation and Development (OECD). (2003). *Information and communication technology (ICT) in poverty reduction strategy papers (PRSPs) as of August 2003.* Global Forum on Knowledge Economy.

Organization for Economic Cooperation and Development (OECD). (2004). *Role of infrastructure in economic growth and poverty reduction: Lessons learned from PRSPs of 33 countries.* DAC Network on Poverty Reduction.

Organization for Economic Cooperation and Development (OECD). (2005). *Integrating ICTs into development co-operation* [Background paper].

Republic of Benin. (2002). *Benin poverty reduction strategy paper 2003-2005* [trans. from French], p. 33.

Republic of Cameroon. (2003). *Poverty Reduction Strategy Paper*, p. 51.

Republic of Malawi. (2003). *An Integrated ICT_Led Socio-Economic Development Policy for Malawi*, p. 7.

Republic of Zambia. (2004). *National Information and Communication Technology Policy* (Second Draft). Ministry of Communications and Transport, p. 2.

Rwanda poverty reduction support credit and grant. (2004). *Document of the world bank. Report No. 29467-RW.* Annex 6, p. 6.

Senegal Country Assistance Strategy. (2003). *Document of the World Bank. Report No. 25498-SE*, p. iii.

Senegal poverty reduction support credit. (2004.) *Document of the World Bank. Report No. 28332-SN*, Schedule 1, p. 11.

Tipson, F., & Frittelli, C. (2003). *Global digital opportunities: National strategies of "ICT for development."* Markle Foundation.

Uganda country assistance strategy. (2000). *Document of the World Bank*, pp. 3-23.

Uganda third poverty reduction support credit. (2004). *Document of the world bank. Report No. 26078-UG*, pp. 68-69.

United Nations Economic Commission for Africa (UNECA). (2003a). *E-strategies national, sectoral and regional ICT policies, plans and strategies.* Paper presented at the meeting of the Sub-Committee on Information and Communication Technology: ICT and Governance, Addis Ababa, Ethiopia.

United Nations Economic Commission for Africa (UNECA). (2003b). *Policies and plans on the information society: Status and impact.*

United Nations Economic Commission for Africa (UNECA). (2004a). *ICT policy environment within the Great Lakes countries.* Paper presented at the Workshop on Creating an Effective Enabling Environment for ICT Development: First COMESA Business Summit, Kampala, Uganda.

United Nations Economic Commission for Africa (UNECA). (2004b). *National informa-tion and communication infrastructure (NICI) plans in Southern Africa.* Report to the Tenth SRO-SA Meeting of ICE, Lusaka, Zambia.

United Nations Economic Commission for Africa (UNECA). (2004c). *National information and communication infrastructure (NICI) plans in West Africa.* Report to the Seventh SRO-WA ICE Meeting, Abuja, Nigeria.

Wild, K. (2003). *A global overview of e-strategies: Making the link with poverty and the millennium development goals.* Paper presented at the Fifth Session of the United Nations ICT Task Force, Geneva, Switzerland.

World Bank. (2005). *African development indicators: 2005.* Washington, DC: Author.

Endnotes

[1]   See, for example, Bedi (1999).

[2]   For further details see *OECD Key ICT Indicators: Contributions of ICT Investment to GDP Growth* available at http://www.oecd.org/dataoecd/20/13/34083403.xls.

[3]   Accenture Consulting, the Markle Foundation, and the UNDP (2001).

[4]   For an overview of donor-agency contributions and programs, refer to the 2003 OCD report *Donor Information and Communication Technology Strategies: Summary Matrix.*

[5]   For example, see, McNamara (2003).

[6]   See http://www.un.org/millenniumgoals/.

[7]   See Gerster and Zimmermann (2003).

[8]   See the AISI Web site for more details at http://www.uneca.org/aisi/.

[9]   For details, see http://www.itu.int/wsis/.

[10]   UNECA has taken the lead in this effort through its National Information and Commu-nication Infrastructure (NICI) Strategies program. For further details, see http://www.uneca.org/aisi/nici/strategies.htm.

[11]   See http://www.opt-init.org/framework.html.

[12]   For further details, see *Summary of NEPAD Plan* available at http://www.nepad.org/2005/files/documents/41.pdf.

[13]   The World Bank defines low-income economies during 2004 to 2005 as those with a per capita GNI of less than $826, and lower middle income as those with a per capita GNI of between $8,265 and $3,255. For more details, see http://www.worldbank.org/data/countryclass/countryclass.html

[14]   For further details, see the World Bank Project Information Document for the Africa Regional Communications Infrastructure Project.

[15]   See UNECA's NICI Web site available at http://www.uneca.org/aisi/nici/graph.htm.

16   UNECA has taken the lead in this effort through its NICI Strategies program (http://www.uneca.org/aisi/nici/strategies.htm).

17   For a more detailed discussion, see Adam (2004).

18   See the Republic of Zambia's second draft of the *National Information and Communication Technology Policy* (2004) available at http://www.coppernet.zm/ictpolicy/draft2nationalictolicyv1.11.pdf.

19   Of these, 21 are PRSPs and 9 are interim PRSPs.

20   See the following World Bank sites for more detail: http://info.worldbank.org/etools/docs/library/108875/toolkit/sector/cas.htm and http://web.worldbank.org/WBSITE/EXTERNAL/PROJECTS/0,,contentMDK:20120746~menuPL:51551~pagesPK:41367~piPK:51533~theSitePK: 40941,00.html.

Appendix: Acronyms

AISI	African Information Society Initiative
ANTIC	National Information and Communication Technologies Agency
CAP	Country Assistance Plan
CAS	Country Assistance Strategy
CCF	Country Cooperation Framework
DAC	Development Assistance Committee
DFID	Department for International Development
DOT Force	Digital Opportunity Task Force
FDI	Foreign Direct Investment
G-8	Group of eight major industrial democracies (Canada, France, Germany, Great Britain, Italy, Japan, Russia, United States)
GDP	Gross Domestic Product
GNI	Gross National Income
HIPC	Heavily Indebted Poor Countries
ICT	Information and Communication Technology
ICT4D	ICT for Development
IDRC	International Development Research Center (Canada)
IFMIS	Integrated Financial-Management Information System
IPRSP	Interim Poverty Reduction Strategy Paper
MDGs	Millennium Development Goals
NEPAD	New Partnership for Africa's Development
NGO	Nongovernmental Organization
NICI	National Information and Communication Infrastructure
NICTP	National Information and Communication Technology Policy

Appendix. continued

NRI	Networked Readiness Index
OECD	Organization for Economic Cooperation and Development
PC	Personal Computer
PRSC	Poverty-Reduction Support Credit
PRSP	Poverty-Reduction Strategy Paper
R&D	Research and Development
RCIP	Regional Communications Infrastructure Program
SAT-3/WASC	South African Telecommunications/West African Submarine Cable
SMEs	Small and Medium Enterprises
SSA	Sub-Saharan Africa
UN	United Nations
UNDP	United Nations Development Programme
UNECA	United Nations Economic Commission for Africa
UNESCO	United Nations Educational, Scientific, and Cultural Organization
WSIS	World Summit on the Information Society

Chapter III

Digital Divide:
Introduction to the Problem

Liudmila Burtseva, Academy of Sciences of Moldova Institute of Mathematics and Computer Science, Moldova

Svetlana Cojocaru, Academy of Sciences of Moldova Institute of Mathematics and Computer Science, Moldova

Constantin Gaindric, Academy of Sciences of Moldova Institute of Mathematics and Computer Science, Moldova

Galina Magariu, Academy of Sciences of Moldova Institute of Mathematics and Computer Science, Moldova

Tatiana Verlan, Academy of Sciences of Moldova Institute of Mathematics and Computer Science, Moldova

Abstract

In this chapter the authors introduce the digital-divide concept to the reader, bring its different definitions, and describe the short history of the problem. The basic figures and facts, which characterize the information and communication technologies' usage in different countries and regions, are given as well. Also, basic indicators that allow the monitoring of the country's advancement on the way to bridging the digital divide are stated.

The main purpose for the authors was to show that the digital divide is not only (and not as much) a technical problem, but rather a social and political one. Hence, the approaches to this problem decision, both in the world community as a whole and in separate countries, are described.

Introduction

"The future belongs not so much to those peoples who have achieved today a high standard of well-being, as to those ones which can induce new ideas in the field of high technologies and in their relations with the Nature. The erudition is necessary for this purpose, and not of separate people, but of the nation as a whole. And this circumstance imposes the special responsibility on a governing body of the state and on the intelligentsia." (N. N. Moiseev, "Universum. Information. Society." Moscow, 2001)

"It is not the gap that divides, but the difference of levels." (Stanislaw J. Lec, "Unkempt Thoughts")

The problem of the digital divide has probably only now begun to be perceived as it deserves. Practically any society can face it. Its manifestations are so various in different countries that it is actually impossible to offer common recipes for its solution. As the problem is basically social rather than technological, the ways of its overcoming depend on the degree of the democratization of a society, on the standard of living of a population, on the level of population erudition, and on cultural and ethnic features of the specific community of people. Certainly, the presence of an ICT infrastructure is necessary, but this is only the necessary condition. This chapter contains a brief history of the problem and various relevant definitions. On the basis of statistical data, the state of the art in the world is shown, the various countries are compared, and some basic ideas of the Genoa action plan are stated.

The necessary steps, without which the solution of the digital-divide problem is impossible, are brought. Positive experiences of the European Union (EU) and other countries are confirmed by examples. Basic indicators of the digital divide that allow the monitoring of the problem solution are brought as well.

A Short History of the Problem

The end of the 20th century and the beginning of the 21st were marked by the rapid development of information and communication technologies, which has led to the avalanche growth of digital information. However, any progressive phenomenon, as a rule, is accompanied also by negative by-products. In this case, alongside the overcoming of existing temporal, spatial, and social borders when using information, society has also received a new problem, the so-called digital divide. There are a lot of definitions of this term, which as a matter of fact are reduced to the following: "the term 'digital divide' describes the fact that the world can be divided into people who do and people who don't have access to—and the capability to use—modern information and communication technology" (*Digital Divide*, 1999).

The world community started talking about the problem of the digital divide and the "have-nots" at the end of the last century (Brown, Barram, & Irving, 1995). The *Oxford English Dictionary Online* (2004) considers that the term digital divide was used for the first time in 1995 in an article of Ohio's daily newspaper *Columbus Dispatch* and gives the following explanation as the commonly accepted meaning of this term: "the gulf between those who have ready access to current digital technology (esp. computers and the Internet) and those who do not; (also) the perceived social or educational inequality resulting from this." At that time, many people refused to take this problem seriously and even spoke about it as a far-fetched problem that promoted further enrichment of computer and telecommunication corporations. By the end of the '90s, the stable concept of the digital divide appeared as the serious, recognized problem that is regularly being studied and periodically being discussed by people all over the world today.

In 1999, in its third survey *Falling Through the Net: Defining the Digital Divide*, the USA National Telecommunications and Information Administration (NTIA) noted that the digital divide became "one of America's leading economic and civil rights issues" (1999, p. xiii).

With time, many international organizations and agencies (United Nations [UN], European Union, World Bank, United Nations Development Program [UNDP], Organization for Economic Cooperation and Development [OECD], International Telecommunications Union [ITU], United Nations Educational, Scientific, and Cultural Organization [UNESCO], Economic and Social Council [ECOSOC]) began to express growing concern that the deepening of the digital divide problem may leave many nations far behind, producing growing disparities between advanced, industrialized countries and developing societies. Therefore, they give a lot of attention, force, and means for studying decisions regarding this problem. The international community carries out international conferences and summits (the Digital Divide Summit by the United States Department of Commerce in 1999, and the World Summit on the Information Society [WSIS] in Geneva in 2003 to Tunis in 2005), organizes various forums, creates specialized sites on the digital-divide problem (http://www.pbs.org/digitaldivide/, http://www.digitaldivide.net, http://cbdd.wsu.edu/, http://europa.eu.int/information_society/eeurope/i2010/digital_divide/index_en.htm), and launches various programs and initiatives. They study the experiences of various countries in overcoming this problem. Their discussions have come to a level of development on which practical recommendations are giving for bridging digital inequality both within an international scope and between separate states as well.

Defining the Concept of Digital Divide

There are a lot of terms to describe the concept of digital divide—digital gap, digital inequality, and rarely, information inequality—but all of them reflect the inequality of access to digital or information technologies.

However, before speaking about the problem of digital inequality, and for easier understanding of its essence and origin, it is necessary to pay attention to inequality in general. The following discussion is widespread and absolutely true. Inequality takes place in all spheres of social life from the moment of the beginning of a society. This is the inequality in access to vital resources (food, raw power, and now to information as well), workplaces, education, medical services, and cultural heritage. The distinctions of people regarding social status, the amount of available money resources, level of education, age, residence, and so forth lay in the basis of inequality. Inequality is the reason for conflicts and social cataclysms of various scales. Therefore, the world community, first of all the advanced countries, makes efforts for the neutralization of threats to global and local stability caused by various sorts of inequality.

In this way. the ensuring of equal access to social, economic, cultural, educational, and technological opportunities is offered for all people and for all states. Thus, they get the potential opportunity to reach an equal social status. However, it is an opportunity only, not the solution of the problem. In fact, certain limited resources (financial and especially human resources), even in the presence of political will, cannot be the sole determining factor as they do not allow the removal of inequality. If the opportunities exist already, then it is the will and efforts of people that will determine whether the actual inequality will proceed or will be eliminated. The consciousness of the person influences his or her will. The comprehension of inequality is already a powerful stimulus for social transformations, and for the development of separate people, social groups, and states as a whole. Therefore, discussion of the problem and the popularization of the necessity of overcoming inequality at all levels—internationally, nationally, and in governmental circles and various social groups—are very important.

Now let us turn to the digital-inequality problem, or as it is put more often, the digital-divide problem.

The attention of researchers of the problem at first was usually focused on the inequality in access to technical equipment. Even the definition given in the UN review (UN, 2003) fixes this position: The digital divide is "the fact that poor people in the industrialized world and almost all in the developing world are excluded from modern (information and communication) technologies" (p. 25).

However, this definition is too elementary to characterize the problem, which, actually, is much deeper and extensive. For today, we may consider, among others, the following aspects of the digital divide as basic ones:

- Property
- Age
- Education
- Territory
- Gender
- Culture

In addition, all these aspects are manifested differently in various countries, irrespective of their well-being and ICT infrastructure development level. From practical experience it becomes obvious that the idea "the more computers, the less digital divide" is narrow.

Irvine M. Warschauer (2002), a professor at California University, analyzed three examples of projects concerning ICT promotion. The conclusion was that providing access to ICT is not enough for bridging the digital divide. Analogously, taking into account each of the factors of the digital division (social factors, age, etc.) separately does not determine the problem. The problem needs to be considered in a complex way, taking into account all relevant factors.

For an illustration, let us examine these projects.

- **Example 1. (Warschauer, 2002, "A Slum 'Hole in the Wall'"):** This project was established in 2000 by the New Delhi government in collaboration with an information-technology corporation. A computer kiosk was set up in one of New Delhi's poorest slums. Five computers were inside a booth, and monitors were placed in holes in the walls. Specially designed joysticks and buttons were provided instead of computer mice and keyboards. Dial-up, 24-hour Internet access was available. There were no teachers in accordance to the concept of minimally invasive education. The idea was to allow children to learn by their own desire and capabilities.

Researchers and government officials appreciated this project as it was one that offered a model for how to bring India's and the world's urban poor into the computer age. However, as M. Warschauer (2002) noted, visits to the computer kiosk indicated a rather different reality. Internet access was of little use since it seldom functioned. There were no special educational programs and no special content in Hindi, the only language the children knew. Children did learn to manipulate the joystick and buttons, but almost all their time was spent drawing with paint programs or playing computer games.

Parents had ambivalent feelings. Some saw the kiosk as a welcome initiative, but most expressed concern that the lack of organized instruction took away from its value. In short, the community came to realize that minimally invasive education was, in practice, minimally effective education.

- **Example 2. (Warschauer, 2002, "An Information Age Town"):** In 1997, Ireland's national telecommunications company held a national competition "Information Age Town." Towns of 5,000 people and more across Ireland were invited to compete by submitting proposals detailing their vision of an information-age town and how they could become one. Four towns were chosen as finalists, and then Ennis, a small, remote town of 15,000 people, was selected as the winner. The prize consisted of over $1,200 per resident, a huge sum for a struggling Irish town.

The proposal planned for the following:

- An Internet-ready personal computer (PC) for every family
- An ISDN (integrated services digital network) line for every business
- A Web site for every business that wanted one
- Smart-card readers for every business, and smart cards for every family

Ennis was strongly encouraged to implement these plans as quickly as possible.

Meanwhile, each of three other towns received consolation prizes of about $1.5 million. These towns were not limited by time.

Three years later, Ennis had little to show for its money. Training programs had been run, but they were not sufficiently accompanied by awareness programs. People were not prepared to use advanced technology. In some cases, well-functioning social systems were broken.

The unemployed had received computers and Internet connections at home so that they could sign in and receive electronic payments via the Internet, thus the necessity to visit the labor registry office fell away. However, these people lost the important social function to overcome isolation. More over, they could not use the equipment, and most others saw no reason to do so. Thus, a good number of those computers were sold.

Meanwhile, the other three towns with far fewer resources were forced to carefully plan the usage of their funds rather than spend them for massive amounts of equipment. Community groups, small businesses, and labor unions participated in the planning process. Much greater effort and money were spent on developing awareness, planning and implementing effective training, and setting up processes for sustainable change. The towns built on already existing networks among workers, educators, and businesspeople to support basic uses of technology. As a result, these three towns actually achieved more success than the winner.

- **Example 3. (Warschauer, 2002, "A Model Computer Lab"):** An international donor project funded by the United States Agency for International Development decided to donate a computer laboratory to the College of Education at a major Egyptian university. The purpose was to establish a model teacher-training program using computer-assisted learning in one of the departments of the college. State-of-the-art equipment was selected, including more than 40 computers, an expensive video projection system, several printers and scanners, and expensive educational software. To guarantee that the project would be sustainable, the Egyptian university would be required to manage all the ongoing expenses and operations, including paying for Internet access, maintaining the local area network (LAN), and operating the computer laboratory.

Before the equipment was installed, it became clear that the college would have difficulty in making use of such a huge and expensive donation. Other departments within the college became envious because of the fact that a single department would have such modern and expensive equipment. The college and university could not easily justify spending the money. No money was available to engage an outside LAN manager or provide Internet access at the proper level. Due to all these difficulties, the expensive state-of-the-art computers sat in boxes in a locked room for more than a year before they were even installed, thus losing about one third of their economic value.

These experiences confirm the idea expressed by Bridges.org that states:

> *providing access to technology is critical, but it must be about more than just physical access. Computers and connections are insufficient if the technology is not used effectively because it is not affordable; people do not understand how to put it to use, or they are discouraged from using it; or the local economy cannot sustain its use.* ("Spanning the Digital Divide," 2001, p. 5)

Thus, we come to the wider definition: "digital inequality is a going deep inequality in access to social, economic, educational, cultural and other opportunities owing to unequal access to information and communication technologies" (Baranov, 2003).

Figures and Facts

A lot of analysis and research was carried out to compare the state of the art in the world. The results allow for the assessment of disparities existing in the access to and use of ICT between different countries (international digital divide) and groups within countries (domestic digital divide).

The existence of the digital-divide problem is recognized already by one and all. However, to compare the problem in different countries and at various times, it is necessary to measure it somehow. There are three basic parameters that are frequently used for measuring the digital divide: the number of ICT users, number of computer users, and number of Internet users.

According to data from the Digital Opportunity Task Force (DOT Force, 2001), 70% of the world's poor live in rural and remote areas, and very often they have scarce access even to a telephone, not speaking about ICT in general. Thus, one third of the world population has never made a telephone call.

In its *Human Development Report* of 1998, the UNDP drew attention to the fact that 109 million primary-school-age children (22% of those in the world) were out of school, 885 million adults (age 15 and above) were illiterate, and 4 copies of daily newspapers were circulated per 100 people in developing countries, in contrast to 26 in industrial countries.

Other impressive comparative statistics include the following:

- On the entire continent of Africa, there are only 14 million phone lines—less than the number in either Manhattan or Tokyo (Nkrumah, 2000).
- Wealthy nations make up only 16% of the world population but possess 90% of Internet host computers (Nkrumah, 2000).
- Sixty percent of world Internet users reside in North America, but only 5% of the world population reside there (Nkrumah, 2000).
- One in two Americans is online as opposed to 1 in 250 Africans ("Falling through the Net?" 2000).

Table 1. World Internet usage and population statistics for July 23, 2005 (Source: The table is made according to the data taken from Internet World Stats, 2005).

World regions	Population (mln) (2005 est.)	Population % of world	Internet Usage (mln), latest data	Usage growth 2000-2005	% Population (penetration)	World users %
Africa	896.72	14.0	16.17	258.3	1.8	1.7
Asia	3622.99	56.4	323.76	183.2	8.9	34.5
Europe	731.02	11.4	269.04	161.0	36.8	28.7
European Union	460.27	7.2	221.60	137.9	48.1	23.6
Rest of Europe	270.75	4.2	47.44	377.6	17.5	5.1
Middle East	260.81	4.1	21.77	311.9	8.3	2.3
North America	328.39	5.1	223.39	106.7	68	23.8
Latin America/ Caribbean	546.72	8.5	68.13	277.1	12.5	7.3
Oceania/ Australia	33.44	0.5	16.45	115.9	49.2	1.8
World total	6420.10	100	938.71	160	14.6	100

In digital-divide studies, Internet-usage numbers are most often cited to describe the divide. Nua Internet Surveys ("How Many Online?," 2002) offers an estimate of the global Internet-user population based on an extensive examination of surveys and reports from around the world. Nua's data on how many people have used the Internet show a clear division. In 2001 in the world as a whole, there were 407.1 million Internet users; by 2002, the online users numbered 605.6 million. The leading regions were Europe (190.91 million), Asia and the Pacific (187.24 million), and Canada and the USA (182.67 million). A comparison with similar data on Latin America (33.35 million), Africa (6.31 million), and the Middle East (5.12 million) impresses.

Internet World Stats (2005), an International Web site, shows up-to-date 2005 worldwide Internet-usage and population statistics for over 233 countries and world regions. See Table 1[1] for world-regions data. These data as well as Nua's ("How Many Online?," 2002) show the identical world tendency: Asia, Europe, and North America remain leaders in Internet usage.

However, one can notice that in 2002, Europe was the leader by the absolute amount of Internet users (though its population makes up only 11.4% of the world's population); in 2005, Asia was the leader in the world (see Figure 1). Nevertheless, speaking about the percent of the country's population using the Internet (see Internet penetration in Figure 1), Asia, the population of which makes up 56.4% of the world's population, is still far behind (8.9%), and Northern America is the absolute leader (68%), though its population makes up only 5.1% of the world's population. By examining the dynamics of Internet users' growth inside each region for 2000 to 2005, one can see that the largest progress during these 5 years was made by the nonmembers of the EU (377.6%); the Middle East follows with 311.9%. However, penetration inside these regions remains at only 17.5% and 8.3%, accordingly. The tendency is characteristic for countries of Latin America and the Caribbean (277.1%), Africa (258.3%), and Asia (183.2%) as well, where the penetration parameter is equal to 12.5%, 1.8%, and 8.9%, respectively. Let us compare the same parameters for North America, with a penetration rate of 68%. In this region for the same period, Internet users' growth was only 106.7%.

Figure 1. Comparison of population and Internet usage for different world regions (Source: Diagram is made by the authors of this chapter using data taken from Internet World Stats, 2005)

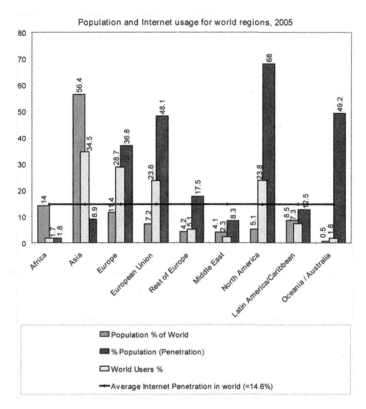

That is, during the last several years, less developed countries of the Middle East, East Europe, the Asian-Pacific region, and Latin America showed a constant increase in the active Internet audience, but not the USA, Japan, and countries of Western Europe. Insignificant growth of the number of Internet users in countries where penetration is already high is quite clear. Additionally, it is not only saturation, but probably an insuperable part of the digital divide that will remain in each society, at least in the near future.

According to the statistics in Table 1, on July 23, 2005, only 14.6% of the world population used the Internet. The reasons for which the other 85.4% are nonusers are interesting. Numerous reviews specify the following reasons: poverty, a badly advanced ICT infrastructure, a lack of education, a misunderstanding of the benefits of ICT usage, bad content, the absence of interesting e-services, and so forth. However, the factor of motivation in using or not using ICT, the Internet in particular, is not less important. The report (Kalkun & Kalvet, 2002) prepared at the order of the Estonia state chancellery contains an analysis of motivation regarding Internet nonuse. Some ideas of this analysis are appropriate for the discussion below.

This report indicates that Internet nonusers constitute about 58% of the Estonian population in the age group of 15 to 74 (February 2002). Every second nonuser acknowledges one or many benefits of computers or the Internet, while one half of the nonusers cannot point out any benefits of Internet.

One third of Internet nonusers are motivated to use the Internet. They have access to the Internet due to ongoing projects. This is because they have a more open attitude to learning new skills on the one hand, and an ability to overcome any barriers to Internet use that may arise on the other hand.

New projects should pay special attention to those two thirds of Internet nonusers who do not associate the possibilities of Internet use with their lives. There are two distinct categories in this group: retired persons and workers, or, as they are called in this report, "passive people" and "blue collars."

- **Passive people** (28% of nonusers)
  - About 60% of people in this group are of 50 or older.
  - They have relatively little interest in matters outside their daily life.
  - They have a very weak relation to the Internet or computers; they see no benefits in the Internet and have no need to use it.
  - They prefer to use traditional media (even if the Internet were cheaper and more convenient); besides a lack of interest, they have a language barrier and are incapable of handling the user interfaces of computers. They are also relatively less able to learn and memorize new things, and are unwilling to change their habits.
- **Blue collars** (27% of nonusers)
  - They are mainly unskilled and skilled workers who do not use computers in their work.
  - About half of people in this group see no benefits in the Internet and would not very willingly change their daily routines as the Internet is unattractive for them.
  - A personal monetary gain would make the Internet attractive for them.
  - There are social and psychological barriers (fear of new technologies, no perception of the need for lifelong learning, a fear of demonstrating their lack of skills to others), skill barriers (lack of computer and ignorance of foreign languages), and economic barriers (income per family member is low).

These groups have not realized a relation between their lives and the Internet yet. That is why the important task is to motivate them, to introduce Internet services adjusted to the habits of these target groups, and to develop suitable Internet services where necessary. It is also important to pay attention to the Internet-skills and Internet-access problems of the passive people and blue collars groups. The rest of the nonusers already have the motivation to use the Internet.

It may be said with fair certainty that the sociodemographic characteristics of the population segments that do not use information technologies are similar to those of other countries. The problem of motivation regarding ICT use arises in many countries, both in the developing and advanced. For example, in Scotland, where the technical base exists and is at a high-enough level, the question about the necessity of projects for the motivation to use ICT arises for those who do not use them (nonusers). Viviane Reding, member of the European Commission, states the same idea. She notes that governments need to encourage the use of new technologies, saying that the public will find new technologies "beneficial but guidance will be needed. The infrastructure exists but is underused: broadband is available on 80% of the European network but has been taken up by only 7% of users" (Raven, 2004).

The authors of the Estonian review fairly remark that if the problems of nonusers are ignored, a part of the population would effectively be excluded from actively participating in economic activities. This implies a decrease in the number of consumers, lower labor quality for the private sector, and, in the worst case scenario, the generation of an army of unemployed for the public sector, which in turn may cause extensive social problems (Kalkun & Kalvet, 2002).

Solutions for the Digital Divide Problem

In July 2000, the summit of the Great 8 (G8) was held in Kyushu-Okinawa, Japan. At this summit, the leaders from G8 countries adopted the *Okinawa Charter on Global Information Society* (2000). This charter established the DOT Force to integrate "efforts into a broader international approach" (p. 5). The DOT Force presented the report *Digital Opportunities for All: Meeting the Challenge* (2001) at the G8 summit held in Genoa in 2001. In that report, a nine-point action plan (Genoa Plan of Action) was proposed as well as a theory of ICT utilization to activate social and economic development.

Since then, the recipes for overcoming the digital inequality in and among countries have found reflection also in a lot of other world community documents ("Spanning the Digital Divide," 2001; UN ECOSOC, 2000). Today, the European Union is aimed to become the most dynamic knowledge-based economy and considers closing the digital divide as a key goal. This idea is reflected in such fundamental EU documents as the conclusion of the European Council in Lisbon 2000 (Lisbon European Council, 2000), the *eEurope 2002 Action Plan* (Council of the European Union & Commission of the European Communities [CEU & CEC], 2000), the *eEurope Benchmarking Report* (CEC, 2002b), and the *eEurope 2005 Action Plan* (CEC, 2002a).

There are many initiatives in the world directed to the digital-divide reduction.

However, it is necessary to understand the idea ("Spanning the Digital Divide," 2001) that solutions that are successful in developed countries cannot simply be copied in the environments of developing countries. The solutions must take into consideration the local needs and conditions. As UN review (UN, 2003) stated, "The UN Millennium Declaration mentions the digital divide issue as one of the symbols of deepening developmental inequality in the world and indeed, finding a comprehensive solution to it belongs to world-making efforts" (p. 26).

Also, the analysis of relevant documents allows drawing a conclusion that the solution to the digital-inequality problem demands a balanced, nationwide-system approach that concentrates on the following basic directions: (a) policy, (b) access, (c) services, (d) content, (e) knowledge and skills, and (f) motivation.

In the Genoa Plan of Action (DOT Force, 2001), special attention is given to the coordination of strategies produced by less developed countries, as well as to involving in the work representatives of both private and state sectors. The states should produce these strategies by themselves, and the strategies' presence in itself is already important for less developed countries. With that, it is necessary to formulate the strategy in strict conformity with national interests.

The many areas of human activity where ICTs can be applied and the many reasons for the digital divide assume many directions to operate and many various forces to involve for its overcoming. In what proportion, when, and what should be preferred depends on features of the specific country. The problem should be solved in a complex way, taking into account and coordinating the actions directed on the elimination of the separate reasons and overcoming any separate barrier. To embrace the basic aspects of the digital divide and to take into account the fact that each society has its own economical, political, social, and historical peculiarities, the following level of reality is necessary to be achieved.

- Physical access (infrastructure, computers, availability of necessary information in the language required on the Net)
- Comprehension of necessity and desire for ICT advantages
- Sufficient degree of society democratization
- Certain literacy level and opportunity for training
- Legislative base (electronic signatures, electronic documents, rights of access to information and protection of confidential information)
- Commercial-structures participation
- Sufficient financing
- State support (political will)

Having in view the objective of achieving this level, experts emphasize the following steps for overcoming the digital divide that are necessary to undertake in the directions listed previously.

1. Formation of national strategy, international and internal policy, and a favorable legislative, public, and economic atmosphere in the fields of informatisation and of ICT use

2. Maintenance of the potential opportunity for the population to access ICT everywhere due to the association of efforts of the state and private sectors of the economy on the development of an information infrastructure

3. Assistance to increase the variety and amount of services for the population and business by means of ICT

4.   Concentration of efforts of the state and society for the creation of public electronic information resources (content) on the basis of national, world, political, economic, cultural, religious, and other types of aspects of development

5.   Ensuring the possibility to get knowledge and skills in ICT use while getting basic special and higher education, and also the creation of conditions for obtaining initial knowledge and skills in this area for all layers of the population

6.   Creation of a system of motivations for ICT application and use, aimed at the formation of wide demand for the use of such technologies in all spheres of society life

In these directions, a variety of avenues have been taken to bridge the digital divide in the world in general and in the EU particularly. Primarily, there have been efforts to promote e-government, encourage technological innovation and the use of existing technologies, guarantee more people Internet access, and advocate media pluralism and creativity. Many of these plans are interesting and noteworthy, but it will take a great deal of political will to accomplish them.

Lately, many high-ranking officials in the EU in their statements express their readiness to undertake the necessary actions to bridge the digital divide. British prime minister Tony Blair, in his speech to the Labour Party Conference in Brighton (Blair, 2004), promised a broadband Britain by 2008. Also, member of European parliament and former French minister of culture and communication Catherine Trautman stated, "Europe must allocate resources for equity of access but also in equipment and in education" (as cited in Raven, 2004). These intentions of high-ranking officials agree with the *eEurope 2005 Action Plan* (CEC, 2002a), which is based on two complementary groups of actions: "On the one hand, it aims to stimulate services, applications and content, covering both online public services and e-business; on the other hand it addresses the underlying broadband infrastructure and security matters" (p. 3).

According to information presented in *People's Daily Online* ("280 Mln U.S Dollars Spent to Eliminate Digital Divide in HK," 2001), the Hong Kong secretary for information technology and broadcasting, Carrie Yau, emphasized that in spite of the fact that the digital-divide problem is not so sharp for Hong Kong as for other countries, the government had formulated clear policies in tackling the issue. She outlined a series of measures taken to bridge the gap or avoid the emergence of a potential gap between various sectors of the community. These include providing education and training, creating a favorable environment for technology diffusion in the community, enhancing knowledge and awareness, and developing e-government. By 2001, the Hong Kong government already expended $282 million to strengthen the community for the exploitation of opportunities in the digital world. Yau noted that a substantial proportion of the local population already had the opportunity to access ICT and the Internet. Half of the households have installed computers. One third of the population are Internet users. The mobile-phone penetration rate has reached nearly 80%.

The new-coming technologies of information transmission are currently applied to bridge the technology and media clusters of the digital divide. The EU's action plan for 2005 includes a thesis for carrying out a cost-benefit analysis of various technological options including space-based ones (CEC, 2002a). In the summer of 2004, the eEurope Advisory Group published *Work Group No.1: Digital Divide and Broadband Territorial Coverage*. The main idea of this paper is that fast data exchange can supply citizens with e-services and help in bridging technological and other clusters of the digital divide. The paper presents recommendations to public authorities for selecting proper and effective technologies that correspond to local conditions. Satellite technologies are proposed for low-density rural areas because of "service costs dependent on the average bit rate usage, and investment costs dependent on peak bit rates" (p. 7). WiFi (wireless fidelity), DSL (digital subscriber line), and fibre technologies are recommended in the case of a medium-density village. High-density rural and urban areas are supposed to be covered by ADSL/VDSL and fibre or cable. The eEurope Advisory Group has examined other alternative technologies such as third-generation mobile/UMTS, power-line communications, broadband wireless access, and digital terrestrial TV, but found out that these technologies are more expensive or offer insufficient bit rates and interactivity as compared with other solutions.

According to these recommendations, "public authorities could also encourage the creation of Public Access Points (libraries, community centres, schools) in order to extend broadband access as much as possible into rural areas" (p. 10).

In particular, WiFi is currently widespread. Several projects based on this technology started during the last 3 years. Both inter-European projects, for example, TWISTER (Terrestrial Wireless Infrastructure Integrated with Satellite Telecommunications for E-Rural; European Space Policy, 2004), and national projects, for example, the Spanish program Rural Public Access Points (Diputacion de Badajoz, 2005), have begun.

Included in the framework of the EU action plan of 2005 was the forum on the digital divide (http://www.techsoup.org/fb). Through this forum, any concerned person can exchange opinions, ask about possible solutions to a problem, or share a solution.

Although the digital-divide problem has become apparent all over the world, it has its own manifestations in each country because of different experiences according to the situation in the respective country.

About Basic Indicators Characterizing the Digital Divide Problem

The sets of indicators for digital-divide assessment differ when mentioned by different organizations. These sets sometimes have some common elements, and sometimes they differ in their composition; however, they are not contradicting in essence, but supplement each other. Even in the evolution of these sets, we can track some consecution and regularity. Thus, at the first stages of studying the digital-divide problem, more attention was paid to the technological aspects. In the course of time, the world community became conscious that this problem is also of human and social character, and that is why the indicators characterizing this problem began to reflect these parts of human activity as well.

Thus, inasmuch as the digital divide was in the first place directly connected with ICT penetration into society life, for digital-divide monitoring and assessment it will be efficient to evaluate ICT development using a range of indicators to benchmark connectivity, access, ICT policy, and overall ICT diffusion. In the Geneva *Plan of Action* (WSIS, 2003), in the section "Action Lines," it is stated, "In the context of national e-strategies, devise appropriate universal access policies and strategies, and their means of implementation, in line with the indicative targets, and develop ICT connectivity indicators." In the section "Follow-Up and Evaluation," the following is stipulated:

Appropriate indicators and benchmarking, including community connectivity indicators, should clarify the magnitude of the digital divide, in both its domestic and international dimensions, and keep it under regular assessment, and tracking global progress in the use of ICTs to achieve internationally agreed development goals, including those of the Millennium Declaration...

All countries and regions should develop tools so as to provide statistical information on the Information Society, with basic indicators and analysis of its key dimensions. Priority should be given to setting up coherent and internationally comparable indicator systems, taking into account different levels of development.

So, each country should develop its own basic indicators to characterize the state of the art of ICT development in it, and to be able to evaluate the development or reduction of the digital divide. Nevertheless, there is a core list of ICT indicators that was developed and is adopted by international organs; it is recommended to be followed, not excluding the indicators elaborated to stress the specific country's peculiarities. Thus, the WSIS Thematic Meeting on "Measuring the Information Society," held in Geneva in February 2005, published the recommended core list of ICT indicators and its broad evolvement ("Final Conclusions," 2005). So, not to overload the space in this chapter but to give an idea of their details, we give the core list of ICT indicators and only some of its subindicators given in the document.

Core List of ICT indicators:

- Infrastructure and access core indicators (CIs)
- CI on access and ICT use by households and individuals
- CI on access and ICT use by businesses

Infrastructure and access CIs (basic core):

- Fixed telephone lines per 100 inhabitants
- Mobile cellular subscribers per 100 inhabitants
- Computers per 100 inhabitants
- Internet subscribers per 100 inhabitants
- Broadband Internet subscribers per 100 inhabitants (fixed and mobile)
- International Internet bandwidth per inhabitant
- Population percentage covered by mobile cellular telephony
- Internet-access tariffs
- Mobile-cellular tariffs

- Percentage of localities with public Internet-access centres by number of inhabitants (rural/urban)

Certainly, the problem of digital-divide evolution is a rather specific one. This problem differs to some extent from the problems of ICT evolution and of information-society evolution. Perhaps it should take into account some specific trends, but these basic trends are useful for assessment, too. Therefore, the indicators mentioned above are taken as the components for the calculation of more complex indicators that take into account the human factor as well. These are e-readiness, e-government, and e-ranking. They were calculated in analytical UN reports during last decade to estimate the level of society informatisation.

For example, we show the structure of the e-government indicator according to its explanation presented in the UN report (American Society for Public Administration & United Nations Division for Public Economics and Public Administration [ASPA & UNDPEPA], 2002).

a.   **Presence on the Internet**

b.   **Infrastructure of telecommunications**

- Number of PCs per 100 persons
- Number of Internet hosts per 10,000 persons
- Percentage of population using Internet
- Number of telephone lines per 100 persons
- Number of mobile telephones per 100 persons
- Number of TV sets per 1,000 persons

c.   **Human resources**

- Human-development index
- Index of access to information
- Ratio between urban and rural population

Tracking all of these indicators is useful for digital-divide monitoring and comparative analysis. These indicators' are indicative for every country, too.

The mentioned indicators for any range of countries or population groups allow carrying out comparative analysis, but do not allow expressing numerically the unevenness of the researched resource distribution between these groups. In the UN report *The Digital Divide: ICT Development Indices 2004* (2005), the authors propose to use Gini coefficients and Lorenz curves in the fields of telephone main lines, mobile subscribers, Internet hosts, PCs, and Internet users for the measurement of digital-divide unevenness.

The Gini coefficient is a measure of inequality. It is usually used to measure income inequality, but can be used to measure any form of uneven distribution. The Lorenz curve was developed as a graphical representation of income distribution and is used to calculate the Gini coefficient. These tools are very visual and can be calculated simply enough, having the values of the researched indicators for the chosen set of countries or groups of population.

In the same report, the calculated Gini coefficients are presented (UN, 2005). These data show changes that occurred during the period from 1995 until 2002 in the fields of telephone main lines, mobile subscribers, Internet hosts, PCs, and Internet users. For example, for telephone main lines, the value of the Gini coefficient in 1995 was equal to 0.688 for 200 measured countries, and it became equal to 0.551 in 2002 for 188 measured countries. For mobile subscribers, these values were 0.822 (195 countries) and 0.609 (194 countries), correspondingly. In other words, the inequality of these resources' distribution between countries had decreased. The same tendency was seen for PCs and Internet users. However, for Internet hosts, the picture is different: In 1995, the value was 0.910 (199 countries), and in 2002, it was 0.913 (204 countries). In this field, the inequality had increased instead of decreased. Perhaps this can be explained by the fact that this resource is the most expensive and requires a strategic approach.

Summarizing all discussed above about digital-divide estimation, we can recommend the use of the simple and complex (e-readiness, e-government) indicators as well as Gini coefficients for digital-divide monitoring and assessment.

In this chapter, the authors described the history of the problem, showed the situation in the world and the large-scale and magnitude of the problem, and set out the traditional, generally accepted views and trends for its solution. Every time, before giving a thesis, the authors endeavored to choose demonstrative examples from the world practice and then, on their basis, to make generalizations and conclusions.

Now, when benchmarking is made, it would be logical and useful to show the application of these judgments and recommendations for specific situations in the example of a typical, average country that is not distinguished by anything. The authors examine the application of these judgments for a specific country in the next chapter of this book. Being an agrarian country with a transition economy (from planned to market), in which the digital-divide problem is especially manifested, Moldova was chosen as such a country.

Conclusion

The analysis of the situations in some countries, made in this chapter, shows that the digital-divide problem has a set of common aspects irrespective of country's development level or other (geographical, demographical, etc.) characteristics. Moreover, this problem is not so much technological as it is even more social and political. Therefore, its solution needs not only technological measures, but social and political ones as well.

- Creation of a system of motivation for ICT usage in everyday life
- Creation by the state and society of national electronic, informational resources, available for the population
- Elaboration of national strategy for information-society development, supported by a system of laws that provide (ensure) the creation of a favorable climate for nondiscriminated access to information for all citizens, for economic activity, and for social progress

References

280 mln U.S dollars spent to eliminate digital divide in HK. (2001). *People's Daily Online.* Retrieved July 8, 2005, from http://english.peopledaily.com.cn/english/200106/07/eng20010607_71990.html

American Society for Public Administration & United Nations Division for Public Economics and Public Administration (ASPA & UNDPEPA). (2002). *Benchmarking e-government: A global perspective.* Retrieved February 29, 2004, from http://www.itpolicy.gov.il/topics_egov/docs/benchmarking.pdf

Baranov, A. (2003). Nad "tsifrovoi propast'yu." *Zerkalo Nedeli, 2*(427). Retrieved July 8, 2005, from http://www.zerkalo-nedeli.com/nn/show/427/37343/

Blair, T. (2004). *Full text of Blair's speech.* Retrieved July 15, 2005, from http://news.bbc.co.uk/1/hi/uk_politics/3697434.stm

Brown, R. H., Barram, D. J., & Irving, L. (1995). *Falling through the Net: A survey of the "have nots" in rural and urban America.* Retrieved July 1, 2005, from http://www.ntia.doc.gov/ntiahome/fallingthru.html

Commission of the European Communities (CEC). (2002a). *eEurope 2005: An information society for all. Action plan.* Retrieved August 5, 2005, from http://europa.eu.int/information_society/eeurope/2002/news_library/documents/eeurope2005/eeurope2005_en.pdf

Commission of the European Communities (CEC). (2002b). *eEurope benchmarking report.* Retrieved August 5, 2005, from http://europa.eu.int/eur-lex/en/com/cnc/2002/com2002_0062en01.pdf

Council of the European Union & Commission of the European Communities (CEU & CEC). (2000). *eEurope 2002 action plan.* Retrieved August 5, 2005, from http://europa.eu.int/information_society/eeurope/2002/action_plan/pdf/actionplan_en.pdf

Digital divide. (1999). Retrieved April 20, 2005, from http://searchsmb.techtarget.com/sDefinition/0,290660,sid44_gci214062,00.html

Digital Opportunity Task (DOT) Force. (2001). *Digital opportunities for all: Meeting the challenge.* Retrieved March 25, 2005, from http://www.labi-berlin.nubb.dfn.de/bibliothek/positionspapiere/dot_force.htm

Diputacion de Badajoz. (2005). *Convocatoria publica para la participacion de los entes locales de la diputacion de Badajoz en el programa "Puntos de Acceso Publico a Internet Ii" (Telecentros.Es).* Retrieved August 2, 2005, from http://www.dip-badajoz.es/municipios/internet_rural/inetrural_convocatoria2005_diputacion.pdf

eEurope Advisory Group. (2004). *Work Group No.1: Digital divide and broadband territorial coverage.* Retrieved August 2, 2005, from http://europa.eu.int/information_society/eeurope/2005/doc/wg1_digi_divide_written_recs_290904.pdf

European Space Policy. (2004). *TWISTER: New project moves to close "digital divide."* Retrieved August 2, 2005, from http://europa.eu.int/comm/space/news/article_730_en.html

Falling through the Net? (2000). *The Economist.* Retrieved April 12, 2005, from http://www.economist.com/surveys/displayStory.cfm?Story_id=375645

Final conclusions. (2005). *WSIS Thematic Meeting on "Measuring the Information Society."* Retrieved November 28, 2005, from http://www.itu.int/wsis/docs2/thematic/unctad/final-conclusions.pdf

Internet World Stats. (2005). Retrieved July 25, 2005, from http://www.internetworldstats.com/stats.htm

Kalkun, M., & Kalvet, T. (2002). *Digital divide in Estonia and how to bridge it.* Retrieved July 1, 2005, from http://unpan1.un.org/intradoc/groups/public/documents/UNTC/UNPAN018532.pdf

Lisbon European Council. (2000). *Presidency conclusions.* Retrieved August 4, 2005, from *http://ue.eu.int/ueDocs/cms_Data/docs/pressData/en/ec/00100-r1.en0.htm*

National Telecommunications and Information Administration (NTIA). (1999). *Falling through the Net: Defining the digital divide.* Retrieved July 18, 2005, from http://www.ntia.doc.gov/ntiahome/fttn99/contents.html

Nkrumah, G. (2000). Digital divide. *Al-Ahram Weekly, 492.* Retrieved April 12, 2005, from http://www.ahram.org.eg/weekly/2000/492/in3.htm

How many online? (2002). *Nua Internet Surveys.* Retrieved March 18, 2005, from http://www.nua.com/surveys/how_many_online/index.html

Okinawa charter on global information society. (2000). Retrieved July 20, 2005, from http://lacnet.unicttaskforce.org/Docs/Dot%20Force/Okinawa%20Charter%20on%20Global%20Information%20Society.pdf

Oxford English dictionary online. (2004). Retrieved June 14, 2005, from http://dictionary.oed.com

Raven, F. (2004). *The European Union on the digital divide.* Retrieved July 15, 2005, from http://www.digitaldivide.net/articles/view.php?ArticleID=41

Spanning the digital divide: Understanding and tackling the issues. (2001). Retrieved April 3, 2005, from http://www.bridges.org/spanning/download.html

United Nations (UN). (2003). *World public sector report 2003: E-government at the crossroads.* Retrieved March 25, 2004, from http://www.unpan.org/dpepa_worldpareport.asp

United Nations (UN). (2005). *The digital divide: ICT development indices 2004.* Retrieved November 26, 2005, from http://www.unctad.org/en/docs/iteipc20054_en.pdf

United Nations Development Program (UNDP). (1998). *Human development report 1998: Consumption for human development.* Retrieved March 17, 2005, from http://hdr.undp.org/reports/global/1998/en/

United Nations Economic and Social Council (UN ECOSOC). (2000). *Development and international cooperation in the twenty-first century: The role of information technology in the context of a knowledge-based global economy.* Retrieved July 13, 2005, from http://www.un.org/documents/ecosoc/docs/2000/e2000-19.pdf

Warschauer, M. (2002). Reconceptualizing the digital divide. *First Monday, 7*(7). Retrieved July 19, 2005, from http://firstmonday.org/issues/issue7_7/warschauer/index.html

World Summit on the Information Society (WSIS). (2003). *Plan of action.* Retrieved February 4, 2005, from http://www.itu.int/wsis/documents/doc_multi.asp?lang=en&id=1160|0

Endnote

[1]   Here and further on, the most recent data available at the moment of this chapter's writing are presented. For example, the data for year 2004 for Moldova are taken when possible from a preliminary report issued in 2005 by the National Bureau for Statistics. If the table or diagram lacks some data for year 2004 for Moldova, it means that the data were not presented in 2004's report and in the preliminary 2005 report. Also, it may be that corresponding data from the preliminary 2005 report were calculated by a different method and disagree with similar data for previous years from the 2004 report.

Chapter IV

Digital Divide:
A Glance at the Problem
in Moldova

Liudmila Burtseva, Academy of Sciences of Moldova Institute of Mathematics and
Computer Science, Moldova

Svetlana Cojocaru, Academy of Sciences of Moldova Institute of Mathematics
and Computer Science, Moldova

Constantin Gaindric, Academy of Sciences of Moldova Institute of Mathematics
and Computer Science, Moldova

Galina Magariu, Academy of Sciences of Moldova Institute of Mathematics and
Computer Science, Moldova

Tatiana Verlan, Academy of Sciences of Moldova Institute of Mathematics and
Computer Science, Moldova

Abstract

*In this chapter, we want to state shortly the basic components and manifestations of the
digital-divide problem, as well as the ways of its solution in a specific country with its
specific regional, social, historical, and political features. Moldova is taken as such a
country. The problem is interesting to consider in the example of such a country because it
is especially manifested in countries of such type: those that are waking up to development
and are limited in means.*

Introduction

"The love for one's country impels and imperiously dictates to everyone, who intends to describe the customs of one's nation, to praise the nation, to which he belongs by birth, and to laud the population of the country which gave him birth (generally speaking, not many strangers know the customs of moldovan people). On the other hand, the love for truth hinders and forbids praising of what is to be condemned upon a fair balance. It will be more useful for country if we will not hide from its citizens' eyes the shortcomings, which are current among them in abundance..."

(Demetrii Cantemirii, "Descriptio Antiqui et Hodierni Status Moldaviae," Petropoli, 1727)

No problem could be explained if we speak only about a problem in general. When putting forward some general conclusions and discussions, one should always examine them with concrete examples. In real life, the problem is manifested by concrete facts, at a concrete place and at a concrete time.

In the previous chapter, we examined basic statements of the digital-divide problem: a short history, the situation in the world, and basic manifestations and approaches to its solution that the world community undertakes and recommends. These discussions were illustrated by some examples from the history of different countries. In the present chapter, the authors base their arguments on the judgments and conclusions stated in their chapter for the examination of the digital-divide problem, and give possible ways to its solution in a specific country. Moldova is chosen as such a country.

Moldova is a country that just now became aware of the necessity to create the information society. Though scientists of the country have told about this for more than 10 years, extreme poverty and instability did not allow people to even think about any purposeful actions in spite of having a comparatively good infrastructure. The concrete, real steps have been started only since the year 2003, although the corresponding rhetoric sounded in different documents and speeches earlier.

The chapter describes the economic situation in the Republic of Moldova (RM) as one of the countries with strongly pronounced symptoms of the digital divide, and describes Moldova's steps in the creation of the information society and the problems that it faces. The chapter shows the degree of the complexity of the digital-divide problem in this country, and what priorities and difficulties occur.

Naturally, national peculiarities are present in Moldova as in any other country. This is not just a type, but a real country. The authors have no pretension about Moldova's oneness, but want to emphasize only that every country, when resolving the digital-divide problem, should take into consideration general statements and the country's individuality as well. In the course of the whole chapter, the authors compare Moldova with other countries by all measured and available indices.

The situation in Moldova is considered in the context of other countries, namely, its direct neighbors (Romania, Ukraine) and a set of other countries from the former socialist camp and that are just passing or has just passed through the phase of transition from planned to market economies (Estonia, Slovakia, Slovenia, etc). Certainly, the analysis includes also those countries in which the solution of the digital-divide problem can serve as a guiding line for ones just starting the problem solving.

On the basis of this analysis, the complex actions that, in the authors' opinion, can provide the solution of the problem in Moldova are offered.

Moldova's E-Place in the World

For more precise understanding of manifestations of the digital-divide problem (in particular, the domestic one) and ways of its overcoming, it is useful to consider it with an example of a specific country. Most sharply, this problem is manifested and more difficult to be tackled in poor countries with a prevailing agricultural population. An example of such a country is Moldova, the small (with an area of 338,000 km^2), poor, agrarian country located in the southeast part of Europe, with its capital Chisinau (see Figure 1). Moldova, formerly part of the Soviet Union, now belongs to a group of underdeveloped countries. According to the preliminary data of the population census from 2004, the population of the country is 3.386 million inhabitants (Biroul National de Statistica [BNS], 2005b). According to the state's official statistical data (BNS, 2005a), the urban population makes up 38.6% of the total population, and rural population makes up 61.4%; the gross domestic product (GDP) per capita has grown from $458 in 2002 up to $719 in 2004.

Let us consider Moldova among other countries according to Web presence and e-readiness. The world community carried out the huge amount of work on the development of methods and the calculation of parameters. For the definition of Moldova's place in the world, the authors of the chapter, in their analytical study (Burtseva, Cojocaru, Gaindric, Magariu, & Verlan, 2004b) made for the United Nations Development Program (UNDP), had based their data on two international analytical reports:

- A UN report (American Society for Public Administration & United Nations Division for Public Economics and Public Administration [ASPA & UNDPEPA], 2002) on the basis of 2001 data

- A review (UN, 2003) made by the Department of Economic and Social Affairs of the United Nations (on the basis of 2003 data)

In 2001, a statistical analysis was done comparing the ICT infrastructure and human-capital capacity for 144 out of 190 UN member states. One hundred forty-three countries from them were listed as using the Internet in some capacity. In 2003, the coverage was expanded to include all UN member states. Only 173 out of 191 member states had a Web-site presence. In both surveys, an assessment of the e-government index was done. Different methodologies were used for this index calculation, but each of them takes into account such important indices as Web-presence measure, infrastructure measure, and human-capital measure, which in their turn are calculated on the basis of several other characteristics. In the 2003 survey,

Table 1. E-readiness, population, and GDP per capita for range of countries (Source: Table is made by the authors of this chapter using data from ASPA & UNDPEPA, 2002; GEOHIVE: Global Statistics, n.d.; UN, 2003)

Country	2001		2003			
	E-Gov Index	Rank of E-Readiness	E-Gov Readiness Index	Population Total (million)	Urban Population (% from total)	GDP per Capita (thousand $US)
USA	3.11	1	0.927	294.04	80.1	37.007
Australia	2.60	3	0.831	19.73	92	26.273
Norway	2.55	7	0.778	4.53	78.6	48.881
United Kingdom	2.52	5	0.814	59.25	89.1	30.293
Netherlands	2.51	11	0.746	16.15	65.8	31.677
Denmark	2.47	4	0.820	5.36	85.3	39.599
Sweden	2.45	2	0.840	8.88	83.4	33.888
Spain	2.30	29	0.602	41.06	76.5	20.363
Estonia	2.05	16	0.697	0.96	69.4	8.739
Russian Federation	1.89	58	0.443	143.25	73.3	3.026
Ukraine	1.80	54	0.462	48.52	67.2	1.021
Slovakia	1.71	40	0.528	5.40	57.4	5.899
Slovenia	1.66	28	0.631	1.98	50.8	13.247
Romania	1.63	50	0.483	22.33	54.5	2.703
Azerbaijan	1.30	94	0.364	8.37	50	0.851
Moldova, Rep. of	1.29	95	0.363	4.27	46	0.460
Honduras	1.20	124	0.280	6.94	45.6	1.005
Guatemala	1.17	109	0.329	12.35	46.3	2.003
Kyrgyzstan	1.01	110	0.327	5.14	33.9	0.338
Kenya	0.90	118	0.299	31.99	39.4	0.433
Madagascar	0.79	144	0.229	17.40	26.5	0.314
Sierra Leone	0.68	167	0.126	4.97	38.8	0.160
Ethiopia	0.57	166	0.128	70.68	15.6	0.094
Bosnia and Herzegovina	-	115	0.309	4.16	44.3	1.673
Albania	-	114	0.311	3.17	43.8	1.934
Liechtenstein	-	154	0.178	0.03	21.6	-
Papua New Guinea	-	136	0.250	5.71	13.2	0.594

Table 2. Population and Internet-usage data for range of countries for year 2005 (Source: The Table uses the data from Internet World Stats, 2005)

Country	Population (million) 2005 est.	Popu-lation % of World	Internet Usage (million) Latest Data	Usage Growth (%) 2000-2005	Popu-lation Pene-tration (%)	World Users (%)
USA	296.21	4.61	202.89	112.8	68.5	21.614
Sweden	9.04	0.14	6.66	64.4	73.6	0.709
Australia	20.51	0.32	13.78	108.9	67.2	1.468
Denmark	5.41	0.08	3.72	90.8	68.7	0.396
United Kingdom	59.89	0.93	35.81	132.5	59.8	3.815
Norway	4.61	0.07	3.14	42.7	68.2	0.335
Netherlands	16.32	0.25	10.81	177.1	66.2	1.151
Estonia	1.34	0.02	0.62	69.4	46.2	0.066
Slovenia	1.96	0.03	0.93	210.0	47.5	0.099
Spain	43.44	0.68	15.57	188.9	35.8	1.658
Slovakia	5.38	0.08	1.82	180.0	33.8	0.194
Romania	21.38	0.33	4.94	517.5	23.1	0.526
Ukraine	46.66	0.73	5.28	1305.0	11.3	0.562
Russian Federation	144.00	2.24	22.30	619.4	15.5	2.376
Azerbaijan	8.33	0.13	0.30	2400.0	3.6	0.032
Moldova, Rep. of	3.90	0.06	0.29[a]	1052.0	7.4	0.031
Guatemala	12.33	0.19	0.40	515.4	3.2	0.043
Kyrgyzstan	5.31	0.08	0.20	287.6	3.8	0.021
Albania	3.09	0.05	0.03	1100.0	1.0	0.003
Bosnia and Herzegovina	4.45	0.07	0.10	1328.6	2.2	0.011
Kenya	33.39	0.52	0.50	150.0	1.5	0.053
Honduras	6.57	0.10	0.27	580.0	4.1	0.029
Papua New Guinea	5.85	0.09	0.07	-44.4	1.3	0.008
Madagascar	17.96	0.28	0.07	135.0	0.4	0.008
Liechtenstein	0.03	0.00	0.02	122.2	57.3	0.002
Ethiopia	70.60	1.10	0.10	900.0	0.1	0.011
Sierra Leone	5.03	0.08	0.02	300.0	0.4	0.002

Figure 1. Moldova's geographical position

the rank of the e-government index and Web-presence measure were determined for each of the 173 assessed countries.

Thus, the e-readiness index (readiness of the countries for transition to e-governance) allows one to estimate in any measure the degree of the use of ICT in the country, and hence to judge about the digital divide between countries. For comparison, the authors chose the following categories of countries:

- Those with the highest values of the e-readiness index (USA, Australia, Norway, United Kingdom, Netherlands, Denmark, Sweden, Spain)

- Geographical neighbors of Moldova, and countries from the former USSR and from the former socialist community (Estonia, Russian Federation, Ukraine, Romania, Azerbaijan, Kyrgyzstan, Slovakia, Slovenia)

- Agrarian countries, where the percent of the rural population is close to (or lower than) the Figure in Moldova (Bosnia and Herzegovina,[1] Albania,[1] Honduras, Guatemala, Kenya, Madagascar, Sierra Leone, Ethiopia, Liechtenstein,[1] Papua New Guinea[1])

- Table 1 contains the following information about the chosen countries.

- E-readiness index values for 2001 (ASPA & UNDPEPA, 2002) and for 2003 (UN, 2003), which allow one to judge about the degree of ICT use in the country

- Population number for 2003 (GEOHIVE: Global Statistics, n.d.), which allows us to judge about the size of the country

- Percent of urban population for 2003 (GEOHIVE: Global Statistics, n.d.), which characterizes the degree of the rurality of the country

Figure 2. Comparison of e-government indices for the years 2001 and 2003 (Source: Diagram is made by the authors of this chapter data from the UN reports: ASPA & UNDPEPA 2002 & UN 2003)

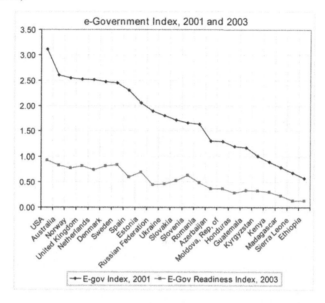

- GDP per capita in U.S. dollars in 2003 (GEOHIVE: Global Statistics, n.d.), which allows one to judge about the level of well-being or the degree of poverty in the country

- Note that because the year 2003 is the latest one for which data on e-readiness are available, the rest of the data in Table 1 were also from this year. To carry out the comparison[2] on the basis of the latest data (year 2005), we took the Internet-users penetration index—the percent of the country's population that use the Internet (see Table 2)—for the same country range as in Table 1.

In Table 1, countries are ordered according to the decrease of the 2001 e-government index so that by the position of the country in that list, we are able to judge about the digital divide between chosen countries.

In 2001 and 2003, calculations were made by using different methods, and therefore absolute values of these indices are incomparable. However, one may observe the ratios of values of each country to the values of others and how these ratios evolved (see Figure 2).

One may notice the progress of Australia, Norway, Great Britain, Holland, Denmark, and Sweden, which came close to the United States. It means that the digital divide between them and the United States decreased. Estonia made considerable progress. Slovakia, Slovenia, and Romania also progressed. Moldova and Azerbaijan remained at the same low level and did not change their positions relative to the other countries. Their ranks in 2003

Figure 3. E-government ranks for the range of countries (Source: Digram is made by the authors of this chapter using data from the reports fo the Center for Public Policy by Darrell M. West 2001-2005)

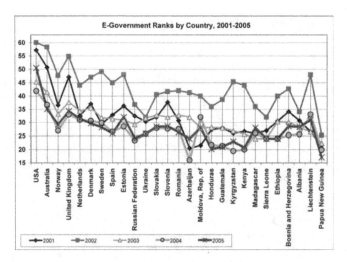

Figure 4. Comparison of levels of urban population and GDP per capita for the range of countries (Source: Diagram is made by the authors of this chapter using data from the Web site GEOHIVE: Global Statistics, n.d.)

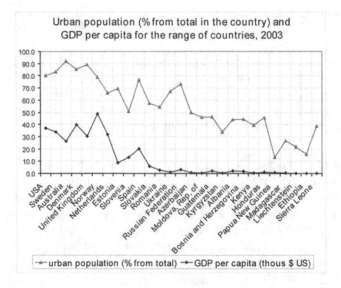

Figure 5. Percentage of Internet users in a country's population for the range of countries (Source: Digram is made by the authors of this chapter using data from the Web site Internet World Stats, 2005)

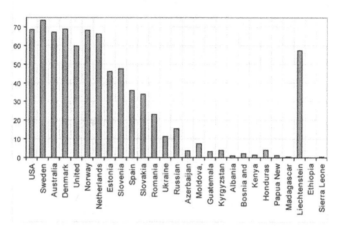

were correspondingly 95 and 94. They remain amongst the countries for which the digital divide is the largest as compared with leading countries.

The global e-government reports (West, 2001, 2002, 2003, 2004, 2005) present annual results on global e-government: the delivery of public-sector information and online services through the Internet. In Figure 3 we show the e-government rank orderings gathered from all these reports for the chosen range of countries.

It is necessary to note once more that the absolute values for different years for the same country are not comparable and not indicative. However, they are indicative of the correlation between countries for one year. So, Moldova in 2001 was situated among lagging countries and occupied the 155th place with an e-government rank value equal to 21.6. Only Azerbaijan came after Moldova in the selected range of countries. In 2002, Moldova occupied the 105th place with an e-government rank value equal to 40.0. Then, nine countries from the selected range came after Moldova. In 2003, Moldova came out at the 62nd place, in 2004 at 21st place, and in 2005 it was at the 61st place. The abrupt improvement in 2004 is evidence not so much of abrupt development acceleration in Moldova as it is of slackening speed in other countries (if we exclude the possibility of the inaccuracy of the data on the basis of which the calculations were made). The fact that the results for the years of 2003 and 2005 are close confirms this conclusion.

Now we shall compare the e-government index (that is, the degree of ICT use) with the percent of the urban population and with the GDP per capita of the countries.[3] Since the data for this comparison are for 2003, it is logical to arrange the countries in decreasing order of e-government index for 2003 (see Figure 4).

One can precisely trace the following dependence: The percent of the urban population and the GDP per capita in the countries with a high degree of ICT use are higher, and vice versa.

Figure 6. Comparison of Internet-usage growth for the range of countries for the period 2000-2005 (Source: Diagram is made by the authors of this chapter using data from the Web site Internt World Stats, 2005)

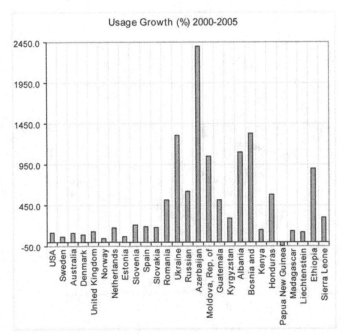

Consequently, the resulted Figures confirm that the degree of the digital divide is influenced both by the ratio of the city population to the rural one, and by the country's standard of living. Moldova, with its poverty and high percent of rural population,[4] alongside other agrarian countries, is at the end of this spectrum.

There are some slight (and quite explainable) deviations from the described tendency. For example, Estonia and Slovenia, by their position in the list of chosen countries, possess high-enough values of the e-government index with a rather low percent of urban population and a low GDP per capita. Slovakia and Romania, with lower percents of urban population than Ukraine and Russia have (and approximately identical GDP per capita), possess higher values of the e-government index. As to Moldova, its place according to the value of the e-government index corresponds to its percent of urban population among the chosen countries. If we analyze the parity of the values of GDP per capita, we see several countries with lower e-government index values but with higher values of GDP per capita: Guatemala, Albania, Bosnia and Herzegovina, Honduras, and Papua New Guinea.

These examples and deviations show that agrarianism and the poverty of the country are not unique factors that determine the digital divide.

Figure 5 helps to draw the conclusion: The rank of the countries based on Internet penetration in 2005 basically meets the same order (the decrease of the e-government index value for

Table 3. General socioeconomic data of Moldova (Source: The Table is made by the authors of this chapter using data from official reports, DSSRM, 2004; BNS, 2005a)

Type of Data	1999	2000	2001	2002	2003	2004	2005
Total Area (thousand km^2)	33.8						
Number of Population[a] (million inhabitants)	3.6493	3.6435	3.6345	3.6272	3.6177	3.6068	3.3860
Population of Urban/Rural (in % of the total)	42.0/58.0	42.0/58.0	41.3/58.7	41.4/58.6	41.4/58.6	41.4/58.6	38.7/61.3
GDP (million $US, current prices)	1170.83	1288.46	1480.71	1661.83	1957.81	2595.00	-
Indices of GDP (previous year = 100)	96.6	102.1	106.1	107.8	106.6	107.3	-
Economically Inactive Population (in % of the total)	53.9	54.6	55.6	55.5	59.2	60.3	-

Note: [a]Data from the official annual report for year 2004 (DSSRM, 2004) are the result of recalculation by the methodology applicable in the periods between population censuses.

2003) with some exceptions. The obvious exception represents Liechtenstein: For its number of Internet users in 2005, this country takes an essentially higher place than the one for its e-government index value in 2003. Some of the less advanced countries have made a greater step forward than more advanced countries. Moldova is among them, too. This proves to be true also by the data on Internet growth as shown in Figure 6. In several less developed countries, the number of Internet users has increased during 5 years by more than 1,000%, including Moldova (1,052%). With that, the index of Internet penetration in Moldova is still very low. Compare the 7.4% in Moldova with the 68.5% in the USA, the 35.5% in Europe, and the 13.9% in the whole world; the index value of usage growth is equal to 1,052% in Moldova, 112.8% in the USA, 151.9% in Europe, and 146.2% in the whole world.

Having considered the position of Moldova among other countries, we shall examine the dynamics of the parameters influencing the digital divide in Moldova, its current condition relative to the digital divide inside the country, what was undertaken, and what is necessary to undertake for overcoming the digital divide. In the beginning, we shall consider the dynamics of the basic socioeconomic indices during the last few years.

The General Socio-Enonomic Data of Moldova

The general socioeconomic data of Moldova from official reports (BNS, 2005a; Departamentul Statistica si Sociologie al Republicii Moldova [DSSRM], 2004) are presented in Table 3.

The data show that Moldova's population is rural to a great extent (61.3%), and the percent of the rural population in the country is growing. The same tendency is true for a number of economically inactive populations. The indices of GDP are slightly growing from year to year, but it is most likely due to inflation. The level of living standard has grown a little, too. Nevertheless, as the data in Table 1 show, the GDP per capita in Moldova is very low.

Figure 7. Distribution of employment by economic activities in Moldova (Source: Diagram is made by the authors fo this chapter using data from offical reports of DSSRM 2004; BNS 2005a)

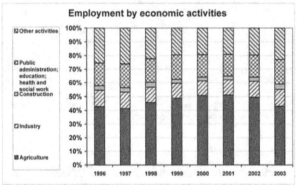

Figure 8. Incomes and living standards of the population in Moldova (Source: Diagram is made by the authors of this chapter using data from offical reports of DSSRM 2004; BNS 2005a)

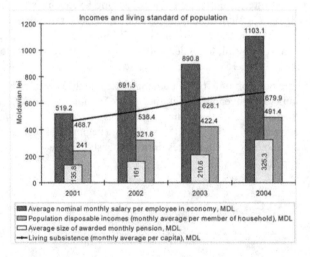

Regarding the employed part of the population, one can see that the rate of the agricultural sector is dominant (see Figure 7).

The comparison of population incomes and its living subsistence also bears eloquent evidence of the population's poverty. The corresponding data are presented in Figure 8. The monthly average per member of a household (not to mention the average size of awarded monthly pension) is essentially lower than the living subsistence.

When estimating the cited data, it is necessary to take into account the situation in the country. For example, part of the population illegally works outside the country, and this number is beyond all calculation. People leave their native places in search of jobs for which they can earn some money to keep their families in Moldova. Officially, this part consists of 366,000

Table 4. Telephone means for public use (Source: The Table is made by the authors of this chapter using data from official reports, BNS, 2005a; DSSRM, 2004)

Type of Data	1996	1997	1998	1999	2000	2001	2002	2003	2004
Number of House Telephone Sets in Public Network or Connected to It (per 100 inhabitants total)	11.5	12.4	12.5	13.3	14.1	15.6	17.3	19.3	21.2
In Urban Network	18.8	20.4	21.5	22.5	24.5	26.1	27.5	29.2	30.3
In Rural Network	5.2	5.5	6.0	6.6	6.9	8.1	10.1	12.2	14.7
% Rural of Urban	27.66	26.96	27.91	29.33	28.16	31.03	36.73	41.78	48.51

Figure 9. Rural-area and urban-area provision of common telephone connection in Moldova (Source: Diagram is made by the authors if this chapter using data from offical reports of DSSRM 2004; BNS 2005a)

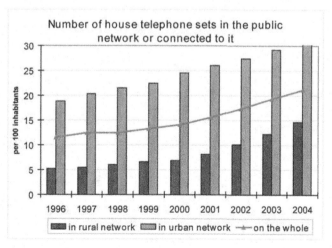

inhabitants, but according to independent experts' estimations, it includes about 1.3 to 1.6 million inhabitants who in 2004 transferred to the country approximately $970 million. So, not all statistical data are present, and those we have are not always absolutely authentic. The data from different sources do not always coincide. Inside the country, the regular gathering and processing of statistical data on all parameters and techniques accepted in the world is not adjusted yet. Nevertheless, the data we have help us to track the tendency and ratio of the parameters we are interested in.

These factors, along with others, constitute the serious obstacles in the way of the implementation of ideas about the information society in Moldova.

Domestic Digital Divide in Moldova by Figures

Table 4 presents the data about the number of house telephone sets in the public network disaggregated by the urban area and the rural one for the period from 1996 to 2004. These data show that during this period of time, the provision of the rural area with common telephone connection is much less than it is in the urban one (see Figure 9).

The same tendency of weak provision of ICT technologies in rural areas is confirmed by the data from the National Regulatory Agency in Telecommunications and Information (NRATI) site (n.d.) about granted licenses. On July 1, 2005, only 1 in 27 holders of the date-transfer license was from the village Bardar. All 21 holders of licenses for IP (Internet protocol) phone services are from the capital of the country, Chisinau. All six holders of licenses for fixed phone services are from Chisinau, too.

Figure 10. Nonuniformity of access to Internet in settlements of Moldova (Source: Data is given by the Department of Informational Technologies of Modova. This data is collected from economical agents only.)

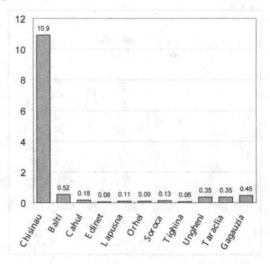

In Figure 10, the data for the year 2003 about the number of registered Internet users per 10,000 inhabitants as distributed by different districts of Moldova are presented. They show the nonuniformity of access to the Internet. It is one of the sharpest problems for Moldova. This urgency has been taken into account by the development of the action plan on overcoming the problem, that is, first of all, to direct efforts and means for the creation of the minimal conditions for inhabitants of rural areas. The state should give to citizens at least a minimal but guaranteed set of services that will allow them to not remain outside of the modern information society.

As a result of current natural, social, historical, economic, and political conditions in the country, it is possible to note the pronounced digital divide, both international and domestic. The Figures indicate the negative specificity of the country, at the same time emphasizing the sharp necessity to pass to modern technologies, and the difficulty to implement these technologies as well.

Figure 11. Ratio of provision of telephone sets in rural areas to this provision in urban areas of Moldova (Source: Diagram is made by the authors of this chapter using data from offical reports of DSSRM 2004; 2005a)

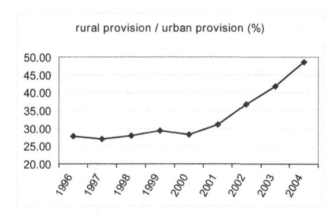

Figure 12. Density of mobile-telephone communication (Source: Data is taken from Annual Report 2004; NRATI 2005)

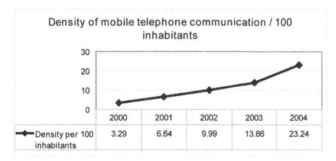

Figure 13. Capacity of service market in the field of data transmission, Internet access, and channel renting (Source: Data is from Annual report 2004; NRATI 2005)

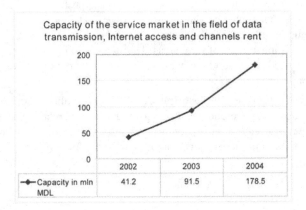

Figure 14. Number of providers of Internet-access services broken down by type of connection (on January 1, 2005) (Source: data is from Annual report 2004; NRATI 2005)

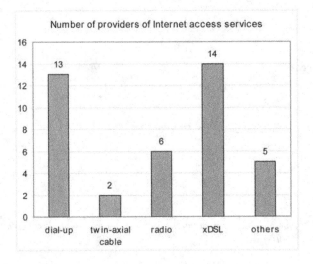

Figure 15. Dynamics of the number of connections for Internet access broken down by type of connection (Source: Data is taken from Annual report 2004l NRATI 2005)

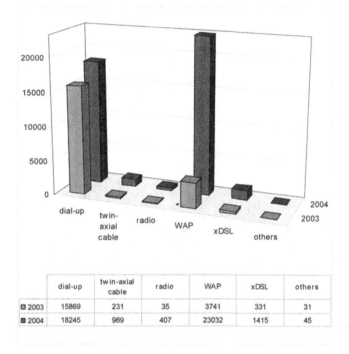

	dial-up	twin-axial cable	radio	WAP	xDSL	others
▣ 2003	15869	231	35	3741	331	31
▪ 2004	18245	969	407	23032	1415	45

Positive Dynamics Toward the Information Society

Although the previous section of the chapter showed that Moldova is at low level of development, the following data demonstrate that the situation becomes better from year to year.

ICT Infrastructure

Let us see the Figures in Table 4 from another point of view: Compare the ratio of telephone-set provision in rural areas to this provision in urban areas. One will see the sTable, positive dynamics from the year 2000 (see Figure 11).

The dynamics of ICT infrastructure development are also demonstrated by data in Table 5.

According to the data for year 2004 (NRATI, 2005), the development of mobile-phone services in RM made essential progress. During the period from 2000 to 2003, the number of new connections in the market grew from 110,000 to 130,000 subscribers per year. In the year 2004, 317,500 subscribers were connected to networks; that is 67.6% more. As a result, in 2004 the density of mobile telephony essentially increased (see Figure 12).

Table 5. Data on ICT infrastructure development in Moldova (Source: The Table uses data from official reports, BNS, 2005a; DSSRM, 2004)

Type of Data	1996	1997	1998	1999	2000	2001	2002	2003	2004
Share of the Length of Lines with Optic Cable in the Total Length of Cable Long-Distance Lines of Telecommunications (%)	17.1	-	23.7	-	23.9	-	43.3	-	-
Share of Channel Length in Total Length of Long-Distance and International Telephone Channels (% of digital transmission systems with optic cable)	8.5 5.7	18.2 15.3	38.6 35.2	49.4* 44.9	69.1 63.3	59.6 55.9	99.6 98.0	100.0 97.8	100.0 100.0
Number of Mobile-Phone Service Subscribers (thousand)	0.92	2.20	8.50	17.93	109.64	224.78	338.30	475.94	786.94
Number of Internet Networks and Access Points	6	10	32	55	223	386	415	415	415

Table 6. NRATI licenses (Source: The Table uses data from NRATI, n.d.)

Data Type	2003	2004	2005 (November 1)
Total	230	247	230
Inclusive for Rural Area	1	21	110

Let us consider the market of telecommunications in Moldova: Services for data transmission, Internet access, and the renting of channels make up about 6.66% of the total amount of services (NRATI, 2005). In 2004, the cost of the market of these services increased in comparison with the previous year by 95% (see Figure 13). Figure 14 presents the distribution of providers of Internet-access services broken down by the type of connection on January 1, 2005.

In 2004, the number of Internet connections increased by 22,004 in comparison with 2003. The progress is due to the following connections: WAP connections grew by 19,291; co-axial cable by 738; xDSL connections, in particular, ADSL (asymmetric digital subscriber line), by 1,084; radio connections by 372; dial-up connections by 505; and other kinds of connections by 14 (see Figure 15).

Table 7. Data on Higher Education Institutions (Source: The Table uses data from official reports, BNS, 2005a; DSSRM, 2004).

Type of Data	1996/ 1997	1997/ 1998	1998/ 1999	1999/ 2000	2000/ 2001	2001/ 2002	2002/ 2003	2003/ 2004	2004/ 2005
Higher University Educational Institutions	24	28	38	43	47	47	45	40	35
Students (thousand)	58.3	65.6	72.7	77.3	79.1	86.4	95.0	104.0	114.6
Students (10,000 inhabitants)	162	180	199	212	217	238	262	288	318
Pedagogical Staff (thousand)	4.4	4.6	4.7	5.1	5.3	5.3	5.5	5.7	5.9

According NRATI (2005), in 2004 the amount of broadband Internet connections increased by 4.75 times, having reached 2,791 connections by January 1, 2005 (compare to 597 connections in 2003). It has taken place, basically, due to the increase in the amount of connections of twisted telephone pairs by 1,084 connections. The increase in the number of connections through the twisted telephone pairs is caused by the development of xDSL broadband technologies, in particular, ADSL. Note that the world community recognizes xDSL as prospective technologies, but the implementation of xDSL services in the CEE 10 is still at a very early stage.

The NRATI data about granted licenses are evidence of ICT infrastructure improvement, particularly in the rural sector. The licenses issued by NRATI (n.d.) are distributed as in Table 6.

Toward the beginning of the second half of year 2005, NRATI had registered 333 holders of the licenses that allow the provision of services of computer science in public places, 84 of them working in rural settlements (Server, n.d.).

The data brought to this subsection confirm that there exists a national satisfactory structure of communication highways, which may serve as a foundation for the implementation of the actions directed to the information society's creation.

Educational Level

According to the data of the UNDP (2003, 2005) human-development reports, the following parameters are evidence of the high literacy rate of the population.

- Literate adult population (older than 15): 99.0% in 2001 (UNDP, 2003), 96.2% in 2003 (UNDP, 2005)
- Literate youth of ages 15 to 24: 99.8% in 2001 (UNDP, 2003), 98.7% in 2003 (UNDP, 2005)

- Net secondary enrollment ratio (number of students enrolled in a level of education who are of official school age for that level as a percentage of the population of official school age for that level): 68% in 2000 to 2001 (UNDP, 2003), 69% in 2002 to 2003 (UNDP, 2005)

- Tertiary students in science, math, and engineering (percent of all tertiary students): 44% in 1994 to 1997 (UNDP, 2003); later data are absent

Note that in spite of economic difficulties, there remains the big craving for higher education in the country. See data on higher education institutions presented in Table 7. The ever-growing number of students in the country testifies to it. Also note that the share of students training in the ICT area is great enough and also grows. One can see it by analyzing the data in Figure 16.

So, regardless of the pauperization of the population, there persists the consciousness of the knowledge necessity. Moreover, a lot of people, not only the young, receive a second (and sometimes a third) higher education, aspiring not only to have the big opportunity to get a prestigious and well-paid job, but also to get more opportunities for self-realization.

The described situation in the country is confirmed by UN report Figures (UN, 2003). From the point of view of electronic-government implementation, Moldova occupies the 95th place among 173 estimated countries. As to presence on the Internet, Moldova occupies the 146th place. It is lower than any European country, although the indices of human capacity are rather high: 0.9 (the maximal one is 0.99).

Figure 16. Graduation of students of higher university educational institutions by groups of specialities related to ICT (Source: Diagram is made by the authors of this chapter using data from offical report of DSSRM 2004)

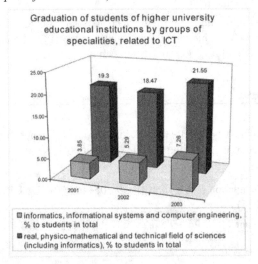

Political Will

An important component on the way to bridging the digital divide is political will. Within the last 10 years, activity in this area in Moldova bore a rather declarative character. At last, during the latest 2 years, the specific steps and results have appeared. The presence of political will in the country is shown by the chronology of the issued decisions of the government and accepted laws.

1. **November 21, 2003:** The parliament of RM passed the law about informatization and state information resources.

2. **March 19, 2004:** The decree of the president of RM about the creation of an information society is issued.

3. **May 2004:** The program SALT, which assumes the maintenance of physical access to the Internet for all schools in the country, is accepted.

4. **July 15, 2004:** The parliament of RM passed the law regarding electronic documents and digital signatures.

5. **February 22, 2005:** RM is among the first countries from the Commonwealth of Independent States to sign in Brussels the plan of action "European Union: Moldova," which has a section about information-society development.

6. **February 23, 2005:** The government has accepted the strategy of information-society creation called "Electronic Moldova" and the action plan for its implementation.

7. **In 2005**, in the structure of the newly elected government, the Ministry of Information Development appeared.

The authors of the present chapter are the eyewitnesses and participants of the process of national strategy development. This document was developed on the basis of numerous meetings, seminars, and round Tables with the participation of scientists, experts, and advisers in the field of ICT, representatives of civil society, and also governmental and commercial structures. Results of the analytical research that has been carried out in various relevant directions by commissions of experts have been taken into account. This process passed iteratively in some stages, thus in full conformity to recommendations of the Genoa Plan of Action, Point I:

> *These strategies, generated by the countries themselves, should be the result of a consultative process involving all relevant interested parties in the country, including the private sector and non-profit organizations (NPOs). Such eStrategies should be regularly reviewed and updated, and benchmarked internationally; they should, where appropriate, be reinforced by regional and sub-regional coordination efforts, notably in the context of economic integration.*

(Digital Opportunity Task [DOT] Force, 2001, p. 13)

There are a lot of programs in which the specific steps, directed at increasing the living standard and improving the life conditions of the population, and connected with ICT introduction into daily life, are stipulated. The examples of such programs in Moldova are the Program of Economic Growth and Struggle Against Poverty, the Moldovan Village, and SALT. Besides these, nongovernmental organizations have their own programs focused on information-society development.

Other Facts and Events

There are also other manifestations in society that testify to the positive dynamics in overcoming the digital divide.

- **Example 1:** The State Office of Public Prosecutor (SOPP) of Moldova is the first and, for the time being, only establishment of RM in which computers on a multifunctional network provide fast and protected information interchange between the SOPP and other state structures (E-uriadnik, n.d.-a).
  - This information-telecommunication center provides Internet services and e-mail on 150 computers that are interconnected and offer opportunity for further expansion. The center is connected to information-telecommunication systems of local public bodies. Furthermore, the connection of all territorial divisions of SOPP and all law-enforcement bodies to the new telecommunication center is supposed.
  - The work is carried out within the framework of the project the Protected Information System of the SOPP of RM with financial support from the European Union (EU) and the UNDP, and at the additional support of experts of the state enterprise the Center of Special Telecommunications.
- **Example 2:** Since June 15, 2005, the Moldavian FinComBank has offered a new service: the payment for municipal services through the Internet (E-uriadnik, n.d.-b). Owners of Visa and MasterCard credit cards can pay for municipal services at http://www.fincompay.com. The client also has the opportunity to view archives, receive extracts from the account, and get information on the rest of the card.
- **Example 3:** On August 19, 2005, the official Web representation of the RM government opened (E-uriadnik, n.d.-c). The governmental Web site http://www.gov.md contains information on the structure of the agency, the ministers' biographies, information on the next government assemblies, and agendas.
  - Citizens can be familiarized with government activity for 2005 to 2009, laws on the state budget, the strategy for economic growth and decrease in the level of poverty, the plan of action European Union: Moldova, and various strategies and plans of activity. One can also access news information as press releases, communiqué, and so forth at the site. The Web site has three language versions: Romanian, Russian, and English.
  - On the basis of cited Figures and facts, and also on the basis of analysis of the level of e-government development and of the volume of e-services rendered

in Moldova (Burtseva, Cojocaru, Gaindric, Magariu, & Verlan, 2004a, 2004c; Cojocaru & Gaindric, 2003), it is possible to consider that the preconditions for information-society creation in the country exist.

The Solutions for the
Digital Divide Problem in Moldova

All the aforesaid shows that Moldova is at a low-enough economic and social level that naturally influences its e-state. Nevertheless, it is possible to take available advantages and to bypass certain obstacles.

The priorities are the following:

1. Attraction, vocation, and orientation of the majority of youth to the information-society technologies
2. Absence of viable alternatives of economy relaunching and the creation of new work-places
3.   Communications facilities and means for data processing have constantly decreasing prices, reduce energy consumption, and are not pollutants.
4. Existence of national structure of communication lines
5. Absence of real dependence on outdated information systems
6. Favourable international context (European, UN, and World Bank initiatives)
7. Still good-enough quality of higher education for relevant specialities

Some vulnerable points include the following:

1. Internet access is expensive and unreliable, and has reduced speed
2. Reduced access to new technologies (caused by the low purchasing capacity of the population), correlated with nonuniform Internet penetration and great discrepancies between urban and rural areas
3. Inertia of officers of central and local public administration
4. Bureaucracy, fraud, and corruption cause some to look at the evolution toward the information society as the irreducible enemy
5. Absence of sufficient information distribution for the general public
6. Massive migration of gifted and qualified youth, accompanied by the growth of the population older than 50
7. Chaotic and noncorrelated mode of informatization of public institutions, as well as the inclination toward individualized solutions that are not harmonized on the basis of unitary conception

8.   Tendency to invest mainly in equipment (to the detriment of management and knowl-
     edge-exploitation tools), without analysis, the preliminary setting of needs, and adequate
     personnel policy

9.   Relatively reduced interest of investors and absence of trust of financial institutions
     that could place investments

10. Presence of the insufficiency of knowledge in relevant domains within secondary
     education

On the other hand, alongside the described manifestations of the digital divide, there are
positive factors in the country promoting the development of is the information society,
such as the presence of political will on the part of the state, a good corresponding ICT
infrastructure, and the high educational level of the population.

In our previous chapter, the basic directions of the balanced nationwide-system approach
to the digital-divide problem are listed as (a) policy, (b) access, (c) services, (d) content, (e)
knowledge and skills, and (f) motivation. Also, the steps to overcoming the digital divide
that are necessary to undertake in these directions are described. In the present chapter,
it is appropriate to consider in detail the state of affairs in Moldova regarding these basic
directions.

1.   The national strategy for building the E-Moldova information society has been formu-
     lated. In all government programs, including those for economic growth and poverty
     reduction, there are sections for information-society creation and the wider granting
     of services to the population by the government.

Moldova actively participates in the Southeast Europe initiative on the integration into the
information society. The parliament accepted the law that stimulates firms working on ICT
development and introduction. The firms dealing with software development received a
"tax vacation."

2.   The state has provided the creation of a communication infrastructure. All regional
     centers are connected by optical cable. There are two rings of optical cable that provide
     communication reliability.

Within the framework of SALT (Jump), 1,364 schools of 1,644 already have physical access to the Moldtelecom network (since February 15, 2006), as the minister of education
V. Tsvirkun asserts (personal communication, February 16, 2006). All 1,364 schools, 140
sport schools, and children's creative houses will be connected to the Internet by the first of
September, 2006. Prime Minister V. Tarlev formed the working group for this monitoring
program.

The relations between the state and local governments and the private sector are still very
weak. There are practically no joint projects for providing information services to the
population. The rate of growth in providing information services (see Table 6) has sharply
increased recently. It especially concerns the rural area. The number of licenses for pro-

viding information services in villages granted during the first half of 2005 is more than the number achieved during the whole year of 2004 (see Table 6). For this period, NRATI granted licenses to 68 companies, 35 of which are working in villages.

3.   Unfortunately, it is necessary to establish the fact that the e-services the government provides the population and business are not enough and do not respond to population demands. These services are limited to providing information: addresses, phone numbers, work schedules, lists and prices of provided services, samples of documents for filling out, and normative and legislative documents related to institution activities (Burtseva et al., 2004b, 2004c). Unfortunately, this information is not always full and updated in time. Interactivity is actually absent.

However, there are successes. For example, take the modern information system at the SOPP (example 1 previously in this chapter). It is the first step to the introduction of automated systems for document circulation in SOPP.

As to commercial structures, there is already an example of interactive services: the payment of municipal services through the Internet (example 2).

4.   For 2005, the government, on behalf of the Ministry of Information Development with the assistance of UNDP, provided the development of the following:

   •   A functioning e-governance-portal model with at least two available pilot services for citizens (e.g., tax payment)
   •   A standard for governmental Web sites and a data-storage and communications protocol
   •   A regulatory mechanism for the implementation of online services

In this development, both the governmental structures and representatives of the scientific organizations, universities, and civil society are involved. This provides taking into account various aspects of Moldova development (national, economic, world outlook, etc.). The first steps are made already, and there are first successes: The site has already opened (example 3). However, for the time being, the site is only informative. The declared interactive services are planned to be available by the beginning of 2007.

5.   Teaching and skills in ICT use are stipulated in all training programs at schools, lyceums, and all university faculties. However, the challenge is that this knowledge is to be sufficient and focused on the future specialist's needs. The president of Moldova has set the objective that in all schools, each pupil will have Internet access. Surely, the objective formulated is general enough. Various ministries carry it out on their own understanding. Having quite a good ICT infrastructure, Moldtelecom successfully supplies cable to the schools. However, the Ministry of Education has not actually started the process of training the teachers (besides those of computer science). One

important problem, for which the Ministry of Education has not yet determined how to approach, is the problem of content. Ensuring that pupils are supplied with the necessary information in their native language is a problem not only of pedagogical science, but also of sociologists, mass media, and the whole society as well.

6.   Problems in the creation of motivation for ICT use remain for the time being without the attention of both the government and the civil society. The program Moldova-e of the public broadcasting company has been carrying out the broadcast of "Information Society" for almost 1 year. But this program, unfortunately, is not thought over enough, and there is no confidence that it will waken the motivation for ICT use in the work of businessmen, farmers, and others. For the present, the most powerful incentive for business is the example set by partners from other countries and the necessity of entering into regional and European structures. Banks and other financial structures, insurance companies, and so forth, in which the level of ICT use is essentially higher than in other branches, can serve as examples. Let us address again example 2 from earlier in this chapter. To implement such an interactive service (the payment for municipal services through the Internet), undoubtedly, it was necessary to use advanced ICT achievements, basing on the last legislative acts concerning electronic signatures, person identification, and the right to use authorization. Motivation is important here, too: Such a service undoubtedly is attractive for the population as it allows one to save time and to carry out this operation in any one moment convenient for the citizen.

Taking into account the weak provision of literature in libraries, it is sharply necessary to create in Moldova an electronic library accessible free of charge for the population. The library should contain educational, national, and classical literature. This action will help to develop the motivation and the long-term habit to use ICT in daily life, study, and work for the majority.

As to daily life, it is not just the most competent people who can find applications of the newest technologies if only the availability of these technologies would be provided. The bright, real episode from village life illustrates this idea well. Two already elderly farmers are talking. The question arises about mobile phones. One farmer tells another, "Yes, mobile phone—it's great! Can you imagine, Ion, I'm pasturing cows far in the field, and suddenly a 'gentleman' became urgently necessary for your cow. I call you by mobile phone and inform: 'Urgently take away your cow. It has alarmed the entire herd!' Now you can act immediately, and the problem is solved!" (P. Pastoohov, personal communication, June 25, 2005)

As regards the motivation for Internet use by the elderly (especially rural) people in Moldova, there also are special reasons. As we already mentioned above, a great number of inhabitants who are able to work have been compelled to leave their families in search of earnings in other countries. To maintain communication with their families—with the grandmothers and grandfathers with whom they have left their children—some of these persons before departure had taught the old men not only to use e-mail, but also to use multimedia means for online conversations.

Complex Conditions Necessary for Overcoming the Digital Divide in Moldova

Note that the basic obstacle in bridging the digital divide is the fact that today in Moldova there is no cooperation between the state sector and private capital. It is possible to understand what the government sees: that the gross national product is very small for the present, that most of the population able to work does not find workplaces in the native land, that industry is not restored yet (production has not reached the level of 1993), that agriculture is noncompetitive, and that import strongly outstrips export. This tendency is being amplified; investments do not grow at the necessary rate. Therefore, clearly, the basic care is an aspiration to raise the standard of life for the population. Unfortunately, not everyone understands that wide introduction of ICT is able to not only promote but also speed up economic growth.

Such problems arise not only in Moldova. Even the World Summit on the Information Society (WSIS) in its *Tunis Agenda for the Information Society*, when writing about financial mechanisms for meeting the challenges of ICT for development, it stated, "We recognize the existence of the digital divide and the challenges that this poses for many countries, which are forced to choose between many competing objectives in their development planning and in demands for development funds whilst having limited resources" (WSIS, 2005a, p. 1).

Nevertheless, it considers ICT development of great importance and writes the following: "We encourage all governments to give appropriate priority to ICTs, including traditional ICTs such as broadcast radio and television, in their national development strategies" (p. 3).

When speaking about complex conditions and the actions necessary for overcoming the digital divide, we shall see that not all of them are carried out. Therefore, it is especially important for a country to find its own way of overcoming deep digital divides.

Let us consider the complex of necessary conditions:

1.   There is a lack of physical access to the Internet. As it was already mentioned, there is an advanced network of optical lines. Within 2 years, all schools will be connected to the Internet. Meanwhile, the share of people having a PC at home is too small. Therefore, the majority of users have access at their workplaces. There are not enough public Internet-access points (PIAPs). Internet access is expensive.

2.   Only a part of the society (those who have graduated from universities during the last 10 years, employees of banks and insurance campaigns, and some employees of state machinery) understands the value and realizes the necessity of ICT use for work. Probably, other parts of the society would like to use ICT, but they are too poor to buy a computer.

3.   According to the reports of the UN and other organizations, the degree of democratization in Moldova for the time being is not too high. However, recent events (elections of the parliament; the accepted laws on liberalizations of the press, radio, and TV; economic activities' liberalization; the law of "guillotine"; and orientation to integration into Europe) convince some that the degree of democratization will increase and be sufficient for information-society construction. It, in its turn, will promote wider democratization of the society.

4.   The level of population literacy is high enough.

5.   The laws accepted during the last 2 years serve as a strong basis for information-society creation.

6.   We already mentioned the weak interaction between state and commercial structures. Practically, each of them works independently. However, commercial structures already give an impulse of ICT penetration into the countryside. In cities, private firms influence ICT distribution, though it is not enough.

7.   The financial assets put into ICT are too small. The basic share of the investment is the resources of private enterprises. However, according to the action plan European Union: Moldova, the action plan for the implementation of the national strategy for information-society development e-Moldova, the budget for 2007 will have the separate expense item for ICT introduction in the economy, education, public health services, and local management.

The problems of attracting investments into e-government development and services provision to the population remain sharp. The United Nations Development Program assists some of the nongovernmental organizations, but it is obviously insufficient. The investments of those who understand that all expenses will be repaid and will result in economic growth are necessary.

8.   If 5 to 7 years ago state support was only declarative, the last 2 to 3 years were the turning points (see subsection "Political Will").

Note that the problem of information distribution among the population remains on the second plan up until now. The state so far is going to invest in systems that will give results quickly. Those stated above, the concrete measures accepted and planned for the nearest 1 to 2 years, and the worldview of people that came into the state structures allow us to offer public Internet-access points as a way to accelerate overcoming the digital divide. Basically, the majority of actors influencing information-society development in Moldova supports these measures; at least we have not met open opponents.

Taking into account the current situation and limited financial opportunities, the coordination of actions in all programs for more expedient use of investments is necessary. As the first stage for such coordinated actions, the opening of PIAPs in all settlements with the participation of the state, nongovernmental organizations, and commercial structures is supposed. It corresponds to Point II of the Genoa action plan (DOT Force, 2001, p. 14):

> *The establishment of public and community ICT access points in developing countries should be supported as a key means to facilitate timely, broad, affordable and sustainable access to ICT; for this purpose facilities such as post offices, elementary schools, Internet cafés or community multimedia centers could be used; emphasis should be placed on providing both access and training...Approaches to promote universal access for rural and remote areas in developing countries should be pursued...*

This question remains the actual one. So, at the last WSIS forum devoted to informa-tion-society problems, including the digital divide, in the Tunis Commitment it was written (WSIS, 2005b, p. 3), "We urge governments, using the potential of ICTs, to create public systems of information on laws and regulations, envisaging a wider development of public access points and supporting the broad availability of this information."

PIAPs could provide the following:

The basic parts of the information society (such as e-government, e-democracy, e-culture, e-medicine, e-commerce, etc.) to be created locally

- Nondiscriminated access of all of the population to information (which is more im-portant)
- Participation in the e-democracy
- Services of e-government

Let us explain now the method of choice in Moldova and consider our propositions about PIAP development, supply, and maintenance.

Description of PIAPs Proposal

The PIAP functionality supposes the presence of necessary items: hardware, software, room, connection, personnel, training, user's payment, traffic cost, and technical maintenance.

Table 8. Public places for PIAPs in different countries (Source: The Table is made by the authors on the basis of an analysis of a number of different Web sources, Burtseva, Cojocaru, Gaindric, Magariu, & Verlan, 2005)

Country	Schools	Libraries	Telecommunications	Other
France			Yes	
Austria	Yes		Yes	
Finland		Yes	Yes	
Greece	Yes			
Croatia	Yes			
Estonia	Yes	Yes	Yes	
Brazil				Yes
Romania			Yes	
Latvia		Yes		
Scotland	Yes	Yes	Yes	Yes
Lithuania	Yes	Yes	Yes	Yes
Slovenia	Yes	Yes		
Moldova	Yes	Yes	Yes	

The implementation of these items requires financial aid and technical efforts. An at-once realization of such a project is impossible with the current situation in Moldova, so we propose to move from stage to stage.

At the first stage, the PIAP creation is offered on the basis of schools (after hours). The following circumstances that are specific for Moldova underlie this choice:

- School is one of not many public institutions that are active in the countryside.
- Schools have their own buildings.
- Schools in the countryside have the necessary ICT infrastructure.
- There is the presence of personnel (informatics teachers) for initial training to use the computer and Internet.

Similar ways were chosen by Austria, Greece, Croatia, Slovenia, Estonia, Scotland, and Lithuania. One can see that Croatia and Slovenia are in this list of countries, and they have similar social-economical conditions. Our closest neighbor, Romania, took another way.

Certainly, each country solves this problem individually, proceeding from national features (Table 8). As a rule, public places convenient for inhabitants that people already visit and also that already are a part of their daily life are being chosen: schools, libraries, post offices, national bank branches, railway and bus stations, airports, shops, cafes, hotels, clubs, churches, and so forth.

The mentioned-above circumstances, specific for Moldova and which cover some necessary items of PIAP, do not resolve the problems of hardware equipment and the technical maintenance of PIAP. Intending to use the school hardware at the first stage, we take in consideration the fact that many of rural schools have no computer class. This problem requires collaboration with state education authorities; in Moldova, this is the Ministry of Education, Youth, and Sport. The payment for traffic and other supplies is also a significant problem. At the first stage, it is supposed that the local budget can be implemented only by persuading the local authorities. The principal companies dealing with Internet-traffic support and electricity can give a discount for state programs. For resolving the problem of PIAP maintenance, we propose to initially get the teachers of computer science for this work, who will receive additional payment. Cascade training (as supposed in SALT as well) be offered by engaging teachers, rural intellectuals, and, further on, people with secondary education.

This stage fulfilling allows the second stage to expand further the PIAPs network by opening these points in city halls, libraries, post offices, and other public places. This way, the necessary supplies can be covered by the corresponding institutions. The state or joint enterprises can be created for PIAP's technical maintenance.

Then, at the third stage, the telecenters can be established in hotels, bars, and so forth. This stage requires business investments from Internet providers, banks, and the ICT sector.

The implementation of the second and third stages would be impossible without mutual coordinated actions of local administration and business. According to this plan, the local administration should find a way to awake business interest to support the PIAPs.

To reduce expenses and ensure the PIAP functionality, we propose the establishment of a standard for the minimal information services guaranteed to each member of society irrespective of whether he or she lives in the countryside or not: e-mail; access to the legislative database; access to the membership of the local networks created for different business branches; weather reports; and so forth. For this, it is necessary to establish Internet content for these services and to provide each PIAP with a minimal software set supporting these services.

Now we argue for our choice of software tool kit for PIAP. This tool kit is set by each country according to its specific social-economic situation. Several initiatives, for example, Cambridge Online City (*About Cambridge Online City*, n.d.), prefer complex solutions by Microsoft. However, we share the position with those who propose open-source solutions.

Open-source software or free software (OSS or FS) are programs that have licenses that give users freedom to run, study, and modify the programs, and to redistribute copies of either the original or modified programs (without having to pay royalties to previous developers; *Open Software License v. 2.1*, 2005).

Many countries accept the OSS solution at their administrative level (Wong, 2004).

- **OSS is used for local government network support:** This choice is made by countries with both high and low levels of ICT. The countries with high ICT levels use OSS mostly because of the necessity for independence from software developers: the governments of the USA (Aitoro, 2005), Australia ("Government Open Source Guide Coming Next Month," 2005), and Italy ("Italian IT Leader Engineering Ingegneria Informatica," 2005). Certainly, countries with low ICT levels take OSS solutions mostly because of financial and copyright reasons. Several specific projects of OSS-usage advancement have been initiated for different regions of the world: Asia (International Open Source Network, 2004), Africa (FOSSFA, n.d.), and so forth. In this context, it is remarkable that such populous countries as China ("China's Bet on Linux," 2005), India (Noronha, 2002), and Indonesia ("Indonesia Government Opts for Open Source," 2004) choose OSS for government networks. The Government Information Technology Officers' Council (GITOC; 2003) in South Africa promotes OSS in its strategy. Brazil's government announced its intention to change from Microsoft's operating system to OSS on 300,000 government computers (Goldmark, 2005).

- **OSS is used for Internet provision at schools:** The corresponding projects were announced in 2005 by the governments of France (Marson, 2005a), South Korea (Ilett, 2005), and New Zealand (Marson, 2005b). In New Zealand, 2,600 state schools will use Novell's software for a reduced price. The Republic of Macedonia in 2005 decided to deploy Linux at 468 schools and 182 computer labs nationwide ("Macedonia Deploys 5,000 GNOME Desktops in Public Schools," 2005). The School-to-School Project in China plans to load nearly 140,000 PCs with a national Linux version ("Largest Asian Linux Rollout Ever," 2005).

- **OSS is used for PIAPs (considered in detail as follows):** There are a lot of reasons for using OSS in noncommercial domains (schools, local government, state PIAPs).

  The first reason for OSS usage for PIAPs and especially for local government networks is the independence from software manufacturers.

Despite the different financial situations in countries that supply PIAPs by OSS, the reason of economy is equally significant. The main objections of opponents are the inadequacy of OSS regarding users' needs and the absence of support. The thesis of inadequacy became baseless with the modern development of OSS. For example, the Microsoft solution for an ordinary PIAP hardware set includes the Windows 2003 Enterprise Server operating system for 25 clients ($1,875); the e-mail server Microsoft Exchange 2000 Server 25-Client Enterprise ($6,899); and the RDBMS server Microsoft SQL Server 2000 Enterprise Edition ($7,500). The prices are from an Internet shop's (Amazon.com, n.d.) price list. However, the corresponding OSS solution, for example, Linux, provides for an unlimited number of clients. E-mail and RDBMS servers are embedded in the operating system. Any OSS scripting tool can be used. So, the OSS now has functional completeness. OSS security can also be set to the due level.

BZ Media LLC, a privately held high-tech media company, issued BZ Research. Its survey of 6,344 software-development managers shows that Linux is superior to Windows for operating-system security attacks, and OSS was in most categories considered equal or better at the application layer ("Linux Wins on Security in survey," 2005). From the point of view of performance and reliability, OSS also shows results that are comparable to or better than the results of commercial software. Eighty percent of the top 10 most reliable hosting providers ran OSS or FS ("Most Reliable Hosting Providers During May," 2004). The performance of "heavy" RDBs like Oracle under Linux was so preferable (Burleson, 2003) that software giant Microsoft with Windows 2003 Server started lagging.

Although OSS has no developer support, this lack can be converted to an advantage, especially in the case of PIAP. The active developing of new OSS products and new versions of existing ones eliminates the main fear of users about update difficulty. The distribution of OSS by free CDs made by state or business-state enterprises, for example, like the French government does, resolves the problem of obtaining software.

So, maintaining the software is the only feature of developer support that remains to be discussed.

Let us consider this feature in the specific situation of PIAPs in Moldova. The backcountry districts are hardly reachable for developers' help. Being in use by nonprofessional persons, computers of PIAPs are always at risk of hardware or software damage. So, the preinstalled type of software is inconvenient. The boxed software versions require the presence of a specialist for software installation, and moreover have a higher price. Usually, this problem is resolved by the creation of easily installable pirate software versions.

The OSS license allows software recompiling without breaking privacy. Recompilation gives the PIAP suppliers wide possibilities to resolve their specific problems. First of all, they can adapt the software exactly to the spoken language, hardware, and executing services of the specific PIAP. As it was mentioned above, the possibility to develop easily installable software is also important. In Moldova, there are professionals who can handle the recompiling process. Moreover, in autumn 2005, a center for Linux training and certification by international standards was opened at the State Technical University of Moldova.

Thus, the OSS license combines the significant financial economy with wide possibilities of maintenance. The software realized under this license today has due functionality and has less of the disadvantages of the early years. The OSS can be successfully used for PIAP supply, especially in financially weak states with poor ICT infrastructure in rural areas. Thus, in Venezuela in 2004, numerous info centers and PIAPs with free software were opened throughout the country (Wilper, 2004). As well, in Romania since 2002, the number of PIAPs and of used Linux servers have been growing (Sandu & Nagler, 2005).

Generalizing the discussion above, we can formulate the solution below. We propose to establish a network of PIAPs with the following characteristics:

- Use the financial support of state and local administrations
- Have a supply of standard software
- Give access to a standard minimal set of services

The standard software tool kit consists of the following:

1. Interactive guides and tutorials (for computer usage, Internet navigation, installed software, and the development and support of personal Web pages)
2. Editors (for text, Web pages, graphics, and presentations) and miscellaneous programs (spell checkers, dictionaries, and support for small databases)
3. Internet browsers (access to a free e-mail service, to global and local search engines, and to online dictionaries and translation systems)

Indices for Digital-Divide Monitoring in Moldova

The WSIS Thematic Meeting on "Measuring the Information Society" resulted in the recommended core list of ICT indicators and its broad evolvement ("Final Conclusions," 2005). Taking into consideration Moldova's specificity and more precise monitoring of the digital divide in Moldova, the following indices can be recommended additionally by this chapter's authors.

1. Number of PIAPs per 10,000 inhabitants
2. * Number (and percent) of settlements that have PIAP
3. * Number (and percent) of PIAPs where inhabitants use services gratis
4. ** Number of computer classes per 1,000 pupils
5. ** Average number of subjects at schools in which ICT are used in teaching

An asterisk identifies specific indicators for Moldova.

Two asterisks identify indicators whose influence will affect the digital divide afterward (they contribute to population training).

The authors of this chapter will endeavour to promote these indices so they will be taken into consideration in the state policy in the process of information-society creation in Moldova.

Conclusion

The digital-divide problem is a reality that is present in any society. It will be present later on as well, reflecting the immanent objective, social, economical, and confessional peculiarities inherent in a country or ethnic groups. A striking example from the life of our country (Moldova) is the fact that some Orthodox believers made a protest and refused to get identity cards with personal codes. Obviously, these persons will not be able to use the opportunities that ICTs give. However, in any democratic society, the tendency to provide every member of the society with equal possibilities will promote decreasing the digital divide.

One should not automatically transfer the methods of the solution of the digital-divide problem from one country to another. Nevertheless, the experience accumulated by some countries is certainly useful for others since the common elements—the necessity of state political decisions, of attracting economic agents and civil society, and so forth—should find reflection in decisions that are specific for each country. Even negative experiences of other countries, for example, the termination of the PIAPs and telecenters on the completion of state or other grants, are rather valuable, too, inasmuch as they reveal those aspects of the problem that would be difficult to deal with.

Starting from the specific economic conditions in our country, we consider that the proposed measures and those that are already being realized in Moldova are able to decrease people's differences regarding the possibilities to take part in public and economic activities; that is, they enable the country's development.

Certainly, it might do well to speed up realizing these measure, but the real possibilities of the country, and chiefly the very low GDP, do not allow the majority of the population to purchase computers (the cost of which is about five average nominal monthly salaries per employee in the economy in November 2005) or Internet connections (the cost of a monthly subscription for the Internet is about 17% of the average nominal monthly salary). From this follows the proposed solution for the rural population (which constitutes 61.4% of the total population):

- Usage of school computer classes as PIAPs
- Local administration participation in PIAP financing
- Determination of a standard for minimal services that are provided for any person in any settlement of the country. It is not an obstacle in the way of widening the provided possibilities when the local administration can permit itself such widening.
- Training the population in necessary skills for working with computers and for Internet usage by using the cascade method
- Along with the European indicators for e-readiness monitoring, the introduction into state statistics the specific indicators for Moldova

Several social programs are carried out nowadays in the Republic of Moldova.

- Program for economic growth and poverty reduction, which includes the establishment of PIAPs along with the measures for economic growth

- Moldova's Village, which includes measures for economic and cultural development, for ethical-norms revival, and for the provision of elementary conditions of life (provision for drinking water and gas in each village)

- SALT, providing schools with Internet connections and equipping them with computers

- European Union: Moldova

The main condition for the successful implementation of each of these programs is the coordination of their actions. Certainly, the problem of the digital divide will be resolved indirectly as well. But the purposeful opening of a PIAP in every settlement by means of attracting the existing infrastructure, the possibilities of local self-government, and the good will of teachers of informatics and volunteers can speed up the solution of the problem.

It is very important to establish a system of statistical indicators for monitoring information-society creation, and in particular, the digital divide.

We hope that Moldova's approach, stated in this chapter, will fill up the "money box" of world experience, too, and that it can be useful in those countries where there are similar conditions, mainly those with an agrarian economy and a mainly rural population, which, at that, has a high-enough educational level and keeps a strong thirst for knowledge. The presence of good ICT infrastructure in combination with the implementation of a state program to connect all schools to the Internet became the precondition of the approach suggested (and proved) by us, based on the creation of PIAPs at schools. We have tried to fix the whole spectrum of problems arising at the acceptance of such an approach and to plan possible solutions to them.

References

About Cambridge online city. (n.d.). Retrieved January 27, 2005, from http://www.colc. co.uk/colc/colc.html

Aitoro, J. R. (2005, June 9). State, local governments to leverage open source. *Informationweek.* Retrieved August 18, 2005, from http://www.informationweek.com/story/ showArticle.jhtml?articleID=164302017

Amazon.com. (n.d.). Retrieved August 25, 2005, from *http://www.amazon.com*

American Society for Public Administration & United Nations Division for Public Economics and Public Administration (ASPA & UNDPEPA). (2002). *Benchmarking e-government: A global perspective.* Retrieved February 29, 2004, from http://www.itpolicy. gov.il/topics_egov/docs/benchmarking.pdf

Biroul National de Statistica (BNS). (2005a). *Moldova in Figures: Short statistical book.* Chisinau, Moldova: Statistica.

Biroul National de Statistica (BNS). (2005b). *Nota informationala Nr. 14-01*. Retrieved April 19, 2005, from http://www.statistica.md/statistics/dat/596/ro/Nr_pop_la1ian_2005. doc

Burleson, D. (2003). *Oracle Windows or Oracle Linux?* Retrieved August 18, 2005, from http://www.dba-oracle.com/oracle_tips_linux_oracle.htm

Burtseva, L., Cojocaru, S., Gaindric, C., Magariu, G., & Verlan, T. (2004a). Electronic services in public administration (e-government): Privacy and freedom of information (Review of study made for situation in Moldova). *Computer Science Journal of Moldova, 12*, 467-496.

Burtseva, L., Cojocaru, S., Gaindric, C., Magariu, G., & Verlan, T. (2004b). *Servicii electronice in sectorul administratiei publice (e-government): Inviolabilitatea informatiei personale si dreptul la informatie* (Tech. Rep.). Chisinau, Moldova: Academy of Sciences of Moldova, Institute of Mathematics and Computer Science.

Burtseva, L., Cojocaru, S., Gaindric, C., Magariu, G., & Verlan, T. (2004c). Sravnitel'ny'y analiz razlichny'h podhodov k realizacii e-pravitel'stva: Uslugi e'lektronnogo pravitel'stva. In *Abstracts on BIT+2004 "IV International Conference on Information Technologies 2004"* (pp. 66-68).

Burtseva, L., Cojocaru, S., Gaindric, C., Magariu, G., & Verlan, T. (2005). Internetul in mediul rural. In *Teze si comunicari de conferinta nationala "Comunitatile Rurale si Renasterea Satului"* (pp. 133-135). Chisinau, Moldova: Academia de Stiinte a Moldovei.

China's bet on Linux. (2005). *CIO-Asia.com*. Retrieved January 28, 2006, from http://cio-asia.com/ShowPage.aspx?pagetype=2&articleid=3015&pubid=5&issueid=71

Cojocaru, S., & Gaindric, C. (2003). *Considerente asupra edificarii societatii informationale in Moldova*. Chisinau, Moldova: Stiinta.

Departamentul Statistica si Sociologie al Republicii Moldova (DSSRM). (2004). *Statistical yearbook of the Republic of Moldova*. Chisinau, Moldova: Statistica.

Digital Opportunity Task (DOT) Force. (2001). *Digital opportunities for all: Meeting the challenge*. Retrieved March 25, 2005, from http://www.labi-berlin.nubb.dfn.de/bibliothek/positionspapiere/dot_force.htm

E-uriadnik. (n.d.-a). *General'naia prokuratura Moldovy poluchila sovremennuiu informatsionnuiu sistemu*. Retrieved July 15, 2005, from http://www.e-uriadnik.org.ua/modules. php?name=News&file=article&sid=2454

E-uriadnik. (n.d.-b). *V Moldove stalo vozmojnym oplachivat' kommunal'nyie uslugi cherez Internet*. Retrieved July 20, 2005, from http://www.e-uriadnik.org.ua/modules. php?name=News&file=article&sid=2322

E-uriadnik. (n.d.-c). *V seti otkrylsea ofitsial'nyi vebsait Pravitel'stva Respubliki Moldova*. Retrieved August 21, 2005, from http://www.e-uriadnik.org.ua/modules.php?name= News&file=article&sid=2596

Final conclusions. (2005). *WSIS Thematic Meeting on "Measuring the Information Society."* Retrieved November 28, 2005, from http://www.itu.int/wsis/docs2/thematic/unctad/final-conclusions.pdf

FOSSFA. (n.d.). Retrieved January 28, 2006, from http://www.fossfa.net/tiki-index. php?page=FOSSFA.

GEOHIVE: Global Statistics. (n.d.). Retrieved August 8, 2005, from http://www.geohive.com/index.php

Government Information Technology Officers' Council (GITOC). (2003). *Using open source software in the South African government.* Retrieved January 28, 2006, from http://www.oss.gov.za/docs/OSS_Strategy_v3.pdf

Goldmark, A. (2005). *Brazil makes move to open source software.* Retrieved January 30, 2006, from http://www.npr.org/templates/story/story.php?storyId=4471963

Government open source guide coming next month. (2005). *LinuxWorld.* Retrieved August 18, 2005, from http://www.linuxworld.com.au/index.php/id;1912876672;fp;2;fpid;1

Ilett, D. (2005). *Korea brings open source to 10,000 schools: No offence to Microsoft...* Retrieved August 15, 2005, from http://software.silicon.com/os/0,39024651,39131 325,00.htm

Indonesia government opts for open source. (2004). *Public sector technology & management.* Retrieved January 29, 2006, from http://www.pstm.net/article/index.php?articleid=224

International Open Source Network. (2004). Retrieved July 25, 2005, from http://www.iosn.net

Internet World Stats. (2005). Retrieved July 25, 2005, from http://www.internetworldstats.com/stats.htm

Italian IT leader engineering Ingegneria Informatica joins Objectweb Consortium. (2005). *OSDIR.COM.* Retrieved August 19, 2005, from http://osdir.com/Article5664.phtml

Largest Asian Linux rollout ever: 140,000-plus PCs deploying to Chinese schools. (2005). *Linux Today.* Retrieved January 30, 2006, from http://www.linuxtoday.com/news/2005100402426NWDTPB

Linux wins on security in survey of 6,000+ software developers. (2005). *LWN.net.* Retrieved August 17, 2005, from http://lwn.net/Articles/131788/

Macedonia deploys 5,000 GNOME desktops in public schools. (2005, December 2). *The Gnome Journal.* Retrieved January 30, 2006, from http://www.gnomejournal.org/article/33/macedonia-deploys-5000-gnome-in-public-schools

Marson, I. (2005a). French students to get Linux CDs. *ZDNet UK.* Retrieved August 17, 2005, from http://news.zdnet.co.uk/software/linuxunix/0,39020390,39212812,00.htm

Marson, I. (2005b). New Zealand's schools to get open source for less. *ZDNet UK.* Retrieved August 17, 2005, from http://news.zdnet.co.uk/software/linuxunix/0,39020390,39209666,00.htm

Most reliable hosting providers during May, ranking by failed requests and connection time, May 1st-31st 2004. (2004). *Netcraft.* Retrieved August 17, 2005, from http://news.netcraft.com/archives/2004/06/02/most_reliable_hosting_providers_during_may.html

Noronha, F. (2002). *The Penguin's flying-carpet: Free/libre and open source software in India.* Retrieved January 29, 2006, from http://www.unesco.org/webworld/portal_freesoft/reports/the_penguin.pdf

National Regulatory Agency in Telecommunications and Information (NRATI). (2005). *Annual report 2004.* Retrieved June 30, 2005, from http://www.anrti.md/index_en.htm

National Regulatory Agency in Telecommunications and Information (NRATI). (n.d.). Retrieved August 15, 2005, from http://www.anrti.md

Open software license (v. 2.1). (2005). Retrieved August 25, 2005, from http://opensource. org/licenses/osl-2.1.php

Sandu, T. G., & Nagler, M. (2005). *A brief overview: Open source software in Romania.* Retrieved February 1, 2006, from http://europa.eu.int/idabc/servlets/Doc?id=23392

Server. (n.d.). Retrieved July 28, 2005, from http://www.server.md/news/11702/

United Nations (UN). (2003). *World public sector report 2003: E-government at the crossroads.* Retrieved March 25, 2004, from http://www.unpan.org/dpepa_worldpareport.asp

United Nations Development Program (UNDP). (2003). *Human development report 2003. Millennium development goals: A compact among nations to end human poverty.* Retrieved March 17, 2005, from http://hdr.undp.org/reports/global/2003/pdf/hdr03_ complete.pdf

United Nations Development Program (UNDP). (2005). *Human development report 2005. International cooperation at a crossroads: Aid, trade and security in an unequal world.* Retrieved September 13, 2005, from http://hdr.undp.org/reports/global/2005/ pdf/HDR05_complete.pdf

West, D. M. (2001). *WMRC global e-government survey.* Retrieved September 28, 2005, from http://www.insidepolitics.org/egovt01int.html

West, D. M. (2002). *Global e-government.* Retrieved September 28, 2005, from http://www. insidepolitics.org/egovt02int.html

West, D. M. (2003). *Global e-government.* Retrieved September 28, 2005, from http://www. insidepolitics.org/egovt03int.pdf

West, D. M. (2004). *Global e-government.* Retrieved September 28, 2005, from http://www. insidepolitics.org/egovt04int.pdf

West, D. M. (2005). *Global e-government.* Retrieved September 28, 2005, from http://www. insidepolitics.org/egovt05int.pdf

Wilper, G. (2004). *Chavez announces that Venezuelan state will switch to "free soft-ware."* Retrieved February 1, 2006, from http://www.venezuelanalysis.com/news. php?newsno=1373

Wong, K. (2004). *Free/open source software: Government policy.* Retrieved January 28, 2006, from http://www.iosn.net/government/foss-government-primer/foss-govt-policy.pdf

World Summit on the Information Society (WSIS). (2005a). *Tunis agenda for the informa-tion society.* Retrieved November 28, 2005, from http://www.itu.int/wsis/documents/ doc_multi.asp?lang=en&id=2267|0

World Summit on the Information Society (WSIS). (2005b). *Tunis commitment.* Re-trieved November 28, 2005, from http://www.itu.int/wsis/documents/doc_multi. asp?lang=en&id=2266|0

Endnotes

[1]   For these countries, the values of the e-readiness index for 2001 are absent. Neverthe-less, they are included in the range of countries because they are agrarian countries close to Moldova in their percent of rural population. In Table 1, they are at the end of the list, and in the comparative analysis presented in Figure 2 they are not included. However, in the subsequent analysis they are examined.

[2]   Not all of the desired data were available for all countries, years, and indices (in par-ticular, for countries from the chosen list), so the authors tried to make the comparative analysis of the state and dynamics of digital-divide development on the basis of the information found to be available. At that, the data are taken from different sources. The data given for the same country by different sources are not always comparable since they are calculated by different methods. However, the authors set for themselves the objective to follow up on the tendency of the development of conditions in the country and between countries. For this purpose, the described state of affairs with data was not an obstacle.

[3]   Moldova's national source (NRATI, 2005) gives the GDP Figure for Moldova in MDL (Moldova's national currency), which, when recalculated in U.S. dollars, differs from the Figure given in GEOHIVE: Global Statistics (n.d.). The difference is not large (compare $541, the result of our recalculation, and $460; GEOHIVE) and does not essentially change the picture. So, in our research, we use the UN statistics.

[4]   The data on the percent of the urban population in Moldova, 46% (GEOHIVE: Global Statistics, n.d.), are a little bit overestimated in comparison with the data given in the national statistical report: 41.4% (DSSRM, 2004). The data from the national statisti-cal report in the greater degree met the described tendency.

Note: [a] The site http://www.internetworldstats.com gives this Figure. However, the national source NRATI (2005) gives the following Figures: 288,000 Internet users in 2003 and 406,000 in 2004. As well, we should say the same about Internet penetration. The Ministry of Informational Development of Moldova gives the following information: According to the sociological questioning made in 2004, the number of Internet users in Moldova constituted 17.4% of the total population. This Figure is closer to the one of NRATI. However, in our research, we use the *Internet World Stats* (2005) data to keep the world picture given there.

Chapter V

Poverty Reduction through Community-Compatible ICTs:
Examples from Botswana and other African Countries

Rebecca Lekoko, University of Botswana, Botswana

Bantu Morolong, University of Botswana, Botswana

Abstract

ICTs are an integral part of both scientific and lay cultures. However, scientific know-how, whose significant features are high expertise and highly trained personnel, is dominant while traditional cultures are gradually receding. The use of ICTs shows great potential for creating access boundaries between the rich and poor. Out of this awareness, this chapter invites readers to rethink basic questions: What are ICTs? What have been their benefits for the rich and poor? While these questions cannot be answered in detail here, few important points are presented emphasizing that ICTs do not function in a societal vacuum. The type of access to ICTs that the poor need is not that which only enables them to be like others in using ICTs. They, much more than other sectors of society, have an increasing need to effectively manage their lives, and community-compatible ICTs can be employed for this purpose.

Background

The key operational concepts in this chapter are poverty, information communication technologies, and community-compatible ICTs. Even though these are concepts in common usage in the various disciplines, for the purposes of elucidation, they are briefly defined in the discussion that follows. For each of the concepts, the definition is expanded to highlight some of the fundamental issues that are relevant to the theme of this chapter.

Definitions and Fundamentals of Poverty and Information Communication Technologies

Poverty

Clearly, many definitions of the word poverty reflect the economic impact of being poor. In Botswana, for example, poverty is seen as a "consequence of a narrow economic base, which limits opportunities for gainful employment" (Republic of Botswana, 2004, p.17). To illustrate, in 1993, an estimated 47% of the population lived below the poverty datum line of approximately P100.00 ($20) per person per month. Poverty here is simply viewed as a state in which a family's income is too low to be able to buy the quantities of food, shelter, and clothing that are deemed necessary (http://www.econ100.com/eu5e/open/glossary. html). Perhaps it is this narrowness of focus that has led Botswana to develop a poverty line (PL) that considers only six categories of items as constituting the basic needs of a family in Botswana, namely, (a) food, (b) clothing, (c) personal items, (d) household goods, (e) shelter, and (f) miscellaneous (Central Statistic Office [CSO], 1991). Such an analysis may mislead because it oversimplifies the complex nature of being poor. It portrays a picture of poverty being measured in monetary and material possessions. Unfortunately, this type of understanding perpetuates a pervasive attitude of looking at the poor as the helpless and hopeless, hence giving those in power unprecedented capacity to determine how the poor should live their lives.

It is observed here that "most countries of the Sub-Saharan Africa are predominantly rural in character: roughly 70 percentage of the population live in the rural areas" (Bryceson, 1995, p. 8). It is in these rural areas where most of the poor people reside. According to the *Botswana Millennium Development Status Report 2004*, the "rates of poverty are higher in rural areas, mainly because of fewer opportunities for formal sector employment" (Republic of Botswana, 2004, p. 21). In these rural areas, the means of survival are relatively nonmonetized and predominantly agricultural. Agricultural production using a plough or hoe and livestock keeping are at a subsistence level. It can fairly be said that "animal and plants constitute human food and their importance is obviously great" in everyone's life (Mbiti, 1988, p. 50); it is thus important to have them among the indicators of poverty, especially in Africa. It seems not right, therefore, to measure poverty solely in terms of money (mostly earned through employment in the formal sector).

A more complex picture may appear if we think and expand the definition of poverty to include poverty in the noneconomic sense, as is the case in this chapter. For purely analytical purposes, poverty in this chapter is understood as a state of lacking and/or being deprived of the essentials of life such as material and monetary possessions, employment, health services, education, and access to required social services and status, such as being responsible citizens who would participate meaningfully in their own development as well as the overall development of their country. It thus covers among others the lack of non-tangible aspects of people's lives such as power, exposure to different forms of violations, lack of access to information, as well as low levels of equality among social groups. These inequalities are mainly based on gender, class, and ethnicity. It should, however, be noted that poverty remains a very elusive concept. For example, in an attempt to accommodate the issue of the degree of poverty, there is always a desire to distinguish between poverty, absolute poverty, and relative poverty.

Generally, poverty is most noticeable in material deprivation and the psychological stigma attached to being poor (Heeks, 1999). Wells (2000) contends that prolonged conditions of absolute poverty are associated with low levels of self-esteem, resulting in identity crisis. In some situations, the poor are described as *"no-good"*, *"incompetent"* and *"stupid"* such that they should expect failure of themselves just as the world expects it from them (Heeks, 1999). In simple terms, poverty is seen as being impoverished or underprivileged. Generally, "to be impoverished is to lack or be denied adequate resources to participate meaningfully in society" (http://www.hsph.harvard.edu/thegeocodingproject/webpage/monograph/glossary.htm). A bias in this chapter is toward analyzing and looking at poverty as it leads to exclusion in the economic, social, and political spheres of people's lives, causing conditions of unemployment, and inadequate health and other social services.

Those critical of the definitions as given in the preceding discussion contend that these definitions have misled national leaders to aim at compensating for these deficiencies by setting up welfare systems. The welfare approach includes food handouts, nutrition, counseling, and family planning that merely aim at contributing to immediate relief of a needy situation. Such services continuously relegate the poor to a position of passive recipients of development projects. Whatever else is said and done for the poor opens the doors widely for a sympathetic attitude (Mtshali, 2000). People who are victims of this pity regard governments as power forces that have to change their situations. It is this status of the poor that the current development initiatives are aimed at addressing. This chapter reviews what the role of ICTs can be at the community level. Within the broad thematic area of ICTs and poverty alleviation, the concept of poverty is used here very broadly to refer to a lack of gainful access to and control over resources, with specific emphasis on ICTs as a socioeconomic resource.

Information Communication Technologies

The adoption of the millennium development goals (MDGs) in 2000 has meant that countries started looking for effective means of fighting the poverty scourge. In their search, the national leaders seem convinced that ICTs can be used to counter the crisis of poverty, especially if they are linked to the complex economic, educational, political, and other challenges facing the poor (Gerster & Zimmerman, 2003). Information communication technologies are generally defined as communication devices or applications encompassing radio, television, cell phones, computer networks, and hardware, as well as the services and applications associated with these (http://searchsmb.teentarget.com). According to Adeya

(2002), it also includes electronic networks and services that embody hardware applied through networks, and services for information accumulation and flow in the public and private spheres. This encompasses Internet services, telecommunication equipment, libraries and documentation centers, and network-based information services. Some have referred to these as the group of technologies that have revolutionized the handling of information. A marked distinguishing feature for these in the current era is their capacity to be available (Gerster & Zimmerman, 2003). Other characteristics of these include (a) interactivity, (b) global reach, (c) reduced costs (cost effectiveness), and (d) usability. According to Gerster and Zimmerman, ICTs also refer to some artifacts, techniques, or knowledge used to create, store, manage, and disseminate information. Heeks (1999) sees them as electronic means of capturing, processing, storing, and communicating information. In discussing sustainable ICTs, Batchelor and Norrish (2002) say that the relevance of ICTs in long-term development goals cannot be realized, achieved, or adequately conceived without considering the three capital assets, which are finances, and physical and social capital.

The approach taken in this chapter in defining ICTs is to consider them in relation to the critical needs for countries to develop. Take, for example, information. In any developing country, one of the prime ingredients of development is information. ICTs provide a platform for information sharing and storage toward sustainable development. Information societies are those societies that have well-developed ICTs to share information for development and innovation (http://cbdd.wsu.edu/kewlcontent/cdoutput/TR501/page59.htm). In Africa, for example, information is disseminated for various purposes: information about new agriculture or land development, community building, public health (e.g., HIV/AIDS), and education information campaigns (http://cbdd.wsu.edu/kewlcontent/cdoutput/TR501/page59.htm). Thus, ICTs in this chapter are those artifacts that make it possible for people to share information in order to create a sustainable information society. In Botswana, for example, Vision 2016 states that to build an open, transparent, and accountable nation by the year 2016, "Botswana must improve the access of all its people to information and new technologies that are sweeping the world; it must introduce a freedom of information act to protect the rights of citizens to obtain and use information" (Republic of Botswana, 1997, p. 12). In terms of relevance and usability, Botswana intends to "introduce universal and national radio and television stations to bring information to all parts of the country" (p. 12). The use of the local media, for example, the newspaper and other print materials, are to be encouraged. In sum, information sharing and dissemination is a critical principle in defining the potential use of ICTs for the poor people.

Education is yet another critical platform on which ICTs can be defined. The process of education is basically related to information dissemination and ICTs because information educates (or information is education), and ICTs disseminate education or information. Through communication via ICTs, the world is a global village where people from one country learn about happenings in many other countries as soon as the news breaks (http://cbdd.wsu.edu/kewlcontent/cdoutput/TR501/page59.htm).

When a country like Botswana invests in education in order to build an educated and informed nation, it does so with the knowledge that ICTs are critical tools in making it achieve this goal. Worldwide, ICTs are used to share educational information among people and countries for development purposes (http://cbdd.wsu.edu/kewlcontent/cdoutput/TR501/page59.htm).

Investment in education is a dynamic investment as the educated are creative enough to use available technology. In other words, education must improve all aspects of people's lives, including their ability to create, invest in, and use ICTs for their development. A long-term vision for Botswana, Vision 2016, for example, states that "products of our educational systems must be independent, productive, innovative with cutting edge skills" (Republic of Botswana, 1997, p. 11). In this era, when cutting-edge skills are mentioned, skills for the effective use of ICTs are part of them. Botswana works hard to ensure that it maximizes the potentials of ICTs in its dream for an educated, informed, and productive nation. The executive summary of the Botswana ICT policy paper *Maitlamo* states that the ICT policy complements and builds upon Vision 2016, saying that Botswana will be a globally competitive, knowledgeable, and informed society where lasting improvements in social, economic, and cultural development will be achieved through the effective use of ICTs. Annual ICT expenditure is estimated at one billion Pula, demonstrating significant domestic demand for ICT products and services. Pula is Botswana's currency. Currently, P5 (five pula) is the equivalent of $1. Realizing this demand, the policy stresses the urgency for increased domestic skills to ensure that young graduates have an ICT career path.

It is in this broad usage of ICTs as information-sharing and dissemination tools for national development that the concept of ICTs is presented in this chapter. Both the current and more traditional forms of ICTs are considered important.

The Concept of Community-Compatible ICTs

Developments in the area of information communication technologies have gone very far. What is equally true, however, is that "those areas of the world with the greatest access to new technologies have been privileged in their power to represent, to interpret and to influence development in ICTs and their use" (Johnson-Odim, 2002, p. 7). Their influences extended from determining what can be called an ICT to rules, standards, and even controls about access and the pace of development in this area. It is against this background that the concept of community-compatible ICTs has gained currency. This concept is used in this chapter to denote ICTs that are accessible to those living in both rural and urban community settings. It also refers to ICTs that are relevant, usable, responsive to communities' needs, and accommodative of their existing ways of doing things as well as their ways of understanding, viewing, and interpreting the world.

The debate on community-compatible ICTs coincides with the thinking about sustainable development, which puts emphasis on people-centered, environmentally friendly, and participatory approaches to development. The basic argument is that with appropriate ICTs, the poor people stand a better chance of benefiting from the contributions of ICTs to development and poverty alleviation. In its general meaning, sustainability implies the capacity of something to continue for a long time (Batchelor & Norrish, 2002), with continued benefits or returns to those using it, in this case, ICTs. However, there is a strong critique on failure in most of the development initiatives to use the locally available resources, knowledge, and ideas. The relevance of ICTs in development initiatives is that they play a major role in the transmission of information. Notable here is that information dissemination is a culturally based practice. It is, therefore, of utmost importance that those in the business of ICTs' design and use take into account the close interaction between the contexts within which ICTs are introduced and the ICTs themselves. For those in the communities who adapt and adopt ICTs, it is suggested that being prepared to draw on the existing, indigenous knowledge technologies is a necessary condition for achieving community-compatible ICTs practices. This is meant to say that concern about community-compatible ICTs is, in a nutshell, a call for an understanding that there is potential for complementarity between the local environment and ICTs' influences from elsewhere. This potential does not seem to have been adequately tapped, leaving ICTs to be seen as a modern invention that the indigenous people fail to understand and apply.

The literature reviewed for this chapter does push forward the distinction between "modern" ICTs and those that are traditional and have existed much longer. Experiences from many contexts of the world confirm this view by pointing to the fact that what are often referred to as simple technologies have been in existence for a long time. These include traditional musical instruments through which messages were transmitted, and tools and implements of art and painting from which we have learned so much about those societies. Among these are the most recent technologies upon which the new technologies have been built. In the African context, the radio is a good example here in its use of the airwaves just like the messengers of the chiefs who used to go to the top of the hill to announce to the community an important message. Both the radio and the messenger of the chiefs rely on the airwaves to transmit the messages. Dei (1999), for example, holds that different bodies of knowledge continually influence each other to show the dynamics of all knowledge systems (p. 111). This is meant to imply in this chapter that it should be expected that some modern ICTs would have been informed by traditional technologies. New and old technologies can do well together.

There is evidence from research that indicates that many of the existing ICTs have their basis in traditional technologies. The radio has been given as an example. Consider the transition from AM radio to the technologically superior FM radio. After World War II, it was clear to industry participants that FM represented the future of radio. However, in spite of the victory of FM, AM radio has not vanished, operating alongside FM (Mendelson, 2001). Thus, many new technologies have some elements of compatibility with the old ones. Since traditional designs were responsive to community needs and environmental factors, we assume that both new and old technologies could be useful tools in addressing community problems such as the reduction of rural poverty. Some of the issues that are often pivotal and controversial when discussing issues of ICTs for poverty reduction are highlighted particularly in the context of the developing world.

Key Issues in ICTs and Poverty Reduction

The issues that can be termed key in the discussion of ICTs, particularly community-compatible ICTs, are many and diverse. One of the determining factors for an issue to be regarded as key in the discussion of ICTs is the context within which it is applied. In other words, one issue might be key in the context of Southeast Asia, but not be so much of an issue in the context of Southern Africa. This is simply because the needs and aspirations of people in the two contexts may not be exactly the same. In this chapter, the few issues selected for discussion are those that present themselves as general across regions of the world. Particular focus is made on the African context using Botswana as a point of reference. Among the issues are the following:

- General access to and use of ICTs
- The dilemma of devaluing African indigenous ICTs
- The expert-led belief in the use of ICTs
- The myths about ICT use and literacy
- Bureaucratic and political dimensions

There is a very close connection between the concept of community-compatible ICTs and the issue of the digital divide, which refers to the disparity in ICT diffusion and use between industrialized and developing countries, or indeed between the rich and poor, men and women, and urban and rural areas within individual countries (Souter, 2004). This divide has in "ironic ways put certain classes of people in touch with one another around the world and totally marginalized others" (p. 10). These digital divides are a reflection of deeper social, economic, and political divides. They have been part of a technological revolution (Gerster & Zimmerman, 2003). Thus, when a new innovation is introduced, the best way to assess its worth is to ask this crucial question: This is a revolution to whose benefit? Failure to answer this question is tantamount to defeating the very same benefits that ICTs are to bring to their users. A lack of compatibility of ICTs with community contexts is noted here as one of the contributing factors to the use of ICTs for social exclusion. The idea that is being advanced here is that ICTs have been applied in different parts of the world without due consideration of the importance of compatibility. Evidently, there has been limited reflection on how much impact ICTs would have on poverty if they were made compatible with community interests.

One of the main indicators for a lack of consideration of the issues of compatibility is the continuing lack of local content in the current application of ICTs at the community level. By local content of ICTs, it is meant "locally owned and adapted knowledge of a community, where a community is defined by its location, culture, history, language, interests and needs" (Gerster & Zimmerman, 2003). For example, we need to consider the current move by the Botswana government to employ locally responsive ICTs. Botswana open-source software (BOSS), for instance, would be used by the Ministry of Education to determine the type of material to include in developing fully local educational software. To this end, financial estimates have been made through recommendations from *Maitlamo* (Mmegi, 2005). The concept of community-compatible ICTs is, therefore, viewed in this paper as an innovative idea through which improvements can not only be made on the types of technologies produced, but can also be made in the strategies for the effective application of these technologies. The next part of this chapter explores the relevance of this issue in the use of ICTs for poverty reduction.

General Access to and Use of ICTs

One of the reasons why the poor cannot reap the benefits that accrue from the use of ICTs is the problem of their limited access to these technologies. Access to ICTs for development is crucial because it is about access to information. In Botswana, for example, the rural and the remote-area dwellers do not have access to electricity and some of the infrastructure that is needed to support the use of new technologies. According to the Republic of Botswana's ICT policy document (2004), 37% of the households countrywide use electricity for lighting. Data also show that this number further falls to only 8% in rural and remote settlements. For computer ownership and Internet usage, the Botswana ICT policy reports a very low-level usage of 3 to 5%. This ownership is expected to be concentrated more in urban than rural areas, indicating that members of the remote communities are marginalized by ICTs to mainstream development efforts. Infrastructural limitations or inadequacies compound the problem of ICT access for the poor, most of whom are rural based. Their situation of poverty makes most sophisticated ICTs such as the Internet unaffordable, with only few sections such as the mines and financial-service institutions making better use of ICTs. Thus, the use of ICTs, particularly in these communities, is sporadic. Just recently, in December 2005, the government of Botswana found it necessary to experiment with one of the deprived regions of Botswana, the Chobe district, by setting up a satellite dish for a radio station and the use of telephones. The number of people who responded to this was alarming, and many expressed disappointment at the end of the experiment. This is a case that indicates that many people who stay in the rural areas (mostly the poor) are deprived of basic things such as means for sharing information. Schilderman (n.d.) asserts that information enables the poor to increase their assets. Thus, when the poor are shut out of the world of information, they are put out of actions. The findings of research funded by Department for International Development (DIFD) and the World Bank and carried out in Peru, Sri Lanka, and Zimbabwe revealed the need to make information available for development by the poor. One of the key findings was that the poor do not seek information unless it is for a purpose: to meet a specific need, such as a need for social services, land, employment, and so forth (Schilderman, n.d.). Thus, they will use technology that addresses their life challenges and other needs.

While new challenges inevitably connect the poor to modern ICTs, generally, access to these new innovations is a farce for these people. It is their economic poverty that makes them great targets for using ICTs as economic boosters. Because rural communities lack certain necessary skills, technical and otherwise, and because they are on average less formally educated than urban communities, they miss out on the empowerment that comes with having information (Sebusang & Masupe, n.d.). When the Botswana government advocates for an informed and educated nation, as stated in its long-term vision, Vision 2016, the rural and the poor people are left out if nothing is done to ensure that they reap the benefits of the ICTs for development. As of now, the rural communities in a number of African countries, Botswana included, do not have access to essential ICTs for development. Most ironically, 80% of the world's population has no access to reliable telecommunications, and the bulk of these are the poor peoples of the world. One third has no access to electricity, while there are more Internet account holders in London than there are in the whole of Africa (Heeks, 1999).

As a result of their limited access to modern ICTs, the poor continue to have gaps in information. Notably, the use of these ICTs is private-sector led and does not always focus on the needs of the poor. Where governments play a lead role in ICT provision, there are recorded cases of their reluctance to provide information that can empower the poor. For example, Schilderman (n.d.) reports that in Zimbabwe and Sri Lanka, ICT-based information is withheld from those living in informal settlements. As governments and the private sector fail to facilitate access to information for the poor through the use of ICTs, the poor have no choice but to continue to depend on traditional social networks for information, which are at times limiting.

It has been noted, however, that governments the world over have at least taken to acknowledging the role of ICTs as they give poverty reduction top priority as a challenge needing immediate attention. In the context of the Southern African Development Community (SADC), commitment to the use of ICTs to address development challenges was summarized by the executive secretary of the SADC. In his opening address at the conference of the International Telecommunication Union Economic Commission for Africa held in Botswana in the year 2004, he said that the harmonization of policies, the establishment of proper legal frameworks, and the development of predictable regulatory regimes are key to attracting private-sector participation in the development and expansion of networks to increase access to ICTs. In addition to ICT policy, he said that infrastructure development and e-export are sine qua non for SADC to be transformed into an information-based region. As part of this context, Botswana is likely to be involved and be in step with regional and international ICT initiatives. It has hosted meetings and other activities of great importance, such as the Workshop on ICT Indicators for Africa in 2004 as well as the World Information Technology Forum in 2005. Botswana also participated in the World Summit on the Information Society (WSIS) meetings, particularly the second phase held in Geneva, Switzerland, in 2005. It is on the basis of these conventions that the president of Botswana, Mr. Festus Mogae, in his state-of-the-nation address at the first meeting of the fifth session of the eighth parliament (November 10, 2003), informed the nation that the top development priority for Botswana is the elimination of poverty. The country's Vision 2016 reflects this focus and goes further to indicate that ICT use is one of the core strategies for the reduction of poverty.

However, one cannot help but sympathize with the efforts that have been made so far in poverty reduction because they seem to be doing very little, leaving us with the fear that poverty is here to haunt the present and future generations. The recent *Botswana Millennium Development Status Report* (Republic of Botswana, 2004, p. 21) states clearly that "[d]espite its macroeconomic success, Botswana has a serious problem of poverty compared to countries of similar economic stature." Policies and program support for poverty reduction are reported to be strong in Botswana. The country alleges that 'a comprehensive system of social safety nets provides adequate welfare cover for the indigent,' yet poverty still lingers on. The 2004 *Millennium Development Status Report* acknowledges that all measures to reduce poverty 'translate in slow progress.' Perhaps Botswana needs to look critically at the ways in which it approaches its poverty-reduction campaigns. It is a well-known fact that in Botswana, ICTs are not maximized like in other developing countries. In general, the current practices with the use of ICTs in a number of African countries have done very little to dispel the more subtle and yet influential attitudes that make access to ICTs difficult or impossible for the poor people. One issue worthy of attention that is closely connected to access to ICTs by the poor is discussed below: the dilemma of the devaluation of the indigenous ICTs in the context of Africa.

The Dilemma of Devaluing African Indigenous ICTs

Several decades have passed since a negative attitude swept across many countries: the devaluing of traditional African practices. In Botswana, the erosion of a traditional support mechanism as the economy modernizes perpetuates the situation of the poor as it is now. For example, there used to exist:

the Mafisa system, through which the poor family could get a small number of livestock, usually cattle from a better off family for the purposes of milking, draught power and possible seed...it is now difficult for poor families to barter their labor for draught power because cash is the dominant medium of exchange. (Republic of Botswana, 2004, p. 23)

The attitude described here also applies to the use of indigenous and locally based knowledge systems including the use of technology.

It is commonly known worldwide that people learn from their ways of living and common practices. They come up with unique indigenous technologies adapted and defined by their culture, environment, and needs. For example, Africans continue to use indigenous knowledge and techniques for food preservation, iron smelting, and the application of local medicines to humans and animals to cure diseases endemic to the community (Semali, 1999). Among terms used to refer to these is the concept of indigenous technical knowledge. According to the National Research Foundation of South Africa, this is the complex set of knowledge systems and technologies existing and developed around specific conditions of indigenous communities and peoples of a particular area.

The African nations also continue to use community knowledge produced from local history and information. For example, "knowledge about flora and fauna" are important literacy skills that are critical to people's survival (Semali, 1999, p.305). As Castle (cited in Semali, 1999) argues, whether the child's habit is dominated by mountain, plain, river, or tropical forest, he or she learns new ways to control the environment, and its dangers, use, and fertility. Technological development in the context of traditional practices means that new knowledge and innovations are continuously developed by the local people as powerful driving forces for their survival. Thus, the richness of the poor should not be defined in terms of material possession or high education, but by their "capacity to generate new knowledge and by their ability to apply such knowledge successfully" (Walshok, 1995, p. 7). The type of knowledge referred to here is the one that derives its "origin or meaning not from an individual but a collective epistemological understanding and rationalization of the community" (Semali, 1999, p. 307). This demonstrates the fact that indigenous knowledge for Africans, like for people in other regions of the world, is about what local people know and do, and what local communities have known and done for generations. In the context of Botswana, indigenous technical knowledge has been applied in agro-pastoral activities to sustain livelihoods in natural resource management and in rural development as we see it today. These include tools and equipment to transmit information, to convey messages through music, and to ferry people from one part of their communities to others. It also includes the whole embodiment of indigenous lifestyles and practices of knowledge and information transmission and management as well as its preservation. Thus, to understand people as knowledge producers is of inestimable value. National leaders should acknowledge the fact that the poor themselves are capable of coming up with innovations to address their priority needs (Chambers, 1993). The creative breakthroughs coming from the poor people are a sign that indeed ICTs are being used by these people, and they can play a vital role in poverty reduction. It is not good to devalue local knowledge, but a combination of modern ICTs and traditional ones can make profound impact in the lives of the poor. In this way, the benefits of ICTs can be felt in all sectors of nations rather than in the urban areas only. Thorough research should be carried out to determine how traditional and modern ICTs can be used concurrently to speed up poverty-reduction activities. The question to address here is what the goal in using ICTs should be Should it be to join the global flow through their use, or to use technologies that are relevant and responsive as poverty-reduction strategies?

As alluded to earlier, the inequalities relating to decisions about which types of ICTs to use, the accessibility of these technologies, and their overall ranking seem to have immensely contributed to the evident notion of expert-led ICTs. This expert-led notion influences the imbalances in terms of decisions about the use of ICTs. The leaders in these decision-making processes are the experts on ICTs. This concept of expert-led belief in the use of ICT is further explored in the following part of this chapter.

The Expert-Led Adoption and Use of ICTs

The use of ICTs is influenced to a greater extent by the ways in which the "educated" or experts think about these innovations. Walshok (1995), for example, contends that the effective use of technology depends on the three critical elements of "new discoveries, highly trained personnel, and expert knowledge" (p. 8). This implies that before national leaders think of using ICTs as one of the national development strategies for poverty alleviation, they should question whether ICTs can function effectively in the absence of highly skilled individuals. Although the concept of a skill may imply the ability to generate information and use it for social and economic progress, the Western idea is that a skilled person is one who has undergone formal training, especially in academic institutions. This type of understanding has deep and pervasive implications for how the ICTs can be incorporated as tools for national development, especially for poverty alleviation. First and foremost, this type of thinking automatically disqualifies the poor's capacity and initiatives in using ICTs. Educationally, the poor people are generally known for having limited or no formal or school-based education.

Where expert-driven ICTs are the norm, the poor are deprived of access to ICTs by some of the factors mentioned earlier, and thus they are reflected as people who cannot think for themselves under those conditions. They are considered unable to help themselves and therefore are in need of experts to assist them (Kroeker, 1995). This happens even between nation states where the economically advanced who are also ahead in terms of highly skilled person power control decisions about ICT use for the less-developed countries. Those who can afford to buy high-priced ICTs are also in a good position to determine who these experts should be. They have the power to influence the types of ICTs for poor people without stopping to analyze the knowledge bases of the poor and to use these as springboards for ICT use in poverty reduction.

The current picture pertaining to the use of ICTs is that it has successfully created a kind of mandarin culture for the haves. With this, it is as if ICTs have not, in principle, always been available (Gerster & Zimmerman, 2003). What is different is the pace at which the modern ICTs advance and change, which is much faster than the traditional systems. This culture of the privileged can be broken into and used to benefit the poor people, especially if indigenous technologies are recognized and used together with the modern technologies. This would be the concept of community-compatible ICTs as applied in this chapter. It is important that national leaders should have respect for the use of local knowledge, experiences, and interests (Bergdall, 1993; Dean, 1999) because it provides them with opportunities to learn from the local practices. If, for example, the poor people are helped to develop confidence and efficiency in using ICTs, such a move may reduce their dependency on the governments. High-priced and expert-driven technologies might not be the best for poverty reduction if they have no relevance to the needs of the community. Community-compatible ICTs are suggested here because the authors believe that the educational status of the poor should not be used to deprive them of the opportunities to use ICTs. The poor in this regard, like in many other development initiatives, have proved to be in a better position to decide on relevant technologies because they "know best their own needs" (http://www.hc-sc-.a/hppb/wired/community.html).

However, we cannot rule out the existence of a close relationship between literacy and use of ICTs. This suggests that changes have to be made in the educational systems of countries such as Botswana in order to lay foundations for the effective use of ICTs for poverty alleviation in communities. In the revised national education policy, Botswana realizes the need to acknowledge the benefits of ICT innovations in education. This follows recommendations as contained in the Botswana draft policy on ICTs. The recommendation being made is that ICTs be introduced to children at an early age and also be mainstreamed into the curriculum so that children can have the benefits of technologies throughout their entire lives (Mmegi, 2005). Also suggested in this context is an ICT-specific syllabus at all educational levels. Poor people need guided access to ICTs. If well perceived and appropriately employed as priority tools in the development of communities, ICTs can play a significant role in ensuring good-quality lives of the rural poor. Also, government-sponsored breakthrough ICT courses for the poor can be developed to give them a broader understanding of ICTs, why we use ICTs, and how modern ICTs can be used for their own development. ICTs-based expanded community participation in policy analysis and the discourse of human development and poverty reduction needs special attention, too.

The Myths about ICT Use and Literacy

The relevance of literacy and numeracy in modern ICT use cannot be denied. The concept of literacy as applied here covers the idea of information literacy, which is sometimes interpreted as a type of literacy that is also a critical one in the 21st century. This type of literacy is associated with information practices. It is an ideal type of literacy in the context of rapid technological changes. This idea of literacy is associated with information practices. It denotes the capacity of those receiving information to use it for their development. This raises the issue that if information cannot be manage and used, then it is not beneficial. It is in this regard that this chapter holds a view that "learning the mechanism of reading and writing is the touchstone that could liberate the poor and uneducated people everywhere from the bonds of ignorance, disease and hunger" (Coombs, 1985, p. 265). For example, in Botswana, literacy has been identified as a "prerequisite if Botswana's other developmental objectives are to be met" (Maruatona, 1998, p. 11). This step has been taken after it was observed that illiteracy stood to hamper any effective national development efforts. Thus, within the context of ICTs, literacy is functional to the extent that people can develop mechanisms to use ICTs in coping with challenges and opportunities in their local environments. This type of literacy is required to transform today's information society into tomorrow's learning society (Bruce, 1999) since it provides learning opportunities that enable people to effectively take advantage of the ICTs.

Even though it is an established fact that there is a direct link between adult literacy and socioeconomic development, there is also evidence to suggest that the ability to use ICTs does not require high education, but functional literacy. Take the cell phone, for example; basic numeracy and literacy skills enable one to use this piece of technology. There are many instances when people with the basic literacy skills (low or no formal education at all) use this device in their own successful way. The same thing applies to the ability to operate a telephone or a radio. The most amazing thing is to see illiterate people being able to watch TV. These could be illiterate children or even adults in Botswana who to a very reasonable extent can understand the language being used or relate to the pictures they are watching. The overt social benefits of employing these technologies need not be underestimated. They include an elevated social status just from owning the technology. This presumably goes with a sense of being empowered and better able to take up the challenges of development in one's own terms. This view marries well with one of the critical issues being raised in this chapter, which is the fact that illiteracy should not be used to keep the poor from using ICTs.

Bureaucratic and Political Dimensions of ICT Use

In many African countries, the rural poor are unable to take control of their lives because of the structural, economical, political, and cultural conditions that oppress them. Such oppression is articulated through centralized bureaucratic structures that make participation by the locals in decision making very difficult to implement. In the absence of participation in its ideal form, and also as a key principle in classical thinking about democracy, the communities are represented by the bureaucrats. In this process, the services that are delivered to them are not always in line with their real needs as target groups. For scientific and technological advances, Brynard (1996) opines that these top-down approaches have contributed to the creation of new problems instead of solving existing ones, especially because of the top-down thrust of the use of these technologies. The same is true for ICT adoption processes, which have a top-down thrust that many governments use to address issues of poverty alleviation.

Instead, these welfare approaches do very little to alleviate poverty. A significant feature of this approach is that it makes it difficult for poor people to take responsibility for their lives. The Botswana government acknowledges that welfarism translates into slow progress in poverty reduction (Republic of Botswana, 2004). A study (Lekoko, 2002) also supports the government's contention. In this case, it was the participants of the study, the community-based extension workers, who alluded to the ineffectiveness of the welfare approach. They refer to it as a "spoon-feeding" approach. A significant feature of this approach is that it makes it difficult for poor people to take responsibility for their lives; it encourages dependency. There clearly needs to be some initiatives that challenge the needy people to realize that they have power to change their circumstances. This applies most strongly to the use of ICTs in which communities usually play the roles of passive recipients as governments spearhead all the pilots and more long-term programs, starting with ICT policies. Thus, when ICTs are considered economic resources, a more participatory framework should be worked out. One challenge for national leaders in the developing world is to look closely at the use of technologies in the context of the local economic and social relations and determine how these processes could be made inclusive, despite the unresolved issue of how and when ICT use could be made beneficial to all in an equitable way. Even though there is much debate about how and when ICTs can work, a timely and relevant use can be beneficial. It is important for national leaders to assess how modern ICTs can be adapted to local innovations and new challenges of the local communities.

Within the top-down approaches, bureaucratic interests often can distort the government's choice of technologies. In many instances, the governments, whose key players are the bureaucrats and politicians, assume themselves to be the sole producers of information and knowledge that is vital for development or poverty reduction. As a result of this, they play the roles of a middle person between the poor and those providing the technologies. The governments usually provide the technology on the basis of free grants or subsidies unrelated to the poor's real needs. An example that readily comes to mind is the use of technologies such as radios, which were provided by the government of Botswana in the 1970s to help in agricultural initiatives and in the tribal land grazing policy initiative as a process of social and economic transformation. Because the poor were not as convinced as the government that such technologies would work, some of the program experiences confirmed the view that inadequate participation by recipients of technologies may lead to poor adoption. Radios were used for other purposes other than the program, thereby distorting the economic value of the technologies.

In general, bureaucratic entities are biased toward large-scale, modern, expensive, and usually imported technologies. In the context of countries of the developing world, governments have limited budgetary power to supply the technologies to the poor. Community-compatible ICTs can, therefore, be viable alternative tools to address this problem. This is not meant to suggest that the communities should not have access to the sophisticated technologies that come in as part of development. However, it is a call for a certain degree of realism about what the key principles of sustainable development embrace. While the central thesis of community-compatible ICTs is being advanced here, we also acknowledge the fact that discrepancies can exist between what the governments think about ICTs and their potential role in poverty reduction and what the local people may think. Where the poor do not appear as convinced as national leaders that certain ICTs can play a vital role in their development, such ICTs should not be imposed on them. The locals need to be convinced of their worth, be listened to on their concerns about these technologies, and be adequately involved in the reformulation of what could work in their context. Furthermore, they should have their capacities tapped and properly aligned with what is required for these technologies to make a positive impact, while at the same time attempts should be made to help people understand the technologies and to make them affordable.

Current Poverty-Reduction Strategies

Countries worldwide are committed to joining the fight against poverty. This is evidenced by their leaders being signatories to the MDGs, which among other things commit countries to reducing by half the number of people living in extreme poverty by the year 2015: that is, reducing the proportion of people living on less than $1 a day (http://www.unmillenniumproject.org/reports/goals_targets.htm). In all, 189 United Nations member states pledged to meet this goal. This was a sign that indeed national leaders worldwide are committed to reducing poverty in their respective countries. The president of Botswana, for example, referred to poverty as the greatest threat of all to our future welfare (Republic of Botswana, 2004). He bemoans societies that are divided between extremes of wealth and poverty. The statistics indicate that about 27% of the sub-Saharan African population lives in poverty. Some other regions, for example, South Asia (47%), record a higher proportion (http://www.marxist.com/Globalisation/growing_world_poverty.html). Pockets of abject poverty are also in existence in developed nations. Central and Eastern Europe, for instance, record 2% of people living on less than $1 a day (http://www.marxist.com/Globalisation/growing_world_poverty.html). The situation of poverty is, no doubt, a key challenge for all nations.

In recent years, some African leaders have realized the fallacy of using the welfare approach to fight poverty. For these countries, poverty-reduction strategies that are now devised go beyond compensation and distribution of schemes for the poor. National leaders are aware that there is a need to instill in the poor the spirit of self-worth so that they become aware of taking care of their own situation. The fundamental tenets of the poverty-reduction strategy for Botswana (perhaps not the best but the most accessible to authors) are given below to illustrate the nature and content of such strategies that are said to aim at aggressively fighting poverty.

To deal critically and creatively with the problem of poverty, strategies for the reduction of poverty have to be conceived in terms of the poor's social well-being, as well as the economic and political dimensions. The legal aspect should be an issue of concern. Africa is caught up in situations in which resources are scarce, unemployment is rising, high levels of illiteracy are difficult to break through, and infirmity is increasing. These situations make Africa a

Table 1. Strategies for poverty reduction in Botswana (Source: Republic of Botswana, 2004).

The Instrument	Year	Objectives
National Poverty-Reduction Strategy	2003	• To link and harmonize antipoverty initiatives • To provide opportunities for people to have sustainable livelihoods through the expansion of employment opportunities and improved access to social investment • To monitor progress (regularly) against poverty
Revised National Policy for Rural Development	2002	• To reduce rural poverty • To promote sustainable livelihoods • To stimulate rural employment and income generation • To diversify the rural economy and reduce dependency on the government • To maintain and improve rural capital, increase agricultural productivity, and promote participation in development

great target for foreign aid. The present situation is that many African countries receive economic and technical aid from rich and/or developed countries, and "this aid is not given free, for there is no aid without bait" (Mbiti, 1988, p. 223). Some African countries thus fall victim to the dos and don'ts of some foreign countries. The consequences of this should not be overlooked. Offering some aid should not mean that the providers should undermine African potentialities to develop their own knowledge of addressing their plight.

The Role of ICTs in Poverty Reduction

The adoption of the MDGs in 2000 has meant that countries started looking for effective means of fighting the poverty scourge. The national leaders seem convinced that ICTs can be used to counter the crisis of poverty, especially if they are linked to the complex economic, educational, political, and other challenges facing the poor. Those who see ICTs as catalysts in poverty reduction make a connection between the absence of ICTs and the high levels of poverty in some parts of the world such as Africa, which is recorded as having less than 0.6% of Internet users (http://www.iconnect-online.org). The discussion on the role of ICTs in poverty reduction is entered into bearing in mind an observation made by Heeks (1999): Like any generic technology, ICTs lend themselves to sweeping statements about what they can do for development.

Programs have been put in place in different countries of the world to show that indeed ICTs can make a positive contribution to the reduction of poverty and the achievement of a better quality of life for the poorest and marginalized groups. Evidence for this in the African context can be drawn from a study that was undertaken covering three countries—Mali, Uganda, and Tanzania—conducted in 2003 under the Building Digital Opportunities Program. This study has demonstrated that ICTs can be important tools for achieving improvements in people's lives in the context of MDGs (iConnect.offline, 2003). In reporting this discovery, a strongly held point of view is that for ICTs to be effective in playing a pivotal role in poverty reduction, they should not be "set apart as a minor part of any development activity" (p. 2); instead, they have to be an integral part of the development process. From this study, the areas seen to have potential for increased benefits from ICT use were health, livelihood, and governance, with a special focus on HIV/AIDS.

In the broad area of improved livelihoods through ICTs, there is evidence to suggest that the overall empowerment of communities is achieved as they engage in agricultural processes using ICTs. Communities are empowered through capacity-building programs with emphasis on face-to-face contacts. An empowered community through access to information is better able to overcome most of the impediments to participation. This has to be noted here, bearing in mind the fact that participation is central to good governance. Worth noting, too, is the interrelatedness between all the areas in which ICTs have a potential to contribute to poverty reduction as mentioned above. ICTs are reported to have given communities a voice in development and poverty-reduction debates. This has to a great extent made it possible for their ideas to be better integrated in development initiatives. It is on record also that being able to participate contributes first and foremost to the betterment of self in all the domains of human development. Even in the debate on sustainable development, people's participation is acclaimed as one of the cornerstones for achieving this ideal.

There are those who hold a view that ICTs per se do not contribute to poverty reduction. They should be valued in as far as their capacity to support civil society is concerned. Rykert (1999, p. 184) says, "Technology in and for itself, will not solve problems. Ethical choices challenge us at every turn as we work for the goals of civic society. Local knowledge has much to contribute to when, why and how ICTs can be applied."

The lesson learned from Rykert's (1999) contention is that technology should be applied for its potential to solve social problems. In his view, there are unanswered moral questions relating to effective ICT applications. Effective application, it is argued here, would be evidenced through combining old methods with new ones, sharing wisdoms, and learning from each other. It is the collective capacity, in the words of Rykert, that truly has impact.

Another factor that is likely to contribute to modern ICTs not making an impact on poverty reduction is the lack of the capacity by the poor to effectively apply ICTs to solve their poverty problems. Aside from knowledge and practical skills, it is argued by Heeks (1999) and others that even the trust and levels of confidence and security to use ICTs are lacking among the poor. This has been one of the major impediments for effective ICT use and for receipt of optimal benefits from the technologies by the poor. Incapacity here is used in a very broad sense to include the poor people's lack of skills, trust, and ability to analyze risks and resources, and their lack of power to influence the direction of decisions. Those with this type of pessimism caution us as this chapter does about overoptimism toward ICTs as they are currently applied. In their view, the information that on the surface ICTs are said to effectively transmit…is a necessary resource for poverty alleviation but it is by no means a sufficient one.

The last impediment that this chapter will highlight relating to effective ICT use for poverty reduction is that of the capacity by the poor to manage the ICTs' generated information. No doubt, information generated by modern ICTs is immense in terms of volume and complexity, and therefore it is often also overwhelming not only for the poor but even for the most sophisticated users. It is most of the time context biased and not very organized, hence the general view that it should sometimes be used with caution, while applying special skills to decipher it for positive impact.

There is a generally held view that the poor do not have adequate skills to effectively manage this information (Rykert, 1999) and therefore they have not been able to adequately exploit the potential it holds for poverty reduction. This state of affairs, we would like to argue, will be significantly accentuated (to the disadvantage of the poor) by the rapid pace at which modern ICTs develop, change, and are redeveloped to suit the ever-changing trends and demands and challenges of development. This presentation questions the view held by those who "seem to behave as if it were possible to pluck ideas relating to ICTs, the types, uses, etc out of cultural contexts and treat them as independent technical facts" (Sillitoe, 1998, p. 228). For example, imported ICTs bring with them cultural biases that contribute to their being well received or not being well received. Sillitoes goes on to say, "we need to establish that it is dangerous to do this and demonstrate the importance of understanding environmental interactions and development opportunities within their socio-cultural contexts" (p. 228). We posit here that this is not possible because cultural influences are pervasive in every aspect of development.

Concluding Ideas and Recommendations

Not too long ago, ICTs were considered marginal to the achievement of national economic growth. But a decade or so later, ICTs are considered a central part of development processes at the individual, national, regional, and international levels. There is evidence to suggest, however, that in the contexts of the developing world, more knowledge is still needed about the most effective ways of developing conducive environments for modern ICT use in poverty reduction.

There is a view that modern ICT use in general has, like development, fallen into a trap of trickle-down approaches with all their known limitations. Therefore, the poor and other disadvantaged groups have still not received the desired benefits. There are even those who argue that ICTs have increased the gaps, particularly in knowledge and information between the haves and have-nots. The viewpoint expressed in this chapter is that if modern ICTs have benefited the rich, there is no reason. They cannot benefit the poor but on one condition: that they are made compatible with community needs and environments.

Duly recognized is the fact that developing and less-developed countries are still less well equipped to exploit the potentials of ICTs for reduction of their poverty. One of the contributing factors to the ineffective use of ICTs in poverty reduction has been identified as the inability by these countries to effectively balance policies, and the evidently expensive investment options for ICTs against other socioeconomic objectives, for example, the MDGs. Suggested in this regard are policy priorities that aim to reduce factors that inhibit the effective use of ICTs for poverty reduction. Some of the inhibiting factors as have been discussed in this chapter are inaccessibility to ICTs, limited capacities by the local communities to use the ICTs, and attitudes about modern ICTs as new inventions that the locals fail to understand. These have resulted in a failure to integrate traditional ICT systems into the new ones, and also inability to see ICTs and their use as part of a complex system of national development. Evidently, the relationship between ICTs and poverty reduction is not as clear cut a relationship as it is often assumed to be. It is suggested that a good starting point for the effective employment of ICTs in poverty reduction is to develop a full understanding of this relationship through multidisciplinary research. This type of research will demonstrate the interactions between economic, social, political, and legal aspects of poverty.

Another critical issue raised in this chapter is that to assume that ICT use is of critical benefit when in fact it has had a similar marginalization effect as other developments is an oversimplification of issues. It is still very hard at this point to go into any convincing discussion of positive impact when the true relationships among all the factors have not been adequately ascertained, for example, through research (not even in the developed world). It is concluded, therefore, that many of the assumptions that underpin current thinking about the role of ICTs in development, in general, and poverty reduction in particular is based on intuition. There is only limited evidence from a narrow range of pilot projects to support these, and not from large-scale impact assessments carried out on a macroeconomic scale. Some authors have also argued that the benefits of ICTs are not in the short term, nor can they be easily isolated from the benefits derived from other factors in a given context.

For the developing world, a big issue is that of the affordability of ICTs by its evidently weak economies. The complicating factor in this regard is that most of the ICTs that are used in this context are imported. They are not only imported, but they are accessed most of the time through foreign assistance. This has made it imperative for this presentation to argue for sustainable applications of ICTs in poverty reduction. For us, it is all the more reason why we believe community-compatible ICTs would be a better alternative because they would reduce the susceptibility of the business of accessing ICTs to all the factors of nonlocal production such as import duties, international market fluctuations, other types of taxes, and regulatory frameworks in the world of trade.

This chapter is concluded by affirming that consensus is growing on the potential positive contribution of ICTs to mainstream development. It has also been used to highlight the fact that the role of ICTs in poverty reduction cannot be limited to improvements in the state of economic deprivation. This is confirmed by Gerster and Zimmerman (2003), who hold that beyond economic benefits, ICTs increase levels of interactions between peoples of the world and therefore they are increasingly becoming a basic need.

References

Adeya, N. (2002). *Information and communication technologies in development.* Paper presented at the Conference on Global Equality: Rethinking ICTs in Africa, Asia and Latin America, Heerlen Maastrisht, Netherlands.

Akosah-Sarpong, K. (n.d.). African cultures in the age of globalization. *Expo Times.* Retrieved August 30, 2005, from http://www.expotimes.net/pastissues/issue000524/saporng. htm

Batchelor, S., & Norrish, P. (2002). *Sustainable information and communication technology (ICT).* Retrieved December 1, 2005, from http://www.sutainableicts.org/Sustainable. htm

Bergdall, T. (1993). *Methods for active participation: Experience in rural development from east and central Africa.* Nairobi, Kenya: Oxford University Press.

Brynard, D.J., (1996). Planning participatory approach, in Bekker, K. (Ed.), *Citizen partici-pation in local government.* Pretoria: J.L. van Shaik.

Bruce, R. (1999). Networking multimedia contents for education. Russian Digital Library Journal 2(3). Retrieved from: http://www.elbib.ru/index.phtml?page=elbib/rus/jour-nal/1999/part3/royan.

Bryceson, D. F. (1995). Wishful thinking: Theory and practice of western donor efforts to raise women's status in rural africa. In D. F. Bryceson (Ed.), *Women wielding the hoe,* (pp.201-222). Oxford: Berg Publishers

Campfens, H. (1997). International review of community development theory and practice. In H. Campfens (Ed.), *Community development around the world* (pp. 11-46). Toronto, Canada: University of Toronto.

Central Statistic Office, Botswana (1991). *Education Statistics 1991.* Gaborone: Govern-ment Printers

Chambers, R. (1993). *Farmer first: Farmer innovation and agricultural research*. London Intermediate Technology Publications.

Coombs, P.H. (1985). *The world crisis in education: The view from the eighties*. Oxford: University Press.

Dean, M. (1999). *Governmentality: Power and rule in modern society*. London: Sage.

Dei, G. J. (1999). Rethinking the role of indigenous knowledge in the academy. *The research network for new approaches to lifelong learning* (NALL), Working paper number 58

Dei, G. (2002). Rethinking the role of indigenous knowledge in the academy. *International Journal of Inclusive Education, 4*(2), 111-132.

Gerster, R., & Zimmerman, S. (2003). *Information and communication technologies for poverty reduction*. Switzerland: Swiss Agency for Development Corporation.

Heeks, R. (1999). *Information and communication technologies, poverty and development*. Manchester: Institute for Development Policy and Management.

iConnect Offline (2003). Applying knowledge to development. iConnect, Issue 10 October 2003. Retrieved July 3, 2006 from http://www.iconnect-online.org

Johnson-Odim, C. (2002). *Africa in the information and technology age*. African Studies Association. Retrieved August 30, 2005, from http://www.africanstudies.org/asa_papercalltheme.html

Kroeker, C. J. (1995). Individual, organizational, and societal empowerment: A study of the processes in a Nicaraguan agricultural cooperative. *American Journal of Community Psychology, 23*(5), 749-764.

Lekoko, R. N. (2002). *Appraisal of Botswana extension agents' work and training experiences: Research-based*. FL: UPBLISH/Universal Publication.

Maruatona, T. (1998). *The evaluation of literacy program in Botswana: A report to Botswana Notes and Records*. Gaborone, Botswana.

Mendelson, H. (2001). *In time new and old technologies can thrive together*. San Jose Mercury News, July 2001.

Mbiti, J. S. (1988). *African religious and philosophy*. London: Heinemann.

Miller, J. G. (1978). *Living systems*. New York: McGraw-Hill.

Mmegi, A. (2005, September 22). Getting ready for e-education. *Botswana Weekly Paper, 139*, B2.

Mtshali, S. M. (2000). Monitoring and evaluation of women's rural development extension services in South Africa. *Development South Africa, 17*(1), 64-65.

Muayle-Manenji, F. (2004). *The effects of globalization on culture in Africa in the eyes of an African woman*. Retrieved August 30, 2005, from http://www.wcc-coe.org/wcc/what/jpc/effglob.html

Ntsatsi, T. (2002). Botswana's quest for an information society, (Concept paper), *Botswana Human Development Report, 2002/3*, United Nations development Programme, Gaborone

Pityana, N. B. (1999). The renewal of African moral values. In M. W. Makgoba (Ed.), *African renaissance: The new struggle* (pp. 137-148). Cape Town, South Africa: Mafube.

Ramsamy, P. (2004). *Official opening address at the international telecommunication union/United Nations economic commission for Africa regional workshop on ICT indicators for Africa held in Botswana.* Unpublished manuscript.

Republic of Botswana. (2004). *Botswana millennium development status report 2004: Achievement, future challenges and choices.* Gaborone, Botswana: Tiger Design and Graphics.

Republic of Botswana, President Task Force. (1997). *Long term vision for botswana: Vision 2016.* Gaborone: Government Printers.

Roberts, E. B. (1991). *Entrepreneurs in high technology: Lessons from MIT and beyond.* New York: University Press.

Rykert, L. (1999). New tools, same values: Information and communication technologies to support civil society. In *Civil society at the millennium* (pp. 179-192). CT: Kumarina and Press.

Schilderman, T. (n.d.). *Can ICTs help urban poor access information and knowledge to support their livelihood?* Retrieved August 30, 2005, from http://www.unhabitat. org/programmes/ifup/conf/Theo-Schilderman.pdf

Sebusang, S. (2001). *Making technology work for poor people,* (Seminar presentation), October 17, United Nations Development Programme and the Department of Economics, University of Botswana, Gaborone

Sebusang, S., & Masupe, S. (n.d.). *ICT development in Botswana: Connectivity for rural communities.* Retrieved November 8, 2005, from http://216.239.51.104/ search?q=cache:zifCMVbuh2AJ:link.wits.ac.za/journal/j0401-sebusang-botswana. pdf+ICTs+in+Botswana+-+rural+areas&hl=en

Semali, L. (1999). Community as classroom: Dilemma of valuing African indigenous literacy in education. *International Review of Education, 45*(3-4), 305-319.

Semali, L., & Kincheloe, L. (1999). *What is indigenous knowledge: Voices from the academy.* New York: Falmer Press.

Sillitoe, P. (1998). The development of indigenous knowledge. *Current Anthropology, 39*(2), 223-252.

Souter, D. (2004). *ICTs and economic growth in developing countries.* Retrieved July 4, 2005, from http://www.oecd.org/dataoecd/15/54/34663175.pdf

Walshok, M. L. (1995). *Knowledge without boundaries: What America's research universities can do for the economy, the workplace, and the community.* San Francisco: Jossey-Bass.

Wanyeka, I. M. (n.d.). *The development of community media in East and Southern Africa.* Nairobi, Kenya: Eco News Africa.

Wells, B. (2002). Women's voices: Explaining poverty and plenty in a rural community. *Rural Sociology, 67*(2), 235-254.

Wolf, N. & Wahab, B. (1996). The importance of indigenous organizations to the sustainability of contemporary Yoruba strip-weaving industries in Iseyin, Nigeria. In P. Blunt & M. Warren (Eds.), *Indigenous organizations and development* (pp. 67-87). UK: SRP Exeter.

Zimmerman, M. A. (1995). Psychology empowerment: Issues and illustrations. *American Journal of Community Psychology, 23*, 581-600.

Chapter VI

The E-Pabelan National ICT4PR Pilot Project:
Experiences and Challenges of Implementation in an Indonesian Context

Alex Robinson, University of Hudderfield, UK

Abstract

The chapter presents a case study of an ICT-based attempt to reduce poverty (ICT4PR) in a rural Indonesian community. Differences between the theoretical approaches adopted by the implementing agencies and the difficulties inherent in achieving these aims in practice are outlined. The chapter is particularly concerned with how issues relating to implementation impact on efforts to move toward greater beneficiary inclusion in socioeconomic networks. Crucially, the chapter stresses the ongoing need in practice to move away from a homogenising digital-divide-style approach to ICT4PR, and to better engage with localised realities and contexts.

Introduction

We have plenty of information. We visit other farmers, talk...listen to the radio, watch television...read books! ~Farmer and local official, male, nonpoor, December 4, 2004

Maybe the telecentre is only for rich people [orang mampu]....Information [in Pabelan] does not flow evenly [tidak merata]—it is only for certain people. So poor people, like me, often do not in fact receive information. ~Occasional child minder, female, poor, February 29, 2005

In recent years, there have been increasing interest, speculation, and debate regarding the potential of information communication technologies to facilitate and contribute toward a process of development (ICT for development, ICT4D). This interest has been accompanied by a plethora of activities seeking to harness the potential of ICTs to a correspondingly varied array of development ends. This chapter focuses on an attempt to utilise ICTs for poverty reduction (ICT4PR) in a rural Indonesian community. Research informing this chapter was conducted at the e-Pabelan national ICT4PR pilot project in the village of Pabelan between October 2004 and August 2005.[1] e-Pabelan (http://e-pabelan.myserver.org/portal) is the initial pilot of the Partnerships for e-Prosperity for the Poor (PePP) programme (http://www.ict4pr. org) of the National Development Planning Agency (Badan Perencanaan Pembangunan Nasional, BAPPENAS) and the United Nations Development Programme (UNDP).

e-Pabelan became operational in May 2004. The project takes the form of a telecentre that was established with five computers providing dial-up access to the Internet, plus ancillary equipment including a scanner, printer, and digital projector.[2] More established ICTs such as a telephone or facsimile machine were not provided. The equipment was provided by BAPPENAS/UNDP as was payment for the Internet connection for the first year, some educational materials, and limited training for some staff and members of the community. The chosen local partner was the Islamic boarding school Pondok Pesantren Pabelan acting through its community development wing Balai Pengkajian dan Pengembangun Masyarakat (BPPM). The pesantren is a coeducational secondary (equivalent) school, which, alongside the emphasis on Islamic teachings and proper conduct, follows the Indonesian national curriculum. Additional emphasis is placed on the teaching of languages, including English, and science classes, as well as a range of extracurricular activities. The pesantren is highly regarded nationally and has attracted students from across the archipelago and from abroad. In its capacity as a local partner, the pesantren provided the use of the BPPM building and payment for electricity. Staff, acting on a volunteer basis at the telecentre, were appointed from within the BPPM as well as some senior students from the pesantren (all male). Usage of the Internet at the telecentre was free for the first year, although there were some complaints that individuals from outside the pesantren had been asked to pay in the early months. The project was, somewhat optimistically, expected to be financially independent after the first year.

The chapter proceeds through presenting a case study of the e-Pabelan project rather than a more theoretical analysis of ICT4PR, and limits itself to issues arising from the implementation and development of e-Pabelan over the project's first year. Enthusiasm for ICT4PR is first briefly situated against a broader backdrop. e-Pabelan is then placed in its local context. The chapter emphasises that such contextualisation is critical. Experiences from the three different stakeholder levels are then outlined: from the implementing agencies, the local partner, and from the intended beneficiary level. Differences in expectations and conceptualisations from these groups urge the need for reflection and realism within ICT4PR. The chapter stresses the need for acknowledging continuities and for approaching ICT4PR as an ongoing development process. In closing, an alternative approach is presented that emphasises the need to better engage with existing networks within communities prior to, and in conjunction with, the establishing of access to external networks mediated via ICTs.

Before proceeding, it is necessary to clarify a number of points. With regard to ICTs, the chapter accepts that ICTs are "electronic means of capturing, processing, storing and communicating information" (Heeks, 1999, p. 3), and is mindful of the fact that ICTs "handle information in digital format. That's all" (Heeks, 2002, p. 2). Within a poverty-alleviation context, the importance of more established forms of communicating and receiving information beyond the digital is acknowledged (Hewitt de Alcántara, 2001). The concept of poverty is similarly viewed in multidimensional terms. It is accepted that ICTs may be used to facilitate improvements in the related spheres of empowerment, opportunities, and security (World Bank, 2000).

The stated aim of e-Pabelan, and PePP, is to reduce rural poverty with a particular reference to the agricultural sector. Project documentation states that this aim is to be realised through a pro-poor process and by "empower[ing] and mobilis[ing] poor communities for economic activities and accessing social services through better access to information and communication" (documentation courtesy BAPPENAS/UNDP, September 2004). Reference is also made to accessing market prices and to the exploitative role of middlemen in agricultural market networks along with the need for the provision of basic information. It is also noted by the implementing agencies that the provision of information alone is not enough and that the pilot project will be "tightly focused," localised," and include capacity-building activities (ibid). On paper, therefore, e-Pabelan reflects widely accepted approaches to ICT4PR and community-oriented rural development. The implementing agencies, however, do not proffer a precise working definition of poverty, although under PePP, at least 30% of the beneficiary community must fall below national poverty lines. It is thus assumed that ICT4PR at Pabelan is targeted at this segment of the local population. In this context, ICT4PR is viewed as the direct introduction of ICTs within a community to bolster flows of communication and information to and within that community in order to improve opportunities, empowerment, and security for the poor.

Summarising the Potential and Limitations of ICT4PR

The related concepts of an information age and information society have spurred increasing interest in the role of both information and technology in development.[3] For the proponents of ICTs, the future is conceived as boundless in a vision of unfettered and immediate access to digitally communicated information (Cairncross, 1997). However, as this book explores, such a situation can lead to both opportunities and costs. The information age and its associated technologies present a double-edged sword that could potentially cut a swathe, for better or for worse, through the development sphere. Increasing interest in ICTs in development circles may be summarised, to a degree, by drawing on the words of the foremost commentator on the information age, Manuel Castells (1999), and through what he sees as the emergence of a "fourth world": "This fourth world of social exclusion, beyond poverty, exists everywhere, albeit in different proportions, from South Bronx to Mantes-la-Jolie, from Kamagasaki to Meseta de Orcasitas, and from the favelas of Rio to the shanties of Jakarta. There is … a systemic relationship between the rise of informational, global capitalism, under current conditions, and the extraordinary growth of social exclusion and human despair" (Castells, 1999, p. 10).

If we accept that the emergence of new digital technologies is a critical factor behind such increases in exclusion, the significance of ICTs in and for development becomes clearer; it is increasing disparities between the digitally networked and the marginalised other. At the same time, the emergence of more affordable and flexible ICTs presents new opportunities for inclusion and for empowerment. Such concerns are reflected in calls to bridge the so-called digital divide. The need to bridge this divide has been widely used to leverage access to ICTs as a development priority as the link between poverty and a lack of access to ICTs is "indisputable" (Flor, 2001), one argument follows. Issues of inclusion are undoubtedly central to attempts to alleviate poverty, but there is also the danger that the adoption of such an approach can lead to an overemphasis on technically oriented fixes in practice.

A more cautious view maintains that the notion of a digital divide is misleading. Prioritising a link between ICTs and poverty confuses cause and effect and pays scant attention to the complexities and underlying causes of poverty and social exclusion (Marker, McNamara, & Wallace, 2002; McNamara, 2003). Viewed in such light, the provision of access to ICTs can be construed as little more than a flirtatious diversion from more deep-rooted concerns. There is also the need to ask what the provision of access to ICTs actually means and on whose terms such access is promoted and established (Gurstein, 2003). An overemphasis on technical access, it has also been suggested, reflects, somewhat ironically, a return to the values of modernisation theory in development thinking (Schech, 2002). Modernisation theory was similarly concerned with imparting knowledge and the transferal of technology from "us" to "them." Modernisation theory may be considered the antithesis of community-based or alternative approaches to development. Although different development paradigms coexist within ICT4D (Houston & Jackson, 2003), at the beneficiary level, alternative understandings and realities need to be better acknowledged (Avgerou, 2000).

With reference to poverty alleviation, we may summarise that enthusiasm for ICTs can obscure complexity and prioritise the dominance of particular values and norms. Such an approach raises issues regarding power, representation, and voice and cannot, therefore, be construed as constituting inclusion in its own right. For the marginalised, there is the risk that without due care, ICT4PR may well mean more of the same. The danger of ICT4PR, as both discipline and practice, is that by prioritising universal approaches and fixes, the realities and actual needs of the poor can be de-emphasised. This is not just a point of theoretical concern, but one that can have very real implications in practice. As this case study illustrates, there is a need for fuller engagement with local contexts within ICT4PR. One size does not fit all. In stressing the need for contextualisation, the context in which e-Pabelan was established needs to be outlined.

E-Pabelan in Context

The village of Pabelan lies roughly 30 km to the north of Yogyakarta near the Buddhist temple complex and world-heritage site of Borobudor. Pabelan borders the market town of Muntilan and straddles central Java's main transport artery. The village is not, therefore, isolated in a broader communicative sense. Within Pabelan, poor individuals also utilise various ICTs. Within the village and immediate vicinity, there are 12 public telephone kiosks (wartel). The telecentre cannot, therefore, be considered to be filling a void in access to basic communication technologies. Clustered around the main road there are also businesses offering photocopying services, two computer rental businesses offering off-line applications by the hour, and more recently, kiosks selling mobile telephones and accessories have begun to multiply. Poor households within the village also reported owning radios (76%), televisions (64%), and at least one mobile telephone (13%). No poor households reported having a fixed-line telephone.[4] A lack of ownership of ICTs, however, does not necessarily equate to a lack of access.

Official statistics place the population of Pabelan at 6,955 within 1,839 households (Badan Pusat Statistik, 2005). Broadly speaking, the majority of livelihoods within the village may be said to be centred on agriculture and related activities, including the home-based production of foodstuffs and small-scale trading. The latter two are particularly important livelihood options for women. There is also a significant handicraft industry producing wood, bamboo, and stone products. However, livelihoods within the village are best viewed in terms of diversity and range from salaried government employees to occasional labourers. Importantly, and contrary to popular opinions, households that own land and make a living solely from farming no longer represent the majority. The inheritance of smaller parcels of land through the generations and a lack of alternative local employment opportunities have resulted in a significant number of villagers seeking work in other areas of Indonesia and as far afield as Saudi Arabia. In some subunits (dusun), villagers complain that youth unemployment runs as high as 70%. Poverty estimates vary but suggest that between 30% and 50% of the population are living in poverty.[5] Pabelan livelihood options and limitations are varied and reflect changing patterns of land ownership and wider structural changes within the Indonesian economy.

The Project

While it may appear unrealistic for e-Pabelan to have had a notable impact on poverty by the end of its first year, the project could not be said to have made significant progress toward achieving that end. During the year, the number of farmers, being the primary target group, recorded as visiting the telecentre (rather than using the Internet per se) amounted to 12. This figure showed little change since early training at the telecentre, and the overall profile of users remained consistent throughout the year. The typical user was male (65%), young (mean 19 years), and educated (73% currently in education). In order to account for poor participation by target groups at e-Pabelan, it is necessary to relate the project's implementation to the local context.

Implementing a Vision

As noted, the implementing agencies stress that e-Pabelan is a pro-poor community-based development project and moves were made to establish local ownership through partnering with the *pesantren*. Nevertheless, ensuring wider community involvement became increasingly difficult to realise as the project progressed. In practice, the social, political, and structural *contexts* into which e-Pabelan was introduced had a considerable bearing on the project.

Initial difficulties arose from differing understandings between the implementing agencies and the local partners. Establishing a partnership with the pesantren was based on two principle notions. First, the BPPM had active community-development activities, and second, the pesantren was a regular source of information for the community. Both of these assumptions were, to varying degrees, misplaced. While it is true that the BPPM was active in the past, this has not been the case for some time.[6] The heyday of the BPPM was from 1986 to 1990. It is the case, however, that the pesantren is a source of religious information (mostly) for some members of the community. For others, the pesantren's relationship to the wider community is seen as increasingly distant. This is primarily due to changes within the pesantren's leadership since the death of the reportedly charismatic founder in 1993. A change of village heads (kepala desa) has also been significant.[7] The current kepala desa (1989 onward) is regarded by many as being less active within the wider community than the former. Both the current and former kepala desa occupied positions in the BPPM. While the status of the BPPM was not checked by the implementing agencies, neither was it clarified by the local partners. One member of the BPPM was later to speculate, with no obvious irony, that "perhaps they [the implementing agencies] got that information from the Web?" (male, March 15, 2005) Regardless, the memorandum of understanding (MoU) was signed, and the broad aims of poverty reduction and community development sealed. Concurrently, the telecentre was implemented through what may be described as established political channels and institutional structures.

Within Indonesia, there is a clearly defined political hierarchy extending from the national level to, and within, the village. Under the New Order regime of President Suharto, these channels proved effective in disseminating information to the level of neighbours (rumah tangah) if needed. Equally, this structure facilitated both paternalism and repression up to Suharto's fall in May 1998 (Schwarz, 2004). Although moves toward decentralisation have been established, e-Pabelan was implemented through essentially the same political structure.[8] However, political and social changes within Indonesia since 1998 have also opened new opportunities for both agency and resistance (Bebbington, Dharmawan, Fahmi, & Guggenheim, 2004). Individuals, therefore, are far more able, and increasingly willing, to question the motives behind, and value of, externally driven interventions.

The implementation of e-Pabelan reflected established top-down approaches to development and stands in contrast to the project's stated participatory and community-based aims. The project was directed from the national level down, opened by the mayor (bupati), and initial open public meetings were dominated by invited officials, village leaders, and selected (some villagers claimed) members of the community. All, naturally, showed their support. The result was that the intended beneficiaries were, or perceived themselves as being, excluded from the process. The paradigm (community-based development) adopted in theory did not materialise at the local level. As one villager offered by way of explanation, the political structure both within and beyond the village serves to maintain the status quo: "The political trick is that there is already an arrangement into levels, from the national level down, in Indonesia…[and] Pabelan is like a mini Indonesia" (handicrafts, male, January 31, 2005). From the beneficiary level, attempts to subsequently market the project to the community appeared as little more than an afterthought. Ten months after the signing of the MoU, it was found that less than 50% of poor households surveyed knew of the existence of the telecentre. Those that did know had, in the main, found out from friends or family or from simply passing the BPPM building. Information regarding the project did not flow to the intended beneficiaries, and what information did reach members of the wider community was partial and superficial. As one farmer tellingly noted, "I've never been told about the project…maybe, that's because it's not for me" (sharecropper, male, February 28, 2005).

The utilisation of related institutional structures was mirrored in the initial trainings (June-July 2004). Early training focused on staff at the pesantren and formal community groups (kelompok). These trainings sought to disseminate both awareness of the telecentre and information from the Internet to the wider community. However, formal kelompok membership by poor households in Pabelan is currently low. The notable exception is the women's group Pendidikan Kesjahteraan Keluarga (PKK) Village level women's welfare and educational group. Addressing the specific target group of farmers, 52% of poor households surveyed had employment in agriculture; however, only seven households reported a family member attending a farmers' kelompok. Poorer farmers, in particular, often complained these meetings were merely formalities for the better off and politically connected. One official (female, August 23, 2005) explained that the reason kelompok in Pabelan are not as active as they once were is precisely because individuals now have better access to information through alternative channels, television and radio in particular. Higher attendance at the PKK meetings can be accounted for by the incorporation of a rotary savings scheme (arisan). The arisan is both a social occasion and an important source of independent capital for many women. The critical point about the early trainings, however, is as one of the telecentre staff (male, November 30, 2004) reflected: "They did not come back."

The community trainings were not always completed and quickly came to an end. Any early impetus was rapidly lost. By September 2004, recorded visitors to the telecentre had dropped to 16 from 273 for the previous month. This fall was also attributable to an array of technical problems that the local partners were ill equipped to deal with alongside falling enthusiasm from some local staff. The elite bias (Chambers, 1997) within the implementation was not without its implications.

Local Partners, Politics, and Responses

From a local-partner perspective, it is not difficult to imagine the attraction of a telecentre and the trappings of modernity it implies. Nevertheless, this does not mean that local partners will be equipped to envisage what such a project may entail in practice. Neither does it imply that they will have the necessary will and resources to respond to difficulties that, inevitably, will arise. Within Pabelan, they did not. Although initial trainings for staff at the telecentre were conducted by some external partners, the trainings were limited in both scope and reach. Difficulties at the local level were exacerbated by the lack of coherent systems for monitoring and evaluation, resulting in sluggish responses as problems emerged.

Neither were there clear mechanisms for providing essential support to the local partners initially established. Furthermore, confusion persisted at the local level over how exactly the telecentre, and the Internet in particular, was to help in reducing poverty and bring material (primarily) benefits to the community. As a result, interest quickly waned.

The fall in enthusiasm also reflects a more specific agenda on the part of the local partners. Interest in the project by the local partners was based on the potential of the telecentre to reconnect the activities of the pesantren to the wider community. That the pesantren is perceived as not having the same links to the community as it once had is not something that local officials are blind to. It is also a situation they wish to change. The telecentre was seen as a potential vehicle to do just this and to rejuvenate (menghidupkan) the activities of the BPPM. However, lacking the BPPM's previous expertise, community links, and external support, the local partners were not well placed to achieve this aim. Difficulties were further compounded by the lack of a clear mechanism for achieving the broad aim of poverty reduction. For the BPPM, it became clear that the telecentre was of limited use unless it was tied to more concrete development goals. As one member of the telecentre team reflected, "they [BAPPENAS/UNDP] just gave us the equipment; the telecentre was placed in a vacuum" (male, March 15, 2005). Despite the theoretical considerations of the implementing agencies, in practice, e-Pabelan was established as if the project would and could in some way have a direct impact on poverty; it was left up to the local partner to join up the dots. Although, the implementing agencies stress that the project was not just about the Internet, at the local level the project very much was.

The local partner's response to difficulties was to reorganise the management structure of the telecentre (January 2005) in order to better incorporate the telecentre into the BPPM and its future activities. The initial focus of the BPPM was to be on education and not on poverty reduction per se. Considering the expertise of the pesantren, the user base of the telecentre, and the value placed on children's education by many poor households, this seemed a wholly reasonable response. At the end of the first year, however, any such plans were very much still in the process. Coinciding with the BPPM's response to difficulties, the implementing agencies' hand was forced and a number of interventions were funded. In March 2005, a local technical administrator was appointed for a period of 1 year. The individual was supported, primarily online, by a BAPPENAS technician in Jakarta. Although the telecentre continued to face technical problems, particularly regarding the erratic Telkomnet Instan dial-up service, this was a significant improvement.

In January 2005, the implementing agencies also agreed to fund a dedicated manager for 1 year. By way of compromise with the local partner, a new management team was finally appointed on a job-share basis in May 2005. The management team (two female, one male) were proposed by, and have previous connections to, the pesantren and the BPPM. Continuity, to a degree, with the BPPM's earlier plans was thus assured. Whilst this was an important development, the choice of management team did not, needless to say, directly increase involvement in the running of the project by the intended beneficiaries.[9] A related development (January 2005) was the starting of a 10-month English-language course and computer-skills course for nonelite youths.[10] The English course significantly helped to boost attendance at the telecentre, reaching a peak of 726 recorded visits in May 2005. However, the English course did not change the overall profile of users. The choice of students for the course was problematic. Members of the community complained that the course was dominated (approximately two thirds) by students from the pesantren and from outside of the community.

For older members of the community, the perception reinforced was that the telecentre was not for them. Any sense that the project might be for the poor community within Pabelan was further eroded as the news of free Internet access spread, attracting young people from neighbouring areas. That the English course should inadvertently cement such perceptions is unfortunate. However, the point of concern is that the situation persisted.

In summary, the choice of local partners presented little more than a facade of local ownership. Local ownership in the sense of ownership by the intended beneficiaries themselves was neither achieved nor moved toward. The officials initially consulted by the implementing agencies seldom visited the telecentre and were yet to use the Internet. For these individuals, the telecentre presented its own opportunity. In contrast to the stated inclusive approach, the development of the project continued to reflect the local political structure and to prioritise the interests of elite institutions within the village. Furthermore, interventions at Pabelan meant that the implementing agencies were forced to extend their financial commitment significantly beyond the project's first year as originally planned. It is highly improbable that the telecentre will be able to employ the additional staff after their contracts end. As the new managers are working toward what they see as a more realistic 3-year time frame, this is somewhat troublesome. Although a business plan was implemented for the telecentre in July 2005, the figures had yet to add up. Considering the current status of e-Pabelan, it is unlikely that the telecentre will be able to cover the costs of the current Internet connection alone.[11] In the absence of significant change, e-Pabelan faces a highly uncertain future.

Beneficiary Contexts and Experiences

Usage of the telecentre was dominated by the young (primarily students from the pesantren), reflecting both the location of the telecentre and the attraction of the Internet for this particular group. The majority of these users were in education, and a large number had previous computer experience. It should be noted, however, that the majority of young individuals from within the village itself have not visited the telecentre. Older educated individuals also seldom visited the centre. Some individuals with previous computer experience, and local computer owners, had also yet to visit. This casts doubts on suggestions that one of the major obstacles to accessing the Internet at Pabelan by poor households is illiteracy and low educational attainment. Within Pabelan, this is not the case, and such arguments reflect taking the head of the household as the point of reference. Within the household, educational attainment has steadily risen with a few poor household members educated to degree level (S1). The situation at Pabelan is testament to overall increases in educational attainment within Indonesia over recent decades (Moertiningsih Adioetomo, 2005). Attainment by gender is also evenly matched, but this is not to imply that all things are equal. At times, circumstances dictate they are not:

> *Every year the cost of schooling goes up. If a farmer has other work, it's not a problem, but if you don't have other work like me, it's very difficult. Before we had children the income from farming was enough, but that was before school. After you have children it's not enough. ....Our son [14 years] goes to school in Magelang; it has computers and the facilities are good, so it's expensive.*

> (husband)

*...Our daughter [11 years] goes to school in Borobudor [lower school fees].
She has registered, but she hasn't started yet because we haven't been able to
pay the fees.*

(wife)

*...Of course, we want both of them to go to a progressive school (sekolah
maju)...but it's just too expensive.*

(husband)

(farming household, July 22, 2005, shortly after new school year began)

Naturally, things could always be improved, but within Indonesia, relatively high levels
of educational attainment should, in theory at least, be conducive to the adoption of ICTs.
While the rising cost of education is a major concern for poor households and represents the
major household expenditure for many, it is a cost that families, and particularly women,
go to lengths to bear. [12]

It is also not the case, as the experience of trainings at Pabelan demonstrates, that after
individuals have been introduced to the Internet they will automatically see its worth:

*I attended the basic training...No, I didn't go back. I don't see the benefit
[manfaat] of the telecentre; also I have a young child and don't have the time.
Also, the PKK has new leaders and is not as active as it was before...The PKK
did find lots of information about KIA [mother and child health] and recipes,
for example...but this was the usual information...that we can already find
everywhere...also the health clinic [bidan] is next door to the telecentre...They
would have been happier if they had found new information [for example] if it
was possible to find information that could raise the income of a family...After
the training, the women were still ill at ease [masih canggung] and scared [of
the Internet]...they need continuous training.*

(housewife, April 29, 2005)

The above illustrates that trainees were taught to access the Internet. This is not the same
as accessing previously identified and processed information that is conveyed in a manner
appropriate to particular needs.[13] An emphasis on technical access can blur this crucial distinction. Furthermore, the utility of any information accessed did little to impress and did not
sustain interest. Not all information is equal, and individuals within the wider community
had more pressing concerns. Furthermore, it is evident that training was not ongoing and
that the importance of such activities for building capacity and nurturing demand within
the community was not sufficiently acknowledged in practice. The choice of local partners
was also decisive in shaping intended beneficiaries' perceptions:

*I want to look for information about [business] capital, training for hairdressing,
but I'm scared [to go to the telecentre] because it is owned by the Pondok and
is only for the Pondok...We don't know what the aims [of the project] are and
people don't know about it...Pabelan [i.e., Pabelan IV] receives lots of help,*

but it never reaches Batikan or Jagalan.[14] ...The information does not reach here...The village head has projects, such as the orchid growing [World Bank funded training] and telecentre project, and there are socialisation programmes for the community, but the issue is that they have yet to ever reach here...The poor community are afraid to speak out against this.

(hairdresser, female, March 1, 2005)

Furthermore, e-Pabelan also had to compete with the established demand for existing technologies, and the Internet does not always have an obvious comparative advantage in terms of either communication or information:

People in the community, especially women staying at home, don't have the motivation to use the Internet...you have to walk to the telecentre, write an e-mail and then wait for a reply. It's more convenient to use a mobile phone [i.e., short messaging service].

(health worker, female, March 17, 2005)

Similarly, existing technologies (television and radio) already provide access to specialised local programming for groups such as farmers. Needless to say, individuals also access information from an array of formal and informal sources. Whether individuals actually do act, or are able to act, on this information is another point entirely, but it is evidently not the case that the poor in Pabelan need access to basic information. To emphasise that they do is overtly paternalistic and homogenising. The information individuals require is specific to particular needs and situations. Such needs are in turn dependent on gender, age, occupation, social status, and the various combinations of these factors.

At Pabelan, any assumed link between accessing the Internet and increasing the security of livelihoods has yet to be demonstrated. At the risk of oversimplification, the fundamental reasons for low participation boil down to some simple home truths. For the poor and non-poor alike, the utility and relevance of the telecentre, and particularly the Internet, remained far from clear. The community voted with their feet; the majority walked straight past the telecentre, and the few intended beneficiaries who did enter left and did not return. All the same, at the intended beneficiary level, this does not imply that there is no need for information. Equally, it should not be inferred that the abstract notion of information is viewed as a priority by the poor. The importance of information is regularly acknowledged, but its immediate relevance remains unclear in the face of efforts to secure daily needs. However, it is the case that a working knowledge of computers and the Internet are seen as important for the future of the community's children, particularly in the face of limited employment opportunities for the young. That the selection of participants for the English course was not more beneficiary focused was an opportunity missed. Again, the intended beneficiaries, along with their aspirations, were passed by:

I feel disappointed [that nobody ever told me about the telecentre] because my children want to learn how to use a computer...and I don't clearly know what the procedure is for using [the telecentre].

(laundry service, female, February 28, 2005)

In contrast to its stated aims, e-Pabelan has not been inclusive. The project has merely accentuated differences and reconfirmed preexisting relations of power. While intentions may have been well placed, e-Pabelan is, in effect, something that "we" have done to "them." The implementation and ensuing development of e-Pabelan over its first year cannot be considered pro-poor. Furthermore, it is unlikely that the Internet will ever entirely replace a visit to the health clinic or a hands-on demonstration by an agricultural extension worker. As elsewhere, sociability is valued highly, information is tested, and trust is accrued through the attainment of tangible results.

From the beneficiary viewpoint, the challenge that ICT4PR faces at Pabelan is how to utilise ICTs to increase employment opportunities (particularly for the young), raise incomes (particularly for women), and improve entitlements (Sen, 1981) to and command over resources. ICT4PR must also engage with widening participation and inclusion in localised networks. In this sense, information clearly has a role to play. However, a blanket approach to poverty that ignores complexity and prioritises the technical will achieves little. The wider lesson from e-Pabelan for ICT4PR is that it is essential that the provision of information does not become subordinated to the mechanisms of information delivery within a project's design. e-Pabelan provides access to the Internet for a minority; it has yet to provide access to beneficial information for the majority. As such, the project finds itself lumbering awkwardly somewhere between promise and utility. There has been no information revolution in Pabelan.

Prioritising and Engaging with Localised Networks

The experience of e-Pabelan illustrates the importance of accounting for, and responding to, local contexts. The danger of a digital-divide approach to ICT4PR is that local contexts can become subordinated to the provision of technical access. The Internet is all too readily perceived as a reified artefact (Hand & Sandywell, 2002) of universal benefit and worth to all. Correspondingly, the poor are glossed as an amorphous mass ready to gratefully receive. Individuals' agency and realities are ignored. The approach also reflects a view that conceptualises information as a "public good" (Olson, 1971). While such an approach may well be worth aiming for, this is not the reality of the poor. Within Pabelan, existing flows of information exclude. The structural and political realities of the poor, therefore, need to be actively engaged within ICT4PR. Outside enthusiasm for ICTs needs to be situated against insiders' realities and perspectives.

It is clear that access to ICTs does not automatically result in accessing relevant information. Also, both the economic and social means to enable individuals to act on any information received (Duncombe & Heeks, 2001) needs to be incorporated into the project design. ICT4PR is not an event addressing problems that are merely and conveniently to be bridged a la the digital divide; it is a process. Policy makers, therefore, need to be clear in what it is that they wish and are realistically able to achieve. A project aimed toward providing access to either the Internet or information is not synonymous with a project directed toward poverty alleviation. The latter is far more likely to be achieved by establishing clearly defined development programmes and targets. The role for ICTs in this sense is one of facilitation. In practice, ICTs and poverty remain uneasy bedfellows. For ICT4PR to be effective, it is suggested that the emphasis needs to be placed back on information. It is yet to be conclusively shown that the provision of access to ICTs alone will directly raise the incomes of the poor, although, as e-Pabelan illustrates, projects continue to be implemented as if they may. In a poverty-alleviation context, ICT4PR's potential lies first and foremost in increasing inclusion and empowerment. Somewhat ironically, this is what efforts to bridge the digital divide imply, but for ICT4PR, to attempt to empower and to include requires the acknowledgement that sociopolitical relations matter. It also requires that the approach adopted in practice is active, ongoing, and context specific. A more fruitful point of departure may be found through focusing on more locally oriented networks.

The Importance of Horizontally Oriented Networks

Within ICT4D as a whole, there is a tendency to prioritise the accessing of external networks. Examples from e-Pabelan include the provision of access to externally produced information and the claim that poor farmers can, irrelevant of capacity and resources, and are willing to, irrespective of established market relations, access distant markets. These external networks are hierarchical in nature. As such, these vertically oriented linkages remain socially, culturally, and economically distant. In short, they are of questionable immediate relevance and utility to the poor. Consequently, ICT4PR needs to become more locally and horizontally focused.

Exclusion from localised networks and institutions is commonplace for the poor. During the initial implementation stage of ICT4PR, an alternative approach would be to prioritise the widening of access to information within the community. The initial focus should not be on the deployment of ICTs per se. It is overtly unrealistic to expect individuals to access external and untested networks from a starting point of exclusion. Empowerment and the building of capacity, therefore, need to be prioritised. In order to achieve empowerment, fuller participation within the design and implementation of the project by the intended beneficiaries is required. The concept of participation is not, of course, without its problems. If the answer has already been decided, for example, in the form of a telecentre, participation can become little more than coercion. However, as e-Pabelan indicates, participation remains critical. ICT4PR needs to draw on wider development experiences, and increasing participation should be (re)approached as a politically empowering act (Parfitt, 2004; Williams, 2004). Without empowering individuals to better participate and engage with local political processes and socioeconomic networks, the potential of ICT4PR is severely curtailed.

A further step in establishing the prerequisite environment for a later introduction of ICTs is the identification of beneficiaries' needs. However, while information needs are often emphasised in ICT4PR, it is the identification of development needs that remains critical. It is also the latter that poor individuals are more likely to relate to and be better placed to discuss and convey. ICTs offer the flexibility to be adapted to the development needs of a community. The community should not be expected to bend and conform to a predetermined outside agenda. As e-Pabelan illustrates, the community will, in all likelihood, not. It may well prove to be ICT4PR in both outlook and practice that requires some adjustment. An initial emphasis on participation and empowerment within a community also provides a foundation from which a project can work outward.

From a localised point of departure, networks should be extended laterally. Although hierarchical relationships (as networks remain prone to differing relations of power) can not be totally avoided, they should be minimised. Partnerships with individuals and institutions with locally relevant expertise and experience should be sought. While partnerships for e-Pabelan were established, these partnerships were high level and again vertically orientated. In practice, these high-level stakeholders had limited community involvement at best. Through extending local networks, a sustainable and accessible network of support for the project can be established. Furthermore, such a network can be drawn on to widen access to alternative sources of information, create critical local content, and provide potential sources of community trainings. Such trainings are again a prerequisite to the introduction of ICTs and should be development focused. Examples of trainings relevant to Pabelan would include locally oriented marketing for microenterprises and farmers, and information relating to child psychology for young mothers from poor households—the point being that the information required is specific and is more likely to be better conveyed through personal interaction. Both of these examples require a degree of trust, and individuals need to be able to actively engage with and question the information received. By starting within the target groups and building networks outward, the utility of ICTs is more likely to be apparent on introduction.

Crucially, the introduction of ICTs should be governed by the prevailing communicative environment. In the case of Pabelan, the utilisation of community-based radio may well have proved more effective in disseminating locally relevant information. A staged introduction of differing ICTs should be considered depending on the needs, receptiveness of the beneficiaries, and the intended development goals. Within a more horizontally focused approach to ICT4PR, it may well be that communities of shared experiences have the information that is required; however, they are unlikely to have access to the Internet. The Internet is, of course, subject to network effects, and without relevant information or a trusted source of information at some other node, it is of no use at all.

The challenge that ICT4PR faces in practice is how to shift the emphasis from being an externally driven, supply-led venture to one that begins with the beneficiaries themselves. For the poor to benefit, ICT4PR needs to shed its neutral apolitical stance and universalising approach, and better engage in establishing a process of empowerment and inclusion for the poor. With regard to the Internet, this is problematic as it is currently hard to envisage a situation where access to the Internet for the poor is not mediated in some shape or form. ICT4PR, therefore, needs to tread with caution, strive for inclusion, and engage with and continually reflect upon local contexts throughout the project process. Despite the simplistic allure of the digital divide, policy makers must be mindful of the fact that ICT4PR offers no quick fixes. To continue to act as though it does shows little understanding of the realities of the poor.

Conclusion

e-Pabelan proved to be far harder to implement in practice than anticipated. Despite acknowledgements of social factors, community engagement, and a pro-poor process, in practice, the project reflected an attempt to bridge the digital divide. e-Pabelan was implemented as if it was an event and was subsequently forced, by necessity, to try to become a development process. ICT4PR needs to be viewed as a coherent and targeted process of development from the outset. This requires both a significant commitment and, perhaps, a shift of emphasis. A way forward may be found through moving away from an emphasis on the external to better engaging with networks and relations of power within communities. Contrary to digital-divide-based promises, e-Pabelan has yet to increase inclusion in either external or internal networks for the poor.

Within ICT4PR, there can be a temptation to focus on the tangible rather than the intangible. While the bricks and mortar of a telecentre are a highly visible use of funding, the fact remains that it is information that lies at the heart of ICT4PR. Needless to say, information alone does not have the same immediate appeal to donors as buildings, hardware, and RAM. It may well not have the same appeal for potential local partners also. However, the experience of e-Pabelan demonstrates that the utility of ICT4PR ultimately rests on the socioeconomic and political environment into which such projects are introduced. ICT4PR is also heavily dependent on the linkages through which such projects are implemented, and the socioeconomic and political networks they seek to influence. Due attention must be paid to these issues if fuller inclusion is to be achieved. An approach that emphasises universally beneficial technical access obscures such critical factors. A start toward increasing the goal of inclusion may be obtained through emphasising horizontal rather than vertical linkages. The danger of ICT4PR is that enthusiasm for the technical can, if left unchecked, lead to ICT4PR riding rough shod over many development fundamentals already accrued. The continuation of such an approach will do few favours for ICT4PR or the individuals and communities that ICT4PR seeks to empower.

References

Avgerou, C. (2000). Recognising alternative rationalities in the deployment of information systems. *The Electronic Journal of Information Systems in Developing Countries, 3*(7), 1-15. Retrieved January 10, 2005, from http://www.ejisdc.org

Badan Pusat Statistik. (2005). *Kecamatan mungkid, kabupaten magelang dalam angka tahun 2004.* Magelang, Central Java: Author.

Balai Kepala Desa (Village Head's Office). (2004, 2005). *Unpublished local poverty figures for 2004 and 2005* [accessed 2005]. Pabelan: Village Head's Office.

Bebbington, A., Dharmawan, L., Fahmi, E., & Guggenheim, S. (2004). Village politics, culture and community-driven development: Insights from Indonesia. *Progress in Development Studies, 4*(3), 187-205.

Cairncross, F. (1997). *The death of distance: How the telecommunications revolution will change our world.* London: Orion.

Castells, M. (1999). *Information technology, globalization and social development* (Discussion Paper 114). Geneva, Switzerland: United Nations Research Institute for Social Development.

Chambers, R. (1997). *Whose reality counts? Putting the first last.* London: Intermediate Technology Publications.

Duff, A. S. (2000). *Information society studies.* London: Routledge.

Duncombe, R., & Heeks, R. (2001). *Information, technology and small enterprise in Africa: Lessons from Botswana.* Manchester, United Kingdom: University of Manchester, Institute for Development Policy and Management. Retrieved February 10, 2005, from http://www.sed.manchester.ac.uk/idpm/research/is/ictsme/full/

Flor, A. G. (2001, August). *ICTs and poverty: The indisputable link.* Paper presented at the Third Asia Development Forum on Regional Economic Cooperation in Asia and the Pacific, Bangkok, Thailand. Retrieved August 7, 2005, from http://www.worldbank.org/html/extdr/offrep/eap/eapprem/infoalexan.pdf

Gurstein, M. (2003). Effective use: A community informatics strategy beyond the digital divide. *First Monday, 8*(12). Retrieved August 7, 2005, from http://firstmonday.org/issues/issue8_12/gurstein/index.html

Hand, M., & Sandywell, B. (2002). E-topia as cosmopolis or citadel: On the democratising and de-democratising logics of the Internet, or, toward a critique of the new technological fetishism. *Theory, Culture & Society, 19*(1-2), 197-225.

Heeks, R. (1999). *Information and communication technologies, poverty and development* (Development Informatics Working Paper 5). Manchester, United Kingdom: University of Manchester, Institute for Development Policy and Management. Retrieved February 10, 2004, from http://idpm.man.ac.uk/publications/wp/di/di_wp05.pdf

Heeks, R. (2002). I-development not e-development: Special issue on ICTs and development. *Journal of International Development, 14,* 1-11.

Hewitt de Alcántara, C. (2001). *The development divide in a digital age: An issues paper* (Technology, Business, and Society Programme Paper 4). Geneva, Switzerland: United Nations Research Institute for Social Development. Retrieved August 7, 2005, from http://www.unrisd.org/unrisd/website/document.nsf/d2a23ad2d50cb2a280256eb300385855/19b0b342a4f1cf5b80256b5e0036d99f/$FILE/hewitt.pdf

Houston, R., & Jackson, M. H. (2003). Technology and context within research on international development programs: Positioning an integrationist perspective. *Communication Theory, 13*(1), 57-77.

Marker, P., McNamara, K. S., & Wallace, L. (2002). *The significance of information and communication technologies for reducing poverty.* Department for International Development. Retrieved February 10, 2004, from http://www.dfid.gov.uk/Pubs/files/ict_poverty.htm

McNamara, K. S. (2003, December). *Information and communication technologies, poverty and development: Learning from experience.* Paper presented at the infoDev Annual Symposium, Geneva, Switzerland. Retrieved August 5, 2005, from http://www.eldis.org/fulltext/sidaictpoverty.pdf

Moertiningsih Adioetomo, S. (2005). Reshaping populations. In T. H. Hull (Ed.), *People, population, and policy in Indonesia* (pp. 125-168). Jakarta, Indonesia: Equinox.

Olson, M. (1971). *The logic of collective action: Public goods and the theory of groups.* Cambridge, MA: Harvard University Press.

Parfitt, T. (2004). The ambiguity of participation: A qualified defence of participatory development. *Third World Quarterly, 25*(3), 537-556.

PT Risadata Utama. (2004). *Report survey and statistical analysis on the baseline survey for e-pabelan for* [sic] *National Development Planning Agency of the Republic of Indonesia (BAPPENAS)*. Jakarta, Indonesia: Author.

Schech, S. (2002). Wired for change: The links between ICTs and development discourses. *Journal of International Development, 14*, 13-23.

Schwarz, A. (2004). *A nation in waiting: Indonesia's search for stability*. Singapore: Talisman.

Sen, A. (1981). *Poverty and famines: An essay on entitlements and deprivation*. Oxford, United Kingdom: Oxford University Press.

Webster, F. (with Blom, R., Karvonen, E., Melin, H., Nordenstreng, K., & Puoskari, E.) (Ed.). (2004). *The information society reader*. London: Routledge.

Williams, G. (2004). Evaluating participatory development: Tyranny, power and (re)politicisation. *Third World Quarterly, 25*(3), 557-578.

World Bank. (2000). *World development report 2000/1: Attacking poverty. Opportunity, empowerment and security*. Oxford, United Kingdom: Oxford University Press. Retrieved August 5, 2005, from http://siteresources.worldbank.org/INTPOVERTY/Resources/WDR/overview.pdf

Endnotes

[1]   The research project combined both qualitative and quantitative methods including direct and participant observation, open-ended interviews, questionnaire surveys, and rural appraisals. The statistics referred to on participation are based on data from the telecentre logbook from July 2004 to June 2005 and include repeat visits. Other statistics referred to in this chapter are based on a randomly sampled survey of 216 poor households in five village subunits conducted at the 95% confidence level.

Included supporting statements are indicative of commonly voiced concerns within Pabelan. However, it should be noted that throughout the research period, awareness of and interest in the telecentre (and the project's aims) remained low within the community. For the vast majority, life carried on as before. This chapter focuses on the intended beneficiaries' conceptualisations and not the minority (predominantly students) who utilised the telecentre. To focus on the latter would require distinguishing what the actual difference is in practice between e-Pabelan, being a poverty-reduction project, and a privately run Internet café (warnet). This remained a troublesome issue, and space does not permit a fuller analysis here.

[2]   The term telecentre is used in this chapter as this is the term often used at the implementing-agency level and exclusively at the local level (alongside TC or tele). It is also a more apt descriptor in this context than, for example, multipurpose community centre.

3   Whether an information society or age actually exists, and in what form, remains the subject of debate. For an overview, see Webster (2004). The term information society probably first emerged from Japan in the late 1960s (Duff, 2000).

4   The most used, and most overlooked, communication technology within Pabelan is the motorcycle. Within Pabelan, there were 375 motorcycles in 2004 (Badan Pusat Statistik, 2005) and growing.

5   Poverty figures courtesy of *PT Risadata Utama* (2004) and local figures from *Kepala Desa* (2004, 2005). Local figures reflect income- or consumption-based approaches to measuring poverty. The external source utilised a somewhat broader composite approach.

6   Two projects originally established by the BPPM are currently running. They are a telephone kiosk and a health clinic near the pesantren. Both now run independently of the BPPM. The current health worker at the clinic was not aware of any links with the BPPM itself, although she started work there in 2000.

7   The local political context is further complicated in that the current village head is the spouse of the leader (pimpinan) of the pesantren.

8   Regional autonomy (Otonomi Daerah) resulting in increased powers at the level of the provinces in Indonesia came into being January 1, 2001.

9   An "infomobiliser" with no previous links to the pesantren was also appointed. Toward the end of the research period, this individual was in the process of conducting appraisals with a view to introducing newly formed learning groups (kelompok belajar) to information from the telecentre and then to the telecentre itself at a later date. Although, at the time of writing, it was too early to gauge the effectiveness of this initiative, it should be regarded as a potentially significant development.

10   The English course was established in association with a Jakarta-based nongovernmental organisation and funded by the Regional English Language Office (RELO) of the United States embassy, Jakarta.

11   In August 2005, the implementing agencies agreed to extend payment for the Internet connection for a further 6 months. Charges for using the telecentre were introduced August 1, 2005.

12   Married women often reported receiving the sum of 10,000Rp (just over $1) per day (but not every day) from their husbands. This is to pay for expenses, including food, bills, clothing, and education for children. While some women have independent income sources, others are dependent solely on such money and informal sources of credit.

13   The contrast with utilising radio for development is striking. No one would expect an individual to benefit from accessing a radio station that was devoid of preprepared relevant content.

14   Pabelan is comprised of 10 dusun. The pesantren and telecentre is located in Pabelan IV, which may be considered the political hub of the village. Correspondingly, the telecentre is not located in one of the poorest parts of the village.

Section II:

How can ICT Promote Development? Lessons from Different Fields

Chapter VII

Enabling the Expansion of Microfinance using Information and Communication Technologies

Narima Amin, Independent Consultant, USA

Abstract

This chapter looks at the origins and evolution of microfinance and explores some of the challenges faced by microfinance institutions (MFIs). It examines the costs and benefits of using ICTs as a means of increasing the effectiveness and efficiency of MFIs enabling expansion and outreach to remote populations. Specific technologies such as smart cards, PDAs, and MISs are explored in detail and case studies are provided. MFIs can also use ICTs to facilitate income-generating opportunities for borrowers, and the case of Village Phone will highlight this potential. It is hoped that this chapter will advance the case for the continued use and research into the synergistic combining of microfinance and ICTs.

Introduction

In the international development community, there have been numerous discussions on methods for reaching the millennium development goals (MDGs)[1] by 2015. Stakeholders from all walks of life have many suggestions for eradicating poverty from this world where 1.2 billion people still live on less than $1 a day.

Poverty-intervention tools will be of vital importance if we are to achieve the MDGs, especially the goal of reducing the number of people living in poverty by half by the year 2015. It is acknowledged that:

> *access to financial services provides the poor with the means to make improvements in their lives—in other words, to achieve most of the MDGs—on their own terms, in a sustainable way. Access to credit, savings, or other financial services is only one of a series of strategies needed to reduce poverty and achieve the MDGs.*[2]

Microcredit and microfinance, which involve providing financial and other services to the poorest[3] people in developing countries, has proven to be a practical way to assist them in working their way out of poverty. Microcredit refers to small collateral-free loans targeted to the poor, provided by a bank or other institution. Microfinance involves not only loans, but also other financial products such as savings, insurance, and transfer services to the poor. Microcredit and microfinance are recognized as effective tools for the reduction of extreme poverty and the creation of sustainable economic development. It is in the best interests of those living in poverty that the most effective strategies for reducing and even eradicating poverty be identified and implemented. Whether poverty is created because of the death of the head of a family, changes in economic policies, wars, or natural disasters such as a tsunami, poverty alleviation requires that the best alternatives be found to help poor people build their lives. As poverty-reduction tools, the strengths of microcredit and microfinance are that they are sustainable over the long term and also encourage the independence and self-sufficiency of their recipients.

The concept of microcredit originated in 1976 in Bangladesh when Professor Muhammad Yunus lent money out of his own pocket to prove poor people were bankable and creditworthy. Over the last 30 years, microcredit has evolved to the point where the United Nations declared 2005 as the International Year of Microcredit. According to a United Nations Development Programme (UNDP) administrator Mark Malloch Brown:

> *microfinance is much more than simply an income generation tool. By directly empowering poor people, particularly women, it has become one of the key driving mechanisms towards meeting the Millennium Development Goals, specifically the overreaching target of halving extreme poverty and hunger by 2015.*[4]

Information and communication technologies are considered tools for poverty reduction. Hans d'Orville (2001, p. 1) states that "in the developing world, information and communication technologies (ICTs) are proving formidable and cost-effective development tools. Properly used they can reduce poverty; empower people; build capacities, skills and networks." ICTs[5] have been identified as mechanisms to help microfinance institutions (MFIs) overcome their operational challenges when expanding in remote and rural areas. Brown (2001, p. 1) said "he is convinced that ICTs can help us reach the targets established by world leaders at September's Millennium Summit, including the goal of halving poverty by 2015."

The challenge for microcredit and microfinance institutions is to fulfill the large unmet demand for financial services. The expansion of financial services to reach large numbers of the poorest of the poor is an obstacle confronting many MFIs. MFIs are faced with high transaction costs and institutional inefficiencies that inhibit their ability to reach the underserved segment of the population in remote rural areas. ICTs working in synergy with MFIs can assist in the efficient delivery of credit to the poor, in creating income-generating opportunities for the poor, and in further enhancing the outreach of MFIs to the marginalized poor in remote rural areas. ICTs can reduce poverty by improving the ability of the poorest people to access financial services. In fact, Attali (2004, p. 1) states that "new information and communications technologies constitute essential factors in the growth and ability of a microfinance institution to build capacity and are consequently vital tools in the fight against poverty."

The need for MFIs to lower transaction costs and to expand the scale of the delivery of their financial services to the remote rural poor in regions such as Latin America, Asia, and Africa make experimentation with innovative technologies by microfinance organizations attractive. The current utilization of ICTs such as the standard management information system (MIS), smart cards, personal digital assistants (PDAs), cell phones, and other technologies allow MFIs to service their clients more efficiently through "the reduced amount of paper work, access to information and ability to compute complex analyses" (Siu, 2001, p. 1). The integration of ICTs into MFIs is a relatively recent development, and there are many unknowns associated with its execution. This chapter explores the implementation of some of these new technologies by MFIs and the associated benefits and pitfalls. One publication[6] concluded that "ICTs will continue to impact microfinance operations worldwide. As prices of relevant technology like ATMs [automated teller machines], biometrics, voice recognition, smart-cards, and PDAs continue to fall, more MFIs will be able to take advantage of the benefits they offer" (p. 4). ICTs show great promise for microfinance institutions with respect to efficiency, scale, and outreach.

There are concerns that providing access to ICTs could exacerbate the existing digital divide. However, it is shown that ICTs integrated through poverty-focused programs has been instrumental in narrowing the digital divide. Broadly, the digital divide is the wide technological disparity between countries (North and South) and between groups (rich and poor, men and women, rural and urban) within developing countries. It is a major challenge for our information- and knowledge-based world to overcome this digital divide; however, there is no question that ICTs can be used to facilitate groundbreaking initiatives for poverty reduction in the developing world. Gilhooly (2001, p. 1) says that "the sooner the world accepts it, the sooner ICTs will play a possible crucial role in the global effort to reduce poverty and create a better life for all." The divide will persist if left alone. Commitment from various stakeholders and sectors can aid in diminishing the divide. As with other stakeholders such as the United Nations, Canada recognizes the growing divide and has a "commitment to closing the digital divide through domestic innovations, an ICT agenda, involvement in the G8 Digital Opportunity Task Force (DOT Force) and investments in developing countries" (*CIDA's Strategy on Knowledge*, n.d., p. 4).[7]

In short, it is widely acknowledged that the business of fighting poverty is not an easy task, and it is equally accepted that neither microcredit and microfinance nor ICTs are answers in themselves for solving all development problems, but they can be used in combination as tools for poverty reduction. Brown (2001, p. 1) says, "as with all tools, the usefulness of ICTs depends on how they are employed." The convergence of the ICT and microfinance sectors strengthens the possibility of reducing the inequities of poverty. Attali (2004, p. 1) further states, "ICT can play a major role in the fight against poverty and at the same time, it is precisely in the context of the fight against poverty that these new technologies can help to reduce the digital gap most effectively." The synergy and partnership of stakeholders in and across both the ICT and microfinance sectors provide huge promise in the attainment of the MDGs, especially the goal of halving poverty by 2015.

The Evolution of Microcredit

The Origin of Microcredit

Professor Muhammad Yunus, an economist and former professor with the University of Vanderbuilt in the USA, is credited with originating the concept of microcredit in 1976. At that time, Yunus had returned to Bangladesh where he was teaching at the University of Chittagong. He realized the economic theories he was teaching were not solving the problems of the poverty-stricken people outside his own classroom. As part of a research project, and out of his own pocket, he loaned $27 to about 42 villagers to finance their tiny businesses or income-generating activities. They all repaid their loans and made a profit. He then used his own savings as collateral with conventional banks, cosigning for more loans to lend to the poor. Despite numerous successful projects in several villages and regions of Bangladesh that demonstrated the poor do repay their loans, Dr. Yunus was unable to convince traditional banks that poor people are creditworthy. To address this situation, he founded the Grameen Bank in 1983, thus starting the revolutionary innovation that came to be known as microcredit. Until this time, poor people were at the mercy of money lenders who charged exorbitant interest rates that often forced the borrower into deeper poverty.

The Grameen Bank is owned by the poor. They are stockholders and hold positions as board members. Grameen Bank has now reached over 6.1 million borrowers in Bangladesh, 96% of whom are women, and has proven itself as an innovative leader in bringing credit without the requirement of collateral to the doorsteps of the poorest of the poor. It has loaned over US$5 billion with loan amounts averaging less than $200, and can claim an exemplary repayment rate of 99%. Fifty-five percent of Grameen borrowers and their families have raised themselves above the poverty line, and the remaining borrowers are moving in the same direction.[8]

The word microcredit means the provision of small collateral-free loans to the poor, most of whom are women, for the purposes of self-employment. Grameen-style credit is based on the philosophy that credit is a fundamental human right, that poor people are creditworthy, and that they have inherent skills and abilities that are underutilized or not utilized at all. Loans are provided for income-generating activities and housing for the poor, but not for the purposes of buying food (consumption). Grameen delivers credit to the poor; the poor do not have to travel to the bank. Other Grameen loan products include savings deposits and insurance. The bank also encourages social empowerment through the formation of groups and centers where women are given the opportunity to take on elected leadership roles, and this leads to borrowers participating in the local government electoral process.

The 16 decisions followed by all Grameen borrowers include the promotion of health, the growing of vegetables for consumption, the selling of any surplus vegetables, and the education of their children.

In 1989, Grameen Trust of Bangladesh was created to support Grameen replication programs worldwide. It provides training, financial, technical, and other support to microcredit practitioners and replicators of Grameen-type credit and savings programs. One hundred and thirty-eight Grameen programs have now been replicated in 37 countries. Some include adaptations suited to a country's unique environment, but each maintains the Grameen Bank's philosophy. In 2004, the Grameen Trust introduced a new program called the Grameen Build, Operate, and Transfer (Grameen BOT) program. Where Grameen Trust normally relies on partnership organizations to implement a microcredit program, it has moved to into directly implementing programs especially in countries in difficult situations. It identifies a country and recruit staff to implement a program with the focus of targeting and reaching the poor and to achieve institutional and financial sustainability. This project has so far reached 7 countries including Costa Rica, Kosovo, Turkey, Zambia, and most recently Indonesia, serving the Tsunami affected individuals of the province of Aceh (Grameen BOT program, n.d.).

Microcredit Evolved into the Future

Microcredit, a concept involving lending or the provision of credit, has become a global initiative and has been adapted by numerous institutions in various regions of the world to include additional financial services or products such as transfers, deposits, insurance, and so forth. Credit with these additional services is often referred to as microfinance. Littlefield (2005, p. 1) further describes microfinance as:

> driven by the simple idea that people in developing economies need access to affordable financial services that allow them to make deposits, transfer funds between urban and rural areas, and protect themselves through crop and life insurance. These services help individuals better manage risk and plan for the future, and provide an important buffer for sudden emergencies, business risks, and seasonal slumps.

Microcredit and microfinance institutions involved in the delivery of credit and other services include nongovernmental organizations (NGOs), cooperatives, credit unions, nonbank financial institutions, and some formal banks.

In the 30 years since the origin of microcredit, it has evolved from providing small loans to the poorest women to fund their income-generating activities into an international movement in which microfinance institutions are encouraged to become sustainable financial entities that serve regions where financial services did not previously exist.

In February 1997, over 2,900 participants gathered in Washington, DC, to launch the Microcredit Summit goal of "working to ensure that 100 million of the world's poorest families, especially the women of those families, are receiving credit for self-employment and other financial and business services by the year 2005."[9] The Microcredit Summit campaign was instrumental in the recognition of microcredit and microfinance as contributing factors for achieving the MDGs and in having 2005 declared as the International Year of Microcredit by the United Nations. In November 2006, the Global Microcredit Summit will be held in Halifax, Nova Scotia, Canada. At this meeting, a report on the progress of the 2005 goal will be presented, and the expansion stage of the campaign in support of the MDGs will be launched.

Many other independent initiatives are under way that emphasize the significance of microfinance as a tool to fight poverty. The World Bank and the Consultative Group to Assist the Poor (CGAP) are collaborating with national committees worldwide. Their goal is "to raise awareness of microfinance as a tool to empower and improve lives, in addition to developing strategies to face the challenge of scaling up resources to reach the estimated three billion people who still lack access to formal financial services" (Littlefield, 2005, p. 1).

Microcredit and Microfinance as Poverty-Reduction Tools

Who are the poorest people? The face of extreme poverty can be seen in Nibha Rani Sharkar, a borrower of the Grameen Bank. In a 1995 interview, she described how the Grameen loan program transformed her life and the lives of her children. Her husband died and she was left to raise their three boys, ages 3, 8, and 12. Before receiving a loan from Grameen, she could not afford to feed her children. She and her oldest son worked at another villager's home as domestic servants, and in return they received a daily kilogram of rice. The children were fed mostly on rice mar, the drained liquid from the boiled rice. With her first loan of $50 from the Grameen Bank, she bought a cow and sold the milk to earn an income. Two years later, she sold that cow, made a profit, and bought two others. Within 5 years, Nibha owned several cows, chickens, and three fourths of an acre of land. Her children are now all in school and eat three healthy meals each day. All microcredit and microfinance programs worldwide—in Asia, Africa, the Middle East, Latin America, and the Caribbean—have similar stories to tell of their programs' impact on the lives of their clients as they lift themselves out of poverty. Microcredit and microfinance work to empower these individuals to lift themselves out of poverty and become self-sufficient.

Microfinance is by no means a panacea, but it is a powerful poverty-reduction tool, and its impact on the MDGs is far reaching. Morduch, Hashemi, and Littlefield (2003) conclude that access to financial services reduces poverty, and its effects are demonstrated in multiple ways. Access to microfinance services therefore become the basis for which other essential interventions depend. This is further explained when they state that:

> evidence from the millions of microfinance clients around the world demonstrates that access to financial services enables poor people to increase their household incomes, build assets, and reduce their vulnerability to the crises that are so much a part of their daily lives (and this) also translates into better nutrition and improved health outcomes, such as higher immunization rates. It allows poor people to plan for their future and send more of their children to school for longer. It has made women clients more confident and assertive and thus better able to confront gender inequities. (p. 1)

In terms of sustainability and the impact on the lives of the poorest people on a large scale, they further say, "Microfinance thus offers the potential for a self-propelling cycle of sustainability and massive growth, while providing a powerful impact on the lives of the poor, even the extremely poor" (p. 1).

The Challenges of Microcredit and Microfinance Institutions

Many of the poorest people worldwide still lack access to formal financial services and still have to rely on informal financing methods such as family members, savings groups, and money lenders. The central challenge is how to address the large unmet demand for microcredit and microfinance services for the poorest people. Magnette and Lock (2005) estimate that in 2004, the demand for microfinance services globally was 500 million clients, of whom only 80 million were served by the estimated 7,000 to 10,000 microfinance institutions that exist. Financial services to these 80 million clients reach mostly the urban and peri-urban areas. MFIs have difficulty reaching the rural, remote, and low population-density areas. They are faced with the challenge of finding ways to overcome these obstacles and increase the scale and depth of their outreach while still operating efficiently.

While the focus is on MFIs to achieve scale and efficiency to enable them to reach large numbers, they equally have to ensure that they are in fact not excluding the target population of the 1.2 billion people that live on less than $1 a day. Reaching and having an impact on the poorest people is not an automatic process. Simanowitz and Walter (2002, p. 60) indicated that "conventional microfinance acts through both deliberate and unintentional mechanisms which exclude the poorest. Programs therefore need to be designed to include the poorest, and to facilitate mechanisms that will lead to poverty impacts." Furthermore, "achieving good poverty outreach is about providing the right products as far down the poverty scale as is possible" (p. 64). Two important measurements of poverty outreach are "working in the poorest areas of the country and working with the poorest relative to the population in an MFI's operational area" (p. 64).

For MFI practitioners who are committed to ensuring both targeting and outreach to the poorest segment of the underserved, there are poverty-measurement tools[10] that exist to help MFIs monitor the depth of poverty reached.

The Impact of Information and Communication Technologies on Microfinance Institutions

What are ICTs?

ICTs are defined as the transfer of information and data and include both old and new converging technologies. *CIDA's Strategy on Knowledge* (n.d., p. 7) states that "ICTs such as radio, television, telephones, computers, and the Internet can provide access to knowledge in sectors such as agriculture, microenterprise, education, and human rights, offering a new realm of choices that enable the poor to improve their quality of life." This section will focus on the new and advanced ICTs as enabling tools for transferring data and information to aid the effectiveness and efficiencies of MFIs in order to extend services to the poorest people in rural and remote areas.

Below are descriptions for a number of enabling technologies that are of potential use to MFIs. An MIS is a core information system that includes such functions as portfolio tracking, internal control, accounting, data analysis, and internal and external reporting functions to help MFIs make appropriate policy decisions and manage information more effectively and efficiently. Credit scoring allows an MFI to analyze a client's historical data, while providing links between a client's characteristics and behavior with the assumption that those links will predict how clients might act in the future. Scoring technology can assist MFIs to analyze past behaviors of clients to better assess loan applications, develop more effective loan-collection methods, create more effective target marketing strategies, and increase client retention.

PDAs are small handheld devices that field officers can use to do financial calculations and manage both client and MFI information. With data electronically stored, loan officers can readily gain access to client information, which assists them in activities such as loan processing, reviewing clients' historical data, and monitoring loan portfolios.

Smart cards are small plastic cards that can easily fit into a wallet. They have an embedded microchip that processes information or stores data and works like an electronic passbook to facilitate savings, deposits, and money transfers.

Point of sale (POS) is a device or system that is located at a physical location often remote from a main branch such as in a retail outlet. It is able to perform some of the financial transactions normally associated with branch banking such as the transfer of funds from one account to another or from a customer to a retailer.

Mobile phones allow clients to use a cell phone to call into an automated system to conduct business transactions and to access and request information. They also allow clients to charge others for use of their mobiles, especially in regions without a regular telecommunications infrastructure.

An ATM is a machine that facilitates banking transactions that would otherwise be serviced by staff. It provides account information, accepts deposits, and aids cash disbursement and balance transfers.

Biometrics technology measures an individual's unique physical or behavioral characteristics such as fingerprints and voice patterns to recognize and confirm identity. This technology is used in association with ATMs and POS.

Interactive voice response (IVR) technology allows clients to access an automated system through standard or mobile telephones to do banking transactions and get other information such as office hours and branch locations.

Internet banking allows clients to perform transactions similar to telephone banking, which include verifying account information, making bill payments and money transfers, and accessing new product information.

Appropriate and Enabling ICTs for Microcredit and Microfinance Institutions

In light of the challenges MFIs are facing in terms of high transaction costs and the lack of outreach to isolated and sparsely populated rural areas in regions such as Africa and Latin America, several microfinance institutions worldwide are experimenting with various new technologies to lower operational and transaction costs, improve efficiency, aid in accurately tracking operations, and expand scale and outreach. Frankiewicz (2003) indicated that in terms of institutional technology usage, CGAP's survey of 150 MFIs worldwide:

found that only about one-third of the MFIs in Southeast Asia and Africa are computerized, compared to more than three-quarters of the MFIs in Latin America, Eastern Europe and Central Asia. Worldwide, 46% of MFIs still have very low-tech systems, either manual or spreadsheet-based MIS. The remaining 56% have more advanced systems, either custom outsourced systems (24% of the institutions surveyed), systems built in-house (20%), or applications purchased off the shelf (10%). (p.p 14-15)

There are MFIs of varying sizes and ranges of experience. Smaller MFIs still utilize manual ledgers and spreadsheets for record keeping. However, the majority of MFIs require information system (IS) technology to help them track, report, and analyze information for internal and external use. ICTs or delivery technologies appropriate for MFIs usually start with the core MIS. Other IS technology includes a handheld device such as a PDA that records client information, smart cards, a client-held device that stores customer information, scoring technology, a means of analyzing and forecasting client behavior, and connectivity technologies (broadband or VSAT, a wireless data connection through satellite) that transfer data to staff and branches.

The more advanced delivery technologies that larger MFIs and some banks use include low-cost and standard ATMs and cell- or mobile-phone banking. POS systems are often placed in public retail outlets for use with credit and debit cards, and allow clients to do electronic payments and other transactions. All of these technologies facilitate customer financial transactions such as deposits and payments, and cash withdrawals and transfers. Biometrics, the fingerprint technology associated with smart cards that assists with verification and security of a client's identification, is also used by MFIs.

Frankiewicz's (2003) seminar report made reference to Elizabeth Littlefield's statement:

Technology certainly has the potential to help us do the one thing that microfinance has not been able to do except in very few places thus far and that is scale up exponentially. It can do this by enabling a rapid expansion in access points through improving operations, profits, customer service and, importantly, outreach to underserved populations, especially in rural areas. (p.73)

The report further recounts the seminar discussions on enabling technologies appropriate for MFIs and access points or contact points where clients can gain access to financial products and services that provide them with greater flexibility and convenience. These enabling ICTs and access points are thus seen as an added bonus for MFIs in terms of customer service. The tables below describe the various technologies, state the requirements for implementation, list any associated advantages or disadvantages associated with use, and therefore suggest the applicability of these technologies for MFIs globally.

In addition, case studies are provided below to further illustrate the scope of available technologies for the delivery of financial services, including the basic MIS system, PDAs, smart cards, POS, low-cost ATMs, biometrics, and mobile phones.

Management Information System

Gibbons and Meehan (2000) claim that the use of MIS will improve efficiency and increase the outreach of microfinance institutions, which suggests it to be a necessary technology

Table 1. Summary of access points and their enabling technologies[11] (Source: AfriCap Seminar: Information Technology as Strategic Tool for Microfinance in Africa; used with permission from AfriCap Fund)

Technology	Description	Requirements	Pros	Cons
Automated Teller Machine (ATM)	A machine that can furnish account information, accept deposits, effect balance transfers, and disburse cash	• Reliable and affordable communications and power infrastructure • Central database • Ability to securely transfer currency to machines	For clients: • Convenient service • Flexible account access • Increased hours of operation For MFIs: • Reduced transaction volumes and costs • No staff needed to complete transaction • Can attract savings deposits	• Expensive to own and operate • Need for integrated systems • Maintenance and cash refilling is costly • Security issues (including transport of cash)
Mobile Branches	An ATM on a truck or a branch in a bus that goes from one village to another in rural areas that can be served infrequently (e.g., once a week). Combines ATM functionality with operational staff	• Should be combined with smart cards and POS devices • MFI staff capable of providing a range of services	• Full range of financial services • Expands branch network to low-density rural areas • Much lower cost than setting up a branch • More secure than a permanent ATM • Not dependent on telecommunication infrastructure	• Clients can only transact when the mobile branch is in the village • Higher per-unit cost than ATMs • Need a staff of two to three to drive and service the mobile branch • Higher operating costs (travel distances, maintenance)
Point of Sale (POS) Device	Small machine located at a point of sale that can be used to authenticate the transfer of funds from customer to the retailer	• Retailer buy in and support • Solid communications infrastructure • Centralized database • Coordination between institutions	• Significant reduction of paperwork • No need for data-entry personnel • Immediate reconciliation of transactions	• Expensive to implement and operate • Need for interinstitutional coordination and shared infrastructure

Table 1. continued

Technology	Description	Requirements	Pros	Cons
Smart Cards	Wallet-sized plastic cards with embedded computer chips that can process information or simply store data	• Reliable electrical and communications networks • Dial-up facility for updates • Software integration between cards, readers, and central MIS • Presence of associated technologies	• Store information • No need for real-time connection • Automated transactions • More secure • Quicker administrative functions • Increased transaction accuracy	• Need to purchase associated technologies • High up-front development costs • Security issues with stored information
Mobile Phones	Permit client to request information from, or conduct business with, an automated system through a mobile phone	• Solid MIS • Centrally stored, real-time data • Network availability at affordable rates	• Not reliant on poor landline phone infrastructure • Permits access to rural clients • Frees staff time • 24/7 accessibility	• Lack of mobile network in rural areas • High cost of operation • Expensive to install and maintain • Need for centralized database
Interactive Voice Response (IVR) Technology	Allows callers to request information from, or conduct business with, an automated system by speaking into a telephone or inputting information through its keypad	• Easy and affordable telephone access for clients • Centrally stored, up-to-date data • Secure databases	• Can serve many clients at once • 24/7 service • Frees staff time for more personalized tasks (business counseling, collection calls)	• Need access to telephone services • Initial costs between $10,000 and $50,000 for in-house system • Need for central system to control personal identification numbers (PINs)

Table 1. continued

Technology	Description	Requirements	Pros	Cons
Personal Digital Assistants (PDAs)	Small, handheld digital computers that can run specialized programs to manage MFI and client data and perform financial calculations	• Well-functioning MIS • High-speed access to MIS data from branch offices • Capable technical support • Solid institution and good products	• Increased productivity of field staff • Applicable to wide range of tasks • Can run various software programs • Can standardize procedures • Reduced volume of paper records • Reduced labor costs	• High initial and maintenance costs • Long development process (9 months to 2 years) • Need for custom-designed database applications
Internet Banking	Internet technology enables users to perform a variety of banking activities, including fund transfers, bill payments, and securities trading	• Solid MIS infrastructure • Centralized database • Reliable and affordable communications and power infrastructure	• Flexible account access • No staff needed to complete transaction • Increased hours of operation • Eliminates need for data-entry personnel	• Need Internet access and connectivity • Need for integrated systems • High initial costs • Typically requires higher income and higher literacy rate
Biometrics Technology	Measures an individual's unique physical or behavioral characteristics to recognize and confirm identity	• Reliable electrical power for card or biometric readers • Solid processes and adequate staff • Software integration between cards, readers, and central MIS	• Greater security • Convenience for clients • Local verification • Speedy verification that does not require staff • User identity is stored safely and is tamper free	• Time, money, and energy required for setup and maintenance • Need to train users • Slow user acceptance or user refusal • System integration may require changes in other pieces of hardware

for MFIs. Therefore, as MFIs scale up activities to reach more clientele, a well-defined and well-functioning computerized MIS is required. A full and complete MIS would include all the systems an MFI would need to help generate, track, and analyze information efficiently on staff and clients, as well as provide management systems for effective decision making. Most MFIs have an MIS consisting of an accounting system and a portfolio-tracking system (financial products such as loans and savings), and other systems on client impact and human-resource management. The MIS provides management with an overview of the organizational performance to guide them toward their goals of poverty reduction and building a sustainable and efficient organization. It helps them review performance on products, staff, and clients. The MIS also aids in external communication.

Although it is not a replacement for good and effective management, MISs provide information that is useful in addressing management inefficiencies relating to staff morale, operational, and procedural problems. A well-functioning MIS can be the basis on which other advanced technologies are built to enhance MFI client outreach. In the case of the Grameen Bank, almost all of their branches (1,315, out of 1,609)[12] have access to a computerized MIS. At weekly meetings, branch field officers have readily available computer-printed information on borrowers' repayment schedules. If clients repay their loans according to the schedule, nothing is written but their signatures; therefore, the field staff spends less time on paperwork and are able to give more time to the clients.

Personal Digital Assistants

PDAs are small handheld computers that run specific programs to manage the MFI, client information, and aid in financial calculations. PDAs are custom-designed to be compatible with the institution's MIS. For PDAs to provide maximum benefit, they need to have high-speed access to data from the MIS at the branch offices. PDAs are not a substitute for an MIS, but a supplementary tool. They allow loan officers to access information from their MFI while in the field. From the field, they can access an electronic list of clients with loans in arrears and arrange for loan collection, see clients who are ready to apply for their next loan, and easily obtain background information including client data and records. From certain locations they can update their client records to the head-office MIS immediately or daily, thus reducing the need for data-entry clerks.

MFIs are exploring the use of PDAs to improve performance on a number of levels such as standardizing the institutional methodology and operating policies, aiding in the effectiveness and efficiency of loan officers, improving accuracy in data collection and reporting, and obtaining access to information while in the field.

As a result of the growing competition in the microfinance sector, particularly in Latin America, many MFIs are forced to lower operational costs and improve services and are therefore looking to PDAs to reduce the relatively high cost of labor. PDAs have been used as a microfinance tool since 1999 when they were first introduced by two Mexican MFIs, Compartamos and FinComun.

A CGAP IT Innovation Series paper evaluated the use of PDAs in 10 Latin American institutions, as well as one MFI in the Philippines and one in India. The findings reported by Waterfield (2004) for the Latin American case studies are as follows.

The findings reported by Waterfield (2004) for the Latin American case studies

MFI	Results
Adopem - Dominican Republic	• Improved client retention • Time frame for loan delivery reduced from 5 to 2 days • 60% reduction in paperwork • 50% reduction in data-entry cost • 35% increase in productivity of loan officers
BanGente - Venezuela Banco Solidario -Ecuador	• Improved efficiency of work flow • Decreased operational cost (both of these results were not quantified)
Microfin - Mexico	• Time saving noted by field staff • Improved consistency of work
Compartamos - Mexico	• Suspended use due to different priorities • Management believed PDAs were implemented too early • Difficulties and interface problems between MIS and PDAs

The Waterfield (2004) survey indicated the following benefits of PDAs:

• Assisted in the standardization of the work process

• Increased the accuracy, productivity, and efficiency of field workers

• Improved loan delinquencies

• Improved management of time by field staff

• Increased accuracy and faster credit-approval process

• Decreased paper records

Smart Cards

Smart cards are similar to debit or credit cards in that they are made of plastic and are sized to fit into a wallet. Microchips (microprocessor and memory chip) are imbedded into the smart cards, and these allow for the storage and processing of data.

Smart cards can be used by MFIs to automate client transactions. They store all client savings, loan, and other product information. They operate like a debit card, an electronic passbook, or a credit card in that transactions are recorded once electronically, and this speeds up the transaction process and increases accuracy. For security purposes, smart cards also store clients' fingerprint images, and these are compared to images taken by biometric scanners during transactions.

Smart cards assist MFIs to reduce the volume of paperwork, decrease transaction times, and reach more clients.

The following are the experiences of three MFIs that used smart cards and combined them with other technologies.

SKS (India)

In 2001 and 2002, Swayam Krishi Sangam (SKS) of southern India implemented a 1-year pilot project with smart cards combined with PDAs. The objective was to increase the productivity of loan officers by saving time during client-centered meetings, decrease the number of errors produced by a manual recording system, and provide quick access to data for reporting and monitoring by management. SKS also intended to create a technology infrastructure through which other services could be facilitated—including emergency loans, credit scoring, automated cash access, and real-time application processing. The smart cards cost SKS $3.40 each.

After 1 year's use of the combined technology (PDA and smart cards), SKS reported an increased accuracy in the recording of transactions and increased efficiency in the delivery of information to the central MIS. However, a significant increase to the productivity of loan officers was not realized as field officers increased their efficiency in manually recording transactions.

SKS suspended its use of smart cards because of the high up-front costs (over $125,000) to develop the technologies. Even though SKS did not continue using this technology because of scarce resources and the high implementation costs, the pilot project proved that poor and illiterate people are able to use and understand technological devices, thus "making technology a viable infrastructure for providing additional services in the future" (Whelan, 2004, p. 3).

Prodem FFP (Bolivia)

In 2000, Prodem FFP, an MFI in Bolivia, partnered with Innova (a local software firm) to introduce smart cards. The goals were to reduce operating costs for services to rural areas and to eventually create a low-cost ATM referred to as Smart ATM (SATM). Innova developed the software to have the smart card furnished with client identification data that included fingerprint templates, and also with client financial data from the Prodem Financial processing system. The smart card facilitated withdrawals, currency exchanges, deposits, money orders, and other services.

A number of benefits were derived from the implementation of smart cards. The smart cards significantly reduced the wait time for clients; for instance, clients no longer had to line up to check their balances. Also, transactions were automated, which increased accuracy and security and helped protect user identity. The smart card served as an electronic passbook, and this eliminated paper transactions and allowed clients to perform a wide range of financial activities such as buying money orders, making currency exchanges, and making deposits and withdrawals. The integrated technologies of smart cards, ATMs, and fingerprint identification (biometrics) provided a competitive edge for Prodem PPF, and it attracted more depositors because of its quick and convenient service. Smart cards hold the flexibility to add other products that may be implemented in the future by Prodem FFP.

Microfinance Networks (Uganda): The Remote Transaction System

In 2002, Hewlett Packard joined with seven organizations (Foundation for International Community Assistance [FINCA] International, ACCION International, Freedom from Hunger, BizCredit, Echange, PRIDE Africa, and Grameen Foundation, USA [GFUSA]) and formed the Microdevelopment Finance Team (MFT) to examine how technology can assist in increasing the scale of microfinance given the challenges that the industry is experiencing, "including the lack of industry-wide standardization, high transaction costs, and the inability to reach out to rural areas" (Magnette & Lock, 2005, p. 1). The MFT created the remote transaction system (RTS), "a combined technology and business process which supports both group and individual lending, online and batch offline processing, and back office synchronization" (Magnette & Lock, p. 1). The goal was to create an industry standard, assist the MFIs in cost-effective outreach to remote clients, and advance microfinance to a new stage of development.

The project was piloted for a 1-year period; however, this did not prove to be a sufficient length of time, even with an advance 3-month preparation period. A local team was hired to manage and implement the project. The RTS was piloted in Uganda with the partnership of three MFIs operating in Uganda: the Uganda Microfinance Union (UMU), a partner of ACCION; FINCA; and the Foundation for Credit Community Assistance (FOCCAS), a partner of Freedom from Hunger.

The RTS involved the use of sturdy handheld devices that communicate through GSM[13] cellular networks, and these were combined with the use of smart cards. The smart cards hold account information and are given to clients and field officers to use with the POS device. Clients insert their cards to do their banking transactions, including making a loan payments, and the POS device provides a receipt. The POS system works off line in the field, but when the device is connected online, financial data is transferred via a server to the MFI's MIS. The server could be something as simple as a basic computer with a straightforward software program that could be easily maintained by branch staff members.

The Remote Transaction System eliminated time spent on manual reporting, thereby reducing rural operating costs. The electronic data collection increased client confidence in the MFIs, as well as aiding in fraud reduction. Additionally, "the system, if used by the industry as a whole, might allow MFIs to take full advantage of latent synergies that exist among geographically and financially diverse institutions" (Magnette & Lock, 2005, p. 1).

The value of RTS was assessed against the practices currently in use in the microfinance industry with group, branch, and individual clients. The results demonstrated that the most commercially-oriented of the three MFIs derived the most benefit from the technology largely because they were ready to adjust their business model to take full advantage of the RTS: "The advantages of the system as implemented included automation of transactions, reduced client time and travel, more frequent payments, reduced cash management risk, and avoidance of costs for 'brick and mortar' branches" (Magnette & Lock, 2005, p. 1).

The RTS Uganda pilot-project implementation was short and only involved hundreds of clients, so the impact in terms of the scale of the technology was not clear. There were benefits to clients in rural areas who would otherwise have been excluded. The Microdevelopment Finance Team confirmed that there were advantages to the formation of nontraditional partnerships among nonprofit organizations, for-profit groups, and development agencies.

Furthermore, "If the potential for enabling remote transactions, expanding services into rural areas, and altering business practices can be achieved, then the RTS could potentially have very significant developmental impact" (Magnette & Lock, 2005, p. 1).

Summary of Benefits of ICTs to Microfinance Institutions

The above case studies suggest a number of benefits that technology can bring to MFIs. Ivatury and Pasricha (2005) also mentioned several benefits from a wide range of technologies employed by various MFIs. These include more informed decision making and better reporting through the use of well-developed and well-managed MIS systems. Lower operating costs are another benefit through the use of a scorecard to predict customer payment patterns. Increased deposits and customer convenience are other benefits that were also demonstrated in Prodem's program. Other benefits include increased flexibility for clients, improved customer convenience, and increased number of rural customers.

The Challenges of Integrating Information and Communication Technologies by MFIs

While ICTs hold the promise to increase the efficiency of microfinance institutions and expand outreach to the rural poor by lowering transaction costs, there are obstacles for MFIs to overcome in the integration of ICTs. Hishigsuren (2006) indicated that many of the current ICT applications in the field are employed by the mainstream financial institutions who may not be serving the poor. For MFIs, whose primary mission is to reach the poor and reduce poverty, many of their ICT applications are still in the pilot stage. Also, those MFIs that have gone beyond the pilot stage of integrating ICTs are limited. It is further suggested that it will be sometime before MFIs will be able to fully utilize all the potential of ICTs, and that they should consider taking small steps and seriously consider the cost-benefit analysis when integrating ICTs in some functions of their operations.

The major challenges for MFIs in incorporating ICTs within their operations is not the availability of ICTs, but rather the costs associated with the implementation of ICTs, and the issues involved in choosing the appropriate technology that would give the maximum return on investment. The benefits associated with ICTs come at a price. Software creation and implementation, including application software and the interface between the handheld or branch systems and the MIS, and hardware costs, as well as the time involved for software and hardware development all must be evaluated by the MFIs. Additionally, MFIs would normally need to hire an external firm to manage the development of the software and user interface: "Delivery technologies have the potential to reduce the costs of serving the poor. But in many countries these technologies have yet to prove themselves more cost-effective than manual operations."[14] Technology systems for long-term support of MFIs are costly, especially when taking into account the need for MFIs to adjust to changes in customer needs and the economic and regulatory situations in which they operate. The price of software and hardware is about 15% of the total implementation cost, but the bulk of the expense involves staff time for training and adjusting to the new system.

Further, Ketley and Duminy (2003) stressed that technology is changing the banking arena and that the poor are increasingly becoming an attractive market for conventional banks.

Therefore MFIs must be aware of this "challenge or risk becoming irrelevant." However, even with the cost factors, "MFIs cannot afford not to develop an appropriate technology integration strategy" (p. 2).

Bridging the Digital Divide: Grameen Village Phone Model as a Case Study

This chapter has focused on ways in which MFIs are using ICTs to expand and strengthen their services. However, MFIs have developed a second method of using ICTs. ICTs are also being used as income generators for borrowers. Grameen Village Phone provides a good example of this type of use whereby borrowers or microentrepreneurs use the loans of the MFI to purchase ICTs, in this case cell phones, which they then use to generate an income by providing services to villagers. In addition, there is future potential for the MFI to be greatly impacted; Frankiewicz (2003) suggests that "such microentrepreneurs can become agent access points for an MFI, facilitating access to certain services at a much lower cost than a traditional delivery channel (i.e., physical branch or permanent field staff) ever could" (p. 53).

The digital divide has become a concern for many in various sectors of international development. The CIDA strategy report states that as "of 2000, 70 percent of the world's poor live in rural and remote areas, where access to information and communication technologies, even to a telephone, is often scarce—over one-third of the world population has never made a telephone call" (p. 8).

The Grameen Bank has developed trust and credibility, and established strong ties with thousands of rural villages and millions of the rural poor served by its microcredit programs. With this established network of clients, Grameen Bank was able to leapfrog into a position of using telecommunication technology to create the Village Phone concept. The Village Phone offers a solution for many remote and rural villages where telecommunications service is nonexistent because of the high cost involved in building and administering services where no fixed telephone lines exist.

The Village Phone methodology was pioneered in Bangladesh in 1997 by the Grameen Telecom of Bangladesh (GTC), a nonprofit organization under the Grameen family of companies. GTC partnered with the Grameen Bank program that provides small collateral-free loans to the poorest people in Bangladesh, and with GrameenPhone Ltd (GP), a for-profit company that is licensed to manage a mobile cellular network in all of Bangladesh. GTC buys bulk airtime from GrameenPhone Ltd. Buying airtime in bulk allows GTC to negotiate better rates, and it is then able to pass on savings to the Village Phone operators who get their loans from Grameen Bank to purchase the phones and use them to generate income by providing a service to customers in the village.

The objectives of the Grameen Telecom Village Phone program[15] are as follows:

1.   To provide all of rural Bangladesh with easy access to telephone services

2.   To offer a new income-generating activity for the villagers

3.   To utilize the maximum potential of information technology, and bring it to the doorsteps of villagers

4.   To use telephones to connect the rural population and bring new opportunities to them, as a new tool or weapon in the fight against poverty

Several social and economic benefits are derived from the Grameen Village Phone program. Richardson, Ramirez, and Haq (2000), in a study commissioned by CIDA, concluded that the Grameen Village program yields "significant positive social and economic impacts, including relatively large consumer surplus and immeasurable quality of life benefits." (pg. 48) The study further indicated that the:

> *consumer surplus for a single phone call ranges from 2.64% to 9.8% of mean monthly household income. The cost of a trip to the city ranges from 1.93 to 8.44 times the cost of a phone call, meaning that the real savings for poor rural people is between 132 to 480 taka ($2.70 and $10.00) for calls that substitute for travel between the village and Dhaka.*
>
> (p. 49)

The social and economic benefits can be summarized as follows:

1.   Bangladesh is a labor-exporting country, and 42% of Village Phone users' calls are made regarding remittances from family members working overseas. Through the use of the phones, villagers have knowledge of the market rates and are able to negotiate better exchange rates on money sent from abroad.

2.   Without the use of a phone, villagers have to travel long distances to provide or receive information. By spending the money to make a phone call, the family saves by not having to send a productive member on a journey that might involve hours of traveling time merely to deliver or receive information. The study shows that the cost to travel for information is up to 8 times more expensive than making a phone call.

3.   Farmers are able to get better prices for their products by directly calling the markets themselves rather than using a middleman.

4.   Village Phone offers microentrepreneurs the ability to link with clients from various regions, providing opportunities to expand their microbusinesses.

5.   Village Phone users generate their own business by reselling the information they gather to other villagers.

6.   Phones have proven to be valuable in emergencies, such as arranging for medical help during natural disasters.

7.   There is clear evidence that Village Phone operators have increased their social status in the village. Cell phones are a status symbol of the rich, and the Village Phone in a poor woman's hand elevates her status significantly. This increased social status is noted when a wealthier villager comes to the poorer woman's house to use the phone. The poorer woman's house becomes the center of activity, with villagers waiting to make or receive calls. The operator also has knowledge of the business of other village members. The additional income made further increases her economic status.

Since the Grameen Telecom Village Phone program's inception in 1997, 150,000 Village Phones have been distributed, and the program has spread to more than 35,000 villages in 61 out of 64 districts of the country. GrameenPhone reaches 3 million subscribers. Yunus (2000) stated that:

> *Bangladesh is the only country in the world which could take mobile telephones to the poor women in the villages in a very successful commercial way because of micro-credit. That has laid the foundation for future inroads of IT services like e-commerce, e-healthcare, e-literacy, e-education, e-jobs etc. to the villages in general, and to the poor women in particular. With IT we can put the whole world in the hands of the poor.* (p. 1)

Replicating the Grameen Village Phone Model

The Grameen Telecom Village Phone program in Bangladesh has proven to be a successful initiative demonstrating that technology can positively affect the lives of many rural villages. The Grameen Technology Center, a project under the Grameen Foundation USA (GFUSA),[16] has started replicating the Village Phone model to prove this model could work outside of Bangladesh. It piloted a Village Phone project in Uganda with four objectives:

1. To provide the rural communities of Uganda with valuable communications services to enable them to break the cycle of poverty

2. To validate, measure, and document the Village Phone model in a single country outside of Bangladesh

3. To establish a generalized replication model for the Village Phone program

4. To disseminate this learning to the commercial telecommunications sector and the worldwide development communities so as to catalyze and establish a global Village Phone movement (Keogh & Wood, 2005)

About Village Phone Uganda

GFUSA collaborated with the local telecommunications provider MTN Uganda. In addition to MTN Uganda, Grameen Technology Center established partnerships with eight microfinance institutions. These MFIs were FINCA, FOCCAS, UMU, Uganda Finance Trust (UFT), Feed the Children, MedNet, Hofokam, and Post Bank. GFUSA's extensive partnerships with the various MFIs permitted MTN Village Phone to reach a scale that would allow for "financial and social sustainability" (Grameen Foundation, n.d.).

The Village Phone operators first began their business in Uganda in March 2003 with the official launch of MTN Village Phone as an independent company in November of that same year. Keogh and Wood (2005) said, "Twelve months into formal operations, Village Phone operators in Uganda were selling an average of six times more airtime than is consumed by a typical MTN Uganda subscriber" (p. 13). FINCA Uganda, one of the partners, claims that "village bankers now have access to a powerful tool that can greatly improve their existing businesses' productivity—or be a new business itself." Below is a success story from one of FINCA's clients.

Sarah Sempa, a married mother of four, operates a small retail shop in the village of Namulesa in the Jinja district. She took her first FINCA loan in 2003 for 100,000 Ugandan shillings ($57) and invested it into her business. When she learned of the Village Phone program, she reasoned that her busy trading center was the ideal venue and decided to diversify. Now she earns an additional $25 to $30 weekly, and estimates that people travel from as far as 2 miles on foot to buy minutes of airtime on her Village Phone. [17]

The replication of the Grameen Village Phone program in Uganda proved successful. The Village Phone model has now been documented, and a manual[18] for replication is available. Another Village Phone replication project is now being piloted in Rwanda.

Microfinance institutions worldwide with knowledge of and existing ties to the rural poor through the provision of financial services can position themselves to become the vehicle through which the Village Phone can be introduced as a new service. The replicable business model for this program starts when a client from an MFI is given a loan to purchase a Village Phone starter kit. The cost of the starter kit ranges from $200 to $250 and includes "a mobile phone, prepaid airtime card, external Yagi antenna, signage, as well as marketing and other materials necessary to get started" (Keogh & Wood, 2005, p. 3). This starter kit is provided by the Village Phone company that has developed a relationship with the MFI to offer products to their clients. The Village Phone company negotiates wholesale rates for airtime with the telecommunication provider, who in turn provides Village Phone operators with access to existing telecommunications infrastructures. The Village Phone operators can offer telephone calls at affordable rates to the individuals in the community. In the business model, there are no subsidies and a win-win situation for all parties involved in the partnership is created. With proceeds from the business, the Village Phone operator repays the MFI loan and also purchases additional prepaid airtime cards. The MFI earns money from the loan and also a percentage of the revenue from airtime sales. The telecommunications provider earns money through volume sales of airtime, and the Village Phone company earns enough money to continue to promote and expand the program.

Keys for Success

Keogh and Wood (2005, pp. 12-14) explain the keys for success:

There are four vital elements to ensure the long-term success of a Village Phone program:

1.   The program should be structured so that all parties benefit.
2.   The microfinance sector should be used as a "channel to market." The social structures encouraged by microfinance institutions through groups, centers, and solidarity guarantees create a ready-made market for end-user consumers.
3.   The telecommunications provider should provide wholesale airtime rates to Village Phone Operators to allow them to provide affordable services while simultaneously earning enough margin to repay their loan.
4.   In-country staff should manage the business.

The Village Phone model has provided a way to bridge the digital divide. Through the use of the microfinance sector, the telecommunications sector is able to gain access to the large untapped rural markets they could not reach before because of the high cost of infrastructure development and maintenance. The Village Phone program potentially targets and reaches the poorest of the poor, women, and the illiterate within developing countries while holding the promise of helping to narrow digital disparities.

Conclusion

Like microcredit and microfinance, ICTs are not a panacea, but a powerful tool to aid microfinance institutions to become sustainable by reducing transaction costs, increasing scale, and expanding outreach to the remote areas, thus closing the gap in the demand for microcredit. The implementation of ICTs by microfinance institutions is still in its infancy, and it is not an easy or inexpensive process. Stakeholder collaboration within and across both the ICT and microfinance sectors and proper business planning by MFIs is necessary for cost effectiveness and to derive maximum benefits in implementation. As the cost for appropriate MFI technologies continues to decline, and the innovation and development of new technologies leads to further reductions in cost, MFIs will be able to reach larger numbers of the poor and more isolated and underserved rural poor. While the synergy of the microfinance and ICT sectors shows great promise for the achievement of the MDG of halving poverty by the year 2015, reaching the 1.2 billion people living on less than $1 a day will also depend on individual MFIs' commitment, mission, and program design to target the poorest.

References

Attali, J. (2004). *Microfinance and new technologies.* Information for Development (I4D). Retrieved February 2005 from http://www.i4donline.net/issue/jan04/microfinance_full. htm

Brown, M. M. (2001). Can ICTs address the needs of the poor? *UNDP Choices Magazine.* Retrieved August 20, 2005, from http://www.undp.org/dpa/choices/2001/june/j4e. pdf

CIDA's strategy on knowledge for development through information and communication technologies (ICTs). (n.d.). Retrieved July 2005 from http://www.acdi-cida.gc.ca/publications-e.htm#Strategies

Cracknell, D. (2004). *Electronic banking for the poor: Panacea, potential and pitfalls.* Retrieved August 20, 2005, from http://www.microsave.org

Daley-Harris, S. (2004). State of the Microcredit Summit Campaign report 2004. *Microcredit Summit E-News, 2*(4). Retrieved August 20, 2005, from http://www.microcreditsummit.org

D'Orville, H. (2000). Knowledge and information: New levers for development and prosperity. *UNDP Choices Magazine.* Retrieved May 20, 2005, from http://www.undp.org/dpa/choices/2000/june/p8-9.htm

FINCA helping bridge the digital divide. (n.d.). *FINCA News.* Retrieved August 20, 2005, from http://www.villagebanking.org/fincanews-uganda.htm

Frankiewicz, C. (2003). *Information technology as a strategic tool for microfinance in Africa: A seminar report.* Calmeadow. Retrieved January 2006 from http://www.africapfund. com/site/IMG/pdf/2004_IT_Seminar_Report-2.pdf

Gibson, D., & Meehan, J. (2000). *The Microcredit Summit's challenge: Working towards institutional financial self-sufficiency while maintaining a commitment to serving the poorest families* (Microcredit Summit Discussion Paper).

Gilhooly, D. (2001). Deconstructing the digital divide. *UNDP Choices Magazine.* Retrieved May 20, 2005, from http://www.undp.org/dpa/choices/2001/june/j8e.pdf

Grameen BOT project. (n.d.). *Build, operate and transfer (BOT) projects.* Retrieved October 5, 2006, from http://www.grameen-info.org/grameen/gtrust/bot.html

Grameen Foundation. (n.d.). *Village phone Uganda partners.* Retrieved October 9, 2006, from http://www.grameenfoundation.org/who_we_are/partnerships/technology_part-nerships/village_phone_uganda/

Hishigsuren, G. (2006). *Information and communication technology and microfinance: Options for Mongolia* (Discussion Paper No. 42). ADB Institute. Retrieved March 2006 from http://www.adbi.org/files/2006.02.dp42.ict.microfinance.mongolia.pdf

Ivatury, G., & Pasricha, N. (2005). *Funding microfinance technology* (Donor Brief No. 23). Consultative Group to Assist the Poor (CGAP). Retrieved December 2, 2005, from http://www.cgap.org/docs/DonorBrief_23.pdf

Keogh, D., & Wood, T. (2005). *Village phone replication manual: Creating sustainable access to affordable telecommunications for the rural poor.* Grameen Technology Center, Grameen Foundation USA. Retrieved August 10, 2005, from http://www. gfusa.org/technology_center/

Ketley, R., & Duminy, B. (2003). *Meeting the challenge: The impact of changing technology on microfinance institutions (MFI)* (Microsave Briefing Note 21). Retrieved August 25, 2005, from http://www.microfinancegateway.org/files/3771_03771.pdf

Littlefield, E. (2005). *Celebrating the year of microcredit* [Press Release]. Consultative Group to Assist the Poor (CGAP) & World Bank Group. Retrieved September 5, 2005, from http://www.cgap.org/press/YOM_083105.html

Magnette, N., & Lock, D. (2005). *What works: Scaling microfinance with the remote transaction system: Increasing productivity and scale in rural microfinance.* World Resources Institute. Retrieved August 15, 2005, from http://www.digitaldividend. org/case/case_rts.htm

Morduch, J., Hashemi, S., & Littlefield, E. (2003). *Is microfinance an effective strategy to reach the millennium development goals* (Focus Note No. 24)? Consultative Group to Assist the Poor (CGAP). Retrieved August 14, 2005, from http://www.cgap.org/ docs/FocusNote_24.html

Rao, M. (2004). *Micro-finance and ICTs: Exploring mutual benefits and synergy.* Retrieved April 25, 2005, from http://www.orbicom.uqam.ca/in_focus/columns/en/ar-chives/2004_avril.html

Richardson, D., Ramirez, R., & Haq, M. (2000). *Grameen Telecom's village phone programme in rural Bangladesh: A multi-media case study.* Ottawa, Canada: Government of Canada.

Salazar, D. (2004). *CGAP IT innovation series: Credit scoring.* Retrieved April 25, 2005, from http://www.microfinancegateway.org/content/article/detail/18047

Silva, S. (2002). Quantum Leap microcredit boosted by technology. *Microenterprise Americas Magazine.*(pp. 32-35). Retrieved September 20, 2006 from www.iadb.org/sds/mic/micamericas/eng/2/autumn2002wb.htm

Simanowitz, A., & Walter, A. (2002). Ensuring impact: Reaching the poorest while building financially self-sufficient institutions, and showing improvement in the lives of the poorest women and their families. In S. Daley-Harris (Ed.), *Pathways out of poverty: Innovations in microfinance for the poorest families* (pp. 1-73). Bloomfield, CT: Kumarian Press Inc.

Siu, P. (2001). Increasing access to microfinance using information and communications technologies. PlaNet Finance 2005. Retrieved September 20, 2006 from development-gateway.org/mircrofinance/rc/filedownload

Talking about the future of microfinance. (2005). *Microfinance Matters Newsletter, 13.* Retrieved March 20, 2005, from http://www.uncdf.org/mfmatters

Waterfield, C. (2004). *CGAP IT innovation series personal digital assistants (PDA).* Retrieved April 25, 2005, from http://www.microfinancegateway.org/files/18045

Whelan, S. (2004). *CGAP IT innovation series: Smart cards.* Retrieved April 25, 2005, from http://www.microfinancegateway.org/files/18049_CGAP_Smart_Cards.pdf

Yunus, M. (2000). *IT can be Bangladesh's super highway to prosperity* (Speech at the North America Conference in Atlantic City). PlaNet Finance. Retrieved October 2005 from http://www.developmentgateway.org

Yunus, M. (2005). *Grameen Bank at a glance.* Retrieved August 2005, from http://www.grameen-info.org/bank/GBGlance.htm

Web Site References

Development Gateway: http://www.developmentgateway.org
Digital Dividend Project: http://www.digitaldividend.org
Grameen Bank: http://www.grameen-info.org
Grameen Technology Center: http://www.gfusa.org/technology_center/
Grameen Telecom: http://www.grameen-info.org/grameen/gtelecom/index.html
Grameen Trust: http://www.grameen-info.org/grameen/gtrust/replication.html
Inter-American Development Bank: http://www.iadb.org
Microcredit Summit: http://www.microcreditsummit.org
Microfinance Gateway: http://www.microfinancegateway.org
Microsave: http://www.microsave.org
Technology Resource Center, Consultative Group to Assist the Poorest: http://www.cgap.org/technology

The Canadian Development Agency: http://www.acdi-cida.gc.ca
United Nations: http://www.un.org
United Nations Capital Development Fund: http://www.uncdf.org/english/microfinance/
Year of Microcredit: http://www.yearofmicrocredit.org

Endnotes

1   http://www.un.org/millenniumgoals/index.asp

2   http://www.cgap.org/about/faq04.html

3   The poorest people, rural poor, unserved, underserved, and other like terms refer to those living on less than $1 a day.

4   Quote from Mark Malloch Brown found at http://www.uncdf.org/english/microfinance/

5   ICTs often refer to both the old and new technologies including radio, television, Internet, and so forth for transferring and storing information. This chapter focuses on the new and advanced technologies appropriate for microfinance institutions.

6   Quote taken from *Lessons from the Field: ICTs in Microfinance* (http://www.digitaldividend.org)

7   CIDA refers to the Canadian International Development Agency.

8   Data taken from http://www.grameen-info.org/bank/GBGlance.htm

9   Quote taken from http://www.microcreditsummit.org

10   For poverty-assessment tools see http://www.povertytools.org

11   Tables are taken from the AfriCap seminar report *Information Technology as a Strategic Tool for Microfinance in Africa* (pp. 47-48). Permission was provided by AfriCap Fund for its use.

12   Information taken from http://www.grameen-info.org/bank/GBGlance.htm

13   GSM is the acronym for Global System for Mobile Communication.

14   http://www.microfinancegateway.org/resource_centers/technology/iss_software/other_technologies/ for the quote and for more information on the various technologies.

15   See http//www.grameentelecom.net for more details.

16   For further details, see http://www.gfusa.org/technology_center/.

17   See http://www.villagebanking.org/fincanews-uganda.htm for full story from the news article "FINCA Helping Bridge the Digital Divide."

18   See http://www.gfusa.org/technology_center/ for the replication manual.

Chapter VIII

Human Rights Movements and the Internet:
From Local Contexts to Global Engagement

John Lannon, AIB Centre for Information and Knowledge Management,
Kemmy Business School, Ireland & the Praxis Centre, Leeds Metropolitan University, UK

Edward Halpin, School of Applied Global Ethics & the Praxis Centre,
Leeds Metropolitan University, UK

Abstract

This chapter looks at the impact of the Internet on the worldwide human rights movement, and examines the opportunities and pitfalls of the technology and its applications for human rights organisations. It argues that the technology is a useful tool in nongovernmental efforts toward worldwide compliance with human rights norms despite the new challenges it presents for human rights defenders and activists, particularly in the South. Conceptualising the movement as a collection of issue-based social submovements, it draws on social movement literature and examples from Africa to describe how the technology and its applications benefit the movement in six key areas of activity. The promises, pitfalls, and difficulties of Internet usage are discussed, with particular emphasis on censorship, surveillance and privacy, and the challenges they pose for human rights activists operating in a digital environment.

Introduction

The worldwide human rights regime has been growing in legal, political, and moral strength ever since the adoption of the Universal Declaration of Human Rights in 1948. But it was only after the end of the Cold War that human rights law and discourse became prominent in local, national, and international agendas, and a growing array of professionalised, non-governmental organisations (NGOs) began to appear (Rosenblum, 2000). Human rights defenders and local activist groups can now look to these for moral and material support, and they in turn can mobilise advocates around the world to act on behalf of victims of abuse and oppression. Through the collective efforts of these individuals and organisations, states and other actors have been forced toward greater accountability, institutional structures have been set up, and a vocabulary of liberation has been provided for people all over the globe.

Human rights activists everywhere share a commitment to compliance with human rights norms that transcend nationality and particular cultural values (Shelton, 2002). Granted, the origins of human rights discourse in a Western, liberal tradition is often seen as either undermining its universal value (Kennedy, 2002) or contributing to its ongoing manipulation (Abdul-Raheem, 2005). But antiuniversalism is refuted by arguments against genocide, slavery, racial discrimination, and other grave forms of abuse (Li, 1996), and by the widespread support that the major international human rights documents enjoy among the states of the world today (Perry, 1997). Certainly, particularities of context are important, and it is only when asserted within each country's tradition and history that human rights can become a reality (Tharoor, 1999). Thus, instead of allowing Western actors to set the agenda, local human rights movements in Africa and elsewhere need to "build sustainable legitimacy through local presence and work" (Abdul-Raheem, 2005).

Today, the international human rights regime encompasses institutional actors such as the United Nations (UN); national legal systems and human rights bodies; national and international criminal tribunals; quasi-governmental truth commissions; international, regional, national, and local (grassroots) NGOs; and academics, lawyers, educators, and activists all over the world (Ball, Girouard, & Chapman, 1997). It is becoming increasingly diverse not only because of the worldwide heterogeneity of cultures, subcultures, and contexts in which it operates, but also because the initial preference given to civil and political rights in the "western doctrine of human rights" (Cassese, 1986, p. 297) has waned. Equal attention is now given to economic, social, and cultural rights, and efforts are being made to place these on national and international agendas. There are also new global challenges to contend with: the integration of markets, the shrinking of states, increased transnational flows of information and people, the spread of cultures of intolerance, the decision-making processes of global institutions like the World Bank and multinational corporations (Brysk, 2002), and international terrorism. In response to these, the human rights movement—the worldwide community of advocates and activists working for the promotion and protection of human rights—has extended, evolved, and diversified. The lines between it and other civil society movements have become blurred, and human rights discourse now permeates, and often underpins, peace, conflict resolution, development, environmental protection, gender, health, and many other areas of civic concern.

The human rights movement has been described as "one of the most potent of contemporary social movements" (Cohen & Rai, 2000, p. 7) based on its implied universal logic. As with other international movements to which similar logic can be applied (such as the environmental movement and the women's movement), subnational, national, and regional struggles are often considered tactical, not strategic, interventions. But while individuals and groups may share an intellectual or moral commitment to the abstract ideal of human rights, Charlesworth (2002) notes that the interests of particular groups and individuals can differ dramatically. The diversity of the actors involved, ranging from a UN high commissioner to grassroots activists, renders attempts to analyse it as a single monolithic entity fraught with difficulty.

States are the primary accountable parties in cases of human rights abuses, and violator states rarely change their behaviour without serious, consistent pressure from other states (Burgerman, 1998). The role that transnational networks of human rights groups and activists play in applying this pressure is an important one. Globalisation creates new opportunities to challenge states "from above and below" (Brysk, 1993), and one way in which human rights networks do this is through the use of information and communication technologies.[1] Indeed, at the 2003 World Summit on the Information Society (WSIS), the UN commissioner for human rights noted that ICTs are crucial to improving the enjoyment of human rights such as freedom of expression, access to information, privacy, the right to an adequate standard of living, education, health, and development (Jorgensen, Lindholt, & Lindholt, 2004). The Internet is one of the most important of these tools.[2] Just as the fax machine became a key tool for the human rights movement in the 1980s (Hick, Halpin, & Hoskins, 2000), e-mail and the World Wide Web became important in the 1990s. Similarly in the early 21st century, blogging (the continuous posting of information to a Web site)[3] created an enormous opportunity for the worldwide dissemination of information about human rights abuses.

This chapter looks at the impact of the Internet on the human rights movement as a whole, and examines the opportunities and pitfalls of the technology and its applications. We conceptualise the movement as a collection of issue-based social submovements, and draw on social movement literature to outline the advantages and disadvantages of Internet usage by component networks and organisations. We then examine how the technology and its applications benefit the human rights movement in six key areas of activity. Examples of products and ICT initiatives are included, with an emphasis on work being undertaken in Africa and less developed countries.

While ICTs like the Internet have an important functional role in human rights movements, as many of the examples in this chapter show, their value can easily be overjudged and is frequently overhyped. Technology is only a tool, and ICTs are simply a means to an end for human rights organisations. Since one of the most important considerations is the way in which human rights organisations use these tools to manage information, we look at how the Internet helps organisations to manage this most valuable of resources.

The promises, pitfalls, and difficulties of Internet usage for the human rights movement are numerous and varied. While we discuss these in general, the related themes of censorship, surveillance, and privacy deserve particular attention. In the context of the ever-increasing counterterror measures being adopted by states, these represent particular challenges to human rights activists and freedom of expression.

In conclusion, we identify a number of key issues that will impact on how the human rights movement can reap the potential benefits of the Internet and other ICTs. It is particularly important to ensure that the technology is used to amplify the voices of the victims of human rights abuse and oppression, and it is in this context that new policies and initiatives should be viewed.

Understanding the Human Rights Movement

The most common approach to dealing with the diversity that exists within the human rights movement is to conceptualise it as a collection of issue-based social submovements that seek political and/or social transformation (Cohen & Rai, 2000). The child rights movement, indigenous peoples' movements, and antitorture movement are all examples of how a particular category of rights has been internationalised by the establishment of a global regime seeking to regulate behaviour on an issue. Like all social movements (as defined by Diani, 1992), they are made up of networks of individuals, groups, and organisations who are formally independent, who understand themselves to have common interests, and who assume a common identity for at least some significant part of their social existence.

The study of social movements has benefited greatly from the application of a network perspective (Diani & McAdam, 2003; Friedman & McAdam, 1992; Gould, 1993). This is the approach taken by Burgerman (1998), who uses the concept of transnational issue networks developed in Keck and Sikkink (1998) to analyse human rights advocacy. She sees networks as single interconnected entities, operating at both international and domestic levels, and made up of individuals and agencies that are connected to each other by shared values, a common discourse, and dense exchanges of information and services. Transnational human rights networks can influence state practice through these exchanges, but for this to happen, domestic human rights activists and the "micro-sites of resistance to practices of power, often disarticulated with reference to the global" (Baxi, 2000, p. 35) must somehow keep their cause on the international agenda and provide information to their international allies (Burgerman, 1998).

While the big emancipatory human rights movements like the women's rights movement and the gay rights movement are still in existence, there has been a greater tendency in recent years toward the formation of networks and movements around a single campaign, or with a specific objective. The international network that built up in support of the Ogoni people of Nigeria in the 1990s is a good example of this. The Ogoni, an ethnic minority living in the Niger River Delta region, were demanding increased political power, economic justice, and control over natural resources. The Movement for the Survival of the Ogoni People (MOSOP) organised the Ogoni and brought world attention to their conflict with the Nigerian government and the international oil company Shell. MOSOP and international organisations such as Amnesty International, Human Rights Watch, Greenpeace, and Friends of the Earth worked together to support the Ogoni efforts and to provide support to human rights defenders inside the country (Bob, 2005).

In Africa, there are a number of understandings of the term social movement (Clarke Brill, 2005), all of which are in evidence in this example. The term is used to refer to broad movements like the human rights movement that work for change on an issue. It is also used to refer to a grouping of people who are not heavily involved with an organisation and who may not see themselves as activists; they are often people like the Ogoni who are faced with oppression in their own everyday lives. Finally, it is used to refer to particular organisations that have a strong representation of people who are oppressed, poor, or experiencing human rights violations first hand. MOSOP and the Treatment Action Campaign (TAC), a post-apartheid South African organisation that campaigns for greater access to AIDS treatment by raising public awareness of the issues involved, are good examples of these.

Within the global human rights movement, all of these movement types exist and interact in increasingly complex webs of movements within movements and networks within networks. For example, the child rights movement contains issue-related movements that focus on child labour, children in armed conflict, the sexual exploitation of children, and so on. It also contains global organisational movements like the Child Rights Information Network (CRIN; http://www.crin.org), which covers the broad issue of child rights but with a strategically limited scope of activities. CRIN disseminates information about the Convention on the Rights of the Child[4] and child rights in general amongst NGOs, United Nations agencies, and other institutions. It has a membership of 1,550 organisations in over 125 countries (Yates, 2005), amongst which there are divergent, and occasionally incompatible, information needs (Halpin, 2003a, 2003b). In this respect, it is typical of a growing number of organisations that service the information needs of the ever-expanding human rights community.

The number of international NGOs active in the area of human rights has increased substantially since the early 1990s (Ishay, 2005; Keck & Sikkink, 1998; Smith, 1997). Organisations like the membership-based Amnesty International (http://www.amnesty.org) mobilise transnational resources to act on a wide range of human rights abuses, and often set up their own internal issue-based networks. Others like OMCT, the World Organisation against Torture (http://www.omct.org) coordinate and support global networks of local, national, and regional NGOs fighting against specific forms of abuse.[5] These international NGOs play a role in international policy networks and work with other like-minded NGOs to ensure their campaigns reach the widest possible audiences. There has been a trend toward increased connectedness of these international NGOs through the 1990s (Kaldor, Anheier, & Glasius, 2003), but formal collaboration between them is a relatively new development. For example, it was as recently as 1997 that the Association for the Prevention of Torture (APT) began organising meetings at its headquarters in Geneva to bring together international NGOs to improve the coordination of torture prevention, direct action, and rehabilitation. The broadest antitorture "coalition network" (Diani, 2003, p. 10) in existence today, CINAT (Coalition of International NGOs Against Torture), was only formed in 1999.

The international NGOs strive to bring international pressure to bear on states and to exert influence at the intergovernmental level. Because of the closer relationship that is developing between these NGOs and the United Nations, they are in a position to undertake research on issues under consideration by the Commission on Human Rights and other bodies; to assist in the drafting of its decisions and resolutions; to supply verified, up-to-date data; and to act as intermediaries between the larger NGO community and the United Nations (Maran, 1998). They have a broad constituency and can impact directly and indirectly on national and international legislators, diplomats and officials, and the public at large. They also fulfill another important function, which is to reinforce grassroots NGOs and to support the development of domestic human rights movements. These tend to work locally and are less concerned with the potential of UN accreditation and lobbying than with the plight of people in their own area. They collect, record, and report information about what is happening in their own country. They also ensure that their societies are working toward long-term human rights protection by building and motivating local actors and networks to advocate for change, and they press governments to live up to their formal commitments. This is often done at great personal risk as human rights defenders draw unwanted attention to the illicit actions of the state or its agents, and seek to bring about unwelcome reforms.

The Impact of the Internet on Social Movements

ICTs and especially the Internet have transformed the capacity of social movements to build coalitions and networks and to advocate for causes, principles, and other people (Hick & McNutt, 2002). They help to share information and place it within contexts while retaining editorial control over information content and external communication (Scott & Street, 2001). They also allow groups and organisations to mobilise beyond their constituency and to precipitate real-world activities. They can be cost efficient, and they allow for high impact without the need for major resources.

The Internet reduces the need for central communication and top-down information flows within social movements, making it suited to a nonhierarchical structure (Selian, 2002; Wasserman, 2005). Using the Internet, action can be organised in a decentralised way, even across borders. This opens up opportunities for local organisations, giving them national, regional, or global reach and impact. The Internet also facilitates the convergence of divergent organisations with different goals and strategies (Cammaerts & Van Audenhove, 2003), something that is important in human rights movements. It also allows the creation of new network organisations in which smaller organisations pool their information, thus greatly increasing participants' access to information resources and outlets. News of crises can be spread very quickly to highly interested and energetic people, and there can be equally speedy support for the movement. This can create opportunities for spontaneous global, collective action to supplement planned activities on the ground.

The frequent underestimation of the importance of ICT-based networks by governments has made them excellent tools for undermining efforts at censoring information entering or leaving a country. One of the best examples of how movements can successfully bypass state control and communicate in a secure environment using ICTs are the ongoing efforts of Falun Gong practitioners to highlight human rights abuses in China. According to the Falun Dafa Information Centre in New York,[6] more than 28,000 cases of serious human rights violations were reported up to March 2004.[7] The majority of these were sent by e-mail or fax despite China's all-encompassing surveillance network (Garden Networks, 2004), and the media and information blockade imposed by the Chinese government in all cases relating to Falun Gong (Amnesty International, 2000; Srinivasan, 2004). Practitioners outside of mainland China have also been using the Internet to break through the country's great firewall and to communicate with practitioners inside the country; the tools and technologies used include e-mail, chat rooms, peer-to-peer technologies,[8] and proxy servers.[9]

However, despite the great promise they hold for social movements and networks, ICTs are no more than an "opportunity structure" (Cammaerts & Van Audenhove, 2003, pp. 8-9). As a means of communication, the Internet can assist activists to mobilise participation by augmenting existing communication methods and overcoming their limitations (Wasserman, 2005). However, the notion that it will bring about radical changes in the way social movements and organisations are ordered is questionable. Agre (2002) and other proponents of the amplification theory contend that the Internet changes nothing on its own, but that it can amplify existing forces, which may, in turn, bring about change. The Internet serves to enlarge and accelerate processes already in place in societies and organisations rather than create entirely new forces. Even Selian (2002), who presents a more utopian view of the power of new communication technologies to bring about social change (which she defines as the enhanced awareness and protection of human rights in the international system), concedes that the way in which power is governed and managed by those who control and regulate various communications apparatus is a decisive factor.

According to Manji, Jaffer, and Njuguna (2000), all technologies have a natural proclivity to amplify inequalities, and the Internet is no exception. By the middle of 2005, only 14.6% of the world's 6.4 billion people had access to the World Wide Web (Internet Usage Statistics, 2005). The global divide in access to information technology is currently widening, but Norris (2001) suggests that over time the gap is likely to shrink as in the case of older communication technologies like the telephone, radio, and television. However, she goes on to say that in relation to the worldwide social divide, which is about income, education, class, gender, and race, the Internet reflects and thereby reinforces, rather than transforms, society.

While ICTs are important for the global participation and visibility of marginalised groups such as resource-poor communities, indigenous peoples, immigrants, and refugees (Sassen, 2004), there are two necessary preconditions. One is the preexistence of social networks built through cross-border communities of activism and practice, academic sharing, migration, organisational links, and so on. The other is the availability of adequate technical infrastructure, applications, and expertise to make it happen. In fact, the latter is a three-stage problem (Surman & Reilly, 2003). First there is the fundamental problem of access: Adequate and reliable bandwidth is necessary, as is a computer with an Internet connection, an Internet café in which one is free from surveillance, or a cell phone with SMS (short-message service). Then there is the adoption and development of basic skills needed to use the technology. Finally there is appropriation or strategic use, where a movement turns the technology to its own purposes, making it its own.

Online networks promise and can deliver inclusion, but there is a need for more conscious and concerted attempts to develop online spaces that are interesting, informative, and inclusive. Web sites like Kubatana.net (http://www.kubatana.net), which allows Zimbabwean activists to provide information resources and perspectives on the current social and political situation in the country, are a valuable public space for civil society in general and human rights movements in particular. Described by Bev Clark (2005) as a "one stop shop for information," it aims to improve access to human rights and civic information in Zimbabwe at a time of great political unrest. Global Voices Online (http://cyber.law.harvard.edu/globalvoices/) is another example; it is a nonprofit global citizens' media project that uses a wide variety of technologies including Weblogs, wikis,[10] podcasts,[11] online chats, and other techniques to bring attention to points of view from around the world.

Social movements have been making effective use of electronic mailing lists since the early 1990s. They have been used to promote causes and campaigns, to keep in touch with networks, to collaborate on projects, and to share information and experiences. They were also used, and continue to be used, to create a sense of solidarity and community. The Womenslink mailing list that linked women's organisations in Northern Ireland and the Republic of Ireland (O'Donnell, 2001) was a case in point. But for many organisations, the time and costs involved in hosting and maintaining a list is still not feasible. For this reason, organisations that have the skills and capacity to host and maintain mailing lists and listservs[12] do so on behalf of smaller, less resourced groups. National and regional organisations like Kabissa (http://www.kabissa.org), which provides African organisations with accessible, affordable, and secure Internet services (including Web-site hosting and discussion groups) enable civil society organisations in less developed regions to use ICTs effectively. They host network mailing lists for organisations that want to facilitate and encourage information sharing or coalition building, and newsletter mailing lists for member organisations that simply want to send regular or irregular mailings to interested parties.

While e-mail, mailing lists, virtual communities, and other forms of computer-mediated communications can create new links, strengthen existing links within networks, and sometimes even facilitate the formation of new activist networks and discussion groups, they can also change the rules, the physical context, and the content of communication, and make cooperation agreements extremely fragile. Many of the success stories of online networks have happened when the primary focus was on sharing tactics, information, or other resources. For example, African gender groups have used ICTs very effectively to establish links and to share resources across geographical and cultural borders (Wasserman, 2005). This is helped by the efforts of regional networks like WOUGNET, the Women of Uganda Network (http://www.wougnet.org), which promotes the use of ICTs as a tool to help groups address gender issues collectively. But for long-term, close collaboration where building togetherness and confidence is important, face-to-face communication systems are still superior to computer-based alternatives. Nonetheless, the WOUGNET experiences show that building capacities in ICTs can help expand the reach and activities of a network.

How Human Rights Movements Benefit from the Internet

Notwithstanding the limitations to its effectiveness within social movements, Hick et al. (2000) state and demonstrate in their book, *Human Rights and the Internet*, that "[t]he Internet is changing the operation of human rights organisations, their use of information, and the relationships between them" (p. 8).

Organisations are using it as a tool for their professional activities, but individual human rights activists and advocates are also using it to fight directly against abuse. The uses are numerous, varied, and often innovative as access to technology and training grows.

Information Dissemination

There a number of identifiable and overlapping areas in which human rights movements can benefit from Internet usage. The first is information dissemination. Human rights workers and domestic grassroots groups use the Internet to supply rapid, accurate, and cheap information about human rights violations to as wide an audience as possible. The traditional media, especially radio and television, may be most effective in informing local communities of a human rights violation, but any mention of it in the traditional foreign media is likely to be in newspapers that appear several days after the event (Katz-Lacabe & Lacabe, 2000). The Internet, on the other hand, can provide an almost instantaneous dissemination of news to a wide audience, thus helping the chances of attracting global attention and getting a faster international response to a human rights abuse. While human rights organisations continue to use the traditional media, the Internet also allows human rights activists to publish more of their information.

Shahjahan Siraj, a former online editor of Banglarights.net (http://www.banglarights.net), an independent Web portal that exposes and challenges discriminations and violations of human rights in Bangladesh, wrote that "ICT, [e]specially [the] Internet, used in collaboration with human rights activism, creates virtual alternative tunnels for the free flow of uncensored information within and out of [a] country" (Siraj, 2005, p. 26). In recent times, blogging has made it easier for human rights activists to disseminate information about abuses and to reach a potential audience of millions. Organisations like Human Rights Watch (http://www. hrw.org) and Global Voices Online provide numerous RSS feeds[13] on human rights issues, usually classified according to theme and region, and updated several times daily.

All around the world, journalists and activists document and blog human rights abuses on a daily basis. Blogs like Realidas Colombianas (http://lacoctelera.com/realidades), which covers the guerrilla war, working conditions, freedom of the press, poverty, child labour, and other issues in Colombia, provide well-researched, critical reports on the happenings in the writer's country. Others like Sudan: The Passion of the Present (http://platform.blogs. com/passionofthepresent/) are a resource for communities like those in Darfur who are experiencing daily suffering and oppression.

Blogs are particularly important in countries where the traditional press is under the control of the authorities. Human rights activists are using them to combat censorship and circulate independent news and information, and they have become a powerful tool for freedom of expression. They are easier to set up than a normal Web site, and can be adapted, configured, and altered without special expertise (although installation can be a little tricky). While organising content is not a problem, engaging the audience it reaches can be. To gain an international audience, the choice of blog community is important, as is the frequency and quality of posts, and the technology used to ensure the blog gets picked up by the main search engines. Nonetheless, content syndication, where a blog's author makes all or part of its contents available for posting on other Web sites, is becoming a far more efficient way of disseminating information than e-mail lists and electronic newsletters.

Locally, the Internet also assists in the distribution of information. For some grassroots human rights activists who find it difficult or dangerous to receive hard-copy reports, accessing them in electronic format can be an effective solution (Whaley, 2000), despite the fact that filtering and blocking techniques used by state authorities often make it difficult for human rights organisations to download or even display online information.[14] Civil society information portals like Kubatana.net, which contains information that is accessible and relevant to local individuals and groups and is actively promoted, can increase the flow of information and news within a country where it is often difficult to access diverse views and opinions.

Taking Action

Disseminating information about human rights violations is the first step in human rights activism; the second and most essential step is action. The Internet is a good place for human rights organisations to encourage action, but it depends on timely and reliable information. Jamie Metzl highlighted this in the 1990s: "…accurate and timely information is an indispensable tool to human rights and an essential precondition for effective responsive action and the promotion of human rights, whether by organisations, individuals, governments or international institutions" (Metzl, 1996, p. 706).

The Internet helps make the responsive action of human rights activists more effective in three ways. First, it is used to promote traditional forms of off-line action such as letter writing, home government lobbying, and so forth. Second, it has provided opportunities to develop new forms of online action. Third, it is an ideal medium for the sharing of tactics.

Electronic urgent-action mailing lists have been operated by organisations such as Derechos (http://www.derechos.org) and Amnesty International for many years. Their objective is to encourage people to send letters and faxes, and to make telephone calls to those responsible for human rights violations. As well as facilitating faster and cheaper distribution, these allow organisations to reach a wider range of international supporters and to issue targeted action appeals. They also allow recipients to take advantage of computer applications to draft letters and to send faxes.

Nowadays, Internet-based activism is becoming more popular than the traditional forms of action. E-mail is taking over as the preferred mode of response for human rights activists to urgent-action appeals. In a survey of key South African Amnesty International activists, conducted at a meeting in July 2004, 64% of the 28 respondents said they were most likely to respond to an urgent-action alert by e-mail, 23% said they would post a letter, and 9% said they would send a fax (Lannon & Halpin, 2005). Organisations like Amnesty, whose main support base is amongst those with access to new technologies, have had to take cognizance of this trend.

Legitimate human rights organisations also engage in other forms of cyberactivism[15] or "normal, non-disruptive use of the Internet in support of an agenda or cause" (Arquilla & Ronfeldt, 2001, p. 241). They do this primarily by organising online petitions and e-mail actions targeting government authorities. Other more disruptive tactics, generally referred to as "hactivism" or electronic civil disobedience (Wray, 1999), are sometimes used by independent human rights activists or groups acting alone; these include tactics like the July 2005 virtual sit-in organised by the Electronic Disturbance Theater against anti-immigrant Web sites.[16] However, these tactics raise questions about ethics and the limits of freedom of expression on the Internet, just as civil disobedience tactics like blocking a road do in the real world (Katz-Lacabe & Lacabe, 2000).

The Internet is also used by human rights organisations to share information on tactics. A good example is the online database set up by the New Tactics in Human Rights project (http://www.newtactics.org/). The project, led by a diverse group of international organisations and human rights practitioners, aims to promote tactical innovation and strategic thinking within the international human rights community. As well as the tactics database, they also provide an electronic newsletter for periodic updates and an online discussion forum in which human rights advocates can discuss their experiences.

Organising, Supporting, and Protecting Human Rights Defenders

A third benefit of the Internet in human rights work is that it helps to organise, support, and protect human rights defenders. It does this by providing a means of communication between human rights workers and NGOs that is cheap, instant, and easy to use. Front Line, an international foundation for the protection of human rights defenders (http://www.

frontlinedefenders.org/), claim that people have been able to contact them from hiding using e-mail, and that the Internet has enabled them to get fast lobbying done in cases where people were imprisoned and in danger of being tortured. Indeed, part of their work is to provide technical assistance to human rights defenders in countries like Tunisia, where access to technology and freedom of association and expression are scarce, so that they can record human rights violations and provide information quickly and directly when they are at risk (Lannon, 2002).

Human rights defenders face the same computer risks as other users, including virus attacks, equipment breakdown, difficult physical environments, spamming, and hacking. During a workshop on information technology, electronic communications, and security at Front Line's 2003 Platform for Human Rights Defenders conference, participants highlighted the need for simple solutions to day-to-day problems like these. They also discussed how governments and other actors that are determined to undermine their work create problems for human rights defenders through surveillance, interception of e-mails, reading of computer files, deletion or distortion of information on Web sites, and identifying them as spammers to service providers (Front Line, 2003; Guerra, 2003).

One of the solutions developed to counteract these problems is the Martus human rights bulletin system (http://www.martus.org/). This is a free and open source technology tool that allows grassroots human rights defenders and activists to document human rights abuses quickly and securely. Anyone with basic experience of e-mail can record incidents; these are stored and replicated in multiple locations to safeguard against possible loss and attacks. Human rights groups can even decide what to make public and what should be kept private as they monitor and strive to reduce incidents of human rights abuse (Paik, 2005).

In Guatemala, where the widespread impunity for past human rights abuses has been seen as a major factor in a wave of new abuses, a number of NGOs have used Martus to help secure and protect information relating to events that took place during the pre-1996 civil war. Other projects include the Arizona Coalition against Domestic Violence's compilation of reports of murder-suicides in domestic-violence disputes, and ongoing efforts by the Human Rights Commission in Sri Lanka to monitor human rights violations in the north and east of the country.

Ultimately, what human rights defenders need is the ability to perform routine monitoring as this is more reliable than recording after a human rights crisis has exploded. New convergent technologies like mobile blogging and audio blogging (posting audio to a blog from a phone) have great potential in this area. Mobile blogs or "moblogs" that can be updated remotely from anywhere using a mobile phone or digital assistant can provide human rights defenders with the ability to record and disseminate information about human rights violations as they occur.

Finally, the importance of testimonies given or recorded by human rights defenders in advocacy work (McLagan, 2003) provides another basis for ICT usage. The use of testimonies grew in the 1990s, and with the advent of ICTs came new opportunities for recording and archiving. One of the more recent forms is video; footage has been used in courts, tribunals, legislative and executive bodies, and human rights commissions, as well as by the media and transnational organisations and solidarity networks. The online Witness archive (http://www.witness.org/) is one of the best sources of video advocacy material; it now consists of more than 1,000 hours of raw footage documenting a vast range of human rights abuses. Local human rights defenders in nearly 50 countries shot these, and they feature first-hand testimonies, interviews, and imagery about rights violations and conflict sites around the world.

Research and Analysis

The Internet is also a valuable research tool for human rights workers. Researchers now use it to retrieve information published by other organisations, to cross-check information with other research groups, and to make their own work available to the human rights community. Even for the general public, Web portals like Human Rights Internet (http://www. hri.ca/) and Banglarights.net can be efficient sources of information on a region, country, or specific human rights issue.

The Web has also become a valuable source of information from local newspapers about background data on legal or economic questions, and about intergovernmental and governmental reports (Whaley, 2000). There is also a growing number of online repositories of human rights information, including databases and documentation centres[16] that provide details of human rights treaties and conventions, case law collections, human rights impact assessment reports, and so on. Some, but not all, recognise that those wishing to access online resources may have limited technology and expertise; they may have unreliable or low bandwidth, or be working with old tools (such as an old version of a Web browser). Even still, attempts to survey what is available over the Internet can be a daunting task for human rights practitioners, given the amount of information and the breadth of online sources. Search engines and Web portals are now making the task of finding required information easier; dedicated human rights search engines like HURISEARCH (http://www.hurisearch.org/), which is hosted by the Swiss-based Human Rights Information and Documentation System International (HURIDOCS),[17] provide a single access point to all human rights information published by organisations worldwide.

While search engines and Web portals have greatly improved the retrieval of published human rights information, the electronic exchange of data and information[18] within the human rights community is less clear cut. In some cases there are nontechnical issues like confidentiality, privacy, and the safety of human rights defenders to keep in mind. In other cases there are tactical reasons why organisations are not willing to share information; it may form the basis for a report that is due for release at a later date, or there may be donor-driven demands to keep in mind. Sharing can sometimes be of great benefit; however, if organisations telling the same story pool their information, they can build a more complete picture of an event and ultimately a more forceful case against the perpetrators.

The key to the successful sharing of data and information within the human rights community is the use of standards. Clarity and meaning is important when human rights information is being shared (Halpin & Hick, 2000); even the inconsistent use of terminology like *inhuman treatment* and *persecution* can be a problem. Language is the most obvious reason for inconsistency, but quite often the difficulty is that the information is not sensitive or relevant to the local culture. HURIDOCS and other organisations have done a lot of work to address this through the development of event reporting standards (Dueck, Guzman, & Verstappen, 2001a) and thesauri (Dueck, Guzman, & Verstappen, 2001b). As more and more of the available information is stored as digital resources, the use of embedded metadata[19] with information about victims, types of abuse, places, and so forth becomes an important consideration.

Human Rights Education and Training

A fifth benefit of the Internet is in human rights education and training. Claude and Hick (2000) explain that human rights education is about more than information dissemination; it is helping people "to analyse the world around them, understand that human rights are a way to improve their lives and the lives of others, and to take action to prevent human rights violations" (p. 226). There has been a growing need and demand for training human rights organisations over the past number of years. As a result, there are now many examples of formal online human rights education programs where documents and lessons are provided online. Planned learning processes, centred around or supplemented by these, are designed to develop awareness of human rights and the capacity to act to further human rights aspirations (CEDAL, 1996).

Human rights education is defined by Flowers (2000, p. 35) as "all learning that contributes to the knowledge, skills, and values of human rights." It includes information dissemination, but it is a much more complex process that requires cognitive, emotional, and active learning (Mihr, 2004). Human rights education resource centres like the Human Rights Education Associates (HREA) Web site (http://www.hrea.org/) now go beyond the provision of teaching material for formal education and training of professional groups like the armed forces, human rights monitors, and health professionals. They also include online forums and links to other organisations and resources, and are designed to address the needs of nontraditional education sectors like community leaders and NGOs.

A collection of Web-based visual aids for human rights learning published online by HREA presents an interesting example of how the Internet can contribute to emotional learning.[20] It consists of an annotated compilation of photographs, paintings, drawings, prints, sculptures, and mixed media on human rights themes (Jawad, 2003), and was put together in order to further human rights learning through the viewing of such images and the environments in which violations take place. The images depict a variety of topics including war, genocide, child labour, and torture, and were created by people of all ages and nationalities.

Human rights education involves analysis through reflection on one's own situation. The mere gathering of knowledge is not enough for this; there also needs to be an awareness-building process, day-to-day examples, experience, and reflection (Freire, 1995).[21] A good example of how the Internet and other ICTs can be used to meet this challenge is Pambazuka News (http://www.pambazuka.org/), a weekly newsletter and platform for social justice in Africa. According to its editor, Firoze Manji of Fahamu (http://www.fahamu.org/), it is a response to the social division "that prevents the experiences of the greater part of humanity from being heard, and which, therefore, under-nourishes the discourse of those who do not have access to the technology" (Manji, 2005, p. 13). It helps organisations to find information and to disseminate their own material online by organising it into categories that reflect the subjects of concern to the constituency (these include human rights, refugees and forced migration, women and gender, health and HIV/AIDS, and education). But, in keeping with the need for emotional and active learning, Pambazuka News has also become a tool for advocacy in Africa. As part of the campaign for the ratification of the protocol on the Rights of Women in Africa, for example, two special issues were produced profiling important aspects of the protocol. In 2004, it also exploited the potential of the growing mobile phone market for social change; a system was developed to enable mobile phone users to sign an online petition, and an SMS service was developed to send information on the protocol to people who wanted to subscribe to the service (Manji, 2005).

The informal human rights education that was traditionally supplied by the media is also being greatly enhanced by participation in online newsgroups, chat groups, and various forms of civic journalism, including blogging. Marginalised and disadvantaged communities are now being supplied with human rights education materials from centralised online sources like Kubatana.net in Zimbabwe, or the Peoples Movement for Human Rights Education (http://www.pdhre.org/). The latter has even developed an innovative Human Rights Cities initiative to examine traditional beliefs, collective memory, and aspirations as related to the Universal Declaration of Human Rights.

Networking and Connectivity

Another very important benefit of the Internet for human rights movements is in networking. Formally constituted networks can have their own Web site, giving members the opportunity to discuss and share information. Even mailing lists and newsletters like Pambazuka News can help create a sense of community with other human rights activists and facilitate joint projects with other like-minded individuals and organisations (Katz-Lacabe & Lacabe, 2000). They also provide the opportunity for discussion with experts or people in the human rights field who may have specific expertise or knowledge.

Human Rights Internet claims that it communicates by phone, fax, mail, and the Internet with more than 5,000 organisations and individuals around the world working for the advancement of human rights.[22] While most of these will probably never engage in direct online communication with each other (not least because of the cost involved), there are plenty of international, regional, and national networks where online information flows between members are important. Networks like the Human Rights Network in Uganda (http://www.hurinet.or.ug/), whose mission is to build stronger linkages and cooperation between human rights groups, use the Internet as one of the mechanisms to achieve this. Interorganisational networks like these are nonhierarchical, and collectively and individually the members benefit from the increased exposure that a Web presence gives them.

Another aspect of the Internet that is proving to be of great benefit to some human rights activists and workers is Internet telephony or voice over IP (Internet protocol). One of the best-known service providers, Skype (http://www.skype.org/), provides a free program for making free calls over the Internet to anyone who also has Skype. This is a cheap and convenient way for activists to communicate, providing they have the bandwidth to support it. Without broadband access, however, its value is severely limited. Because the majority of the world's population does not have broadband access, they do not get to make free calls (Burnett, 2005).

The Importance of Information

While ICTs like the Internet have an important functional role in human rights movements, their value can easily be overjudged and is frequently overhyped. Technology is only a tool, and ICTs are just a means to an end for human rights organisations (Ball et al., 1997; Fleming, 2002; Manji, 2005). One of the most important considerations is the way in which these tools are used to manage information, since this is at the heart of what they do (Weyker, 2002). Coupled with the need to communicate, collaborate, and organise, it should provide the basis for ICT investment within human rights organisations.

The ability to access background information, training material, and other documentation online is an important asset to human rights organisations. From a network or movement perspective, being able to share information is equally important. Gauthier (2000) notes that in parts of the world where there is a lack of resources to set up and access traditional documentation centres, being able to feed data into online documentation centres where it can be analysed, classified, and redistributed means organisations are not working in isolation. To be usable, these centres must be well organised, of course, and ideally they should use standard formats to store and present information. HURIDOCS guidelines for recording information about human rights violations (Noval, 1993) are now being used by human rights and like-minded organisations all over the world, including large organisations like the UN High Commissioner for Refugees and the Council of Europe, NGOs like Amnesty International, and smaller groups. However, a lot more needs to be done to ensure consistent and effective management of human rights information throughout the movement.

While the Internet facilitates the gathering and dissemination of information, it does not help in its analysis. In fact, its use can contribute to another problem if the information is not managed properly: that of information overload. There is now more information available through which to build a campaign than ever before (Stoecker, 2000), but finding it, sifting it, evaluating it, and using it can be a time-consuming distraction. Search engines, Web portals, well-organised databases, and RSS aggregators all help, but for human rights organisations that have floods of electronic information pushed toward them, it is becoming increasingly necessary to "weed out or edit lower quality documents, ensure that action is coordinated, that the source is accurate, that follow-up is completed, and that processing is done effectively" (Sottas & Schonveld, 2000, p. 79).

When dealing with information online, reliability can also be a problem for human rights activists and organisations. The Internet environment lends itself particularly well to fabrication and distortion of information, anonymous information, and plagiarism (Chabanov, 2004; Dahlberg, 2001; Warnick, 1998). Some organisations might even be tempted to exaggerate the extent of human rights violations because of the competition for grants. There is even a concern that human rights data are viewed by some organisations as a private, commercial commodity to be used primarily for raising the organisations' own fundraising potential (European Co-ordination Committee on Human Rights Documentation [ECCHRD], 2001). Because of this, the circulation of information in open networks is in some cases diminishing rather than growing.

A lack of objectivity can also be a problem with many online information sources. Blogs, for example, generally represent one person's views, and while they often offer valuable commentary and insight into denials of human rights, their content cannot always be viewed as independent or impartial.

Audience Building and the Internet: Promises and Pitfalls

In Africa, the average cost of a local dial-up Internet account for 20 hours a month in 2005 was about $60 (including call charges). This is higher than the average African monthly salary (Manji, 2005). Nonetheless, despite the high initial costs necessary for the purchase of equipment and the price of connecting to the telecommunications network, Gauthier (2000) saw the Internet as providing African human rights organisations with a new method for working under very difficult conditions.

There are a variety of service-provision options and alternatives for human rights NGOs seeking to take advantage of ICTs. One is e-riders (http://www.eriders.net/), an ICT consultancy solution for small, mission-focused NGOs that cannot afford a full-time technology support person.[x] There are also projects that provide recommendations and software distribution based on a grassroots approach, such as NGO-in-a-Box (http://www.ngoinabox.org). This provides CD box sets of tools and materials based on the experiences of informed practitioners and field experts, and aims to tackle two primary issues: appropriate software selection, and access to such software and related documentation (Tactical Technology Collective, 2005).

One of the primary goals of NGO-in-a-Box is the promotion and distribution of free and open source software (FOSS) to the nonprofit sector. The free software concept, which refers to the user's freedom to run, copy, distribute, study, change, and improve the software (Lutfy, 2004), is based on the notion of adding to what others have done before. Like the human rights movement, it strives to remove restrictions on freedom, cooperation, and information sharing.

While ICTs, and in particular the Internet, are unrelated and irrelevant to the daily struggles of many poor and oppressed communities, they can still be useful for representative NGOs. Wasserman (2005) indicates that for the TAC, an organisation that appeals to the middle class despite its roots in the poor communities, the Internet has been instrumental in establishing and maintaining an important support base. Using the Internet to reach elites means it can build capacity, even beyond activist circles. However, in giving some groups increased access to elites, transnational human rights networks, funding agencies, and other key players, the Internet can sometimes create a greater disparity between the ICT haves and the have-nots. Unlike their counterparts in the North who benefit greatly from the instantaneous flow of information over the Internet, the majority of the Southern hemisphere, and in particular sub-Saharan Africa, lags behind in terms of technological development. There, NGOs often have extremely limited access to telephone lines, let alone computers or international connections. Out of necessity, therefore, Southern NGOs often allow their larger Northern counterparts to set the agenda and make key decisions. Thus, while ICTs like the Internet aid collective decision making, they also serve to concentrate power within a few organisations that collect human rights information and transmit it between the local groups and the transnational community.

Another difficulty faced by human rights movements and organisations is information protection. According to the Benetech Institute (2001), which developed Martus, much of the data collected by human rights groups never reaches its full potential or intended audience because a large part of it is lost. Reasons for loss include confiscation or destruction, neglect, passage of time, and lack of resources within grassroots groups to document and communicate violations systematically and securely. Computers eliminate some of these but introduce other risks like equipment failure, user errors, computer viruses, power surges, and arson attacks. While training and support for grassroots groups is part of the solution, other measures such as off-site storage must also be considered. Here again, the Internet becomes useful by providing the basis for software tools like Martus, which allows users to back up human rights data over the Internet to a secure server located in a different part of the world.

Censorship, Suveillance, and Security

Given the sensitivity of much of what they possess and the threat it could pose to the authorities, human rights organisations in many parts of the world are vulnerable to deliberate external attack. These attacks can take the form of communications interception, monitoring of activities, or physical raids by state agents or others opposed to the organisation's work (Mobbs, 2002)

In a February 2002 *New York Times* article, the human rights writer Michael Ignatieff (2002) observed that since September 11, 2001, the strength and relevance of the human rights movement has been under threat. In the post-September 11 reshaping of international order, human rights has been disconnected from questions of national security (Wilson, 2005), and their protection has been demoted by states all over the world in the interests of a worldwide "war on terror." Freedom of expression has also suffered; while it was not in an ideal state before September 11, there has been a vast increase in detentions and domestic spying powers over the past 5 years, justified as a part of the war on terror (Bhagwat, 2005). In Syria, Iran, Zimbabwe, China, Uganda, Tunisia (which hosted the second phase of the World Summit on the Information Society in 2005), and scores of other countries, the authorities censor the media and impose restrictions curtailing freedom of access to information, freedom of association, and freedom of movement of human rights defenders. Even in countries of the democratised West, including the United Kingdom, Australia, and the United States (where it is now permissible for the authorities to request all kinds of personal and private information), antiterrorism legislation severely restricts the freedom of speech of those who question or oppose government policy.

The expansion of counterterrorist activities has also accelerated the rise of a more bureaucratic cybercontrolled society (Ishay, 2005). Most authoritarian regimes now have the technical means to censor the Internet. Material deemed to be illegal or subversive is automatically blocked by filters in countries like Vietnam, where it is not possible to access Web sites that criticise the government, expose corruption, or talk about human rights abuses (Reporters

Without Borders, 2005). While activists and bloggers are increasingly making use of the Internet, e-mail, and text messages to publicize human rights abuses, organise protests, and exchange political information and ideas, Human Rights Watch (2005) reports that in many countries like Iran, the government regularly detains and imprisons online journalists, bloggers, and Web-site administrators.

In environments like these, human rights organisations need to be particularly vigilant about their information security. As Mobbs (2002) notes, those seeking covert access to an organisation's information repositories will be often deterred by good access barriers because of the additional time required to circumvent them. However, when the state acts, it does not have this problem. It works openly and generally has the staff and specialist tools to gain access. Still, while securing an organisation's premises, computer room, storage devices, and data files does not provide protection, these access barriers can provide vulnerable NGOs with time to take other action, like calling legal assistance or alerting international solidarity networks.

Governments can also easily intercept electronic communications. They can do this by trapping transmitted information packets at publicly accessible Internet nodes through line tapping or disclosure by Internet service providers, or by intercepting the main lines that connect their country to the rest of the world. To protect transmitted information and messages from being read or altered, encryption, a means of encoding information so that it cannot be decoded without a "key," has become a necessary and seamless part of e-mail usage and Web browsing.[y] However, there is now a real danger that the use of difficult-to-crack encryption technologies for the electronic transmission of information may be outlawed. Criminalizing the unauthorised use of these strong encryption products is a threat to the work of human rights organisations as the Internet becomes a more integral part of how they operate (Lane, 2000; Marthoz, 2002).

New tools and techniques are being developed and deployed to address the security needs of human rights defenders and groups. These include Web-based services to allow sending and receiving secure e-mails (Hushmail at http://www.hushmail.com is one example), proxy servers and anonymous Internet communication systems that protect Web browsers against Internet surveillance (such as Tor, http://www.tor.eff.org),[z] and firewall tools to protect against unauthenticated access from the outside world.[aa] Without these, activists working hard to secure human rights might actually be jeopardizing their cause as well as the safety of individuals they are trying to protect (Mladen, Guerra, & Young, 2002). Within the human rights movement, the cost of leaving information unprotected, or of transmitting communications without privacy and security, can often be very high.

Conclusion

Despite globalisation, ICTs, and the tremendous expansion of the human rights regime, international attention to human rights issues remain "spotty" (Bob, 2002). On the one hand, the Internet offers the potential to address this imbalance by providing grassroots organisations with the opportunity to create global awareness and strengthen their own efforts. On the other, the ability to exploit its potential is linked to the infrastructure, resources, and skills at the organisation's disposal, and the freedom they are allowed to exercise their own rights to organise and communicate.

Efforts to reduce the gap between communities who can make effective use of ICTs and those who cannot is seen as essential for development (United Nations Development Program [UNDP], 2002). In this context it can also be viewed as essential for the enjoyment of human rights, particularly economic and social rights. As these rights are inextricably linked to all other rights, including civil and political rights, the use of ICTs to increase civic engagement and to challenge oppressive and discriminatory state practices is also a fundamental component of development for all.

Internationally, the human rights movement has always been quick to explore new opportunities presented by ICTs. Human rights NGOs that enjoy widespread moral and financial support have, over the decades, used fax machines, e-mail, Web sites, and aggregated news feeds to disseminate targeted information, rally popular outrage, and bring pressure to bear on norm-violating governments. In open societies, human rights initiatives have benefited from the increased visibility provided by ICTs (Ishay, 2005). The fast, global spread of images of abuse in Abu Ghraib prison, Iraq, in April 2004 showed how new forms of information dissemination lead to international outrage and ultimately to effective pressure on the perpetrators of the abuse.

International network movements like CRIN and OMCT offer grassroots organisations online information, expertise, and solidarity. But for domestic movements of people living in poverty and experiencing human rights violations first hand, accessing these resources is not always easy. While ICTs make it possible to maintain links and share resources across geographical and cultural borders, NGOs need to be skillful at using limited bandwidth effectively. The difficulties are compounded by restrictions imposed on democratic social movements, and in particular human rights movements, which have increased since September 11, 2001. Even when human rights defenders do manage to get online (often at great risk to themselves and those whose rights they are defending), it can be hard for them to be heard amongst all the "noise" in cyberspace. Knowing what to do with sensitive data, who to send communiqués to, and how and where to post information are all critically important. For groups who are working to build their cases, being able to access online information efficiently can be a major factor in how successful they are. Without the training and support that enable them to do all these effectively, attempting to use the Internet can be like walking into a marketplace blindfolded.

The international intergovernmental and nongovernmental organisations have a role to play in helping grassroots human rights activists use the Internet effectively. They need to be cognizant of the resources that are at the disposal of their partners in developing countries: in their Web-site design and e-mail transmissions, as well as in their content management. They need to avoid crowding out the weaker participants in the online human rights networks, and to provide a space for everyone to contribute to the human rights discourse. The use of ICTs to communicate and inform implicitly favours the dominant voices of the North. For this reason alone the global human rights movement needs policies and initiatives that promote a more egalitarian use of ICT resources so that grassroots organisations and activists can ensure the movement remains relevant to their struggles.

Overall, the Internet helps human rights movements to bring greater pressure to bear on norm-violating actors. It does this through targeted information flows, and new and increased levels of activism. It allows more data to be gathered and recorded securely, and it provides access to background reports and information. It also presents greater opportunity for organisations to pool resources and to benefit from the experiences and expertise of others in the movement. But organisations in the South need help in overcoming access, adoption, and appropriation problems. Developing expertise within local and regional NGOs on how to gather human rights data in a secure environment, analyse the data themselves, build their own databases, and exchange information if and when they wish to is crucial. It is also important that everyone in the human rights movement uses a common language to exchange human rights information; if everyone is using the same words, then data can be collected more efficiently, and information can be accessed more easily.

Organisations like HURIDOCS started working on standards for human rights event reporting in the 1990s. It now needs to be taken a step further by looking at new Internet technologies and opportunities for data gathering and information exchange. This includes the use of metadata to embed usable data into normal Web pages in order to link human rights information from sources all over the world. Using the right technologies, human rights organisations telling the same story with different information can potentially pool together their information and build a more complete picture of what is happening in any part of the world.

Ultimately, one of the keys to the effective use of the Internet by human rights organisations is the development of the necessary information management and research skills within the movement. What is important is not the technology; it is being able to define relevant information, to know how and where to seek it, and to have the capacities and skills to use it. Organisations should not base strategies on technology, but rather they should identify their information needs based on an understanding of what they can manage. The processes they put in place in support of strategic objectives should allow them to take advantage of technologies like the Internet, but the tools should not dictate the strategy.

Further research is required into whether or not technologies like the Internet have made a difference to information and communications flows within human rights movements. One way to do this might be to look at new advocacy movements such as those working on rights issues surrounding HIV/AIDS and compare them to the pre-Internet movements like antitorture. Without question, there are other factors at play in determining the strategies and tactics adopted by these newer movements, but the role of the Internet is one that cannot be discounted.

References

Abdul-Raheem, T. (2005). Africa: The many challenges to human rights in Africa. *Pambazuka News, 233*. Retrieved December 19, 2005, from http://www.pambazuka. org/index.php?id=30839

Agre, P. A. (2002). Real-time politics: The Internet and the political process. *Information Society, 18*(5), 311-331.

Amnesty International. (2000). *People's Republic of China: The crackdown on Falun Gong and other so-called "heretical organizations."* Retrieved August 4, 2005, from http://web.amnesty.org/aidoc/aidoc_pdf.nsf/Index/ASA170112000ENGLISH/$File/ASA1701100.pdf

Arquilla, J., & Ronfeldt, D. (2001). *Networks and netwars: The future of terror, crime and militancy.* Santa Monica, CA: RAND.

Ball, P., Girouard, M., & Chapman, A. (1997). Information technology, information management, and human rights: A response to Metzl. *Human Rights Quarterly, 19*(4), 836-859.

Baxi, U. (2000). Human rights: Suffering between movements and markets. In R. Cohen & S. M. Rai (Eds.), *Global social movements* (pp. 33-45). London: The Athlone Press.

Benetech Institute. (2001). *Martus: Human rights bulletin system. Summary.* Retrieved August 4, 2005, from http://www.benetech.org/download/Martus_1-Pager_Eng_070201.doc

Bhagwat, N. (2005). *Freedom of expression in an era of state terror.* Paper presented at the Forum of Writers, Poets, Publishers and Human Rights Organizations at the Fourth Conference on Freedom of Expression, Istanbul, Turkey.

Bob, C. (2002). Globalization and the social construction of human rights campaigns. In A. Brysk (Ed.), *Globalization and human rights* (pp. 133-147). Berkeley, CA: University of California Press.

Bob, C. (2005). *The marketing of rebellion: Insurgents, media, and international activism.* Cambridge, United Kingdom: Cambridge University Press.

Brysk, A. (1993). From above and below: Social movements, the international system, and human rights in Argentina. *Comparative Political Studies, 26*(3), 263-265.

Brysk, A. (2002). Globalization and human rights: Transnational threats and opportunities. In A. Brysk (Ed.), *Globalization and human rights* (). CA: University of California Press.

Burgerman, S. D. (1998). Mobilizing principles: The role of transnational activists in promoting human rights principles. *Human Rights Quarterly, 20*(4), 905-924.

Burnett, P. (2005). Talking to the world for free, or talking at the world's expense. *Pambazuka News, 230*. Retrieved December 2, 2005, from http://www.pambazuka.org/index.php?id=30400

Cammaerts, B., & Van Audenhove, L. (2003). *ICT-usage of transnational social movements in the networked society: To organise, to mediate and to influence* (No. ASCoR/TNO-STB). Amsterdam: EMTEL2 Key-Deliverable.

Cassese, A. (1986). *International law in a divided world.* Oxford: Clarendon Press.

CEDAL (Centro de Estudios Democráticos de América Latina). (1996). *Towards a pedagogy of human rights education.* Paper presented at the International Consultation on the Pedagogical Foundations of Human Rights Education, La Catalina, Costa Rica.

Chabanov, S. (2004). *Information: An obstacle for human rights?* Retrieved December 27, 2004, from http://www.eumap.org/journal/features/2004/infohr1/infohr2/

Charlesworth, H. (2002). Author! Author! A response to David Kennedy. *Harvard Human Rights Journal, 15*, 127-131.

Clark, B. (2005). Kubatana.net: Creating a "one stop shop" for information. *i4d: Human Rights and ICTs, 3*(7), 15-16.

Clarke Brill, M. (2005). Africa trip report: Exploring the emerging social movements in Africa at the Third African Social Forum. *Africa Action.* Retrieved February 24, 2006, from http://www.africaaction.org/resources/page.php?op=read&documentid=855&type=6&issues=3

Claude, R. P., & Hick, S. (2000). Human rights education on the Internet: Its day has come. In S. Hick, E. F. Halpin, & E. Hoskins (Eds.), *Human rights and the Internet* (pp. 225-237). Houndmills: MacMillan Press Ltd.

Cohen, R., & Rai, S. M. (2000). Global social movements: Towards a cosmopolitan politics. In R. Cohen & S. M. Rai (Eds.), *Global social movements* (pp. 3-17). London: The Athlone Press.

Dahlberg, L. (2001). Computer-mediated communication and the public sphere: A critical analysis. *Journal of Computer-Mediated Communication, 7*(1). Retrieved September 17, 2006, from http://jcmc.indiana.edu/vol7/issue1/dahlberg.html

Diani, M. (1992). The concept of social movement. *The Sociological Review, 40*, 1-25.

Diani, M. (2003). Social movements, contentious actions and social networks: "From metaphor to substance"? In M. Diani & D. McAdam (Eds.), *Social movements and networks: Relational approaches to collective action* (pp. 1-18). Oxford, United Kingdom: Oxford University Press.

Diani, M., & McAdam, D. (Eds.). (2003). *Social movements and networks: Relational approaches to collective action.* Oxford, United Kingdom: Oxford University Press.

Dueck, J., Guzman, M., & Verstappen, B. (2001a). *HURIDOCS events standards formats: A tool for documenting human rights violations* (2nd Rev. ed.). Versoix, Switzerland: HURIDOCS.

Dueck, J., Guzman, M., & Verstappen, B. (2001b). *Micro-thesauri: A tool for documenting human rights violations* (2nd ed.). Versoix, Switzerland: HURIDOCS.

European Co-ordination Committee on Human Rights Documentation (ECCHRD). (2001). *Minutes of the 24th Meeting of the European Co-ordination Committee on Human Rights Documentation (ECCHRD).* Retrieved August 4, 2005, from http://www2.law.uu.nl/english/sim/library/ecchrd/Minutes%20in%20pdf/minutes%2024.pdf

Fleming, S. (2002). Information and communication technologies (ICTs) and development in the south: Potential and current realities. *Electronic Journal on Information Systems in Developing Countries, 10*(1), 1-10.

Flowers, N. (2000). *The human rights education handbook: Effective practices for learning, action, and change.* Minneapolis, MN: University of Minnesota, Human Rights Resource Center.

Freire, P. (1995). *Pedagogy of hope, relieving pedagogy of the oppressed.* New York: Continuum.

Friedman, E. J., & McAdam, D. (1992). Collective identity and activism: Networks, choices, and the life of a social movement. In A. D. Morris & M. McClurg Mueller (Eds.), *Frontiers in social movement theory* (pp. 156-173). New Haven, CT: Yale University Press.

Front Line. (2003). *Coping with surveillance, electronic communications and security: Practical security measures for HRDs.* Paper presented at the Second Dublin Platform for Human Rights Defenders. Frontline: The International Foundation for the Protection of Human Rights Defenders, Dublin, Ireland.

Garden Networks. (2004). *Breaking through the "golden shield."* Retrieved December 27, 2004, from *http://www.eumap.org/journal/features/2004/infohr1/infohr2/*

Gauthier, J. (2000). The Internet in Africa: A turning point in the struggle for human rights? In S. Hick, E. F. Halpin, & E. Hoskins (Eds.), *Human rights and the Internet* (pp. 91-103). Houndmills: MacMillan Press Ltd.

Gould, R. V. (1993). Collective action and network structure. *American Sociological Review, 58*(2), 182-196.

Guerra, R. (2003). *Information technology, electronic communications and security.* Paper presented at the Second Dublin Platform for Human Rights Defenders. Frontline: The International Foundation for the Protection of Human Rights Defenders, Dublin, Ireland.

Halpin, E. F. (2003a). An evaluation of the Child Rights Information Network: Examining information management in a global NGO. Part 1. *Canadian Journal of Library and Information Science, 27*(3), 25-39.

Halpin, E. F. (2003b). An evaluation of the Child Rights Information Network: Examining information management in a global NGO. Part 2. *Canadian Journal of Library and Information Science, 27*(4), 31-54.

Halpin, E. F., & Hick, S. (2000). Information: An essential tool for human rights work. In S. Hick, E. F. Halpin, & E. Hoskins (Eds.), *Human rights and the Internet* (pp. 238-250). Houndmills: MacMillan Press Ltd.

Hick, S., Halpin, E. F., & Hoskins, E. (Eds.). (2000). *Human rights and the Internet.* Houndmills: MacMillan Press Ltd.

Hick, S., & McNutt, J. (Eds.). (2002). *Advocacy, activism and the Internet.* Chicago: Lyceum Press.

Human Rights Watch. (2005). *False freedom: Online censorship in the Middle East and North Africa.* Author.

Ignatieff, M. (2002, February 5). Is the human rights era ending? *New York Times,* (late ed.), Section A, p. 25.

Internet usage statistics: The big picture. World Internet users and population stats. (2005). *Internet World Stats.* Retrieved August 4, 2005, from http://www.internetworldstats.com/stats.htm

Ishay, M. R. (2005). Promoting human rights in the era of globalization and interventions: The changing space of struggle. *Globalizations, 1*(2), 181-193.

Jawad, R. (2003). *Web-based visual aids for human rights learning.* Retrieved February 13, 2006, from http://www.hrea.org/erc/Library/visualaids.htm

Jorgensen, R. F., Lindholt, H., & Lindholt, L. (2004). *Information and communication technologies as human rights enablers.* Retrieved December 14, 2004, from http://www.eumap.org/journal/features/2004/infohr/iactahre/

Kaldor, M., Anheier, H., & Glasius, M. (2003). Global civil society in an era of regressive globalisation. In H. Anheier, M. Glasius, & M. Kaldor (Eds.), *Global civil society yearbook 2003* (pp. 3-33). Oxford, United Kingdom: Oxford University Press.

Katz-Lacabe, M., & Lacabe, M. (2000). Doing human rights online: The Derechos cyberbirth. In S. Hick, E. F. Halpin, & E. Hoskins (Eds.), *Human rights and the Internet* (pp. 65-75). Houndmills: MacMillan Press Ltd.

Keck, M. E., & Sikkink, K. (1998). *Activists beyond borders: Advocacy networks in international politics.* Ithaca, NY: Cornell University Press.

Kennedy, D. (2002). The international human rights movement: Part of the problem. *Harvard Human Rights Journal, 15*, 101-125.

Lane, G. (2000). Human rights and the Internet in Europe. In S. Hick, E. F. Halpin, & E. Hoskins (Eds.), *Human rights and the Internet* (pp. 116-128). Houndmills: MacMillan Press Ltd.

Lannon, J. (2002). *Technology and ties that bind: The impact of the Internet on non-governmental organisations working to combat torture.* Unpublished manuscript, University of Limerick, Ireland.

Lannon, J., & Halpin, E. F. (2005). *The evolution of human rights activism in the Internet age.* Paper presented at the Association of Internet Researchers. Internet Research 6.0: Generations, Chicago.

Li, X. (1996). "Asian values" and the universality of human rights. *Report from the Institue for Philosophy and Public Policy, 16*(2). Retrieved September 25, 2006, from http://www.publicpolicy.umd.edu/IPPP/li.htm

Lutfy, M. (2004). Free software for NGOs. *Virtual Activism E-Newsletter, 12.* Retrieved December 28, 2005, from http://www.virtualactivism.org/articles/freesoftware-matthieu.htm

Manji, F. (2005). Human rights in South Africa: Harnessing ICTs for social justice. *i4d: Human Rights and ICTs, 3*(7), 12-14.

Manji, F., Jaffer, M., & Njuguna, E. N. (2000). *Strengthening human rights organisations in Africa: Challenges of the new technologies.* Canada: International Development Research Centre (IDRC).

Maran, R. (1998). The role of non-governmental organisations. In B. Dunér (Ed.), *An end to torture: Strategies for its eradication.* London: Zed Books.

Marthoz, J.-P. (2002). *11 September 2001: The aftermath. Consequences on freedom of information.* Retrieved December 21, 2005, from http://www.unesco.org/webworld/points_of_views/050802_marthoz.shtml

McLagan, M. (2003). Human rights, testimony, and transnational publicity. *The Scholar and Feminist Online, 1.* Retrieved December 21, 2005, from http://www.barnard.edu/sfonline/ps/printmmc.htm

Metzl, J. F. (1996). Information technology and human rights. *Human Rights Quarterly, 18*(4), 705-746.

Mihr, A. (2004). *Human rights education: Methods, institutions, culture and evaluation.* Institut für Politkwissenschaft, Otto-von-Guericke- Universität.

Mladen, C., Guerra, R., & Young, J. (2002). Privacy and security: New technologies for NGOs. *Rights News Online, 24*(1). Retrieved September 25, 2006, from http://www. columbia.edu/cu/humanrights/publications/publications.htm

Mobbs, P. (2002). *Participating with safety briefings no. 1: Introducing information security.* Association for Progressive Communications.

Norris, P. (2001). *Digital divide: Civic engagement, information poverty and the Internet worldwide.* New York: Cambridge University Press.

Noval, A. M. (1993). *HURIDOCS standard formats for the recording and exchange of bibliographic information concerning human rights.* Versoix, Switzerland: HURIDOCS.

O'Donnell, S. (2001). Analysing the Internet and the public sphere: The case of Womenslink. *Javnost: The Public, 8*(1), 39-58.

Paik, S. (2005). Martus human rights bulletin system: Witness for social justice. *i4d: Human Rights and ICTs, 3*(7), 6-7.

Perry, M. J. (1997). Are human rights universal? The relativist challenge and related matters. *Human Rights Quarterly, 19*(3), 461-509.

Reporters Without Borders. (2005). *Handbook for bloggers and cyber-dissidents.* Author.

Rosenblum, P. (2000). Teaching human rights: Ambivalent activism, multiple discourses, and lingering dilemmas. *Harvard Human Rights Journal, 15*, 301-315.

Sassen, S. (2004). Local actors in global politics. *Current Sociology, 52*(4), 649-670.

Scott, A., & Street, J. (2001). From media politics to e-protest? The use of popular culture and new media in parties and social movements. In F. Webster (Ed.), *Culture and politics in the information age: A new politics?* London: Routledge.

Selian, A. N. (2002). *ICTs in support of human rights, democracy and good governance.* International Telecommunications Union.

Shelton, D. (2002). Protecting human rights in a globalised world. *Boston College International and Comparative Law Review, 25*(2), 273-322.

Siraj, S. (2005). ICT and human rights promotion in Bangladesh: Democratising force of ICT. *i4d: Human Rights and ICTs, 3*(7), 27-29.

Smith, J. (1997). Characteristics of the modern transnational social movement sector. In J. Smith, C. Chatfield, & R. Pagnucco (Eds.), *Transnational social movement and global politics: Solidarity beyond the state* (pp. 42-58). Syracuse, NY: Syracuse University Press.

Sottas, E., & Schonveld, B. (2000). Information overload: How increased information flows affect the work of the human rights movement. In S. Hick, E. F. Halpin, & E. Hoskins (Eds.), *Human rights and the Internet* (pp. 76-88). Houndmills: MacMillan Press Ltd.

Srinivasan, S. (2004). *Blocking the truth: The Chinese government is sending up a satellite to block transmissions about Falun Gong.* Retrieved August 4, 2005, from http://english. epochtimes.com/news/4-3-17/20365.html

Stoecker, R. (2000). *Cyberspace vs face to face: Community organizing in the new millennium.* Paper presented at the COMM-ORG: The On-Line Conference on Community Organizing and Development.

Surman, M., & Reilly, K. (2003). *Appropriating the Internet for social change: Towards the strategic use of networked technologies by transnational civil society organizations.* Information Technology and International Cooperation Program, Social Science Research Council.

Tactical Technology Collective. (2005). *NGO-in-a-box Phase 2: Concept paper.* Retrieved December 21, 2005, from *http://ngoinabox.org/system/files?file=NGO-in-a-box-ConceptPaper2.pdf*

Tharoor, S. (1999). Are human rights universal? *World Policy Journal, 16*(4), 1-6.

United Nations Development Program (UNDP). (2002). *Driving information and communications technology for development: A UNDP agenda for action 2000-2001.* New York: Author.

Warnick, B. (1998). Appearance or reality? Political parody on the Web in campaign '96. *Critical Studies in Mass Communication, 15*(3), 306-324.

Wasserman, H. (2005). Connecting African activism with global networks: ICTs and South African social movements. *Africa Development, 30*(1 & 2), 163-182.

Weyker, S. (2002). The ironies of information technology: The opportunities and pitfalls of information technology for human rights. In A. Brysk (Ed.), *Globalization and human rights* (pp. 115-132). CA: University of California Press.

Whaley, P. (2000). Human rights NGOs: Our love-hate relationship with the Internet. In S. Hick, E. F. Halpin, & E. Hoskins (Eds.), *Human rights and the Internet* (pp. 30-40). Houndmills: MacMillan Press Ltd.

Wilson, R. A. (2005). Human rights in the "War on Terror." In R. A. Wilson (Ed.), *Human rights in the "War on Terror"* (pp. 1-36). Cambridge, United Kingdom: Cambridge University Press.

Wray, S. (1999). On electronic civil disobedience. *Peace Review, 11*(1), 107-111.

Yates, V. (2005). Child Rights Information Network (CRIN): "Right" from the beginning. *i4d: Human Rights and ICTs, 3*(7), 12-14.

Endnotes

[1]   Information and communication technologies is a broad term, usually understood to encompass all the technologies that facilitate the processing and transfer of information and communication services.

[2]   The Internet refers to both the technical infrastructure of worldwide digital networks, and the use to which this infrastructure is put. Current uses include, but are not limited to, sharing computer resources independently of location, distributing and accessing information via the World Wide Web, and communicating using electronic mail, distribution lists, and newsgroups.

3   A Weblog or blog is a personal Web site on which information is posted by an indi-
     vidual, as in a diary. Postings in a blog are typically arranged in chronological order,
     with the most recent additions at the top of the page. The activity of updating a blog
     is known as blogging.

4   The Convention on the Rights of the Child was adopted by the United Nations General
     Assembly Resolution 44/25 on November 20, 1989.

5   OMCT is the world's largest coalition of nongovernmental organisations fighting
     against arbitrary detention, torture, extrajudicial executions, forced disappearances,
     and other forms of violence. Its global network includes almost 300 local, national,
     and regional organisations.

6   Falun Gong is also known as Falun Dafa.

7   S. Chinn, Falun Dafa Information Centre, New York, personal communication, March
     24, 2004

8   Peer-to-peer technologies refer to networks in which computers can share information
     without having to go through a third computer (server).

9   A proxy server is an intermediary between a Web user and the Internet. One of its main
     functions is to keep the user's local area network secure through the use of firewall
     software. It is also useful in cases where anonymity is needed since it hides the local
     network and user's identity.

10   A wiki is a collection of Web pages that can be created and edited by anyone through
     a browser. The term comes from the Hawaiian term *wiki wiki*, meaning rapidly.

11   The term podcasting comes from an amalgam of Apple's *iPod* and *broadcasting*. It
     is a method of publishing files to the Internet and allowing the receipt of new files
     automatically using an iPod device. It is used mostly for audio files.

12   A listserv is a communication tool that offers its members the opportunity to post
     information, comments, or questions on predetermined topics and discussions to a
     large number of people at the same time. When something is posted to the listserv, it
     is distributed to all of the other people on the list.

13   RSS (really simple syndication) is a family of file formats for Web syndication of
     information links that is used by news Web sites and blogs. Internet users or other
     Web sites can subscribe to Web sites that provide RSS feeds of information of interest
     to them instead of browsing to find the information.

14   For a comprehensive description of censorship and how to circumvent it, see Reporters
     Without Borders (2005).

15   Alternatively called electronic advocacy, netactivism, and e-advocacy (Hick & McNutt,
     2002)

16   A virtual sit-in consists of people using software that automatically requests a Web
     page over and over in an attempt to make the Web page unavailable to other users.
     According to the Electronic Disturbance Theater, over 27,000 people took part in the
     July 2005 action. See http://www.thing.net/~rdom/ecd/ecd.html (retrieved February
     24, 2006).

17   A database is a collection of records held on a computer. It contains structured infor-
     mation organised in a consistent manner. A documentation centre, which may or may

not be computer based, contains free-form text information. Databases are organised in such a manner as to facilitate searching for a particular record or set of records, whereas documentation centres rely on cataloguing and/or classification of documents to make information retrieval possible.

[18] HURIDOCS is a global network that facilitates the handling, dissemination, and exchange of information by other human rights organisations. It functions as a decentralised network in which human rights organisations can handle information according to their own requirements. It also develops tools and techniques for information handling and provides support for the establishment and maintenance of information systems and documentation centres by other organisations (http://www.huridocs.org/).

[19] Data are raw materials that are used to produce information; information is data that has been organised, processed, and interpreted so one can draw conclusions and understand implications.

[20] Metadata are data about data. They describe how, when, by whom, and in what format data were recorded. Metadata are added in a Web page or stored in a database; they are available for searching but are not displayed.

[21] See http://www.hrea.org/erc/Library/display.php?doc_id=1257&category_id=18&category_type=3 (retrieved February 13, 2006)

[22] Cited in Mihr (2004)

[23] See http://www.hri.ca/about/intro.shtml (retrieved December 20, 2005)

[24] Ungana-Afrika, a South African service provider, is one example of an organisation providing e-rider solutions (http://www.ungana-afrika.org/).

[25] While the integrated use of encryption techniques such as pretty good privacy (PGP) can successfully hide the content of a message transmission, they do not always guarantee complete anonymity or protection. For example, most e-mail programs that use PGP will encrypt the message contents but not the details of the sender or recipient that are contained in the message header.

[26] Tor uses a concept known as "onion routing," which takes the idea of proxy servers to an additional level of complexity. Each request made through an onion-routing network goes through 2 to 20 additional randomly selected computers, making it difficult to discover what computer originated a request (taken from Reporters Without Borders, 2005).

[27] The security edition of NGO-in-a-Box (http://security.ngoinabox.org), prepared by Front Line Defenders and the Tactical Technology Collective, includes most of these tools. This project provides a variety of FOSS to help organisations and individuals improve their computer and information management operations, stability, costs, and security.

Chapter IX

ICT-Enabled Education in Africa:
A Sober Reflection on the Development Challenges

Shafika Isaacs, SchoolNet Africa, South Africa

Abstract

This essay prompts critical thinking on the way ICT-enabled education programs in Africa have been conceptualized and implemented. It reflects mainly on the experiences of the African SchoolNet movement over the past decade. It highlights important lessons and demonstrates the beneficial effects of technology-enhanced learning programs on African learners and teachers who have had the privilege of being included in SchoolNet initiatives. However, it also shows that the accumulated interventions and programs to date remain insignificant in scale to catalyze a resounding shift toward resolving the crisis in Africa's education systems; it makes the case for integrated system-wide, locally led approaches that soberly takes account of the challenges imposed by globalization. The chapter traces the historical evolution of frameworks to promote African inclusion in the information society, and allusions are specifically made to the emergence of the NEPAD eSchools, and the Global eSchools and Communities Initiative of the UN ICT Task Force, which hold the potential for advancing the frontiers of learning in Africa. Here, the author emphasizes, however, that these new initiatives need to draw on the accumulated learning and experience of the SchoolNet movement over the past 10 years in Africa to succeed. Finally, the chapter raises the dearth of evidence-based research made in Africa by Africans who would verify or refute the case for stronger investment in ICTs for education. It then proffers suggestions on areas for further research.

Introduction

Human resources are the essential infrastructure, without which technology means nothing. (Castells, 2001, p. 155)

The current practice of applying new information and communication technologies in the education systems in Africa is cause for concern. Much of the existing interventions have largely, although not exclusively, been informed by the discourse on bridging the digital divide, ICT for development (ICT4D), and their concomitant supply-side approaches mainly suggested by international donors, and private-sector and development agencies. Often these engagements have not clarified Africa's vision for technology-enhanced learning beyond the setting of numerical targets for universal access and ICT literacy; neither have they been integrated within debates on achieving development goals beyond the narrow scope of digital-divide issues. Indeed, ICTs offer the potential for substantial improvement in education access and delivery, particularly in a developing-economy context. However, there remain obstacles of a systemic nature that militate against the realization of this potential. This systemic context is influenced by a parallel Northern-led discourse on bridging the digital divide on the one hand, and, in contradiction, an imposing framework of globalization that continues to foster social exclusion on the other hand.

This chapter critically discusses Africa's experiences with ICT for education (ICT4E) initiatives in current schooling systems. Because the author has been intimately involved in the African SchoolNet movement, there is a strong bias regarding this experience over the past 10 years. The chapter treats examples of the successful application of ICTs in African schools and their actual and potential developmental spin-offs with caution and warns of the disconnection with glaring social, infrastructural, economic, and political realities that militate against further system-wide success. The chapter further provides perspectives on future potential trends in ICT for education in African schools and concludes with proposals for Africa to proceed far more ambitiously in its drive to make the next century a truly African century.[1]

Context

The global context within which ICTs enhance and support education systems in the developing world is influenced by complex global, economic, political, and social forces that are intertwined with rapid technological innovation and diffusion. The emergence of globalization, shifts in learning and education paradigms, and shifts toward neoliberal economic-policy frameworks to support education delivery combine as powerful contextual influencing factors that affect the way in which ICTs have been adopted and diffused to support learning, teaching, and education systems in Africa.

Globalization and the Digital Divide

A general consensus prevails, albeit not unchallenged, that the world economy is in transition toward a global knowledge-based society that has been profoundly influenced by economic, social, political, and cultural globalization over the past three decades. It is widely believed that the rapid growth and impact of digital technologies have created the impetus for globalization and fueled exponential growth in society's ability to produce, consume, exchange, and distribute information and knowledge.

Castells (1999) asserts that new ICTs are at the root of new productivity sources, new organizational forms, and the construction of a global economy where brain power is seen as a prime resource and an increasingly dominant source of trade and global competitive advantage. Mansell and Wehn (1998) suggest that the term knowledge society has been coined to shift the emphasis from ICTs as determinants or drivers of change to technologies designed and implemented by people within their social, economic, and technological contexts. The rapid growth, innovation, and diffusion of ICTs takes place within existing uneven, embedded social relations, and a number of processes within the ICT sector contribute to continued disparities in the global distribution of wealth and economic power.

The digital divide is a broad allusion to the skewed distribution in the production, access, and consumption of ICTs as mechanisms for social and economic development between and within countries. The concept also incorporates disparities in skill levels in the production and consumption of ICTs, literacy levels in the use of ICTs, varying constraints in enabling environments to promote ICT access and use, and the disparities in digital local content, particularly in countries with diverse multilingual communities. Hewitt de Alcantara (2001) correctly asserts that the digital divide is a function of existing development and socioeconomic divides, and within the digital divide itself, there are further manifestations of social imbalances biased against people in non-Latin language groups, rural communities, and girls and women. Hafkin and Taggert (2001) demonstrate how the digital divide is also a gender divide through extensive differential access, use, and production of digital technologies between girls and women in comparison with boys and men.

Table 1. The new schooling paradigm (Source: Haddad & Draxler, 2002, p. 8)

From	To
A school building	A knowledge infrastructure (schools, labs, radio, television, Internet museums...)
Classrooms	Individual learners
A teacher (as provider of knowledge)	A teacher (as a tutor and facilitator)
A set of textbooks and some audiovisual aids	Multimedia materials (print, audio, video, digital ...)

Shifts in Learning Paradigms

The transition toward a global knowledge-based economy has also coincided with a paradigm shift in learning and education systems. Information competencies and knowledge-society attributes are increasingly important requisites for participation in the knowledge economy, and education systems globally have begun to restructure to accommodate these requirements. The shift in learning and education systems is manifest in the growth of computer science as a school-based subject, the reform of curricula to suit the needs of a developing knowledge-based economy, and the application and integration of ICTs in learning and teaching practice as well as the growing predominance of learner-centred, self-directed, social constructivist learning philosophies. The shift from traditional pedagogy premised on the transfer of knowledge by the teacher, didactic methods, and rote learning to outcomes-based, learner-centred, facilitative learning takes place both independently and under the influence of the growing application of ICTs. These changes are partly due to the development of ICTs and their specialized functionality in facilitating networking and collaborative learning, knowledge sharing, and interactive learning. ICTs are purported to support new ways of learning, provide lower costs for the delivery of education, facilitate flexibility in learning with diverse learner populations, and allow access to vast quantities of education resources. These are the much-vaunted advantages of e-learning or technology-enhanced learning that usher in new learning paradigms. Haddad and Draxler (2002) capture succinctly the way in which the paradigm shift would affect schooling in particular, illustrated in Table 1.

Neoliberalism and the Education Sector

There is also a widely held and contentious view that the predominance of macroeconomic policies premised on neoliberal economic principles have profoundly affected public-goods sectors like the education sector on a global scale. Neoliberalism is an extension of the free-market economic framework propounded by Adam Smith with reference to the efficacy of market mechanisms to regulate economies. The framework promotes reduced state involvement in the economy, thereby allowing greater leeway for market regulation. Since the 1980s, there has been a notable shift away from Keynesian macroeconomic policy frameworks that promote state ownership of public-goods sectors and state welfare programs toward liberalized market economies that have also been a lynchpin of globalization. The effects on classical public-goods sectors like health, education, and indeed telecommunications cannot be ignored. Globally, governments have embarked on cuts in spending on education for programs to privatize public education and promote the increasing involvement of private companies in existent public-education institutions. The growth of private universities, schools, colleges, and even private preschools across the world as well as the availability of learning products and services by a growing number of private companies, particularly in the educational technology sector, are manifestations of this. Klein (2001) talks of the "branding of learning" with reference to the interventionist role of private corporations in education institutions in the USA and Canada, which are increasingly becoming manifest in the developing world and in Africa as well. In demonstrating the corporatisation of education, she says that the corporations "are fighting for their brands to become, not the add-on but the subject of education, not the elective but the core curriculum" (p. 89). She explains that private corporations have been allowed to let their branding interventions in schools largely because schools are "starved of new sources of income" (p. 95), but that school governing bodies have also attempted to impose limits on corporate intervention, especially if they threaten to affect the educational activities in the school.

Additional features of the neoliberal economic paradigm include the progressive liberalization of trade since the 1980s and early 1990s as expounded by the World Trade Organization's General Agreement on Trade and Tariffs, which now includes the General Agreement on Trade in Services (GATS). GATS also includes trade in education services. Daniel, Kanwar, and Uvalic-Trumbic (2005) note the effect of the GATS on cross-border higher education, and they reference two of the four modes of trade in the GATS that allude to cross-border supply and commercial presence as the most contentious in view of their effects on developing countries. Daniel et al. provide three examples of experiences in India, Jamaica, and Sierra Leone in demonstrating how huge unsatisfied demand calls for the expansion of access, how for-profit cross-border providers are active, and how these providers are of low quality despite the high costs of their offerings.

The flexibility of the global labor market, including the global teaching profession that encourages greater mobility of teachers, particularly from the South to the North, is another salient feature of the global economic system. Analysts have written about the "brain drain" in Africa and the developing world with reference particularly to Africa losing numbers of qualified and skilled teachers. The decline in government expenditure on social services, privatization, and the sale of public goods, including in the education sector, are further manifestations of a trend toward a liberalized global markets. The social implications of these policies globally are profound. Fiscal constraints in education have influenced job losses among teachers, downward pressure on salaries of teachers, and a stratification of education access rendering formal education increasingly out of the reach of poorer communities. In Africa, these developments are pivotal in influencing the extent to which new learning paradigms via technology-enhanced learning can make significant inroads in improving education systems and reaching larger numbers of African youth and teachers.

Defining the Development Challenge

Governments have globally been challenged with meeting the growing demand for the delivery of affordable education services to its populace. Compared to global trends, African education lags behind dramatically with weak physical and institutional bases, the effects of natural and human-made disasters and conflicts having placed extreme pressure on African education systems. Many countries in Africa have also been victims of austere structural-adjustment programs that led to cuts in educational expenditure. Together with increasing debt burdens, problems with governance and democracy, the challenges imposed by globalization, and the devastating impact of HIV/AIDS, the basic human right of access to education has been denied to many (Addo, Butcher, & Isaacs, 2002).

Current debates also point to the need to look beyond the achievement of universal primary education to address the need for increasing enrollment and retention in secondary education. The latter is considered important for the socialization of young people and for their preparation to participate in the labor market. However, the achievement of universal primary education alone is a mammoth task. It is estimated that approximately 50% of youth of school-going age in Africa are not in school. According to the United Nations Development Program (UNDP) Human Report Office (2005), there is an estimated 43 million youth not in the formal school system in sub-Saharan Africa, of which an estimated 50% are girls. These categories of youth not in school are mainly child ex-combatants, "street kids," nomadic children, and child laborers.

In 2002, in 19 out of 44 African countries, more than half of all children did not complete primary education (United Nations Educational, Scientific, and Cultural Organization [UNESCO], 2005). HIV/AIDS, disability, conflict, and child-labor practices put millions of children at an extreme disadvantage. In sub-Saharan Africa, more than 11 million children under the age of 15 have lost at least one parent to HIV/AIDS. Their opportunities to learn are seriously obstructed by the need to care for sick family members or contribute to household income (UNESCO, 2004).

The African region has a gross enrollment ratio in secondary schools of less than 40%, which is the lowest in the world despite the fact that the number of pupils has grown by 5.3% in fro 1998 to 2002 compared to 4.4% growth in from 1990 to 1995. This low rate can be explained by the fact that an estimated 58% of children live in countries in Africa where lower secondary education is not compulsory (UNESCO, 2005).

Moreover, the quality of education is seriously undermined by a shortage of teacher supply globally, which is more acute in Africa. Shortcomings in the teacher professional development system, poor wages for teachers, and the recruitment of African teachers by developed economies are contributing factors. Above all, the HIV/AIDS pandemic appears to be eroding the teacher population dramatically. Recent figures from a World Bank report indicate the "HIV/AIDS kills teachers faster than they can be trained, makes orphans of students, and threatens to derail efforts by highly-infected countries to get all boys and girls into primary school by 2015." [2] That women constitute the majority of the teacher population in most countries also points to the gender disparities within this debilitating crisis.

This report quotes figures that illustrate a disturbing trend. For example, in the Central African Republic, 85% of teachers who died between 1996 and 1998 were HIV positive. In Zambia, 1,300 teachers died in the first 10 months of 1998 compared with 680 teachers in 1996.

HIV/AIDS will rewrite the teacher supply and demand equations on current projections. The implications are as yet poorly understood but evidently very extensive. New systems of training and deployment are likely to be needed to meet this challenge. Whilst this issue is outside the scope of this essay, the devastating effects of the HIV/AIDS pandemic on education systems in Africa is crucial in absolute terms when considering the facilitative role ICTs can play. Acevedo (2005) expands on various ways in which ICTs can be applied in the design of development programs including in health and education that can support strategies to combat the devastating effects of the HIV/AIDS pandemic. The Mindset Network[3] in South Africa, with its dedicated multimedia HIV/AIDS channel, is one example of the effective use of ICTs in sensitization and awareness raising for issues of prevention and treatment of the disease.

The Digital Divide has an African Face

The digital divide has its most extreme expression in Africa. Jensen (2002) states that of Africa's total population of 816 million in 2001, it is estimated that: •

- 1 in 4 had a radio (200 million).
- 1 in 13 had a TV (162 million).
- 1 in 35 had a mobile phone (24 million).
- 1 in 39 had a fixed line (21 million).
- 1 in 130 had a PC (personal computer; 5.9 million).
- 1 in 160 use the Internet (5 million).
- 1 in 400 have pay TV (2 million).

These figures, he emphasizes, do not take account of the widespread sharing of resources. For instance, a whole village may use a phone line. Jensen explains that the general low level of economic activity means that technology is often unaffordable. Many African countries still have irregular or nonexistent electricity supplies, which makes ICT use problematic. Rail, road, and air transport is limited, and this infrastructure is needed to implement and support ICT infrastructure, as well as the increased social and economic activity that this technology should stimulate. Many tax regimes define computers and cellular phones as luxury items. This adds to the price of these goods, the vast majority of which must be imported, thus making the technology even more unaffordable for most people. In addition, as noted above, the lack of skills together with the problem of the brain drain also makes widespread adoption of new technology difficult. All of the above issues are further complicated by a business climate that does not always encourage investment in Africa in ways that benefit the continent (Addo et al., 2002).

The digital divide in primary and secondary education is evident from the disparities in PC penetration in schools. It is estimated that the PC-to-student ratio in OECD (Organization for Economic Cooperation and Development) countries averages about 1:10 at the lower end and 1:5 at the higher end of the spectrum, according to a recent survey (OECD, 2005). In contrast, a country like Mozambique has 7,000 schools, of which in 2006, 80 schools had PCs, making the average PC-to-student ratio 1:630. Table 2 gives a general picture of PC access in African schools based on fieldwork guesstimates of the author in the absence of readily available accurate data. Hopefully, in the coming period, more accurate data will

Table 2. Computer penetration ratios at schools in selected African countries (2006)

Country	Number of schools	Schools with computers	Percentage of schools with computers
Egypt	26,000	26,000	100%*
Ghana	32,000	800	2.5%
Mozambique	7,000	80	1.1%
Namibia	1,580	350	22.1%
South Africa	28,000	6,000	21.4%

*Note: * These are based on figures obtained from the Ministry of Education in Egypt, 2006.*

become available as increasing numbers of government ministries adopt comprehensive education-management and information-system programs. For now, the guesstimates in Table 2 will have to suffice.

Of these countries, Egypt has the highest percentage of computers in schools at 100%. The Egyptian Ministry of Education reports that each primary school has at least one multimedia lab with one PC, and each preparatory and secondary school has a computer lab of at least 10 PCs. This contrasts with the more economically developed South Africa, where only 6,000 schools currently have access to computers out of a total of 28,000. Howell and Lundall (2000) note the following factors in the South African context (but relevant generally, too) that prevent schools from using computers for teaching and learning.

- Insufficient funds
- Insufficient numbers of computers
- Lack of computer literacy among teachers
- Lack of subject teachers trained to integrate computers into learning areas
- The absence of a properly developed curriculum for teaching computer skills

While a number of inroads have been made since 2000 in South Africa, including dedicated rollout programs in various provinces and an e-education white paper, these factors remain as key obstacles in the achievement of universal access to ICTs in South African schools.

In addition, many of those schools that do have computers still do not have access to the Internet due to the exorbitant cost of bandwidth. The Internet can provide a wealth of learning resources that many African schools at present are not yet able to access because the costs of Internet access are prohibitive. In South Africa, of the estimated 6,000 schools that have access to PCs, only an estimated 2,500 have Internet access. The main obstacles faced by African schools with respect to Internet access specifically are the following:

- Lack of infrastructure generally and network infrastructure in particular
- High telephone and Internet costs

- Limited expertise and ICT skill levels
- Lack of enabling policy environment (Isaacs, 2002a)

The main barriers to ICT access in general relate to the small number of computers relative to the large numbers of teachers and students per school, the high cost of Internet access, and a dearth of technical skills to assist with troubleshooting and maintenance when computers break down. Notably, within this digital divide, greater gender disparities exist. Research of the experience in Africa shows that girls are further limited from school computer laboratories in some countries. A study commissioned by World Links for Development found that, in reality, it is harder for girls to access computer laboratories, particularly in Uganda and Ghana, especially after school hours (Gadio, 2001). These findings have been corroborated by Derbyshire (2003) and Isaacs (2002b).

The above is not a comprehensive overview, yet it succinctly captures the nature of the development challenge in African education.

African Frameworks to Achieving Quality Education through ICTs

Already in 1948, education as a fundamental human right was proclaimed in the Universal Declaration of Human Rights. In an attempt to describe a vision for educational achievement in Africa, the international development community established the millennium development goals[4] (MDGs) in 2001. The goals related to education follow:

"Goal 2:   Achieve universal primary education

Target 3:   Ensure that, by 2015, children everywhere, boys and girls alike, will be able to complete a full course of primary schooling

Goal 3:   Promote gender equity and empower women

Target 4:   Eliminate gender disparity in primary and secondary education, preferably by 2005, and to all levels of education no later than 2015."

(UN General Assembly Resolution A/56/326, September 6, 2001)

The details of the MDGs have their roots in the Dakar Framework of the World Education Forum. The Dakar Framework for Action set six "education for all" goals, which include the following:

- "Expanding and improving comprehensive early childhood care and education, especially for the most vulnerable and disadvantaged children;

- Ensuring that by 2015 all children, particularly girls, children in difficult circumstances and those belonging to ethnic minorities have access to and complete free and compulsory primary education of good quality;

- Ensuring that the learning needs of all young people and adults are met through equitable access to appropriate learning and life skills programmes;

- Achieving a 50% improvement in levels of adult literacy by 2015, especially for women, and equitable access to basic and continuing education for all adults;

- Eliminating gender disparities in primary and secondary education by 2005, and achieving gender equality in education by 2015, with a focus on ensuring girls' full and equal access to and achievement in basic education of good quality;

- Improving all aspects of the quality of education and ensuring excellence of all so that recognized and measurable learning outcomes are achieved by all, especially in literacy, numeracy and essential life skills." (UNESCO, 2000)

However, educationists have criticized the MDGs and EFA for their lack of sufficient reference to education quality. Whilst it is an issue of much debate informed by varying philosophies and traditions of educational thought, it appears that a broad, standard definition as defined by UNESCO is for now generally accepted. Here, the definition of quality in education identifies the cognitive development of learners as the major explicit objective of all education systems. The role of education is to promote values and an attitude of responsible citizenship, and to nurture creative and emotional development (UNESCO, 2004). There is commonality in this definition with international legislation on quality such as the Convention on the Rights of the Child (1990) and the International Covenant on Economic, Social, and Cultural Rights.

From ISAD to NEPAD

However, the disconnection appears in clarifying the vision for technology-enhanced learning within a development context and linking such a vision to that espoused by the EFA, the MDGs, and related international conventions. Yet, in the many initiatives established to bridge the digital divide in Africa, almost all make reference to the importance of education in the context of developing an African response to the knowledge society. The historic Information Society and Development (ISAD) conference held in South Africa in 1996 officially introduced the African development community to the potential of ICTs. ISAD was a launching pad for the African Information Society Initiative (AISI), a framework that established the African mandate to use ICTs to accelerate economic and social development. The AISI called for the creation of an African Learning Network that would comprise three pillars: the VarsityNet at the tertiary level, the OOSYNET for out-of-school youth, and the SchoolNet Africa.[5] Since then, both the global and regional environment promoting ICT4D have grown. The New Partnership for Africa's Development (NEPAD), which represents a strategy for Africa's economic, social, and political renewal led by African heads of state, established an eSchools Program in 2002. One of its leading spokespersons announced that the vision of NEPAD eSchools is for every African secondary-school graduate to be ICT literate by 2014.[6]

Dearth of Evidence-Based Research

There is extensive literature on the experiences with the adoption and diffusion of ICTs in schools in both developed and developing economies in general. Usually, African economies are included in the general references to developing economies. However, it is widely known that many African economies are significantly poorer, with more than 40 referred to as the least developed countries and the highly indebted poor countries by the World Bank. The available literature on African experiences with ICTs in schools is limited mainly to desk-top reviews with a dearth of evidence-based research that is premised on actual fieldwork reflective of the diversity of the continent. Within the limited research available, there is a substantial body of knowledge on the South African experience, and with this, the danger of extrapolating South African experiences as representative of the rest of the continent. There is also a very strong Anglophone bias in existing literature on ICTs in education in Africa with very little, if any, references to experiences in Francophone, Arabic, and Luso-phone regions of Africa. A study of SchoolNets in nine African countries conducted by the IDRC (International Development Research Centre) in 1999, which also includes a French report on the experiences in Senegal, represent one of the few field-based research works conducted by African researchers (James, 2004). Given the research limitations, perhaps this explains what appears to be a disconnection between general scholarly debates on development and education in Africa and policy and practitioner-based discussions at conferences on ICT for education. Hewitt de Alcantara (2001) correctly asserts that often the realities of the broader developmental challenges are not considered when addressing digital-divide issues, which are a function of the limitation with which notions of the digital divide have been conceptualized.

Debating the Benefits of ICTs for Education in Africa

Given the knowledge-production limitations with reference to Africa, the existing literature demonstrates increasing recognition of the developmental and educational benefits of intro-ducing ICTs to schools (Alverez et al., 1998; Byron & Gagliardi, 1998; Haddad & Draxler, 2002; World Bank, 2002). Some of these benefits include the following:

- ICTs can enhance education access and hence offer the potential for supporting the attainment of the Education for All goals. In places where books and qualified teach-ers are scarce, ICTs can provide access to vast quality educational resources and can facilitate the delivery of educational resources to large numbers of educators and learners relatively easily and cheaply. Importantly, though, access to educational resources should not be confused with automatic access to learning capability.

- ICTs enable access to networks of local and global learning and teaching communities, thereby facilitating collaborative learning.

- ICTs can enhance the quality of learning and teaching by offering new and different learning opportunities through synchronous and asynchronous communication.

- ICTs support learner-centred, individualized, self-directed learning.

According to the African SchoolNet tool kit, ICTs also enable the development of knowledge-society attributes in students such as higher order thinking skills, lifelong learning habits, and the ability to think critically, communicate and collaborate, and access, evaluate, and synthesize information. They allow for the development of ICT skills and competencies in students as preparation for operating in an ICT-rich workplace and society, and they have the potential to address structural problems and deficits in education systems, such as using ICTs to enhance administrative and teaching efficiency; alleviate underresourcing in specific areas (e.g., a lack of textbooks or learning support materials); address equity issues through enabling equality of access to knowledge, resources, and expertise; or support teachers who may be underequipped to deal with new teaching challenges (SchoolNet Africa & the Commonwealth of Learning, 2005).

Some have challenged the approach to the application of ICTs in education in Africa. Enslin, Lelliot, and Pendlebury (2000) contend that globalization, the learning society, and their related interconnected ideas on productivity, change, lifelong learning, and the learning organization have been theorized and conceptualized based on experiences and development in developed economies. They suggest that these concepts have a very different purchase in Africa and the way in which these ideas are currently theorized tend to distort our understanding. For them, patterns of educational provision, styles of teaching and learning, patterns of inclusion and exclusion, and empowerment and disempowerment in Africa have differed from those of Europe and North America. They argue that access to ICT brings on new forms of exclusion and risks that make stern demands on distributive justice because they represent an opportunity cost for money not spent on food, shelter, and basic education.

They refer to a gung ho approach to ICTs in education that offers simplistic truths in a populist fashion, and suggest that the promise held by ICTs for the benefit of education and social change are false and misleading. They do not provide a concrete demonstration of these "truths," however. They also refer to the very notion of learning as being undertheorized in some of these pivotal concepts and suggest that those who espouse the advantages of ICTs for education and social change do so from the perspective of developed economies where basic levels of education have already been universally achieved.

In education, they say that in practice, the claims on ICTs are neither strong nor self-evident: They offer superficially simple solutions to complex economic, education, and political challenges.

For them, ICTs are overspecified in terms of their technological sophistication. ICT programs have not considered local knowledge production or the functionality of education institutions, and concerns about the way political, social, and individual interests are differently served by different patterns of deploying technology in schools and institutions have not been considered.

Whilst this essay may share some of these concerns, it also proposes that Enslin et al.'s (2002) observations are insufficiently substantiated and outdated, and they have not researched the successes within African education adequately to justify such a pessimistic view. Evidently, no reference is made to any of the experiences of African SchoolNets and related organizations in any of the African countries in Enslin et al.'s paper.

Indeed, with the limited experience and codified knowledge of African interventions on ICTs in primary and secondary education under conditions of severe educational deprivation, one has to treat the potential of ICTs with caution. This is important also in considering the vastness and diversity of the African continent and the varying local education contexts and abilities for the adoption and diffusion of ICTs in their education systems. Moreover, whilst ICTs may have potential for educational inclusion of Africa's youth, they may create new forms of exclusion. Some still believe that ICTs represent an opportunity cost compared to spending on more basic requirements such as teacher salaries and school infrastructure.

The fundamental question with reference to the developmental potential of ICTs remains thus: How can ICTs contribute toward the achievement of the educational vision to attain universal quality education under conditions of extreme educational deprivation? In the absence of a coherent African vision and strategy on ICT-enabled education in general and in formal primary and secondary education in particular, this question can only be answered based on what has been tried.

School Networking in Africa

A number of African governments who subscribe to the UN system have developed EFA plans and strategies to attain the MDGs. Where reports of these are available, including the Global Monitoring Reports of UNESCO, very little, if any, is mentioned of progress made in the use of ICTs. In spite of this, however, even though they are not clearly linked to the attainment of EFA and the MDGs, various initiatives to promote ICTs in African schools have emerged over the past decade; chief amongst these are SchoolNets.

The African SchoolNet tool kit describes SchoolNets as country-level programs that operate at the interface between education and ICTs. SchoolNets promote the development of knowledge societies by connecting schools to the Internet; building connections among learners, teachers, and schools; sharing information and resources; and supporting e-learning in online networked environments. In Africa, up to 33 countries have some form of School-Net process under way, all of whom participate in an umbrella network called SchoolNet Africa[7] and related regional and international education networks. They assume various organizational forms—from government agencies located in ministries of education to nongovernment organizations—and they vary in size and scope of intervention depending on resource availability and local conditions.

Foremost among the concerns of SchoolNets is the promotion of universal access to ICTs in schools as a crucial starting point for the involvement of learners and teachers in ICT-supported learning opportunities. Here, access to infrastructure including electricity, telecommunications, and PCs are important prerequisites. Because most SchoolNets in Africa are products of donor and development-agency funding support, their interventions to achieve system-wide networked access to ICTs in schools have been extremely limited. At most, the total number of schools reached in Africa is estimated at 27,000 mostly secondary schools out of a total estimate of 600,000 schools on the continent. The majority of these schools are located in South Africa and Egypt, leaving an estimated 2,000 schools reached for the rest of Africa. Here, schools reached refer mainly to the existence of at least one PC lab consisting of at least 10 PCs. The PC-to-student ratios referred to earlier on are very high as a result (Isaacs, 2005a). As stated above as well, these do not always refer to PCs networked to the Internet.

Over the years, the African SchoolNet movement has revealed the fact that physical access to ICTs alone does not translate into enhanced educational outcomes, and that a number of related activities need to be established in order for a technology-enhanced learning system to work effectively at both the micro and macro levels. These include the following:

- The development of extensive technical-support capacity
- The professional development of teachers to be able to use ICTs as a learning-support tool
- The availability of appropriate digital education content and integration into school curriculum
- The availability of sustainable income streams to maintain the ICT infrastructure
- The establishment of monitoring and evaluation mechanisms for ongoing improvement
- The existence of an enabling policy environment that promotes access and use of ICTs in education

Given strong gender, rural-urban, and linguistic biases, conscious effort is also required to integrate these dimensions in a holistic approach to learning through the use of ICTs. These activities are depicted more clearly in a SchoolNet Value Chain, which was eventually established to encourage an integrated approach to the use of ICTs in African schools (SchoolNet Africa & the Commonwealth of Learning, 2005). The SchoolNet value chain is graphically depicted in Figure 1.

Importantly, too, the integration of ICTs in the learning process in the formal school system needs to be linked to their integration in the rest of the education pipeline to ensure continuity. This should include a strategy for ICT integration at the adult-basic, tertiary, and further education levels. Perhaps most importantly the connection of such a strategy to an overall macroeconomic plan geared toward the creation and development of a knowledge-based labor market to absorb and retain entrants flowing from the education sector is a crucial determinant of success. Few countries in Africa have adopted this holistic approach, albeit only at a policy level. These include Namibia, Botswana, Ghana, and South Africa. However, in practice, at the behest of the enormity of the development challenges, implementation has been very limited.

The current scale of intervention on ICTs in African schools is insignificant for any resounding widespread educational and developmental impact systemically. The scale varies from country to country, particularly when some countries like Namibia and Botswana have scales to their advantage given the lower school population relative to larger countries. However, within the confines of the limited scale of operations, considerable gains have been made in the promotion of online learning and the development of the knowledge-society attributes described above, which warrants serious consideration for further large-scale systemic interventions.

The main issues, successes, and challenges of some of the African SchoolNet organizations are documented elsewhere (Isaacs, 2004, 2005a, 2005b; James, 2004; SchoolNet Africa & the Commonwealth of Learning, 2005; SchoolNet South Africa, 2002).

Figure 1. The SchoolNet Value Chain

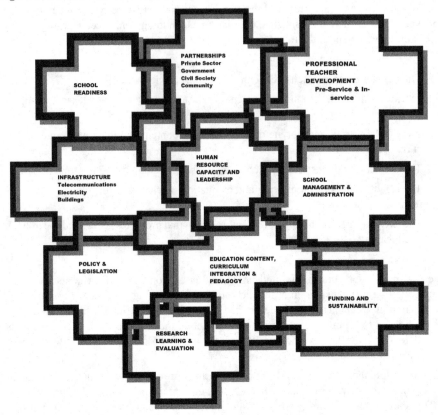

Lessons Learned

One of the first lessons learned was that the attainment of universal access to ICTs needs to be part of an integrated strategy that considers the following:

- Subsidized rates for Internet access (called e-rates) to schools
- The use of both second-hand, refurbished PCs and new PCs
- The use of a range of ICTs not only confined to PCs, but that includes handheld devices such as cell phones, televisions, video, radio and print media
- The reduction of tariffs on imported ICTs designated for schools
- The use of free and open-source software and/or significantly subsidized proprietary software
- The establishment of effective technical support systems involving learners and teachers at a school level as well as technical service centres that provide education solutions to the school at least at the provincial and national levels

- The involvement of both school and nonschool communities to support cost recovery

- Multistakeholder partnerships with the private sector, NGOs, community organizations, and government agencies at local and national levels

Almost all of these issues, with reference to sustainable ICT access alone, have been contentious and furiously debated within the network of practitioners and policymakers in Africa. On a small scale, various successful and sustainable models have been established such as that of the eSchools Network in South Africa, SchoolNet Namibia, SchoolNet Nigeria, and Computers for Schools Kenya (Isaacs, 2005a, 2005b).

It is argued that the SchoolNet movement (which includes those linked to the World Links program) has been technology-centred in its approach to ICT-enabled education in schools, and that less consideration has been given to the learning aspect of the technologies, and more importantly, their integration into improving the social systems at the school level. There is truth in this concern because the attempt at using ICTs in the first place resulted in a preoccupation with issues of technology access, without which there can be no integration of any kind. Within this, the quest for workable technology solutions that were low cost and affordable, and which had the support of the major stakeholders, was an uphill battle that also required considerable learning over time. It would be myopic to suggest that these models can automatically be replicated and extended on a wide scale. However, within them lie ingredients of successful technology solutions for Africa that can be considered in the development and implementation of system-wide strategies.

The second major lesson is that teacher professional development, particularly in terms of ICT literacy and the use of ICTs to support learning, is central to their effective use in the learning process in schools. In practice, there have been many and varied teacher training programs (see research paper by SchoolNet Africa on teacher training, 2004) that focus both on ICT literacy as well as ICT use in learning and teaching. Again, the scale with which teacher training has taken place is extremely minimal. Here, African-owned models such as the Educator Development Network of SchoolNet South Africa, which is also available in French and Portuguese as well, and the pan-African and global teacher networks such as the African Teachers Network of SchoolNet Africa are examples of successful strides made in this arena. However, teacher training in many ways has also developed in a relative vacuum with limited consideration to the social and economic conditions of teachers. One example that stands out here is the dire lack of integration with the effects of the HIV/AIDS pandemic on the lives of teachers and learners and their professional development to use ICTs to enable learning (Isaacs, 2005d).

The third major lesson is that whilst content is king, more important are the learning strategies devised to ensure the educational use of the content. With reference to education content, however, there is a plethora of available curriculum-based content, mainly in English, that have been produced in the developed economies. Notably too, a growing movement toward open education resources that make digital learning resources such as lesson plans, courseware, and so forth freely available on the Internet for use, reuse, sharing, and adaptation is a welcoming trend in e-learning globally. Indeed, it fosters an underlying principle of learning through sharing and highlights greater potential for access to learning resources for poor communities. Daniel (2005b) correctly highlights the accessibility, appropriateness, accreditation, and affordability of open education resources. An important lesson is that strategies that focus on the adaptation of content produced elsewhere together with strategies on the production and consumption of local curriculum content is an essential ingredient for the successful use in schools. Examples of content adaptation are the ways agencies in Kenya are adapting the curriculum content developed by Learnthings, which is based on the curriculum in the United Kingdom. The Thutong Portal, Mindset Learn in South Africa, and CurriculumNet in Uganda are examples of good practice in the development of local, digitized curriculum content on multimedia platforms coupled with strategies for learners and educators to use the resources. However, a few issues require considerable development and learning. These include a coherent approach on the use of local, indigenous languages in the development and use of education content and the need for policies on open education resource content and creative commons licensing. Given the critical discussion on education quality earlier on, it is also evident that processes of quality assurance and assessment in many existing content-related programs remain extremely limited.

What about the Learners?

Because much of the literature focuses more on the school and SchoolNets as units of analyses and less on the perspective of learners, one of SchoolNet Africa's learner-based SchoolNet projects is discussed here: ThinkQuest Africa (TQA) typifies interventions that specifically aim to develop knowledge-society attributes among learners.

TQA (more recently called the Mtandao Afrika program)[8] is a learner-centred educational contest based on an award system that promotes learning through the collaborative development of educational Web sites by teams of learners from different African countries, supported by teacher coaches. The process of involvement includes the selection of the team members, communicating with them over the Internet, the selection of the research topic, conducting research, and the technical development and design of the Web site. These activities require competencies in cross-cultural communication, planning, and Web design and Web-site development. One of the main objectives of the program is to encourage African learners to be producers of local knowledge through the production of African education content. A special award is presented to teams who also focus on the development of content in local, indigenous African languages. This Africanised approach to the ThinkQuest program was very important at the outset given that it was integrally linked to an international program, ThinkQuest Internet Challenge, which originated as a program in the USA in 1996, and which increasingly gained international recognition over the years. TQA as the African chapter of the contest was also designed to encourage more African participation in the program.

The program has been criticized for its focus as an Internet-based program that excludes the vast majority of African learners, thereby reinforcing the notion of new forms of exclusion espoused by Enslin et al. (2002). That it also assumes the form of a contest was cause for concern because it meant that some learners would be winners and others would be losers. Also, the program applied an elitist model of learning relative to a mass model that may be more relevant in an African context. The program also laid claim to the production of education content although the quality-assurance process was reduced to the subjective considerations of the judges in the contest. With these criticisms in mind, SchoolNet Africa commissioned a study to determine the learning value of the program for African learners. The study conducted by Broekman (2002) asked the following important questions. What are African learners' experiences of participation in the ThinkQuest competition? What do they feel they have learned and what do learners believe they have contributed to online learning?

Broekman found that the learning that happened was extensive for the learners interviewed, and it included changes in attitudes and skill development. For most coaches and learners in the study, the social learning experiences were particularly significant, such as cultural sensitivity, new social understandings, tolerance, communication, creativity, and agency in a way that goes beyond the dynamics of the classroom, and which is developed primarily through working within a team as equals but with diverse backgrounds across race, gender, culture, geographical divides, resource divides, and histories. The program competition and its prizes, the opportunity to travel and meet participants, were major motivating factors for participation in the program. The participants also saw the program as more than a competition, but an opportunity for learning, "for changing thinking, outreach, and for an investment in national as well as personal development" (Broekman, 2002, p. 3). She found that the criteria for judging the sites produced by the learners included redress, inclusivity, and outreach. Furthermore, the competition was designed to motivate students to excellence, hence intrinsically limiting participation, but it also has broad educational goals, which imply mass participation. She noted a tension, however, between the notion of elitism used in this study as providing awards to a few, and mass participation, where many are recognized for their efforts. Here, she suggests that mass participation would require considerable scaling up of the program at significantly increased costs. She proffers suggestions on ways to render the program more conducive to mass participation such as focusing on marginalized groups of learners working around connected centres in various African countries. That there has been a low number of African entries in the international contest historically, suggests that the program appeals more to an elite few, but also that African learners can produce excellent Web sites. She also found that in the competition, learning is learner driven, though in other models Web-site production is more coach or teacher driven.

Importantly, both learners and coaches in disadvantaged areas reported a sense of satisfaction with competing successfully against the more advantaged, for example, doing well by using older technology. An assessment of the sites produced suggested that they "put Africa on the map" through the production of local content. The production of quality Web sites are a resource for a wide range of target users as teaching and leaning resources, indicated by the comments of visitors to sites.

With the benefit of hindsight, the TQA program developed over the past 3 years to the extent that it involved larger numbers of African participants each progressive year. In 2004, the contest involved 1,034 learners and teachers compared to 709 during the previous year. The challenges faced by the TQA program are typical of all SchoolNet programs in Africa. The challenges of converting this extracurricular program into a mass program are linked to the challenge for universal access to ICTs in general. In the absence of mass access to ICTs, any SchoolNet program can be misconstrued as exclusive and elitist. The reality in Africa is that even primary education is a privilege.

If the alternative is to discourage SchoolNet-type initiatives in the face of severe poverty, then this means that the limited numbers of learners and teachers reached by SchoolNet programs would be denied the learning possibilities, albeit limited, presented by these programs. This cannot be an alternative.

Instead, the limited strides made in Africa need to be encouraged as attempts at an extension to and in support of universal access to primary and secondary education. Herein lies the challenge.

Drawing on experiences from the World Links for Development Program, Hawkins (2002) details 10 lessons for ICT and education in the developing world.

- Computer labs take time and money but they work.
- Technical support cannot be overlooked.
- Noncompetitive telecommunications infrastructure, policies, and regulations impede connectivity and sustainability.
- Wireless technologies are usually more effective.
- Get the community involved.
- Private-public partnerships are essential.
- ICT initiatives should be linked to broader education reforms.
- Training is fundamental.
- Technology empowers girls.
- Technology motivates students and energizes classrooms.

Hawkins' study corroborates the findings of Broekman (2002) and the research conducted by James (2004).

Future Trends

The disconnections referred to extensively above will in all probability prolong for a while. The perspective for the next few years suggest that more and more African countries will in all likelihood develop national policies on ICTs in education in particular. There will be more debates on the value-added issues relating to open content and quality assurance in technology-enhanced learning, which opens the way for more research that would direct policy and practice in these areas.

There is hope for an expansion of ICT-enabled education programs in African schools, particularly with the prospect of growth of the NEPAD eSchools initiative given its more direct linkages with education decision makers at the highest level and its focus on reaching the remotest schools in rural areas. Furthermore, the emergence of the Global eSchools and Communities Initiative established by the UN ICT Task Force over the past year, with its bias toward Africa, holds the promise of increased qualitative intervention in the promotion of learning and teaching in schools and their surrounding communities.

Furthermore, a number of African countries are also taking bold steps both in collaboration with and independently of the NEPAD and Global eSchools initiatives. Countries like Namibia, Botswana, and Rwanda are cases in point. However, the success of all of these initiatives depend on the rigor of the conceptual framework and implementation strategies with which issues of ICTs in primary and secondary education are programmed in Africa. Here, the importance of drawing on the accumulated learning of 10 years of experience in the African SchoolNet movement is imperative.

In addition, in order for African ICT-enabled programs to yield developmental benefit and tackle the dire crises that they face, a combination of factors identified by Marcelle (2005) in her appraisal of the experience in the Caribbean would be worth considering. She suggests that ICT planning processes need to incorporate a combination of factors for success, which include the following:

- Strategic thinking
- Creative leadership
- Policies that are developmental in their objectives and that put people first
- Emphasis on impact evaluation and continuous monitoring
- Building on existing strengths and assets and facilitating continuous learning in planning and implementation
- Focus on sustainability and institution building
- Effective engagement with the global ICT community

Marcelle (2005) also suggests that it has been shown theoretically and practically that the market alone cannot ensure optimal provision or equitable distribution of public goods. Planning has to take account of market failure. However, Daniel (2005a) indicates that public goods like education need not only be supplied by the state. Governments alone do not have the resources to meet growing demand for education and are compelled to draw in stakeholders in the supply and sourcing of the education system. Daniel states this challenge pithily: "In an era of lifelong learning, there is simply no way that governments can provide at no cost, all the education that people will need throughout life. Governments will have to focus their contributions" (Daniel, 2005b, http://www.col.org/speeches/JD_0602IFCDinner. htm). Education has become both a public and a private good, but the onus still lies with the state to provide the leadership in the involvement of private firms in education in ways that foster greater access and affordability.

There still remains a need for more sober-minded reflection that can be supported by more evidence-based research that takes cognizance of Africa's rich cultural and linguistic diversity, where knowledge production is the domain of local African researchers. Here, more work on the connections between the developmental realities, the educational challenges of reach and quality, and the role of ICTs is important, particularly from the perspective of the so called end users, that is, the learners.

Conclusion

The approach to ICTs for education in Africa has strongly been influenced by supply-side, external interventions. Often, this assumes the form of global funding becoming available or global institutions promoting the setup of projects in African countries with a predominantly Northern perspective on the South. Often, too, these initiatives assume the form of a given sum of money available for delivery within a short period of 3 years with limited strategy toward longer term sustainability. This causes problems systemically, some of which have been highlighted by this essay.

Linked to this approach has also been a predominant preoccupation with process issues and product development, and less with implementation and product use, perhaps because within a short time frame, process-related and product-development deliverables are less challenging than implementation-based deliverables. Here, the convention of numerous multistakeholder conferences, which, at huge costs, have often lent themselves to aggrandizement, rhetoric, and posturing with a conspicuous absence of follow-up action plans, have been a salient feature of the ICT4E and ICT4D sectors. It has been cynically implied that this sector is perhaps the most "conferenced" of sectors. Indeed, engagement in conceptual and practical issues among a community of practice and building networks that these conferences also achieve is important. However, the convention of practitioners and policy makers in a manner that adds concrete value to local implementation is potentially a more constructive way to utilize available resources.

Also, a number of global institutions would develop models, tool kits, portals, and such products with the expectation that they will be utilized in Africa, but with no investment in the active involvement, awareness raising, and training that would encourage local ownership, which in turn would facilitate better use of the products in question. Above all, it can also be argued that so much investment is going into products and processes, but very few programs are taking seriously the attainment on a mass scale of access to the technologies. Without a strategy to attain universal access to ICTs by the mass of African youth and teachers, there can be no use of portals, tool kits, or e-learning models.

It is absolutely imperative that this paradigm shifts toward long-term, demand-led, locally owned and locally led systemic application that responds directly to local conditions and that can be converged with global processes. The establishment of SchoolNet Africa and later the NEPAD eSchools initiative have been attempts to promote models that foster this shift in paradigm. For example, SchoolNet Africa's campaign for 1 million PCs for African schools has been one attempt at highlighting the importance of adopting a mass model that focuses on implementation.

Within this context, African leadership is unquestionably the lynchpin of success. Leadership that encourages the shift of current global supply-side approaches toward engagement and support of demand-led programs, leadership that fosters convergence of the myriad of parallel in-country projects toward coordinated investments of local resources and programs, leadership that redirects global investment and partnerships more toward mass implementation—this is perhaps the single most important ingredient in taking us one step closer to making this century the truly African century espoused by President Thabo Mbeki.

References

Acevedo, M. (2005). *Pandemics in the network society: ICT in the time of AIDS.* Retrieved March 31, 2005, from http://www.undp.org/surf-panama/egov/docs/programme_activities/pmapping/ict_time_of_AIDS.pdf

Addo, H., Butcher, N., & Isaacs, S. (2002). *SchoolNets in Africa: A baseline scan.* Johannesburg, South Africa: SchoolNet Africa & IDRC.

Alverez, M. I., Roman, F., Dobles, M. C., Umana, J., Szuniga, M., Garcia, J., et al. (1998). Computers in schools: A qualitative study of Chile and Costa Rica. *Education and Technology Series, 1*(1).

Broekman, I. (2002). *Learning possibilities of ThinkQuest in the African context.* Johannesburg, South Africa: SchoolNet Africa.

Broekman, I., Isaacs, S., & Mogale, T. (2004). Contextualizing education in Africa. In T. James (Ed.), *The role of ICTs in networking institutions of learning: SchoolNet. Information and communication technologies for development in Africa* (Vol. 3). Senegal: IDRC & CODESRIA.

Butcher, N. (2001). New information and learning technologies in South Africa: Pitfalls and possibilities. In C. Stilwell, A. Leach, & S. Burton (Eds.), *Knowledge, information and development: An African perspective.* Pietermaritzburg, South Africa: University of Natal School of Human and Social Studies.

Byron, I., & Gagliardi, R. (1998). *Communities and the information society: The role of information and communication technologies in education.* Paris: UNESCO & International Bureau of Education (IBE).

Castells, M. (1999). *Globalisation, information and social development* (Discussion Paper No. 114). Geneva, Switzerland: UNRISD.

Castells, M. (2001). Information technology and global development. In J. Muller, N. Cloete, & S. Badat (Eds.), *Challenges of globalisation: South African debates with Manuel Castells.* Maskew Miller Longman.

Cawthera, A. (2001). *Computers in secondary schools in developing countries: Costs and other issues.* London: Department for International Development (DFID), World Links for Development (WordLD), & the Human Development Network of the World Bank.

Daniel, J. (2005a). *The private supply of public goods: Contradictions, challenges and choices.* Retrieved August 15, 2005, from http://www.col.org/speeches/JD_0602IF-CDinner.htm

Daniel, J. (2005b). *Speeches by Sir John Daniel and colleagues.* Vancouver: Commonwealth of Learning.

Daniel, J., Kanwar, A., & Uvalic-Trumbic, S. (2005). ODL in an international context: Trends, prospects and challenges. In J. Daniel (Ed.), *Speeches by Sir John Daniel and colleagues.* Vancouver: Commonwealth of Learning.

Derbyshire, H. (2003). *Gender issues in the use of computers in education in Africa.* London: Imfundo & DFID.

Enslin, P., Lelliott, A., & Pendlebury, S. (2002). Promises of access and inclusion: Online education in Africa. In N. Blake & P. Standish (Eds.), *Enquiries at the interface: Philosophical problems of online education.* Oxford: Blackwell Publishers.

Gadio, C. M. (2001). *Exploring the gender impacts of world links in some selected African countries: A qualitative approach.* Washington, DC: World Links.

Haddad, W. D., & Draxler, A. (2002). *Technologies for education.* Paris: UNESCO & the Academy for Educational Development.

Hafkin, N., & Taggart, N. (2001). *Gender, information technology and developing countries: An analytic study.* Washington, DC: USAID & Office of Women in Development.

Hawkins, R. J. (2002). *Ten lessons for ICT and education in the developing world.*

Hellman, J. A. (2003). *The riddle of distance education: Promise, problems and applications for development* (Technology Business and Society Program Paper No. 9). Geneva, Switzerland: UNRISD.

Heppell, S. (2000). The online learning revolution in schools and beyond. In B. Lucas & T. Greany (Eds.), *Schools in the learning age* (pp. 51-56). London: Campaign of Learning.

Hewitt de Alcantara, C. (2001). *The development divide in a digital age: An issues paper.* The Hague, Netherlands: United Nations Research Institute for Social Development.

Howell, C., & Lundall. (2000). *Computers in schools: A national survey of information and communication technology in South African schools.* Cape Town Education Policy Unit, University of the Western Cape.

International Labour Organization (ILO). (2001). *World employment report: Life at work in the information economy.* Author.

Isaacs, S. (1997). *Consultancy-based SMME support programmes in Europe: What can South Africa learn?* Sussex, United Kingdom: University of Sussex Science Policy Research Unit.

Isaacs, S. (2002a). ICTs in African schools: A multi-media approach for enhancing learning and teaching. *TechKnowLogia*, 32-34.

Isaacs, S. (2002b). *IT's hot for girls: ICTs as an instrument in advancing girls' and women's capabilities in school education in Africa.* Retrieved August 10, 2005, from http://www.un.org/womenwatch/daw/egm/ict2002

Isaacs, S. (2005a). Against all odds: Critical reflections on SchoolNet Africa. In *ICTs for education.* New York: United Nations ICT Task Force.

Isaacs, S. (2005b). Empowering women in the information society: Towards a more concerted global and local effort. In G. Milward-Olivier (Ed.), *Maitland +20: Fixing the missing link.* United Kingdom: The Anima Centre.

Isaacs, S. (2005c). Reaching MDG2: SchoolNet Africa. *I4D Online.* India: Centre for Development and Media Studies.

Isaacs, S. (2005d). School networking in Africa. In V. Naidoo & H. Ramzy (Eds.), *Emerging trends in school networking.* Vancouver: Commonwealth of Learning.

Isaacs, S., & Naidoo, V. (2003). *A Schoolnet value chain for Africa: An integrated model enhancing education through the use of ICTs.* Vancouver: The Commonwealth of Learning.

James, T. (Ed.). (2004). *The role of ICTs in networking institutions of learning: SchoolNet. Information and communication technologies for development in Africa* (Vol. 3). Senegal: IDRC & CODESRIA.

Klein, N. (2000). The branding of learning. In *No logo.* United Kingdom: Flamingo.

Mansell, R., & Wehn, U. (Eds.). (1998). *Knowledge societies: Information technology for sustainable development.* New York: Oxford University Press for the United Nations Commission on Science and Technology for Development.

Marcelle, G. M. (2000). *Transforming information and communication technologies for gender equality* (Gender and Development Monograph Series No. 9).

Marcelle, G. M. (2005). Making the link between ICT and development: Lessons from the Caribbean. In G. Milward-Oliver (Ed.), *Maitland +20: Fixing the missing link.* United Kingdom: The Anima Centre.

Organization for Economic Cooperation and Development (OECD). (2005). *Are students ready for a technology-rich world? What the PISA study tells us.* Retrieved January 28, 2006, from http://www.oecd.org/dataoecd/48/61/36002531.ppt

SchoolNet Africa & the Commonwealth of Learning. (2005). *African SchoolNet toolkit.* Retrieved January 28, 2006, from http://www.schoolnetafrica.net/1500.0.html

SchoolNet South Africa. (2002). *Audit of major educational ICT projects in South Africa.* World Economic Forum Global Digital Divide Initiative.

United Nations Development Program (UNDP) Human Report Office. (2005). *Sub-Saharan Africa: The human costs of the 2015 "business-as-usual" scenario.* Retrieved December 30, 2005, from http://hdr.undp.org/docs/publications/background_papers/2005/HDR2005_Note_Africa_Child_Mortality.pdf

United Nations Educational, Scientific, and Cultural Organization (UNESCO). (2000). *The Dakar framework for action, education for all: Meeting our collective commitments.* Paris: Author.

United Nations Educational, Scientific, and Cultural Organization (UNESCO). (2002a). *EFA global monitoring report 2002: Is the world on track.* Paris: Author.

United Nations Educational, Scientific, and Cultural Organization (UNESCO). (2002b). Statement of commitment. *The Eighth Conference of Ministers of Education of African Member States (MINEDAF VIII).* Retrieved April 24, 2005, from http://www.unesco.org

United Nations Educational, Scientific, and Cultural Organization (UNESCO). (2004). *Education for all: The quality imperative. Summary: EFA global monitoring report 2005.* Paris: Author.

United Nations Educational, Scientific, and Cultural Organization (UNESCO). (2005). *Global education digest 2005: Comparing education statistics across the world.* Montreal, Canada: UNESCO Institute of Statistics.

World Bank. (2002). *Distance education and ICTs for learning in Africa.* Washington, DC: Human Development Group, Africa Region, the World Bank.

Endnotes

1   Reference made in an opening speech delivered by Thabo Mbeki, president of South Africa 1999, delivered at the Conference on Education for African Renaissance in the 21st Century

2   _http://lnweb18.worldbank.org/news/pressrelease.nsf/673fa6c5a2d50a67852565e20 0692a79/d85862c24b5d549d85256bb2006e517e?OpenDocument

3   http://www.mindset.co.za

4   http://www.milleniumgoals.org

5   The AISI attempted a framework for intervention in education in Africa and proposed initiatives that would reach the tertiary, primary, and secondary levels as the basic education sectors. Hence, VarsityNet, OOSYNET, and SchoolNet in Africa as part of a broader African learning network were proposed. The formation of SchoolNet Africa is in fact a direct outcome of this proposal.

6   Speech by Professor Peter Kinyanjui at ICTs in African Schools Workshop, Botswana, 2003. For a full report see, http://www.schoolnetafrica.net/fileadmin/resources/Workshop_Report.zip.

7   http://www.schoolnetafrica.net

8   http://www.mtandao-afrika.org

Chapter X

Peering into the Black Box:
A Holistic Framework for Innovating at the Intersection of ICT & Health

Ben Bellows, University of California at Berkeley, USA

Aman Bhandari, University of California at Berkeley, USA

Mahad Ibrahim, University of California at Berkeley, USA

Jaspal S. Sandhu, University of California at Berkeley, USA

Abstract

This chapter begins with an overview of public health in developing regions. From this population-level perspective, we discuss the information challenges in each of the four domains of public health: research, education, health-care delivery, and disease surveillance. We introduce health-related use classes—categories of specific use cases—to provide a structured presentation of health and information communication technologies in developing regions. In this regard, we define and discuss the following six use classes: (a) surveillance and information gathering, (b) research, (c) provider to provider, (d) provider to patient, (e) education, and (f) logistics. Defining ICT broadly, we argue that the design or selection of technology requires consideration of the cost, ease of use, infrastructure, culture of ICT use, penetration of different ICTs, and population health profile. All of these factors vary among resource-scarce settings, and each factor can greatly impact the appropriate choice in any given setting. We discuss the following three types of assessment, each of which plays a crucial role in project evaluation: systems issues, usability, and health outcomes. Designing ICT for health applications in developing countries requires a deep understanding of various contextual factors, such as health and ICT infrastructure, disease burden, and sociocultural issues. With this in mind, and with some understanding of future trends in health and ICT utilization, we provide forward-looking recommendations for practitioners, researchers, funders, and policy makers.

Introduction

Human and societal development without health is not sustainable. The World Health Organization (WHO) defines health as "a state of complete physical, mental and social well-being and not merely the absence of disease or infirmity" (WHO, 1948, Preamble). Public health can be categorized into four domains: research, education, health-care delivery, and disease surveillance. In this chapter, when we refer to public health, we refer to the bundle of health-related activities that fall under those four domains, which have an impact on the individual (e.g., delivery of medical treatment or health education) and the larger population (e.g., health-care infrastructure capacity or tracking HIV infections).

Unhealthy people have difficulty being productive members of their communities, and unhealthy nations cannot be productive partners in the global community (Deaton, 2003; Hancock, 1993). For many developing economies, disease burdens debilitate entire populations and have a significant impact on a range of factors such as economic growth and development (Baldacci, Clements, Cui, & Gupta, 2005; "Health and Wealth," 2002; Sachs et al, 2002). Poor infrastructure, lack of health systems, lack of access to medical care and medical goods, and financing are major barriers to improving population-wide health and national development. According to the WHO (2004), in 2002 the combined public and private per capita health-care spending in developing countries averaged $70 per year compared to $3,055 in high income countries. The global disease burden comes from a variety of causes such as malaria, HIV, diarrhea, tobacco-induced chronic diseases, poor sanitation, and lack of clean water. The scope and scale of challenges facing such regions is great and requires innovative solutions. This is the context in which information and communication technologies must operate, and in this chapter, our aim is to discuss the promises and challenges of using such technologies to tackle global health problems in low-income regions.

ICT for development has received considerable interest outside of public health for a variety of applications that are discussed elsewhere in this book, such as in education and governmental affairs. While the application of ICT into health care has been on the periphery of ICT innovation, the intersection of ICT and health may be one of the greatest means to positively enhance development. Information access, exchange, and brokering are central to the delivery of health care on both an individual level via clinical providers and a macrolevel via policy makers. Access to information has a significant impact not only on the delivery of health care, but also on increasing equity in health, and thus ICT intervention offers promise in improving health care (e.g., in education, delivery, and clinical outcomes). This promise, however, is tempered by the complex interface of the design, development, and maintenance of ICT, and the nature of public health in developing regions. The application of ICT to improve health similarly depends on access to relevant, reliable knowledge in forms that are appropriate, readily assimilated, and easily applied, whether by a biomedical researcher, a nurse, a doctor, a midwifery student, or a mother.

A range of applications involving ICT for health have been undertaken in recent years. Activities range from the Ptolemy project that links full-text clinical journal access from the University of Toronto with a network of several dozen East African surgeons, to a satellite-based radio feed across Asia with health-education local programming run by Equal Access, a nonprofit organization focused on low-cost technology (Beveridge, Howard, Burton, & Holder, 2003; Camaran Pipes, Program Coordinator [personal communication, August 30, 2005). Various ICTs such as the Internet, radio, and mobile phones can be utilized to build research, training, and implementation capacity. The broad diversity of applications and end users (from surgeons to illiterate patients) in this context presents great opportunity as well as significant challenges and ethical considerations (e.g., access, cost, connectivity, and culturally appropriate content delivery).

The existence of distinct technology use classes or groupings of use cases (e.g., provider to provider, provider to patient, and surveillance) distinguishes ICT for health from other domains. Each use class implies a different set of implementation costs and benefits. Furthermore, much attention has been directed toward the latest Internet-enabled technologies, but public health practitioners have at their disposal a much broader set of ICTs. Public health must focus on the context and goals of health and the capabilities of particular ICTs rather than on being technology driven. Finally, the infrastructure needed for public health intervention is quite complex, varying significantly over both disease categories and physical context. This complexity creates multiple barriers to technology access from social, economic, and political factors rather than technological ones.

In this chapter, we seek to move beyond the limited focus in much of the literature on ICT and health informatics to provide an integrative and expanded framework and analysis of the role of ICTs in public health. Specifically, we will describe each of the distinct use classes, emphasizing their impact on the design, deployment, and maintenance of ICT. We lay out a comprehensive map between ICT and public health. Moreover, we seek to make explicit the multiple barriers to technology access present in the public health infrastructure. Our specific goals are as follows:

1.   Indicate the appropriate roles that ICT can play in improving multiple public health domains, specifically delivery, education, research, and surveillance

2.   Describe the multiple use classes for ICT, highlighting these with concrete examples

3.   Provide recommendations for practitioners, discussing promising applications of technology and meaningful assessment of initiatives

4.   Discuss future trends

Table 1. Barriers to effective ICT utilization in health

Individual	Organization	Population/Society
Experience	Lack of administrative data	Per capita spending on health
Language	Lack of personnel capable of	Policies that disincentive
Economic instability	undertaking research	research
Rural location	Human resources	Regulatory framework
Distance from points of	Incentives	(possibility of getting sued in
service	Funding	U.S.)
Lack of trained personnel	Infrastructure	Policy framework (UK, Canada)
to provide service	No educational or training institutions	Lack of national funding to
Cultural strictures against	Networks	document population health
receiving service	Decision making (information over	Organizational infrastructure
Economic inability to	load)	Physical infrastructure
access service	Capital resource constraints	Underinvestment in education
Lack of trainers to educate	Labor constraints	Policy environment
individuals	Information quality constraints	Technology availability
	Human resources necessary for	Resource availability
	maintenance of equipment, network	Language
	Cultural concepts regarding gender and	Education
	ethnicity	Culture
	Ethical constraints to implementation	Politics
		Gender
		Socio-demographic differences
		Ethical constraints to
		implementation

Information Challenges in Public Health

Much of the discussion of ICT within the sphere of public health in low-income countries has been limited to remote diagnostics and vertical health information systems that report to the central government disease and death events, patient load, and other tasks that fall under medical services and disease surveillance. The discussion of ICT in public health could expand to include health education strategies, effective research tools, and interactive surveillance and response data systems. For many developing countries, the health sector is significantly tied to donor agencies' priorities, which often place a premium on public-sector implementation, individual project reporting, and short-term crisis response.

From a consumer or patient perspective, however, the single largest challenge to public health is access. Low utilization of health services is a function of both underfunded demand and poor supply of high-quality services. ICT can play a significant role in addressing both supply- and demand-side constraints; however, a greater understanding of the barriers to the effective use of ICT in public health applications is needed. Table 1 identifies challenges to public health activities at various levels of social organization. ICT can help overcome those barriers.

Surveillance

Health data are necessary for informed decision making and the allocation of scarce health resources. Disease trends change rapidly, and surveillance systems need to capture those trends to accurately forecast emerging threats to the public's health. The challenges to the implementation of ICT solutions to data collection on population health are exacerbated by centrifugal mandates that devolve power from the central authorities to regional health agencies, and in some cases, to nongovernmental actors. These regional data collection agencies often lack the training, experience, and resources to adequately collect data, much less mount a response to rapidly emerging situations. New surveillance systems should be modular, decentralized, and connect an array of information suppliers on a competitive basis.

Research

Health research essentially is the experimental and observational functions of testing health products, services, and policies. The supply and demand of ICT in health research is inhibited by the same infrastructural challenges facing other public health domains. The ICT challenges to conducting research are exacerbated by ethical quandaries, such as balancing the great need for innovative solutions to pressing public health problems against the protection of communities and individuals in the research.

Fostering the production of health research in developing countries represents a critical challenge of the global public health community. ICT offers a cost-efficient platform for disseminating health research originating from the developing world; however, the cost of dissemination is far from the only barrier. Only 10% of global health research funding is targeted toward 90% of the global disease burden (10/90 gap), which translates into a 1/99 gap for health information (Godlee, Pakenham-Walsh, Ncayiyana, Cohen, & Packer, 2004). It is clear that a significant part of the problem is a result of infrastructure challenges that inhibit both the creation of health research and also the submission of relevant health research into appropriate forums. A few of these infrastructure challenges can be alleviated by the implementation of certain ICT. For example, wired and wireless Internet systems can bridge problems with inadequate and costly postal systems. However, according to one study, the publication barriers faced by developing-country researchers extend beyond purely poor infrastructure. As Horton (2000) noted, developing-country researchers faced broader challenges to both initiating research and disseminating their results, such as the following:

- Lack of a culture of research, thus little reward
- Absence of a peer group to stimulate debate and review work
- Bias in favor of developed countries from journal editors and reviewers
- Lack of interest from editors concerning diseases that are prevalent in developing countries, but not in the developed countries
- Bias toward high-tech, lab-oriented research

Education

There is the need to improve the quality of health-care information in terms of its reliability, relevance, and usability. One barrier to health education is the lack of information demand. Limited demand is a function of any of the following factors: a poor reading culture, low motivation associated with poor working conditions and poor prospects for career development, lack of awareness of evidence-based health care, long-term professional isolation, and long-term lack of access to information leading to the view that whatever is available is adequate (Godlee et al., 2004).

The lack of demand is related in part to the poor quality of much of the information supply (scientific and technical journal papers, reports, theses, conference papers, and bibliographic, factual, and full-text information, for instance). Poor supply worsens educational performance, lowers demand, and creates a negative feedback loop (Easterly, 2002; Edejer, 2000). Godlee et al. (2004) see improved electronic access to essential information for health professionals, such as drug formularies and evidence-based handbooks, as critical to improve health services. Information supply challenges include access to the technological tools for information retrieval, such as high-bandwidth Internet connections. The lack of infrastructure at the societal or economic level is a significant handicap. For instance, global communication networks continue to expand, but remain too costly for many low-income communities. Another supply barrier is the lack of clearly evolved educational standards and norms, including the encouragement of research into better ways of teaching that would enhance the ease of use and value of the content often streamed in from high-income countries (Arunachalam, 2003).

Medical Services

Medical treatment is costly in terms of human resources and money. Providing medical services to improve population health requires a highly trained professional corps and a highly productive infrastructure. The reality in most developing countries is an urban core of highly trained medical professionals that treat a wealthy minority in private practices. Underfunded public clinics close at midday so that staff can open shop to private patients in the afternoon. The financially lucrative, yet non-essential treatments and services sold in many private practices appeal to the paying patients but are not the services that would be prioritized if the national health funds were distributed among the entire population (Walsh & Warren, 1980).

The most useful and urgently needed services in any low-income population often are simple and repetitive. They are such because the enormous costs in treating large numbers require that the service be effective and efficiently provided. Childhood vaccines are classic examples of the type of medical service that is both effective and efficient for large low-income populations (Walsh & Warren). It is a form of triage as those same low-income individuals would benefit just as well from the personalized attention provided to rich patients if they were ever presented the opportunity.

ICT Uses and Applications

There is a long history of ICT applications in industrialized countries; telemedicine (or telehealth) dates back to the late 1960s in the United States. Research and implementation from industrialized regions may prove useful to new initiatives in developing countries. At the same time, the unique constraints within developing countries and evolving technologies allow for new uses and applications. The Institute of Medicine defines telemedicine as "the use of electronic information and communications technologies to provide and support health care when distance separates the participants" (*Telemedicine: A Guide to Assessing Telecommunications in Health Care*, 1996).

Telemedicine initiatives in industrialized countries, such as Norway and the United States, have often sought to serve groups separated by distance from medical resources, but distance separating participants is not an essential quality of the applications we will discuss in this chapter. The following retrospective on the failures of telemedicine in its infancy is highly relevant to our current discussion (Bashshur, 1980, pp. 13-14):

> *Many telemedicine projects begun in the early seventies were discontinued because they were not self-sustaining. Some were hastily conceived, almost assuring their eventual demise. In some instances this is not surprising since they were implemented without a clear definition of mission, an identification of the specific niche they would occupy in the existing health care system, or the unique contribution they would make to it. Moreover, the serious questions dealing with the economic viability of this mode of practice...were not addressed....[T]hese projects were designed as self-limiting experiments without intention of continuation beyond the experimental stage.*

As we review current initiatives and look to the future, it is important to develop a framework for discussing the applications. Perhaps more than other ICT application areas, such as education and governance, health applications involve a variety of users of various backgrounds and technical proficiency. Professional software systems designers often employ use cases, stories describing the detailed use of a system, to determine the functional requirements of that system. The use case has evolved from a concept introduced by Jacobson, Christerson, Jonsson, and Overgaard (1992) in *Object-Oriented Software Engineering* to a fundamental tool in software design.

In this work, we define use classes as groupings of use cases with similar traits. Applications with common human and organizational elements, for example, linking providers to patients, belong together in a use class. It is important to cluster applications into such use classes because, although the use classes themselves are agnostic with respect to the specific technology, the applications within a particular class may utilize some of the same technologies or approaches as one another. This is because of commonalities in the ability of users, physical constraints, and technical requirements.

For ICT applications in health, we define six primary use classes; though these are by no means exhaustive, they do cover the majority of current and upcoming applications. These use classes are (a) surveillance and information gathering, (b) research, (c) provider to provider, (d) provider to patient, (e) education, and (f) logistics.

A Multitude of Use Classes

Surveillance and Information Gathering

The practice of public health cannot exist under a state of ignorance; however, in many developing societies, this is the predominant condition because of the lack of reliable disease surveillance and other critical health data. The systematic gathering and analysis of clinical, environmental, and behavioral information represents a key user class. This type of information gathering allows public health to move from being reactive to responsive, with an end result of saving and improving lives. The Centers for Disease Control and Prevention (CDC) (2005) define public health surveillance as "the ongoing systematic collection, analysis, and interpretation of health data for the purposes of improving health and safety. Key to public health surveillance is the dissemination and use of data to improve health."

The key components in the labor- and information-intensive practice of public health information gathering are the following:

1.   The systematic and comprehensive collection of information on communicable and noncommunicable diseases, environmental factors, and behavioral and other health-risk factors

2.   The integration and analysis of disparate data sources to identify public health events and problems

3.   The dissemination of the results to the public health community so that a response can be developed

Perhaps the most well-known type of information gathering is the surveillance of communicable diseases. These types of diseases are of great importance because of the potential for rapid global spread without proper intervention (e.g., severe acute respiratory syndrome [SARS] or avian influenza subtype H5N1). In 2005, the Uige Province of Angola experienced the largest and deadliest outbreak of the Marburg hemorrhagic fever ever. There is no cure or effective treatment for the Marburg virus, but there are techniques for limiting the exposure and spread of the virus. In Angola, these measures were implemented months after the initial outbreak because of poor performance in the technical and social aspects of the national surveillance infrastructure (Ndayimirije & Kindhauser, 2005). A major gap was the lack of a functioning surveillance system that might have generated action reports concerning the existence of abnormal clinical cases. In the end, Dr. Maria Bonino, leveraging her experience, reported potential hemorrhagic fever cases to the government and international agencies with the assistance of the district health administrator Dr. Matondo Alexandre (LaFraniere & Grady, 2005). Months after the first cases, the existence of Marbrug was confirmed, allowing for a full-scale response by the collective expertise of the Global Outbreak Alert and Response Network (GOARN) operated by the WHO. This case illustrates serious gaps in the collection of surveillance data. The public health information infrastructure relies on data collected from a variety of sources (Lumpkin & Richards, 2002).

1. Medical data is derived from clinical encounters and includes patient history, physical findings, and clinical tests.

2. Environmental data is derived from ongoing monitoring programs of the environment, for example, tests for the level of air pollutants in a given community, or the capturing of insects, birds, and animals to test for particular diseases.

3. Survey data is designed to fill in the gaps of the other primary methods of gathering data. Surveys can be conducted via direct clinical intervention, the phone, or other mechanisms. Examples include the demographic and health surveys, or national HIV serosurveys.

Health data collection can be a Herculean task in industrialized regions, but in developing regions, severe resource constraints often turn the best plans of systematic data collection into a patchwork of incomplete data sets and missing information. However, a surveillance infrastructure does exist for certain types of diseases due to significant international attention and intervention. In Angola, the GOARN network, in their response to the Marburg outbreak, used the existing basic infrastructure for poliomyelitis eradication to aid their efforts (Ndayimirije & Kindhauser, 2005). In Uganda, one innovative method of using ICT to bridge these obstacles is the use of handheld computers and wireless connectivity technologies to allow consistent transmission of health data between rural health workers and the national authorities. Uganda has a poor wired communication infrastructure, but the mobile-phone network offers comprehensive coverage throughout the country; thus, by using technologies from Wideray Corporation (http://www.wideray.com), health workers are able to transmit information locally via 802.11b wireless connections to a server (Wideray jack server). Those data are then passed onward to data repositories located in the Ministry of Health in Kampala via GPRS (general packet radio service) on the GSM (Global System for Mobile Communications) network (Taggart, 2003).

Voxiva presents another approach to bridging the immense infrastructure challenges for data reporting in developing countries. An organization that frames itself as a service provider, Voxiva allows for its partners to collect real-time data from disparate locations using whatever technological means are available (Casas, LaJoie, & Prahalad, 2003; Voxiva, 2005). Furthermore, they enable effective communication using this same strategy, focusing on the use of available technology. Paul Meyer, founder of Voxiva, originally noted that the telephone was a much more widespread, accessible, and thus practical tool than the Internet; based on this, Voxiva began a disease surveillance initiative, Alerta, in Peru in 2002. This enabled better reporting in terms of yield, frequency, and data quality without investment in infrastructure or technology at the edges of the network. Today, Voxiva's solutions continue to allow heterogeneous forms of interaction for data reporting, including the Web, telephone, fax, e-mail, and SMS (short messaging service). Since they operate as a service, their partners (or clients) are not responsible for technical issues or maintenance: simply interfacing with the system as users. Today, Voxiva has international health surveillance initiatives in

Table 2. Essential sources of health-related information (AbouZahr & Boerma, 2005)

1.	A census.
2.	Continuous monitoring of births and deaths with certification of cause of death. Where universal coverage and medical death certification is not feasible, consideration should be given to sample vital registration systems (i.e., registration of vital events in randomly selected samples of the population) coupled with verbal autopsy.
3.	A surveillance and response system focused on epidemic and vaccine-preventable diseases (e.g., cholera, HIV, and polio) as well as emerging diseases (e.g., SARS).
4.	A programme of household surveys designed to measure use of healthcare services and important household or individual behaviors, covering both demographic and health surveys and other surveys that can be used to generate health-related information, such as surveys of living standards.
5.	A system of service generated data derived from facilities and patient-provider interactions covering aspects such as care offered, quality of care and treatments administered.
6.	Mapping of public health facilities and services at national and district levels.
7.	Behavioral surveillance focusing especially on risk factors such as smoking, unsafe sex and malnutrition.
8.	National health accounts.
9.	Financial and management information.
10.	Modeling, estimates and projections.
11.	Health research, including clinical, health systems and operations research.

Peru (Nacer for maternal and child health); Tamil Nadu, India (post-tsunami Health Watch); Andhra Pradesh, India (Acute Encephalitis Syndrome Surveillance Information Management System [AESSIMS] for Japanese encephalitis); and Rwanda (Treatment Research and AIDS Centre [TRACnet] for HIV/AIDS).

Surveillance and information gathering are ultimately concerned with generating knowledge about the state of health in a given area. As has been discussed, the collection of data is critical to this endeavor, but equally important is the proper analysis of collected information to ascertain actionable knowledge. A large part of the analysis equation involves the presence of personnel skilled in epidemiological techniques and data analysis, but ICTs do have a role in assisting analysis. In particular, geographic information systems (GISs) have been increasingly used to map data to improve analysis and decision making in developing regions. One example is the HealthMapper application, a geographic database, information-management, and mapping application, developed by the WHO to support the surveillance needs of national Guinea worm-eradication programs. As the software was designed for public health needs, it can be applied to numerous disease surveillance applications incorporating surveillance-specific data as well as data relating to population settlements, social and health services, and the natural environment (WHO, 2005). Developed by researchers at the Centers for Disease Control and Prevention, EpiInfo represents a similar effort to create freely available software for surveillance data management and analysis (2005).

Research

Information gaps in health research in developing countries exist in both the consumption and production of research. However, the global public health community often focuses only on the consumption of health research information as the key information gap facing developing countries. Thus, providing access to critical health research through free or reduced-price access to journals is the principal intervention. This point of view neglects that information gaps are often a result of multiple problems, and health research is no different. Journals are often the least valuable information sources for health professionals (Godlee et al., 2004). The focus on access clouds the issue of information needs, and there is often a considerable gap between information and useful knowledge. Being able to select the information that is necessary and appropriate given the particular local context is the critical issue. Access to appropriate knowledge is complicated by two factors: (a) most health information sources are produced and hosted in developed nations, and (b) there exists scant research on the ecology of information for health workers in developing nations: "Notwithstanding an often rudimentary computing environment, users in developing countries should be empowered to produce digital library collections themselves, not just consume information produced elsewhere…In the developing world, digital libraries represent a killer app for computing technology" (Witten, Loots, Trujillo, & Bainbridge, 2001, p.84).

Applications are needed for analyzing surveillance data, evaluating health interventions and related projects, and conducting analysis of clinical trial data. One thought has been to focus on creating parallel knowledge networks so that developing-country researchers can exchange information amongst themselves, but in many countries of Africa for instance, these initiatives face severe infrastructure bottlenecks. It is often easier and cheaper in many African countries to communicate with Europe using the telecommunications system than it is to connect to their neighbors. As is evident, ICTs have the potential to assist in improving some of the barriers related to the production and consumption of health research, but many challenges are beyond the realm of the technology.

Provider to Provider

The need for health care is universal; however, the quality, availability, needs, and health service delivery mechanisms differ greatly across the world. Health-care providers are the human interface and play a central role in large regional and local health-care systems. Differences in service quality among health-care providers are one of the key distinctions between developing and developed nations. Health-care providers as referred to in this chapter are service professionals or semiprofessionals responsible for delivering some form of preventive and curative care. Health-care providers tend to be differentiated both by specialties and severity of care (e.g., primary, secondary, and tertiary), as well as the economic model of their affiliate institution: public, for profit, and nonprofit.

Guided by standard health policy and high-income-country precedent, many low-income countries have focused on the development of a distributed public-sector health-care infrastructure based on primary care. However, a substantial portion of health-care services in developing societies are delivered by private providers on a fee-for-service basis (Hanson & Berman, 1998; Prata, Montagu, & Jefferys, 2005). "Private" providers are defined as those who fall outside the direct control of government, and can include both for-profit and non-profit providers (Hanson & Berman). Many of these private providers tend to be small and independent, for example, individual doctors and drug shops. This informal private sector serves a significant portion of many low-income populations, and could potentially improve the quality of their services through the adoption of low-cost ICT strategies. As AbouZahr and Boerma (2005) note, "ICTs have a significant role to play at the level of individuals and communities, for effective clinical management and for assessing the extent to which services are meeting the needs and demand of patients and communities" (p. 529).

Health-care service providers have two broadly defined information needs. The first area is the collection, processing, reporting, and use of pertinent health information. The second information need is to consult, coordinate, and diagnose across disparate locations, specialties, and levels of care. It is assumed that poor provider service is simply due to a lack of information, but the reality is more complex. Several factors impact the demand and supply of health information, and ultimately the efficacy of provider services:

- **Many actors, many needs, and unequal power:** At inception, the Health Information System (HIS) of Mozambique was heavily centralized, and information policy emphasized reporting from the primary levels to the central authority (Braa et al., 2001). Later, Mozambique adopted the WHO-recommended primary health-care strategy, which focuses on the district and local delivery of health care, thus there is greater use of information at these levels rather than through upward reporting. However, local use of information is hampered by two factors: (a) an underfunded local infrastructure and (b) the dependence of Mozambique on foreign donors for a substantial portion of their resources, creating yet a different set of information needs.

- **The lack of capacity to utilize information effectively:** Health workers have little or no training to interpret health data in a useful manner. In the Cuamba district of Mozambique, the health center had cumulative data on each point in the DPT (diphtheria, pertussis, tetanus) immunization campaign; however, those data, if interpreted properly, would have shown a dropout rate of 55% by the last required immunization and only 10% coverage for the target population of 2,500 children (Braa et al., 2001).

- **Infrastructure problems:** Technical infrastructure is handicapped by irregular electricity access, the lack of skilled technical personnel, and the inability to fully implement comprehensive communications infrastructure.

- **Absence of strong provider networks:** Developing societies are characterized by a single public health-care entity and an array of small, independent private providers that account for most health-care contacts. These informal and unregulated health-care markets present both data collection and health policy enforcement difficulties.

Similarly, we also find challenges in the supply of health information:

- **Lack of a strong health information infrastructure:** The health information infrastructure (HII) refers to the organizations, technologies, and policies responsible for the use of information relevant to health-care services. Due to the lack of financial and technical resources in many developing countries, the HII infrastructure is inadequate or nonexistent.

- **Gaps in data due to intermittent and noncomprehensive data collection:** This is largely a result of failed governance. Developing-country governments are unable to enforce surveillance reporting from the health sector (public and private).

- **Pertinent information and data spread among diverse group of stakeholders:** Essential health information is not derived from one source, but is the responsibility of many domestic and international actors.

- **Lack of agreement on an essential data set:** An essential data set is the most important data elements chosen from all primary health programs routinely reported by health service providers. The essential data set is guided by two principles: (a) The number of data elements should be limited to 100 or 150, and should enable the calculation of 80 to 120 indicators, and (b) the essential data set should integrate the needs of various programs. When building the data set, one must ask two important questions: (a) Why do we want to collect this information? (b) How will we use it? (Shaw, 2005)

The need to collect, process, report, and use information is a crucial part of any health-care information system. The continuing improvement in the quality, cost, and capabilities in modern ICT has allowed an entirely new type of information exchange: remote consultation, coordination, and diagnosis. While this type of ICT application is in its infancy, certain applications have showed the promise of ICTs to extend the reach of health services. While urbanization is accelerating across the developing world, significant populations remain in rural or underserved areas. Though many issues are beyond the reach of technology, many challenges in remote consultation, coordination, and diagnosis are a direct result of deficiencies in the technical infrastructure.

A remote hospital in Yugoslavia received a donated ultrasound unit from Dartmouth-Hitchcock Medical Center (USA) for use in the examination and diagnosis of patients (Dartmouth Medical School, 2005). While there was a definite need for the ultrasound machine, the hospital did not possess the capacity to read the images. A doctor and medical student from Dartmouth Medical School attempted to remove this barrier by designing a system for remote image reading. In their pilot study, 50 images were compressed, transmitted, uncompressed, and reviewed by two attending radiologists, as well as one radiology resident and medical student. In 64% of the cases, the reviewer could not tell the difference between the two types of images. Image compression was critical to the feasibility of the transmission of large images over a slow link; however, increased data compression affects different aspects of image quality, which can be highly problematic for clinical applications, such as radiology. The study found that 67% of the images were suitable for diagnostic purposes, and of the remaining images deemed unsuitable, the machine, rather than the image compression, may have caused the problem.

Another similar example demonstrates the use of annotated images (via a Web-based referral system called EyesTalk) in order to refer difficult ophthalmologic cases to centers of excellence within the Aravind Eye Care System (AECS; Bhandari, Ibrahim, & Sandhu, 2004). For example, a complex case of childhood glaucoma was referred to one of the system hospitals with a pediatric glaucoma specialist; this referral included the referring clinician's comments as well as two digital images of the child's condition. The receiving ophthalmologist reviewed the information, spoke with the referring doctor over the telephone for further information, and made his recommendations.

In the industrialized world, health-care systems are dominated by strong public and private entities (e.g., National Health Service, United Kingdom). These strong entities are capable of implementing information policies and management both internally and externally; however, as has been shown, many developing societies are entirely different. Small, independent providers in developing countries have an inability to communicate for reasons that go well beyond ICT, but ICT in collaboration with programmatic and policy-level change can have an impact on more effective service delivery, particularly in resource sharing and the sharing of information to improve clinical management and response.

Provider to Patient

Connecting providers directly to patients was a major objective of many of the telehealth initiatives in the United States and other industrialized countries over the past 40 years. In all cases, the aim was largely the same: to connect health-care providers to patients who would otherwise be inaccessible due to distance or transportation. This communication could be used for a variety of services, including the provision of health information, diagnosis, and treatment follow-up. In fact, telephones were first used for diagnosis almost as soon as they were invented, with a pediatrician diagnosing a child with croup over the phone in 1897 (Fosaelli, 1983). Successful diagnosis is more appropriate to some medical disciplines than others; to date, primarily in industrialized countries, these disciplines include dermatology and mental health (radiology also, but that falls under the provider-to-provider use class).

Newer communication technologies include asynchronous modalities (where there is a delay in communication), e-mail, for example. This introduces dynamics into the proposed applications that have not been witnessed previously. Synchronous communication technologies, for example, telephones and audio-video links, are largely intuitive for new users, are more comfortable for patients because of direct interaction with providers, and have been used extensively in a variety of medical disciplines. Asynchronous methods have not been used extensively, and bring both advantages and disadvantages.

E-mail as an example makes better use of resources, including bandwidth and the provider's time, making it more cost effective and potentially allowing for consultation with a wider range of providers; with little need for scheduling, and given the lower time investment, consultation with specialists around the world is a possibility (e.g., Graham et al., 2003), but the sustainability and scalability of such a model is still in question. Furthermore, the utility of information that may be conveyed using a combination of text and images is subject to the abilities and/or training of the user or mediator, such as a kiosk operator. Evaluating the health outcomes based on these different modalities in a developing setting would be very useful for planning effective ICT initiatives in the future (see Whited, 2001, for an evaluation of outcomes in a developed setting). Patient satisfaction is another issue that may vary with differing modes of interaction. Finally, and perhaps most importantly, e-mail incurs a delay in response. Where transportation is costly, as it is for many rural people in the developing world, a delay between medical service events often prevents the patient from following up; in the case of e-mail being used for diagnosis of a ophthalmic condition at a kiosk in a larger village in India, the patient may not be able to return to the kiosk for lack of time and/or funds.

The Aravind Eye Care System, among other ICT initiatives, has experimented with remote diagnosis (see Figure 1). AECS is one of the largest providers of eye care in the world, located in Tamil Nadu, India, and focused on the eradication of preventable blindness in underserved populations. In 2003, AECS partnered with n-Logue, a private company created by Professor Ashok Jhunjhunwala of the Indian Institute of Technology, Madras, to establish rural information kiosks throughout India. The partnership was aimed at providing another mechanism for screening patients and directing them to the hospital for care. Many of Tamil Nadu's residents live in rural settings where transportation to urban centers for treatment represents a significant burden. Much like the eye camps that AECS runs, this initiative was aimed at bringing the diagnosis to the people. Under the supervision of one of the doctors at their Madurai hospital, AECS designated several counselors to deal with requests for consultation made from the n-Logue kiosks.

At present, the system has not met with widespread use due to several factors. The n-Logue wireless technology was good at providing connectivity across distances cost effectively, but bandwidth was severely limited. Each kiosk owner was provided with a bundle of technologies, including a digital camera, but its resolution often proved insufficient for proper diagnosis of anything beyond the most mature cataracts. Furthermore, patients preferred synchronous communication mechanisms such as videoconferencing sessions with the counselors to detailing their problem to the kiosk owner who relays the information via e-mail along with a picture. The bandwidth restrictions of the n-Logue system made it difficult to hold satisfactory videoconferencing sessions, though attempts were made to deal with poor performance. Another problem was the kiosk owners themselves because they served as the

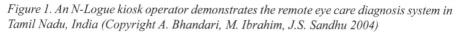

Figure 1. An N-Logue kiosk operator demonstrates the remote eye care diagnosis system in Tamil Nadu, India (Copyright A. Bhandari, M. Ibrahim, J.S. Sandhu 2004)

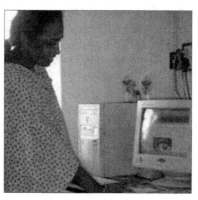

*Figure 2. Women in Kunduz, Afghanistan being trained to use Equal Access Satellite Receiver
(Copyright Equal Access 2005, reprinted with permission)*

key point of contact with the rural communities. If they did not buy into the potential of such services, or were unwilling to provide the assistance necessary to facilitate such contacts, the system was effectively useless. This was the case with many kiosk owners; but in cases where a motivated kiosk owner existed, positive results were seen by AECS (Bhandari et al., 2004). There exists potential for this system to be used additionally for follow-up care and the dissemination of information (including education), but this potential is yet unrealized aside from some experiments.

Connecting providers to patients, via any modality, must be accompanied by proper support and follow up; training mediators, such as kiosk operators, to assist with diagnosis or screening is critical to the success of such operations. Furthermore, practitioners should realize that this is of more value to some medical specialties than others, and that digital imaging can play a very important role in the feasibility of operations for some of these disciplines.

Education

As we have already indicated, education is one of the major areas of public health. As a use class, education presents more usability challenges than the other classes because of the diversity of end users. Health education can be subdivided into two subclasses: (a) continuing education for medical staff and semiskilled training for paraprofessionals, and (b) direct population education. Each of these subclasses represents a distinct but diverse set of users with different needs, values, and abilities.

- **Health worker education:** Chandrasekhar and Ghosh (2001, p. 851) indicate the need for "education and lifelong learning that will enable doctors in developing countries to be informed about and trained in the use of advances in knowledge." Pakenham-Walsh, Priestley, and Smith (1997, p. 90) further develop the need to educate a broader set of health workers: "Providing access to reliable health information for health workers in developing countries is potentially the single most cost effective and achievable strategy for sustainable improvement in health care." The challenges are in providing that reliable access, but also in allowing for ownership of information, in other words, for health workers and others to actively participate in, and contribute to, the educational process rather than passively assimilate information created in a different context. In either case, ICT has not been adequately used to date to accomplish the task of continual training for medical professionals and paraprofessionals. The end users of such systems have a wide variety of abilities and informational needs, from skilled surgeons to midwives.

- **Population education:** As we have already noted, the goal of health education is to change peoples' behavior in order to benefit community health. Unfortunately, such health promotion has always been a very difficult proposition, given any medium. Recent trends toward using culturally appropriate entertainment have proved more successful than traditional means of education, such as the presentation of facts (e.g., Brown, 2004; Farr, Witte, Jarato, & Menard, 2005, for HIV/AIDS). ICTs are well-designed for entertainment and are often used for this purpose across the developing world, so leveraging this in order to develop meaningful health education initiatives is promising.

Equal Access' educational initiatives use satellite radio to enable community women (see figure 2) to create audio content and broadcast it to a wide geographic area (Bellows & Sandhu, personal communication, 2005). Their system is being used to develop locally created programs that enable health education in Nepal, Afghanistan, and India. Satellite radio as a medium allows them to create their own content at a much lower cost than traditional broadcast radio, and to reach a much broader audience. The drawbacks are the cost of program creation and the equipment cost. In other settings, educational kiosks have been used in urban health clinics in Mexico City to educate women about prenatal care (Langer & Catino, 2003). In direct education of populations at large, the users are highly varied. In many cases, they may not be literate, or they may speak many dialects and languages over a small geographic area, but this is very country dependent. For example, Cuba and Mongolia both have literacy rates of more than 97%, while Nepal's rate is 45% and Niger's is less than 20% (CIA, 2005). This makes the development of appropriate educational material difficult. While some technologists approach this problem by developing content (or devices) that communicate in all manners to all people, another approach is to view the community's collective assets (in terms of both literacy and linguistic ability) as an element of the system (Sandhu, Hey, Newman, & Agogino, 2005). Rather than creating ICT that can communicate with every person, ICT that can communicate with every community can have greater population impact, if designed carefully.

Logistics

Logistical systems form the backbone of the major areas of public health. Logistic systems supply not only products, but also health professionals who provide key services. As a use class, logistics has two general subclasses of end users divided into (a) disaster-relief systems for emergency and temporary medical services, and (b) permanent population health services that enhance health systems. Both of these subclasses represent a distinct but diverse set of users with different needs, values, and abilities.

- **Disaster relief logistics:** In the December 2004 Indian Ocean tsunami, there was a need for both short-term disaster relief and long-term systems enhancement. The logistics of relief include collecting immediate surveillance data, funneling resources to set up medical services, creating systems to inform the affected populations about treatment and prevention of contagion, and evaluating the process to continue squeezing more efficiency from future missions. Various organizations specialize in developing the necessary systems and skills for logistics relief programs. The Fritz Institute, for example, focuses on developing and deploying humanitarian logistics software, and addressing the problem of aid delivery, supply-chain management and coordination, and operations research. Such logistical organization of services and goods is critical to both public health relief efforts and health systems in general. As *The Economist* noted:

  what is special about this tsunami is the geographical extent of the devastation and the number of countries affected. Earthquakes produce terrible consequences, but normally of a highly localised sort…the damage stretches across thousands of miles and involves millions of people. That produces a huge logistical challenge for international organisations and aid agencies: how to get relief supplies and, later, reconstruction assistance to so many places at more or less the same time. Much more of the money and planning will have to be devoted to planes, helicopters, trucks and supply lines than in "normal" disasters and relief efforts.

  ("Asia's Devastation: Reflections on a Rare but Terrible Calamity," 2004, p.9)

The tsunami operation highlighted the complexities of getting relief across borders in the shortest possible time and with maximum efficiency. Humanitarian organizations not only had to cope with damaged infrastructure, they were also dealing with 12 different governments and 12 different sets of customs regulations. Delays in getting aid to those who needed it cost lives (Bannon, 2005). Coordinated efforts via ICT applications such as humanitarian logistics software applications are starting to gain attention. Recent crises demonstrate that ICTs can improve the delivery of health and disaster-management services to poor and remote locations (Chandrasekhar & Ghosh, 2001). However, the opposite is also true, and ICTs should be supported by contingency plans when ICT-dependent operations fail. In the 2005 U.S. Hurricane Katrina relief effort, mobile medical services could not be seconded quickly to disaster areas in part because the communications infrastructure had been decimated resulting in an inability to coordinate human efforts to drive the placement of such extra resources. The service providers and volunteers, however, expected the systems to be ready, and the absence of any effective response system led to immediate criticisms of federal and state inaction (Marchione, 2005).

- **Long-term population health services:** There are a variety of logistical ICT applications that can enhance health systems. The discussion of each would require detail beyond the scope of this chapter; however, several general examples should be mentioned. Systems to assure consistent medical goods and information supply are critical for every aspect of public health. For example, "stock-outs," when inventory levels reach zero in the face of continuing demand, are a constant problem for public clinics in many developing countries, and having a basic communications link in place can help alleviate this problem. In another example, effective surveillance and subsequent logistical coordination requires a data supply chain to deliver information to decision makers and resource-allocation centers. Furthermore, health services are only operational if clinical data are accessible by health-care workers. Some other examples of supporting health-care delivery and systems include the implementation of mini medical records via smart-card applications that capture clinical data. Some efforts are being made to have personal health data carried on a card to clinics of the patient's choice. All of these applications should be designed with two major goals in mind: the enhancement of decision-making capacity and the organization of services for patient care.

A Variety of Technologies

In July 2005, *The Economist* asserted that the mobile phone, not the personal computer, was the key to alleviating the digital divide ("Business: Calling an End to Poverty," 2005). Even C. K. Prahalad claimed in that same issue, "Emerging markets will be wireless-centric, not PC-centric," but wireless technologies alone will not offer a means for tackling all problems. Though the article cites a World Bank report indicating that 77% of the world's population lives within range of a mobile network, this is in fact an optimistic estimate; 60% is more accurate (*Financing Information and Communication Infrastructure Needs in the Developing World: Public and Private Roles*, 2005). Additionally, many of the people in this 60% do not have access to the networks because of the prohibitive handset cost. Furthermore, building mobile networks that will reach the remainder of the population will be difficult as this represents the poorest, most rural populations, and as the quality of access will necessarily be worse. Sharing devices where appropriate will certainly help alleviate some of these problems, but the reality is that heterogeneous methods integrating multiple technologies with more traditional forms of communication will be necessary to achieve the apparent goal of improving lives as Voxiva is now doing with health surveillance in Peru and India. It is important to recognize that a variety of ICTs exist, each with its own set of strengths and weaknesses. Furthermore, the requirements of each use class within the health sector vary greatly, so no single ICT will prove decisive.

A particular ICT activity can similarly be enabled by multiple technologies, depending on the setting; for example, television can be relayed via traditional terrestrial broadcast, via the Internet on a personal computer, or via satellite using a dish. In this television example—in addition to different platforms and broadcast mechanisms—there can also be different applications, such as entertainment, news, or education. Although the end result may be similar, the cost, ease of use, infrastructure, and penetration might be extremely different. These factors can greatly impact the appropriate choice in a given setting.

Assessment

Health ICT involves the intersection of technology, health, and local context and thus requires a multifaceted approach to answering the question of how best to judge these technologies. In other words, an assessment of the technology alone is not likely to yield a sufficient analysis because without improved health outcomes, the overall benefit will be negligible. These issues of technical and population health performance impact both design and assessment. As health ICT operates at the intersection of several fields, we must clarify what is meant by assessment. Assessment includes systems-level issues, health outcomes (or relevant proxies for health outcomes), usability, and technical evaluation; however, we will only discuss the first three of these as technical evaluation (e.g., reliability, performance, interoperability) is well established. Each of these factors plays a critical role in the successful deployment of a sustainable health ICT solution.

Systems Issues

How do we assess these various technologies? In order to judge any technology one must first ask questions concerning the initiative, project, or intervention. The following are systems-level issues, where systems are comprised of people, organizations, and technology:

1. What are the system goals?
2. What are the needs of the target users?
3. What are the capabilities of this target population?
4. What are the needs of the critical stakeholders (often not the users)?
5. Who has ownership of the technology? Is there sufficient local investment in the initiative to provide for sustainability?
6. What is the duration of the project and how will the system evolve?
7. How will maintenance and support be provided?
8. What are the assumed modes of interaction with the system, and are they feasible?
9. What is the source of financing, what are the real operation costs, and is it economically sustainable?

The answers to these questions should be used during the systems design phase, and should be answered prior to undertaking any initiative. At the same time, these questions can and should be revisited during the progress of such an initiative in order to assess its effectiveness as it is implemented.

Health Outcomes

Different assessment strategies are appropriate for different ICT initiatives in health, both by the nature of the application and the purpose of the project. A one-size-fits-all assessment strategy is not practical and may be somewhat harmful. Why conduct assessment? In some cases, assessment is no more than program evaluation and is used to improve the ongoing processes of an initiative. Beyond this, program evaluation may help others undertaking similar initiatives. In the most rigorous sense, as is often appropriate in a more experimental initiative, formal research methods can be used to elicit intervention effects in order to add to the greater body of knowledge and to plan a strategy for similar initiatives elsewhere.

Randomized control trials (RCTs) of products and even services are the most rigorous means of assessing the potential. The gold standard, double-blinded RCT, may be impractical or unethical in many settings (Smith & Pell, 2003). An intervention might be randomized against a placebo or compared to the current gold-standard product or service in what are called equivalency trials. For example, an equivalency trial might compare in-person cataract diagnosis (the gold standard) against remote diagnosis using e-mail with digital imagery. Randomized intervention trials require the measurement of effects at the scale of an individual, or perhaps a community; as such, this methodology does not lend itself easily to particular ICT applications (e.g., changing from paper to electronic medical records at a particular health center).

Evaluating medical interventions has traditionally considered efficacy and clinical outcomes. Increasingly, there is also concern with cost and effectiveness in the field. For public health evaluators, the ultimate goal is verification of health outcomes: alive or dead, sick or healthy. However, other indicators often suffice to answer questions of program functionality. For example, health education evaluations rely on measuring changes in knowledge, attitudes, or behaviors (in increasing order of difficulty), but do not have time to wait for health events to validate the intervention.

Ethical issues also arise, particularly in the design of RCTs. International standards require prior informed consent of study participants; furthermore, research cannot assign harm to study subjects (United Nations, 2005). Withholding a service that is known to be beneficial from a population when there are sufficient funds to provide the service to this population may be unethical. A more comprehensive discussion of RCT ethics is not appropriate here, but ethical issues should be at the forefront of any research design.

Committees for the protection of human subjects (CPHS), also known as institutional review boards (IRBs), were established in the hope that peer review would reduce the likelihood of abusive research. Community advisory boards (CABs) take research oversight one step further with active community participation in research design and implementation. Community-based participatory research (CBPR) is a loosely defined field in which the community forms an active partnership in, and in some cases leads, research efforts (Minkler, 1997). Rather than limit participation to the CAB, CBPR calls for community involvement from the first efforts at framing the research question to the dissemination and publication of findings. Critics argue that this gradient of increasing involvement from IRB to CBPR compromises the quality of objective inquiry; however, there are compelling counterarguments noting the greater ethical validity of study participants playing an active role in research design and implementation. Though there are some similarities, CBPR is distinct from the participatory methods that have been used in other development-related work (e.g., Narayan & Srinivasan, 1994).

Usability

Usability refers to the ease with which people can utilize a product or service for a particular purpose. Though the term is often applied to artifacts, it can apply to any designed system, of which technology is often only a part.

Voxiva represents an excellent example of a system that has adequately addressed issues of usability. They circumvented many usability issues by focusing on existing technology: their system users were already familiar with the technology as it was readily accessible and required no further maintenance. However, in the case of other applications, such as electronic surveillance systems, it may be necessary to develop new technology. In such cases, it is imperative to follow systematic usability design and assessment strategies. Good usability alone will not make a project successful, but poor usability of health ICT does not only plague projects, it can actually harm individuals (e.g., see Koppel et al., 2005).

Various methods exist for assessing the usability of products or services, primarily from the fields of human-computer interaction and human factors engineering. A treatment of these methods is outside the scope of this chapter, so for a more comprehensive review of usability, including usability assessment, the reader is referred to Kuniavsky (2003), Nielsen (1994), and Norman (2002). Beyond this, Karsh (2004) provides a topically relevant, comprehensive overview of issues related to technology acceptance.

Design is inherently an iterative process, and integrating systems usability testing into this process leads to more robust, lean, and ultimately useful products and services. The key is to involve users early and often in the design process, in particular eliciting and addressing their unique needs as system users.

Overall Considerations

In the short term, information technologies essentially "introduce new channels of communication and transactions in healthcare" (Demiris, 2004, p. 145). Effective delivery of health services requires a plethora of data. Measuring population outcomes, monitoring service delivery outputs, and managing health systems all require large, often complex, information flows. Technologies that manage information and communication increase the efficiency of information flows, and ultimately save lives and money. The ability to coordinate a health system and delivery of care is predicated on the ability to communicate and have access to information. In the long term, health ICT "refers to a fundamental redesign of healthcare delivery" (Scott, 2004, p.1). Health ICT applications and principles promise to rebuild health industries in profound ways. However, the challenges are significant because emerging economies impose resource constraints on ICT development that are not present in wealthier societies. In addition to resource constraints, there are a number of other very important challenges, including the match between design and cultural context, systems infrastructure, and disease characteristics.

It is necessary for design purposes to know the local context and variety of applications. In one example of the challenges to public health, researchers identified four critical factors in telehealth transfer to Ethiopia: national ICT policies, ICT infrastructure, telehealth implementation factors, and culture-specific beliefs and values and differences in technology cultures between the developers in rich countries and the users in poor countries (Tan et al., 2005). Heeks (2002) highlighted a "design-actuality gap," which he defined as the match or mismatch between information systems designs and local user reality. Two further illustrations make similar points. First, according to Jayasuriya (1999, p. 335):

> *Factors that led to the failure [of the Philippine computerized information system (IS)] included ambiguity in the organization and in responsibility for the project, lack of capacity to undertake large information systems development projects and inability to retain appropriate staff. However, when the historical and contextual issues were revealed and the interplay between the content, process and context of the change was analyzed it was revealed that the content of the IS was not responsive to the changes in the wider health system. The case study confirms the need to analyze and understand organizational, environmental and cultural issues in adopting models and procedures used elsewhere when managing information systems in developing countries.*

Second, according to WHO (2001a):

> *New technologies hold great potential for improving health care, primarily by increasing the quality, relevance and delivery of information to health personnel. Unfortunately, this potential is far from being realized in many countries, partly because of the financial, technological and infrastructure challenges of the "digital divide," but also because the real and greatly varying needs of the users are often overlooked.*

ICT development, use, and implementation can face infrastructure-level barriers that not only include the lack of a highly skilled workforce and appropriate financing, but also other factors that fall under the broad umbrella of ICT governance; some examples include issues such as the sustainability of ICT systems, training and management capacity, constant maintenance of software systems, establishing data standards, adequate and appropriate power supply, and privacy and security of particular types of sensitive health data (e.g., pregnancy or HIV test results). In the West, there are regulatory systems in place that guide rule enforcement, and policy initiatives that protect privacy such as the Health Insurance Portability and Accountability Act (HIPAA) regulations in the United States. Innovative solutions must be generated in order to have a high level of ICT governance that also encompasses ethical considerations. Furthermore, because of the lack of health-care infrastructure in many developing regions, product design must be appropriate to the particular context. For example, having robust hardware (e.g., for power-supply issues, having longer life batteries or alternative power options) or proper management is more critical.

In the developed world, various insurance and governmental schemes generally pay for most of health care; however, in the developing world, the individual can bear over two thirds of the cost (Lewinberg, 2003). The lack of third-party payers for medical infrastructure in these regions is a significant barrier. The annual total expenditure per person in the world's developing regions is less than $75 on all health expenses (Quick, 2003; Trouiller, Olliaro, Torreele, Orbinski, Laing, & Ford, 2002). Since the consumer does not bear the actual cost of substantial portions of health care in developed nations, the demand for medical care and new technologies is very high (Cutler & McClellan, 2001). Clearly, this is not the case in developing nations. However, even if the cost of technology or particular types of care was significantly reduced, the lack of infrastructure would make it very difficult to distribute, administer or use, and properly sustain the use of various medical goods (Hongoro & McPake, 2004). Furthermore, there are significant indirect costs, including waiting time, transportation costs, lost wages, poor-quality health services, and many others (Melese, Alemayehu, Friedlander, & Courtright, 2004; Russell, 2004). These indirect costs are substantial and are significant deterrents to utilizing health care. These factors will substantially impact any sort of ICT for health initiatives and should be taken into account.

Alternative health finance strategies are being piloted. The World Bank, German Development Bank (KfW), and others are considering a mechanism called output-based assistance (OBA). Instead of using input-based global budgets, which allocate funds for supplies, labor, and other goods and services to the provider, an OBA approach gives patients the means to choose their preferred health-care provider. Patients use vouchers for health services at qualified government and nongovernment facilities. Providers are reimbursed on a per-patient basis, the clinic's output, as long as quality criteria are met in delivering the service. OBA has been lauded as a strategy to put aid in the hands of those who need it most while freeing service providers to develop competitively priced high-quality health services (Campell, Janisch, Potts, & Bellows, 2005; Sandiford, Gorter, & Salvetto, 2002; Yamamoto, 2004). ICT reporting systems will improve the efficiency and reduce fraud of future iterations of this strategy.

The nature of a particular disease will dictate not only ICT design and health finance structures, but also a host of other factors such as intervention, sustainability, complexity, and costs. In general, the public health community categorizes diseases as either acute (HIV) or chronic (cardiovascular diseases); however, one must go beyond such categories and understand the true natural history of disease and its treatment. For example, an SMS-based (mobile phone) medication reminder may result in very different levels of compliance after several months for tuberculosis patients, who are generally asymptomatic, when compared with diabetics, who can become symptomatic very quickly. Also, the course of diabetes is a chronic condition requiring a lifetime of treatment and vigilance.

Major barriers to information-technology access and development include disease characteristics, appropriate accompanying technology, sociocultural considerations, and poor health-care infrastructure. ICT for health projects should be mindful of the overall goals of public health in developing countries, which is to reduce population-wide morbidity and mortality. When building such projects, designers should consider the net impact of any particular ICT implementation on a disease or health issue, and whether extremely scarce resources are being used wisely. Initiatives should also attempt to build in cost-reducing, efficiency-increasing systems for health care, and avoid redeploying an entirely different way of delivering care.

Trends and Conclusion

Future trends will be affected by the dynamic nature of both technology and the shifting disease burden. There are several likely stages of ICT utilization for health in developing countries that will be dependent on the state of the infrastructure available.

In the short term, it is practical to assume that the state of the ICT infrastructure (lack of infrastructure in many cases) will be relatively stable; however, the utilization of the existing infrastructure will be somewhat variable. We anticipate an increase of currently available services: more health worker training, more telehealth applications, improved frequency of data gathering for surveillance, and more sites using information technology for effective management. Skilled medical staff, particularly in urban areas, will gain increasing access to health information, but this will still be tempered by the cost of accessing some of the most relevant content (e.g., health journal research).

In the long term, we expect ICT infrastructure to develop and overcome current bottlenecks. The diffusion of modern ICTs—mobile telephony is the most prominent example today—have allowed many populations to leapfrog older technologies (such as terrestrial telephony) because of the lower access costs. In a similar fashion, we expect mobile telephony, WLL (wireless local loop), WAN (wide area network, including Worldwide Interoperability for Microwave Access [WiMAX]), and other such technologies to enable wider access to information and communication channels. Thus, we expect a proliferation of the number

Table 3. Change in the rank order of disease burden for 8 leading causes worldwide, 1990-2020 (Lopez & Murray, 1998)

Rank	Disease or Injury	
	1990	2020
1	Lower respiratory infections	Ischemic heart disease
2	Diarrheal diseases	Unipolar major depression
3	Conditions during the perinatal period	Road traffic accidents
4	Unipolar major depression	Cerebrovascular disease
5	Ischemic heart disease	Chronic obstructive pulmonary disease
6	Cerebrovascular disease	Lower respiratory infections
7	Tuberculosis	Tuberculosis
8	Measles	War

and type of health services, but this will occur over a time scale that is largely paced by the natural diffusion of the technology.

While economic viability plays a central role in the sustainability of any health ICT initiative, technology itself plays another critical role. Computing and communication technologies—from software applications to mobile phones to networking equipment—are constantly evolving. The highly dynamic nature of technology and the obsolescence of the technology left in its wake are of paramount concern as new technology often requires further capital investment and personnel training. Using older technologies with local support is appropriate as long as the technology is meeting the necessary requirements, and maintenance does not depend on components that can no longer be acquired. Technological sustainability and obsolescence are key concerns because of the often critical nature of health services that may grow dependent on the technology.

We need to understand not only technological change, but also dynamic health issues. The global burden of disease (GBD) forecast for 2020 (see Table 3) provides a gross indication of the changing face of disease and injury. Notably, depression will climb to second on the list in the face of prevailing global stigma and discrimination against those who suffer from it (WHO, 2001b). Road traffic accidents will represent the third highest disease burden, and while health ICT initiatives may serve to improve response to such accidents, prevention will be equally as important. Though these forecasts were compiled by a group of world experts, they were developed with disparate data and many strong assumptions, and are subject to regional differences; however, the importance of this data to our discussion is not the actual changes in the GBD, but that there will be a change, and that ICT initiatives, or the use of ICT more generally, must adapt to these changes.

Health disparities within countries and regions will explode over the upcoming years. For the first time, many health technologies, including ICT, will be available in country, but only to those who can afford them (e.g., Apollo Hospitals in India). It is yet unclear whether having these technologies present in country will have any impact on population health at the national scale, but is nonetheless an important trend to watch.

In order to successfully develop and integrate ICTs for public health applications, it is crucial to approach the process holistically, addressing human factors with respect to organizations, cultural context, and end users. Comprehensive ICT strategies should integrate more "basic" technologies (terrestrial phones, conventional radio, and television) with new opportunities. Multipronged assessment is critical to addressing locally relevant issues as well as to providing information for others who may undertake similar initiatives. All of this ICT development and integration should consider the use classes as a starting point for applying these lessons to research, education, health-care delivery, and surveillance in public health.

References

AbouZahr, C., & Boerma, T. (2005). Health information systems: The foundations of public health. *Bull World Health Organ, 83*(8), 578-583.

Arunachalam, S. (2003). Information for research in developing countries: Information technology: Friend or foe? *Bulletin of the American Society for Information Science and Technology, 29*(5), 16-21.

Asia's devastation: Reflections on a rare but terrible calamity. (2004, December 29). *The Economist*, p. 9.

Baldacci, E., Clements, B., Cui, Q., & Gupta, S. (2005). What does it take to help the poor? *Finance and Development, 42*(2), 20.

Bannon, V. (2005, January 12). Red Cross: Disaster donors must focus on local volunteers. *Wall Street Journal*.

Bashshur, R. (1980). *Technology serves the people: The story of a cooperative telemedicine project by NASA, the Indian Health Service and the Papago people.* Washington, DC: National Aeronautics and Space Administration.

Beveridge, M., Howard, A., Burton, K., & Holder, W. (2003). The Ptolemy project: A scalable model for delivering health information in Africa. *BMJ, 327*(7418), 790-793.

Bhandari, A., Ibrahim, M., & Sandhu, J. S. (2004). *Remote eye care delivery via rural information kiosks* (white paper). Berkeley, CA: University of California.

Braa, J., Macome, E., Mavimbe, J. C., Nhampossa, J. L., Leopoldo da Costa, J., Jose, B., et al. (2001). A study of the actual and potential usage of information and communication technology at district and provincial levels in Mozambique with a focus on the health sector. *Electronic Journal on Information Systems in Developing Countries, 5*(2), 1-29.

Brown, H. (2004). UN urges broadcasters to air AIDS programmes. *The Lancet, 363*(9405), 295.

Business: Calling an end to poverty. Mobile phones and development. (2005). *The Economist, 376*, 53.

Campell, M., Janisch, C., Potts, M., & Bellows, B. (2005). *The need and potential for output-based assistance in health and family planning.* Unpublished manuscript.

Casas, C., LaJoie, W., & Prahalad, C. K. (2003). *Voxiva case study.* MI: University of Michigan Business School, Department of Strategy and Corporate Business.

Centers for Disease Control and Prevention. (2005). *EpiInfo.* Retrieved March 21, 2005, from http://www.cdc.gov/epiinfo/

Chandrasekhar, C. P., & Ghosh, J. (2001). Information and communication technologies and health in low income countries: The potential and the constraints. *Bull World Health Organ, 79*(9), 850-855.

Central Intellegence Agency (CIA). (2005). *World fact book.* Retrieved on September 27, 2006 from https:www.cia.gov/cia/publications/factbook/index.html

Cutler, D., & McClellan, M. (2001). Is technological change in medicine worth it? *Health Affairs, 20*(5), 11-29.

Dartmouth Medical School (2005) *Ultrasound images transmitted over the phone allow radiologists to diagnose patients in poorer countries in real time.* Press Release. May 17, 2005.

Deaton, A. (2003). Health, inequality and economic development. *Journal of Economic Literature, 41*(1), 113-158.

Demiris, G. (2004). Preface. In G. Demiris (Ed.), *E-health: Current status and future trends* (Vol. 106, pp. 145). Washington, DC: IOS Press.

Easterly, W. (2002). *The elusive quest for growth.* Cambridge, MA: MIT Paperback Press.

Edejer, T. T.-T. (2000). Disseminating health information in developing countries: The role of the Internet. *BMJ, 321*(7264), 797-800.

Equal access: Satellite radio programming in South Asia. (2005). (pp. personal communication). San Francisco.

Farr, A., Witte, K., Jarato, K., & Menard, T. (2005). The effectiveness of media use in health education: Evaluation of an HIV/AIDS television campaign in Ethiopia. *Journal of Health Communication, 10*(3), 225-235.

Financing information and communication infrastructure needs in the developing world: Public and private roles. (2005). Washington, DC: World Bank, Global Information and Communication Technologies Department.

Fosaelli, P. (1983). The telephone in pediatric medicine: A review. *Clinical Pediatrics, 22*(4), 293-296.

Godlee, F., Pakenham-Walsh, N., Ncayiyana, D., Cohen, B., & Packer, A. (2004). Can we achieve health information for all by 2015? *Lancet, 364*(9430), 295-300.

Graham, L., Zimmerman, M., Vassallo, D., Patterson, V., Swinfen, P., Swinfen, R., et al. (2003). Telemedicine: The way ahead for medicine in the developing world. *Tropical Doctor, 33*(1), 36-38.

Hancock, T. (1993). *Health, human development and the community ecosystem: Three ecological models.* Oxford, United Kingdom: Oxford University Press.

Hanson, K., & Berman, P. (1998). Private health care provision in developing countries: A preliminary analysis of levels and composition. *Health Policy and Planning, 13*(3), 195-211.

Health and wealth. (2002). *Nature Medicine, 8*(2), 89.

Heeks, R. (2002). Information systems and developing countries: Failure, success, and local improvisations. *The Information Society, 18*, 101-112.

Hongoro, C., & McPake, B. (2004). How to bridge the gap in human resources for health. *Lancet, 364*(9443), 1451-1456.

Horton, R. (2000). North and south: Bridging the information gap. *The Lancet, 355*(9222), 2231-2237.

Jacobson, I., Christerson, M., Jonsson, P., & Overgaard, G. (1992). *Object-oriented software engineering: A use case driven approach.* Wokingham, UK: Addison-Wesley.

Jayasuriya, R. (1999). Managing information systems for health services in a developing country: A case study using a contextualist framework. *International Journal of Information Management, 19*(5), 335-349.

Karsh, B. T. (2004). Beyond usability: Designing effective technology implementation systems to promote patient safety. *Quality and Safety in Healthcare, 13*(5), 388-394.

Koppel, R., Metlay, J. P., Cohen, A., Abaluck, B., Localio, A. R., Kimmel, S. E., et al. (2005). Role of computerized physician order entry systems in facilitating medication errors. *JAMA, 293*(10), 1197-1203.

Kuniavsky, M. *Observing the user experience: a practitioner's guide to user research.* San Francisco, Calif.: Morgan Kaufmann, 2003.

LaFraniere, S., & Grady, D. (2005, April 17). Stalking a deadly virus, battling a town's fears. *New York Times*, p. 1.

Langer, T. A., & Catino, J. (2003). *Improving prenatal care in Mexico City: Impact of an interactive computer-based education and empowerment tool.* Paper presented at the XVII FIGO World Congress of Obstetrics and Gynecology, Santiago, Chile.

Lewinberg, A. (2003). *Guide for policy makers and researchers: Understanding the challenge making essential medicines available to the world's poor.* Toronto, Canada: University of Toronto, Centre for Innovation Law and Policy.

Lopez, A. D., & Murray, C. C. (1998). The global burden of disease, 1990-2020. *Nature Medicine, 4*(11), 1241-1243.

Lumpkin, J. R., & Richards, M. S. (2002). Transforming the public health information infrastructure. *Health Affairs, 21*(6), 45.

Marchione, M. (2005). *Doctors hamstrung in relief efforts.* Retrieved September 4, 2005, from http://news.yahoo.com/s/ap/20050904/ap_on_he_me/katrina_health_1

Melese, M., Alemayehu, W., Friedlander, E., & Courtright, P. (2004). Indirect costs associated with accessing eye care services as a barrier to service use in Ethiopia. *Tropical Medicine and International Health, 9*(3), 426-431.

Minkler, M. (Ed.). (1997). *Community organizing & community building for health.* New Brunswick, NJ: Rutgers State University Press.

Narayan, D., & Srinivasan, L. (1994). *Participatory development toolkit: Materials to facilitate community empowerment.* Washington, DC: World Bank.

Ndayimirije, N., & Kindhauser, M. K. (2005). Marburg hemorrhagic fever in Angola: Fighting fear and a lethal pathogen. *New England Journal of Medicine, 352*(21), 2155-2158.

Nielsen, J. *Usability engineering.* San Francisco, Calif.: Morgan Kaufmann, 1994.

Norman, D. A. (2002). *The Design of Everyday Things.* New York: Basic Books.

Pakenham-Walsh, N., Priestley, C., & Smith, R. (1997). Meeting the information needs of health workers in developing countries. *BMJ, 314*(7074), 90-.

Prata, N., Montagu, D., & Jefferys, E. (2005). Private sector, human resources and health franchising in Africa. *Bull World Health Organization, 83*, 274-279.

Quick, J. D. (2003). Ensuring access to essential medicines in the developing countries: A framework for action. *Clinical Pharmacology Therapeutics, 73*(4), 279-283.

Russell, S. (2004). The economic burden of illness for households in developing countries: A review of studies focusing on malaria, tuberculosis, and human immunodeficiency virus/acquired immunodeficiency syndrome. *American Journal of Tropical Medicine and Hygiene, 71*(Suppl. 2), 147-155.

Sachs, J., Ahluwalia, I.J., Amoako, K.Y., Aninat, E., Cohen,D., Diabre, Z., et al. (2002). *Report of the Commission on Macroeconomics and Health: Investing in health for economic development.* Geneva, Switzerland: World Health Organization.

Sandhu, J., Hey, J., Newman, C., & Agogino, A. (2005). *Informal health and legal rights education in rural, agricultural communities using mobile devices.* Paper presented at the IEEE Technology for Education in Developing Countries (TEDC) Workshop, Kaohsiung, Taiwan.

Sandiford, P., Gorter, A., & Salvetto, M. (2002). Use of voucher schemes for output-based aid in the health sector in Nicaragua: Three case studies. *Public Policy for the Private Sector, 4*, 1-4.

Scott, J. (2004). Message from James K Scott, director of the European Union Center at the University of Missouri. In G. Demiris (Ed.), *E-health: Current status and future trends* (Vol. 106, pp. 1-2). Washington, DC: IOS Press.

Shaw, V. (2005). Health information system reform in South Africa: Developing an essential data set. *Bull World Health Organization, 83*(8), 632-639.

Smith, G. C. S., & Pell, J. P. (2003). Parachute use to prevent death and major trauma related to gravitational challenge: Systematic review of randomised controlled trials. *BMJ, 327*(7429), 1459-1461.

Taggart, K. (2003). Ugandan doctors pilot electronic communications. *Medical Post, 39*(37), 6.

Telemedicine: A guide to assessing telecommunications in health care. (1996). Washington, DC: U.S. Institute of Medicine, Committee on Evaluating Clinical Applications of Telemedicine.

Trouiller, P., Olliaro, P., Torreele, E., Orbinski, J., Laing, R., & Ford, N. (2002). Drug development for neglected diseases: A deficient market and a public-health policy failure. *Lancet, 359*(9324), 2188-2194.

United Nations (UN). (2005). *Declaration of Helsinki: Ethical principles for medical research involving human subjects.* World Medical Association.

Voxiva. (2005). Retrieved August 30, 2005, from *http://www.voxiva.net*

Walsh, J. A., & Warren, K. S. (1980). Selective primary health care: An interim strategy for disease control in developing countries. *Social Science & Medicine [Med Econ], 14*(2), 145-163.

Whited, J. (2001). Teledermatology: Current status and future directions. *American Journal of Clinical Dermatology., 2*(2), 59-64.

Witten, I. H., Loots, M., Trujillo, M. F., & Bainbridge, D. (2001). The promise of digital libraries in developing countries. *Communications of the ACM (Association for Computing Machinery), 44*(5), 82-85.

World Health Organization (WHO). (1948). *World Health Organization constitution.* Geneva, Switzerland: Author.

World Health Organization (WHO). (2001a). *United Nations millennium action plan: Health InterNetwork.* Retrieved September 15, 2005, from *http://www.healthinternetwork. net/src/millenium.php*

World Health Organization (WHO). (2001b). *The world health report 2001. Mental health: New understanding, new hope.* Geneva, Switzerland: Author.

World Health Organization (WHO). (2004). *Health expenditure data.* Retrieved September 15, 2005, from http://devdata.worldbank.org/external/dgsector.asp?W=0&RMDK=1 10&SMDK=473886

World Health Organization (WHO). (2005). *HealthMapper.* Retrieved September 15, 2005, from http://www.who.int/health_mapping/tools/healthmapper/en/

Yamamoto, C. (2004). *Output-based aid in health: Reaching the poor through public-private partnership.* Washington, DC: World Bank.

Note

The author list does not imply the usual meaning with regard to the level of contribution. This chapter was truly a team effort with equal contributions from all.

Chapter XI

Computer-Based Health Information Systems:
Projects for Computerization or Health Management? Empirical Experiences from India

Ranjini C. R., Lancaster University, UK

Sundeep Sahay, University of Oslo, Norway

Abstract

Large investments are being made to reform the health sector in developing countries as the potential of ICTs in achieving health goals is being increasingly recognized. However, there have been various reports that indicate this potential of ICT is not being fully realized on the ground in particular settings. In this chapter, an empirical investigation of the introduction of health information systems in the primary health-care sector in India is reported. Three cases—the India Health Care Project, Family Health Information Management System, and Integrated Health Information Management Systems—are presented. The authors argue against adopting a technocentric approach during the development of the HIS and suggest that these efforts should be sensitive to the sociotechnical context. Furthermore, a variety of constraints are identified. The chapter concludes with a discussion on the potentials of integration to address some of the identified constraints.

Introduction: The Challenges of HIS in Developing Countries

The plural of datum is not information.

~ Anonymous

Information and communication technologies in primary health-care settings offer a number of opportunities to enhance the efficiency of administration and improve the delivery of health-care services. Health information systems (HISs), geographic information systems (GISs), telemedicine, Web-based initiatives, and the development of health-care databases (see Bodavala, 2002) are examples of a few ICT-based initiatives currently ongoing in the primary health sector in India, and also in other developing countries. Despite the undoubted potential that ICTs provide, obtaining their practical benefits on the ground is a very complex undertaking, and there are various reports of total, partial, sustainability, and replication failures (Heeks, Mundy, & Salazar, 2000). Contributing to this unrealized potential are a number of complex interrelated issues such as inadequacies in both the computer-based infrastructure (for example, Nhampossa, 2004) and physical infrastructure of roads and transportation, which are required for the transmission of reports (Mosse & Nielsen, 2004); that is, there is a lack of proper network infrastructure, the persistent presence of legacy systems embroiled with different institutional interests (Nhampossa), weak human-resource capacities both in numbers and skills (Chilundo, 2004), heavy workload of health staff who need to give priority to providing care over administrative tasks like reporting (Mosse & Sahay, 2003), and a culture of information use that sees periodic reports as primarily fulfilling the needs of the bureaucracy rather than using the information to support action (Quraishy & Gregory, 2005). All these contextual influences make the challenge of introducing ICTs in the health-care sector a very difficult one in practice (Sahay, 2001).

The critical role that HISs can play in public health has been emphasized since the early 1980s in attempts to integrate data collection, processing, reporting, and use to strengthen management at all levels of health services (Lippeveld, Sauerborn, & Bodart, 2000). HISs in most developing countries have been described by researchers and also policy documents emerging from international agencies as being grossly inadequate (for example, Lippeveld, Foltz, and Mahouri, 1992; World Health Organisation [WHO], 1987). Sauerborn and Lippeveld (2000) argue that this ineffectiveness stems from various reasons including the irrelevance and poor quality of data being gathered, duplication and waste among parallel HISs, lack of timely reporting and feedback, and poor use of information. As a result, what we typically find is HISs that are data led rather than action led (Sandiford, Annett, & Cibulski, 1992); in this sense data is an end in itself rather than a basis for planning, decision making, and evaluating interventions. Institutionally, HISs in developing countries are situated in rather centralized structures (Braa, Heywood, & Shung King, 1997; Braa & Nermukh, 2000; Braa et al., 2001) in which local use of information is not encouraged (Opit, 1987). This has led Sandiford et al. to comment that what is needed is not necessarily more information but more use of information.

While as a part of various health reform efforts, including HIS, ICTs are being actively introduced by international agencies and national and local governments, what is often found is that the focus of such efforts are primarily on the means, computerization, rather than the ends of what needs to be achieved: strengthening information support for health management. Introducing ICTs in the development of HIS is not necessarily the silver bullet that solves the efficiency problem of the health services (Sandiford et al., 1992), and over the years research has emphasized that critical issues to be addressed in the implementation of IS are social and organisational, not solely technical (Anderson & Aydin, 1997; Walsham, 1993). As Helfenbein et al. (1987) have argued, changing the way information is gathered, processed, and used for decision making implies making changes in the way an organisation operates. They also suggest that producing and utilizing information more effectively will affect the behaviour and motivation of all personnel.

Policy makers (for example, under the sector-wide approach policy) and also researchers (for example, Piotti, Chilundo, & Sahay, 2005) propose that the integration of an HIS provides mechanisms to address some of the existing inefficiencies of HIS and to develop new forms of health data analysis. For example, the management of HIV programmes requires data from various sources such as the mother, child, and HIV-specific programmes. Rather than developing new HISs, it is argued that the existing systems should be effectively integrated. However, integration of HIS is a complex task. In a study on a national STI (sexually transmitted infections)/HIV/AIDS programme in Mozambique, Piotti et al. (2005) analysed the multiple reporting systems that were in place. Systems for the prevention of mother-to-child transmission, volunteers, counseling and testing, blood-transfusion services, AIDS patients under follow-up for the treatment of infections and/or antiretroviral therapy, rural-district AIDS inpatients, and AIDS patients under follow-up for home-based care were among the many reporting systems that they identified. Despite formal instruments to support the reform efforts to integrate the HIV/AIDS HIS, the multiplicity of reporting systems continued to exist, each with its own practices and processes. The integration of the HIS is not merely a technical or social task, but it is sociotechnical in nature.

We argue that taking a technological determinist perspective on HIS development implies a lack of sensitivity to the sociopolitical and institutional context, and contributes significantly to the unrealized potential of the computerization of HIS in developing countries. There is an urgent need to shift this focus from computerization itself to the question—What is it that we want to achieve through computerization?—in order to strengthen these HIS-focused reform efforts. Analysis of this question helps to develop an argument against the adoption of a technocentric approach to the development of HIS and to instead approach this effort with a focus on integration and sensitivity to the sociotechnical context. Introducing computers does not in itself lead to better handling and use of information, and the challenge is to initiate a parallel informational reform process where information is seen as a resource for action rather than for fulfilling the needs of the bureaucracy.

The present chapter analyzes empirically some of these challenges, drawing upon a study of three specific HIS initiatives introduced in primary health-care settings in Andhra Pradesh (AP; a state in southern India): The India Health Care (IHC) project, the Family Health Information Management System (FHIMS), and Integrated Health Information Management Systems (IHIMS). In the following section, we provide a brief summary of the broad context of the health sector and HIS in India. We next describe the research setting followed by a narrative of the HIS projects. Later, we present our analysis and discuss the challenges and opportunities inherent in shifting the focus of HIS efforts from computerization itself to how it can support health management. Finally, some brief conclusions are presented.

The Indian Health Sector Context

The goal of health policy in India has been stated as supporting universal and free primary health care for all (Gupta & Chen, 1996). A primary health centre was conceived in India as an institutional structure to provide integrated preventive, promotional, curative, and rehabilitative services for the entire rural population. The primary health sector includes primary health centres (PHCs), subcentres (SCs), community health centres, and upgraded PHCs in some areas. Each PHC is expected to provide health care for a population of about 30,000, whereas in practical terms, this ranges from 20,000 to 70,000. More details on the health sector in Andhra Pradesh are provided later.

The health staff in the PHCs and SCs generate considerable amounts of data about the services that they render, collate them on a weekly or monthly basis, and report them in prescribed formats, sometimes duplicating the same report format to different departments or programme managers. These informational activities take up a considerable amount of the health staff's time. Moreover, frontline health assistants are mere producers of data rather than its users. While the focus on reporting serves to fulfill the needs of the bureaucracy and their dependencies on international aid agencies, and the potential need for epidemiological analysis, information is rarely ever used to guide local action at the level at which the data are collected (Sahay, 2001). There are also quality-related issues that inhibit the active use of data. For example, data collected at every level are aggregated, and by the time these data reach the higher levels of the health system, the specific situations in the peripheral areas are completely masked (Quraishy & Gregory, 2005). The flow of data is largely unidirectional from the lower levels to the higher ones (see Figure 1), with very little constructive feedback being given to the local levels to strengthen their work processes. Instead, often the only feedback is in the form of a reprimand, where health staff are pulled up for not meeting their (rather unrealistic) targets. Mechanisms to facilitate mutual exchange of information are also minimal.

Acknowledging these limitations of the existing HIS during the launch of a new programme named the National Rural Health Mission, the prime minister of India, Dr. Manmohan Singh, called for reorienting the HIS to support local action (April 12, 2005):

> *The monitoring systems have to become oriented outward towards the community and not upward towards the bureaucracy. For example, so far the health information we have in our country through the National Family Health Services Reports are seen at State and Central levels and hardly ever at district and below district levels. If information is to lead to action, it should be available and used at the local level. We must reorient the information system to support an accountability-structure by developing district health reports, state health reports and so on.*

While the challenges to HIS reform are now being recognized at the policy level, the harder task is to address them on the ground. With this as the backdrop, we now shift to describing the specific research setting and the particular HIS implementation efforts.

Figure 1. Health Information Flow (Source: Sahay & Walsham, 2005, p. 44).

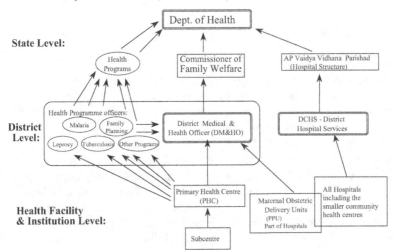

The empirical material reported here is derived from a situational analysis of the implementation of three HIS projects in AP, a state with a population of 75.7 million (http://www.censusindia.net). Figure 1 provides a broad structure of the health-sector network and an overview of health information flows in Andhra Pradesh.

Subcentres have been established under the PHCs at a rate of one for every 5,000 people in rural areas, and one for every 3,000 people in tribal areas. One or two health assistants (auxiliary nurses and midwives) work at the SCs and are responsible for outreach programmes. They travel from one village to another to provide services such as immunisation, antenatal care, family planning, information and education activities, and school health programmes to the rural population. PHCs serve as the hub for implementing national programmes such as population control, and disease-control programmes like malaria, tuberculosis, leprosy, and gastroenteritis among others. Mainly, however, the PHCs are the cornerstone of the maternity and child health programme, now integrated into the reproductive and child health programme.

For example, one district, Chittoor, has a population of about 3.75 million served by 84 PHCs, each theoretically catering to a population of about 30,000. Each PHC has under it about four to seven SCs, each of which in turn is supposed to cater to a population of about 5,000. In practice, the PHC population varies from 25,000 to 40,000, and the SCs from 4,000 to 8,000. The state has about 1,386 PHCs, of which 470 PHCs are expected to provide round-the-clock services for safe deliveries. There will also be 268 hospitals, dispensaries, community health centres, and mobile units, and 10,568 SCs spread across 23 administrative districts, covering an area of about 246,793 sq km. In Andhra Pradesh, there are about 2,848 medical officers, 506 community health officers, 1,686 multipurpose health extension officers, 1,621 female multipurpose health supervisors, 614 public health nurses, about 11,000 multipurpose health assistants (also called auxiliary nurses and midwives), and 500 other administrative staff at the primary health centre level (family welfare [FW] departmental manual).

Research Settings:
Ongoing HIS Initiatives in Andhra Pradesh

Over the last few years, HIS projects have been initiated in the Family Welfare Department (FWD) in AP to help provide electronic support tools to the health staff at different levels of the organisation. These HIS efforts of the state government were initiated with the backdrop of larger good-governance reform policies initiated by the former chief minister Chandrababu Naidu within the framework of SMART governance (Simple, Moral, Accountable, Reliable, and Trustworthy). As a component of this ambitious good-governance policy, the chief minister drew up vision statements for every government department. The government's IT vision states, "Andhra Pradesh will leverage Information Technology to attain a position of leadership and excellence in the information age and to transform itself into a knowledge society." The vision document also established ambitious and demanding goals for the health department to be achieved by the year 2020. These goals were, among others, to achieve infant and child mortality rates of 10 per 1,000 (live births) and 20 per 1,000, respectively, a total fertility rate of 1.5 (average number of children per woman), and population growth of 0.8% a year. Good governance and the use of ICTs in public administration were emphasized to help achieve these goals.

In January 2002, the government of Andhra Pradesh brought out a strategy paper on governance and public management that forms the basis for governance reform activities in the state. In the book *Good Governance Initiatives in Andhra Pradesh* (Mohanty, Jones, & Rao, 2004), 28 projects have been documented to disseminate examples of good practices in the field of governance and public-sector reforms. The introductory chapter notes that:

> *governance involves mechanisms, processes and institutions, through which people articulate their characteristics of good governance to include: rule of law, participation, transparency, responsiveness, consensus, equity and inclusiveness, economy, efficiency and effectiveness, and accountability...The government of Andhra Pradesh has adopted an approach of combining knowledge, technology and citizen-centricity as the key strategy to improve governance in the state.* (p. iii)

This focus on good governance to reform public services is indeed welcome. However, there is a need to shift the focus from merely elaborating on the content of reforms to the feasibility of implementing them on the ground. Implementation of these modern and managerial models to support good governance and best practices is complex and problematic (Madon, Sahay, & Sahay, 2004). Given the excessive focus on the provision of infrastructure rather than on implementation and use, asymmetries exist between macro-level governance policies and the micro-level implementation of particular ICT projects (Madon, Sahay, & Sudan, 2005).

Toward a Computerised Health Database: Vision and Reality

In Andhra Pradesh, toward achieving Vision 2020 and the SMART objectives, the government undertook a number of IT initiatives, some of which had had direct implications for the health initiatives under study. One such initiative was the Multipurpose Household Survey (MPHS).

The MPHS was an ambitious project of the government of Andhra Pradesh to build a massive name-based database of 75.7 million citizens and 76.5 million land records to help provide a social-security identification number for every citizen of the state. The survey was originally compiled in 1995. It was later computerised and the data was hosted on a central server for public access. The citizen's database with about 130 data elements has been installed in 1,125 mandal[1] revenue offices. Although this database was created by the state revenue department for its own purposes, the government passed a directive that MPHS should be used as a standard database by all government departments and other agencies in an attempt to prevent multiplicity of databases. In order to comply with this directive, other departments started to add data from their own databases to the MPHS.

Creating a name-based database with various socioeconomic indicators for a population of 75.7 million is a challenging task. A consultant in the revenue department explained that this database was compiled in 1995 by conducting a household survey, and subsequently between 1998 and 2003 two private companies were given contracts to update these data and also to include other data such as deaths, births, migration, and so forth. Additional data (such as the number of school-going children and the number of working children in the age group 6 to 14) from another survey called the Human Development Survey (HDS), which was conducted by the planning department, was integrated with the MPHS data in January 2000. Integrating the data from the HDS into the MPHS database had inherent problems because the basic unit for the MPHS was the village and that for the HDS was the habitation.[2] In the HDS, data were collected on total numbers and not on the details of all individuals in a family. For example, details about a family included the total number of children in the age group of 0 to 5, the number of illiterates above 15 years, and the number of family members above 65 years, while in the MPHS, data were collected about every individual member. There were commissions and omissions because of the migration of people, and also because some people were reluctant to give their details for the survey. There were also quality issues raised about the HDS data as they had been collected by school children. As a result, the database was not accurate, and the quality of data was very poor.

In addition, with regard to our main concern here, the HIS, the PHC as the fundamental unit for the state health department did not match with the fundamental unit of the revenue department (the owners of the MPHS), the village. As a result, many of the health parameters necessary for health services were not included in the MPHS database, and it had to be updated with these data subsequently.

Around the time that the MPHS was being upgraded, in June 2000, Infodev (the Information for Development Programme), an agency of the World Bank, granted $250,000 in funding for the first of the projects under study here: the IHC project. The key objectives of the IHC were to reduce or eliminate the redundant entry of data prevalent in paper registers, to generate monthly reports automatically for health assistants, and to make data electronically available for further analysis and compilation at higher levels of the health-care system. The project was eventually implemented in 200 subcentres (spread across 32 PHCs). The larger objective of the initiative was to reduce infant mortality and maternal mortality by improving the quality of antenatal care and child health through improved information management.

The second project under study here, the FHIMS, was an offshoot of the IHC project. One district, Nalgonda, out of the 23 districts in the state was selected to pilot this project. It took off simultaneously in all 67 PHCs in the district in 2002. The information needs at different levels forced the family welfare department to embark on a more elaborate project to have information systems not just at the PHCs, but also in the district offices and the state office. The overall aim of the project was to "computerize the activities of the PHCs as a whole to take care of (a) Family Welfare needs (b) control of communicable diseases and (c) PHC management" (CFW, Office of the Commissioner of Family Welfare, 2003).

As already mentioned, during the initial days of the IHC project, it was decided that MPHS should form the basis for a name-based health registry, and that instead of conducting a new survey, the health staff should update the MPHS. The survey data were crucial for both the projects because they were to be the foundation of the name-based IS. This name-based system (with details such as, for example, who has malaria) was to replace the earlier one in which data were collected based on numbers (for example, how many cases of malaria in a region). In the FWD, the family or household was the basic unit of analysis, and it was expected that the database would maintain this unit of analysis, along data on births, marriages, family planning methods, antenatal and postnatal cases, immunisation of children, deaths, and diseases. It was argued by the proponents of the name-based system that it was necessary to provide targeted health care, especially in following up with antenatal cases, immunising children over a period of time, and in tracking patients. While the officially stated aim of the FHIMS was to improve patient-specific care, in practice, as one doctor said, the rationale underlying FHIMS was to try and "prevent the manipulation of figures by the health staff, since with names it is easier to track whether or not the right numbers have been filled."

Apart from these data-related issues, there were also software challenges. A consultant in the revenue department explained:

> *Quality problems with the software are because each department hires an agency on its own to get the necessary fields from the MPHS. That company may not know the design of the MPHS data completely. They are given a very short time, say a month or so, to deliver the product. Understanding a huge database and to know how to do it takes time. Quality suffered because of this.*

Another software programme was developed to download the MPHS and print the MPHS data on habitation in the form of a household register. A software engineer of the IT company that had been involved in the development of the software for the FWD said, "Nobody knows about the accuracy of the data. The survey was initially done for the revenue department. We did not know the software codes because it was done many years back. We cannot assure the accuracy of the data."

The development of the FHIMS software was contracted to an IT company located in the state capital at a cost of about $68,500, and the requirements included 17 modules (such as family welfare activities, tuberculosis control, leprosy eradication, budget monitoring, personnel information, etc.). The software was developed on an Oracle back end using Visual Basic. Although the project itself was delayed (because the household survey, which was expected to be completed by December 2003, was still ongoing in March 2004 in many PHCs), the software was expected to be deployed toward the end of 2003. The health department mobilised about $7.3 million for the project through a consortium of funding agencies including the World Bank to buy about 1,500 computers and install it in every PHC and district office, and in the state office, and load the computers with Oracle software (with a license fee of about $200 per computer) and Microsoft software.

The idea of computerization was that the MPHS data would be loaded in the FHIMS software, and using this health survey, data could be entered (based on names). It was soon realized, however, that the MPHS data was unsuitable because of quality issues and the fact that the data did not match the needs of the health department. As already mentioned, this was because the MPHS was conducted by the revenue department and hence did not have all the data that were necessary for the health department.

This process of collecting data for such a massive population, as can be imagined, was a complicated task and involved multiple challenges. When the health staff took the MPHS survey books to their respective habitations, they found them afflicted with many errors. Many health assistants complained that names were missing or inaccurate, ages of family members were wrong, or sometimes data on entire habitations were missing. Sometimes there would be a Muslim name for the head of the household, and the family members would have Hindu names (a quite unlikely possibility!). In another instance, the same name (of a head of the family) was in all the families in a particular habitation. Also, since house numbers were not arranged in an order in many villages, the health assistants had to rely on the names of people to locate their families.

Health assistants were expected to do the survey in addition to their regular work. Some of the health assistants said they were ordered to conduct this survey at their own cost and time. However, higher officials disagreed and said doing such surveys is part of their job. The health assistants would go in the evenings after work to conduct the survey, and had to be accompanied by their husbands because they had to travel after dark. Also, as the list of names in the forms (printed from the FHIMS database) given to them did not match the people who were physically located in the habitations, they found it easier to buy new books and write the names by pen themselves. However, in the absence of any financial support, the health staff had to buy these books at their own cost. Because of time constraints, and the fact that they had to enter whether a person had (or had not) a list of about nine diseases and particulars of physical disability (six types) in code numbers, the assistants would typically simply enter "no" for all. A project coordinator of the FHIMS explained some of these difficulties experienced by the health assistants while conducting the survey during the pilot phase of the project as follows:

The other big difficulty that our staff faced is that they were given registers…per habitation, per village like that. Each book runs, depending on the size of the habitation, anywhere between 500 and 600 pages. Some habitations are really big and have 10,000 people. Our health assistants have to go to the field with these registers, not knowing on which page the family they have to survey is on because the books do not have any index. Addresses are not printed in a serial order as to how they are located nor are the names listed in an alphabetical order. So the health assistant practically had to turn all the 600 pages or 10,000 pages every time to locate a family. And she couldn't just tear all the pages and arrange it one after the other…She knows perfectly well which house comes next to which… That was also not possible because in one sheet we had two to three families. Later, in replication phase we have made sure we get only one family per page and we now have an index for every bound book…in an alphabetical order.

After the house-to-house survey, the next stage of the project was to enter the data into the computerised database, which was a time-consuming and arduous task given the already heavy workload and time constraints of the health assistants. The data entry into the household database, which would then be imported to FHIMS, was outsourced to a private party. This private agency further recruited data-processing operators (data operators; at a salary of about less than $100 per month) to do the data entry.

During the pilot phase of the FHIMS project involving data entry, there were many omissions because the work of the data operators was not well monitored. While the health assistants were instructed to be present with their registers when data were being entered by the data operators to oversee the process, the health assistants would simply leave their registers with the data operators and go away to fulfill other duties. The data operators, for their part, found it difficult to make out the handwriting of the health assistants and the variety of informal symbols they had made in the registers. A retired district officer, who was appointed as a consultant for the project, explained why this lack of oversight of the data-entry process occurred as follows:

On many occasions health assistants were not present when the data entry was done. If the health assistant sat with the data operator with her register, that would slow down the data operator because his work would be constantly double-checked. On the other hand, work would proceed faster when the health assistant was not present because the data operator would worry less about whether he was entering the records correctly or not. Remember his payment was based on the number of records he entered per day. So naturally, his interest was not whether data he entered was right or wrong, his interest was to enter as many records as possible in a day and collect his money. The health assistants were not able to sit with the data operators, oversee and clarify, because she had so many other priorities. Moreover, that sort of accountability and sense of responsibility was not there among most of the field staff. So, in effect, the data entry was not done in a systematic manner.

As the project expanded, data entry was moved to the respective PHCs. Now, a new set of problems caused delays in the process. Multiple software bugs, especially due to software incompatibility between the household survey module and the FHIMS database, were some of the problems encountered. The result was that certain data, for instance, data on antenatal women who did not reside in habitation or data on pregnancies leading to abortion or medical termination, could not be entered into the database. In some PHCs, the household survey module could not be linked to FHIMS database, leading to discrepancies between the population figures that were entered and what was actually displayed in FHIMS. In fact, although it was claimed that all the data had been entered, close examination revealed later that data entry was done only for the FWD module and even then for only a portion of it.

The India Health Care Project

The IHC project was started as a pilot in three health centres in the Nalgonda district where health assistants were given personal digital assistants (PDAs) and another health centre was selected to pilot the same application on a desktop computer. Subsequently, PDAs, which are mobile computing devices, were given to about 200 women health assistants. Typically, health assistants spend a considerable amount of time collecting, collating, and reporting health data to different officials. This paperwork is time consuming and cumbersome, and historic data are difficult to manage, retrieve, and use. The health assistants submit several reports of the services they have offered to the supervisors and medical officers at the weekly and monthly meetings, generally organised at the PHCs. At times, they also submit reports on different health programmes to different functionaries and agencies. The stated objectives of the project were to reduce manual paperwork and eliminate redundant data entry, and thereby free up assistants' time for health-care delivery. The application was also expected to facilitate the generation of schedules with information pertaining to immunization and antenatal services for the health assistants, which would help them to geographically identify antenatal cases to be visited and children to be immunized. The system was also supposed to help the health assistant in tracking the history of the patients and enable her to take preventive measures such as treating high-risk pregnant women or giving timely vaccinations to children. The schedules also highlighted pending cases and those who had been missed by her in previous visits. This was supposed to help the health assistant to prioritise her work so that she could attend to cases that needed immediate attention. The PDAs were expected to eventually replace paper registers. Thus, the use of these mobile computing devices was projected as providing ample opportunities for assisting health staff in their routine work. At the PHC level, it was expected that the data from PDAs would regularly be transferred and uploaded onto desktop computers located at the PHCs and support the routine HIS.

However, the use of the PDAs was largely unsuccessful for a variety of reasons. For one, the memory supplied was insufficient (16MB). There were problems with charging the batteries in the rural areas. Many health assistants said the device was slow, and since using the device while on the job was time consuming, a few health assistants would do the data entry later in the bus on their way back from work or at home. One health assistant said she would ask her children to do the data entry at home. Those health assistants with eye-sight problems complained that they found it difficult to read small letters on the black and white screen, and said that a colour screen would have been better. Also, while standing with the PDAs in the sun made it difficult for the health assistants to see the screen clearly. Since they had to deal with long lines of people waiting to get their attention, they found it troublesome to spend time trying to enter data into the PDAs. Added to the poor quality of the MPHS and the database, there were technical problems during the uploading of data into the database. The PDAs were perceived to be costly, and the health assistants were scared that they might lose them and they would have to pay for it from their pockets. Due to these and other problems, PDA use has now stopped. A health worker shared her experience:

> *The PDAs which were supplied were low in memory. When we started using PDAs it was taking a lot of time to search the name, or open the screen or save the entry. When we had a long queue of patients, mothers holding their small children waiting for us to give the children immunization shots, if we were operating a PDA which was slow, the patients would be frustrated. If I don't attend to them, they will go away. So, very soon I realised this PDA was not much of use when I was on the job. So I resorted back to writing in my old book. What I did was I would go home and then again enter all the day's entry into the PDA. To tell you frankly, though it has helped me in getting schedules, it has also increased my work load.*

A doctor working at a health centre also shared a similar opinion on the reasons for nonuse of the devices:

> *The health assistants are reluctant to use PDAs because the operating system is such that if the power is discharged or if a health assistant forgets to recharge it, all the data will vanish. She has to come to the PHC and upload the data from the desktop to the PDA. In this division, the reason for reluctance of health assistants to use computers is that we got the PDAs first and desktops later. So whenever data vanished, the software engineers would take the PDAs to Hyderabad (the state capital) and would feed the data there into the PDA. The second problem was memory. Third problem is when we said the memory is not sufficient, they changed the software so only the target population is there in the PDA. There are many software problems because of this. The health assistants who are really interested even today are not able to use them because some records are not captured properly.*

Another doctor who was involved in training and supervising the project said both technical and nontechnical factors contributed to the failure of the PDA project:

> *The processing capacity of the PDA was slow. The intention of giving PDAs was that the health worker would give immunisation and immediately enter that data in the field. But that did not happen in practice. People won't wait. So they wrote manually in their registers. Once the immunisation session was completed, the health workers would have to again enter the data, come to the health centre and then upload the data (into the desktop). Only after that could they get the*

schedule. In that schedule few names would be missed because some records would be rejected. So due to all these issues health assistants were not able to use the PDAs comfortably. If these technical problems could have been solved, the percentage (of health assistants using the PDAs) would have been about 70-75%, but not 100%, because you cannot make everyone use that device. Also, battery has to be replaced after every two years or so. All these issues were not taken into consideration.

The reason to do a pilot is to try out a technology on a small scale in order to identify problems and resolve them before making a large investment. However, about 200 PDAs were brought by the IT company all at once. The consultant of the IHC project said:

The irony of it is we started the project in three PHCs initially as a pilot. So they could have procured the PDAs only for those 3 PHCs. When we raised this problem of memory they could have procured higher memory PDAs later. After having gained experience during this pilot phase they could have bought the rest of the PDAs. Anybody would do that. But the software company said they have bought all the PDAs at once. For half of the district, it was 200+ PDAs.

The poor quality of the survey database, recurring software problems, insufficient memory capacity, and the absence of timely and ongoing technical support and maintenance gradually led to nonuse of these devices on the job. The health assistants who were trained and were enthusiastic initially gradually lost interest and reverted back to their earlier manual system of recording health data. The project was neither sustainable nor was it scalable because of the costs involved. Out of 200, only about 9 health assistants were using PDAs in March 2004 during a field visit by one of the authors. During the visit, the health staff took out the PDAs from locked cupboards and showed the researcher blank PDAs that had not been used for months. In some other PHCs, we saw the children of the health assistants playing with these devices.

The aim of the project was to provide support tools that would allow health assistants to reduce the time spent doing paperwork. However, in practice, it actually increased their work. The second aim was to increase the accuracy of the data flowing up from the health assistants; however, this could not be achieved because the quality of the multipurpose survey data itself was poor. The third aim was to provide a means for getting health-care data at the village level into electronic form and generate reports. This was too ambitious to achieve because shifting from a manual to an electronic form was difficult for the reasons cited above. Finally, the project aimed to provide health assistants with information that allowed them to provide more targeted and effective services to the people. Health assistants need more than just support tools, however, but also support to use those tools. In the absence of this, they were not able to use these devices effectively. As the consultant said, "it works only if the supporting staff trouble-shoot problems promptly and in a reasonable period. But this did not happen, so gradually the health assistants lost interest and developed a negative attitude towards computers." So when plans to expand the computerisation project to the whole state were being drawn, it was decided not to opt for PDAs because of these problems, and also because it was considered too expensive.

Family Health Information Management System

The FHIMS project was conceived based on the experience of the IHC project. While the IHC project covered only one aspect of the work of the health assistants (family welfare services), it was decided by the FWD that a comprehensive HIS was necessary, and that it should include the different activities of PHCs including family welfare services, various health services (disease control, for example), and administrative aspects (such as budgets and logistics support). The department in its official circular (CFW, 2003) outlined the key objectives of this project as follows:

- To provide a name-based follow-up of family welfare services including antenatal services and immunization, and the early identification and timely referral of high-risk antenatal cases

- To improve the full immunization rates and thereby contribute to the reduction of infant mortality rates and maternal mortality rates

- To facilitate the health assistants to easily get schedules of services to be rendered in each habitation during a month; that is, to provide schedules on pregnant women and children to be visited by the health assistants in their respective subcentres

- To reduce the burden of manual record keeping by the field staff and all the higher levels

- To contain the spread of communicable diseases and blindness by tracking incidences of diseases

- To improve the functioning of PHCs by facilitating effective service delivery

- To streamline inventory and infrastructure management at the health centres

- To manage career and training issues of field personnel

The project was conceived over the following phases: the pilot at the Nalgonda district (December 2001-November 2002), and the state-wide replication (June 2003-ongoing). We discuss these two phases followed by a summary of the identified implementation challenges.

The Pilot Phase of FHIMS at the Nalgonda District

The pilot phase of the FHIMS project was started in 67 PHCs in December 2001 about a year after the IHC project in the same district. A software engineer who had been involved throughout the design and development of IHC and also FHIMS explained that elaborate consultations were held with health officials at different levels, including health assistants, during the design of the software. However, when we spoke to many doctors, they typically said that the process had been largely top down with limited involvement of PHC-level doctors.

After the software was installed in all the PHCs, the department appointed data-processing operators (data operators) on a temporary basis for a period of 9 months to do the data entry and to train the staff during this transition period. Although data operators initiated the data-entry process, they did not seem to have the capacity to take on the role of change agents and to motivate the health staff. Although the district administration had instructed every PHC to identify a competent person as a system administrator who could act as a leader and be trained by the data operators from the beginning, this did not happen. Also, the role of systems administrators was not clearly defined, and adequate guidelines were not given to them on how to manage their regular work (for example, as lab assistants) with these additional responsibilities. Additionally, no incentives were provided to concurrently carry on both this task and that of a system administrator. The system administrators also complained that the training that was provided was inadequate and focused primarily on computer awareness with hardly anything on the FHIMS and nothing on health management itself. A coordinator for FHIMS who was involved in conducting training sessions confirmed this exclusion:

> *Initially, all the cadres were trained in all the modules. That was not really useful. For example, a health assistant need not know about the budget module, or vehicle or personnel module. If she knows about the family welfare module and one or two national health programmes, that should be enough. Similarly, a pharmacist need not know about budget or family welfare modules. If he knows about his stores, inside out, it is more than enough. It won't take more than 2 days. He will be more than happy if he is thoroughly trained for 2 days on his module. But they were called for 5 days and were taught all the modules. By the time they came to their module, they had probably lost interest.*

The doctors said they were not fully involved in the project from the beginning and were unaware about the aims of the project. A FHIMS coordinator, who is also a doctor said:

> *From the beginning, the doctors did not have ownership of the data… since the time the survey started. Training on updating the registers was given only to the health assistants, and the doctors did not know what the training was about. Had the doctors at the PHCs been told about the registers, all about the project, and given guidelines as to how a health assistant has to go about her work, this is where you as a doctor have to guide them…then things would have been different. However, the doctor was bypassed. The data entry was done at a central point (not at PHCs). The doctor lost track there again. That's how they drifted slowly. They could have probably fallen back on track when the software was installed, but that didn't happen due to many reasons. Hence the doctors did not own the project.*

Online data transfer took place initially for sometime, but then stopped. The coordinator of FHIMS explained why:

Online data transfer was going on in 50% of the PHCs for sometime. But the thing is, the district administration is still taking only the manual reports. It is not taking the reports generated from FHIMS because all the data are not being entered into FHIMS. So, whatever report you get from that (software), it is not complete. We can generate only one report, Form B from FHIMS. But that had a few errors. And even if you could correct one or two errors with a pen, you need the other data. And where will the other data come from?

In March 2003, the authors visited 12 PHCs, one community health centre, and the district office. The health staff complained that many software- and system-related problems were identified but not addressed. In many PHCs, the health staff did not know the passwords, and did not know how to burn CDs and save the data. At the time of our visits, a majority of the health staff were not using the computerised system, were not entering and updating the health data regularly, and hence were not generating computerised schedules or reports. The projects in most PHCs had stopped when the data operators left after their temporary tenure.

State-Wide Expansion of FHIMS

State-wide replication of the project involved the extension of the Nalgonda project to all the other 22 districts and 1,319 PHCs. The expansion phase of the project, which started in 2003, involved the computerisation of all the PHCs, district medical and health offices (DM&HOs), and the offices of the Director of Health and the Commissioner of Family Welfare at the state level (Circular I, CFW, 2003, p. 1). The replication involved the conduct of a household survey (to replace the MPHS data as was done in Nalgonda), the installation of computers and the FHIMS, the entering of survey data, training for the health staff, and the initiating of the other activities (such as identifying private agencies for printing MPHS books or team building) necessary for starting the project.

Based on the experience of the pilot, many changes were made during the replication phase. Survey registers were printed with an index and in alphabetical order. A team of 16 people were trained in each district, who in turn trained the health staff at the district level on how to conduct the household survey. Doctors were involved and system administrators were identified. Videoconferencing facilities were used regularly by the commissioner to coordinate and give instructions to health officials in the district, and to obtain status reports on the data-entry process. A number of circulars were sent to every PHC regularly, giving detailed instructions at different stages of implementation.

The computers were introduced in September 2003 in the PHCs, and the initial plan was to start the project by December 2003. In July 2005, one of the authors and his team conducted a situational analysis of the status of the implementation of FHIMS in 84 PHCs in another district (called Chittoor). This evaluation report, which was provided to the collector of the district, the DM&HOs, and the state-level authorities, identified a number of ongoing problems in the implementation of FHIMS contributing to it being far behind

Table 1. Summary of the implementation challenges

* Improving data-collection approaches
* Developing a culture of using information to support local action
* Providing adequate training not just in using computers to generate regular reports, but also in interpreting data
* Providing on-site training (at PHCs) for the health staff on a regular basis
* Adopting an iterative process to improve technical features of the software
* Managing the workload of the staff
* Getting health staff to start doing data entry rather than data-processing operators
* Initiating collective participation to facilitate ownership of the systems
* Motivating health staff to change existing work practices
* Encouraging system administrators and doctors to take on the role of change agents
* Building the capacity of health managers for evidence-based decision making
* Providing timely hardware and software support
* Addressing infrastructural issues
* Switching over to online reporting
* Sustaining the project over time by involving officials at the state, district, and local levels
* Managing interdependencies (for example, the building of the health database was dependent on MPHS, which was developed by another department)

schedule. The evaluation identified that all the PHCs had reported software bugs of varying levels of complexity. Although household data had been entered, service data remained grossly incomplete. None of the PHCs were generating any of the reports that were needed to be sent to the district. This was because, except for one report, other reports could not be generated through the FHIMS. Although in a few cases schedules for health assistants were being printed, the demand for these schedules did not come from the health assistants themselves, but the schedules had been printed by the data operators (before they had left) and given to the health assistants. The study also revealed that on average only three or four people per PHC had received training in computer awareness through the 5-day training programme. No formal training was given to the PHC staff on FHIMS. In some cases, the data operators had provided some basic training to the system administrators. In more than 50% of the PHCs, none of the staff knew the username and password to enter the FHIMS modules after the departure of the data operators.

In summary, various factors have been identified that have impeded the implementation of the HIS initiatives discussed. These complexities are sociotechnical in nature. While some of these problems are expected given the extreme complexity of the projects, some, we believe, can be addressed by providing increased care and attention to the sociotechnical issues. In Table 1, we summarize some of these key challenges, and in the following section, we discuss how they were addressed.

Discussion

One of the key recommendations of WHO (2005) in *Health and the Millennium Development Goals* is to improve the information basis on which health management decisions are made. The report notes, "making available information concerning the location, functioning, and performance of health services should also improve transparency and accountability in the management of the health sector" (p. 79). Accurate information can support better management and enhance the efficiency of health-care delivery. HIS can contribute to human development by supporting health management. Jacucci, Shaw, and Braa (2005) argue that the overall sustainability of a standards-based HIS is dependent on the quality of data and the skillful use of data at the level of collection. Local sustainability of the HIS requires the information to be of relevance not just for the managers, but also at the local level. This requires training health staff not just on the mechanics of using software, but also on public health-related topics of information use, data quality, significance of health indicators, validation, analysis, and interpretation of data, and linking these with interventions on the ground.

The implementation of HIS is not just a matter of introducing technology, but is also dependent on the social, organisational, and political issues that need to be addressed on an ongoing basis. Several authors have emphasized the need to understand and analyse information systems from a sociotechnical perspective (Coakes, Willis, & Lloyd-Jones, 2000; Kling & Lamb, 2000; Walsham, 1993). For example, Kling (1987) and Kling and Scacchi (1982) utilize Web models to take into account the social relations between the set of participants, the infrastructure available for its support, and the previous history of commitments in the organisation around computer-based technologies. Walsham (1993) provides an analytical framework for understanding the mutually shaping linkages that exist between content, social context, and social processes of IS. Over the years, several authors have both applied Walsham's structural framework and also expanded it by including various facets of the economic, cultural, and political context (e.g., Avgerou & Walsham, 2000; Jarvenpaa & Leidner, 1998; Madon, 1993; Sahay, 2000; Walsham, 2001). Avgerou and Madon (2004) argue "for broadening of the perspective of situated research to make explicit the contextual origins of the meanings, emotional dispositions, and competencies actors bring to bear on the interactions that constitute these processes" (p. 176).

Even though a participatory approach was stated to have been adopted to a certain extent during the design and implementation of the FHIMS, in practice, this did not evolve into effective and sustainable partnerships resulting in end users owning the new system. As an example, the HISP team conducted a situation analysis in the 84 PHCs of the Chittoor district in August 2005 after the contracts of the data-processing operators responsible for the FHIMS implementation were discontinued. The analysis revealed that in about 50 of the 84 PHCs, the FHIMS system had not been used since the departure of the operators because the PHC staff did not even know the password to log into the system, indicative of the absence of a partnership between the implementing team and the end users, and the lack of local ownership of the system. This raises the need to adopt complementary or alternative approaches that can facilitate the creation of local capacity and ownership. This requires the trainers to play multiple roles from building technical capacity to motivating the staff, and facilitating the change processes at multiple levels (Tomasi, Facchini, & Maia, 2004).

Building these capacities is a slow and gradual process, but they are crucial and fundamental for the collective ownership of the project. This requires the need to shift the focus from being primarily on technology to the various surrounding processes required to strengthen the informational basis of health management. Some ways in which these challenges are being addressed in the FHIMS case is now discussed.

Shifting Focus from Technology to Information: Empirical Experiences from IHIMS

In order to address the various implementation challenges, the State Health Department endorsed in July 2005 a project called Integrated Health Information Management System (IHIMS) through a Memorandum of Understanding (MoU) with HISP India[3] (a not-for-profit society set up by the University of Oslo). HISP is an ongoing, large-scale action research initiative that operates as a global network across a number of developing countries. HISP was started in India in December 2000, and was operating in some limited areas parallel to the FHIMS project, which had a state mandate. Since FHIMS was the official state project, and HISP was seen primarily as a university research and development project, HISP was always vulnerable to being terminated by the state in favour of FHIMS. As a strategy to protect itself against such an event, the HISP management proposed to the state the IHIMS project, which would integrate the individual capabilities of the FHIMS and HISP projects and develop synergies to contribute to the overall health information management in the state. The integration logic argued by HISP was informational rather than technological. While FHIMS was a name-based software, the District Health Information Software (DHIS), a not-for-profit customised open-source software developed by HISP, was a facility-based system. By linking the two technological systems, it was argued that an integrated informational analysis could be carried out both at the level of individuals and health facilities. Also, since the DHIS was linked to the Web and GISs, the integrated system could provide visual representations of the information on the Web and maps, something not currently possible with FHIMS.

Technically, the integration was developed in the following way. With its focus on name-based data, FHIMS was capable of generating subcentre-based reports and schedules to help the health staff identify which households to visit and when. The name-based household data was entered into the FHIMS, through which the subcentre-based reports were generated. The data were then aggregated and imported into the DHIS by facilities (subcentres) and processed, which resulted in the generation of various analysis reports, including on the GIS and Web. The integration was thus proposed to convert some of the raw (household based) data into useful information through the use of analytical tools, and to improve the representation of the data using GIS-generated maps. In arguing for the integration, the HISP team emphasized that map-based reports would be useful for district- and state-level officials, for example, in resource-allocation decisions (such as opening a new facility or buying an ambulance). The conceptual schema of the integration proposed, and subsequently accepted, through the MoU under the IHIMS project is depicted in Figure 2.

The IHIMS implementation commenced in August 2005, and the first phase of the project was a situation analysis to try to understand the status of the earlier FHIMS implementation

Figure 2. The FHIMS-HISP integration

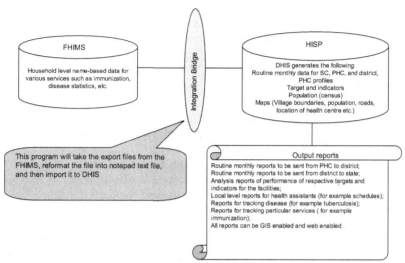

and the underlying challenges. A key problem identified was that the operators who had been working previously in the PHCs under the FHIMS project had operated as independent islands and had not involved the health assistants in the PHCs. As a result, there was little development of local expertise and ownership of the system. As mentioned earlier, in nearly 50 of the 84 PHCs, even the passwords to log on to the system were not known to the staff in clinics there. In contrast to the approach of the operators whose focus was on data entry, the HISP's emphasis was on system facilitation whereby the data entry and report generation was not done by the trainers, but by the health staff themselves, supported and facilitated by the trainers. Also, there was a difference in the focus of the training content, which was not limited to the mechanics of the software, but also to issues of how information can be made useful to support local action.

After the situation analysis in August, the HISP trainers were assigned to a cluster of four to five PHCs and were responsible for providing ongoing support to the staff on site in each of the PHCs. This on-site training approach was radically different from the earlier FHIMS training strategy of one large district-level 3- to 5-day training programme followed by liter-ally no support to the staff in the course of their everyday work. From August to November, a key focus of the IHIMS project was on completing the huge amounts of backlog in data entry in the FHIMS database, and trying to change the mindsets of the health staff from FHIMS to IHIMS, which included both DHIS and FHIMS. At the end of November 2005, an evaluation of the IHIMS indicated that 68 of the 84 PHCs had completed the backlog of data entry, and they had generated the Form B, mother and child report, and also the Forms A and C, for communicable diseases and other health services. The way IHIMS worked was that data for the Form B was entered into the FHIMS, and the report accordingly generated. However, the data required to generate Forms A and C were directly entered into the DHIS database, and the reports were generated through the DHIS. The FHIMS technically was not capable of developing the Forms A and C, but through the integration of the two systems, the whole suite of reports could be generated. Another evaluation at the end of December indicated that the number of PHCs that had generated the Forms A, B, and C was now 75, and the remaining 9 had serious structural problems (lack of staff or very large PHCs). Also, some of the PHCs, in addition to the routine reports of Forms A, B, and C, had also started to generate some analysis reports such as those for conducting inter-subcentre comparison. The HISP's training focus in the future was to be increasingly on the analysis reports and the use of information for action.

The relative success of the IHIMS programme can be attributed to three key reasons. First, by linking up the FHIMS and DHIS, the state government gave opportunities for the different people involved to pool their strengths and capacities rather than fight with each other. Second, the individual capabilities of the two systems could be innovatively combined so that the FHIMS software was used for generating subcentre-based reports while the DHIS provided the facility-specific reports and also incorporated different forms of representation including the Web and GIS. Third, alternative training approaches could be included through the integration. Unlike the FHIMS project, in which training focused primarily on the use of computers, HISP emphasized the use of information, including the generation of reports, the analysis of data, and the use of GIS to make visible spatial correlations in health data. Also, HISP tried to develop the capacity of the health assistants and other staff at the PHC in the local use of information. This effort is part of a larger and long-term process of developing an information culture where data is not just seen as a mindless effort to fulfill the needs of an uncaring bureaucracy, but a resource that can strengthen the everyday local work. This approach is compatible with Sandiford et al.'s (1992) argument:

> the ability to analyse and interpret data is indispensable but insufficient to overcome the inertia of the status quo to ensure that the information is translated into decisions and action....The need to tailor the presentation of information to the intended audience must be recognised. (p. 1085)

The analysis capabilities of the DHIS could be emphasized through various preprogrammed tools that provided the user with the ability to make comparisons and present data in the form of graphs, charts, and maps. Similarly, GIS provided particular analytical tools that enabled the mapping of health status and diseases, programme planning, displaying healthcare coverage, planning health infrastructure and maintenance, and comparing performance indicators across PHCs (Sauerborn & Karam, 2000).

Prior research in the domains of IS and HIS, both in developed and developing countries, has emphasized that integrating systems is no easy task as it involves aligning social, technical, and political linkages, and fostering coalitions and building synergies (Chilundo, 2004; Hanseth, Ciborra, & Braa, 2001). We agree with Chilundo, who has argued that the integration of ISs is not only a technical exercise, but involves the creation of a heterogeneous network comprised of various groups of people, technological artefacts, medical practices, and different information systems. While, at one level, integration can be seen as an attempt to reduce some of the heterogeneity in the system arising from a multiplicity of information systems, by adopting a modular approach to integration, heterogeneity can be encouraged rather than neutralized. While both the DHIS and FHIMS were capable of operating independently, in combination they were able to produce the whole set of reports required by the health department. Integration of not only the technical systems also implied bringing together different training approaches and also the pooling of financial and human resources. For example, the system administrators, a post created to support the FHIMS implementation, now were made the focal persons under the IHIMS and became responsible for the generation of the reports from both the DHIS and FHIMS systems.

In summary, we argue that the integration of systems can provide potential opportunities to address some of the implementation challenges discussed earlier. However, the philosophy underlying the integration attempts should not be to neutralize or eliminate one system, but to see how synergies can be created through drawing upon the positive aspects of both the systems and associated resources. For example, through IHIMS, the positive aspects of FHIMS, which were the name-based service schedule and summary reports, and DHIS, which was the facility-based reports, could be meaningfully incorporated toward the broader goals of health management.

Conclusion

The case studies presented earlier provide evidence of the importance of adopting a sociotechnical and integrated approach to the development of HIS. Too often, the introduction of ICTs is equated with development as an end in itself rather than as a means for supporting health management, which can in practice support development. These projects end up as largely computerisation projects and unsuccessful ones at that, rather than effective health-management initiatives. The introduction of computers, and the development and implementation of HIS in itself are not sufficient. Rather, the focus should be on how to develop and improve the informational base whereby information comes to be seen as a resource at all levels—at the local, district, state, and national levels—rather than just for bureaucracy.

There is typically an overemphasis on technical aspects during the implementation of HIS, and a relative neglect in addressing problems of information support that is necessary for better health management. The challenge is to move away from this pattern and to adopt a more integrated, holistic, and comprehensive approach to reforming informational and organisational practices. Introducing a HIS, particularly a name-based system, without addressing issues related to information generation, management, and use (analysis, interpretation, and evidence-based decision making) does not solve existing problems of poor quality of data, or the manipulation of figures, because health staff working in the field may have their own logic, stakes, and priorities that might not align with the goals of the promoters. That is, introducing information technology and systems does not in itself necessarily lead to better information practices or better health management. The challenge is not just to have adequate information, but to make better use of it and have a greater ability to act on it.

A grand vision to have a unified system (one-for-all purposes), as in the case of MPHS and FHIMS, may be attractive, but it brings with it numerous problems and is difficult to put effectively in practice. Instead, a more realistic approach should attempt to recognise what exists, what works well, and at what costs new systems are being built. While the name-based approach of the FHIMS is useful at the community level to track patients and provide targeted health care, HISP emphasizes the use of analytical tools for better health management and for capacity building of health staff. Initiating synergies between the FHIMS and DHIS through an integrated approach, as is being empirically attempted, provides opportunities to develop more sustainable health information systems that either of the systems by themselves cannot provide. These opportunities come through increased technical functionalities to serve different needs, a pooling of financial and human resources, and the incorporation of different and complementary training approaches.

Acknowledgments

The authors would like to thank Professor Lucy Suchman for her helpful comments on previous drafts of this chapter. We would also like to thank the officials at the office of the Commissioner of Family Welfare, Andhra Pradesh, all the health staff and members of HISP India, and the FHIMS team for their support.

References

Anderson, J. G., & Aydin, C. E. (1997). Evaluating the impact of health care information systems. *International Journal of Technology Assessment in Health Care, 13*(2), 380-393.

Avgerou, C., & Madon, S. (2004). Framing IS studies: Understanding the social context of IS innovation. In C. Avgerou, C. Ciborra, & F. Land (Eds.), *The social study of information and communication technology: Innovation, actors, and contexts* (pp. 162-182). Oxford, United Kingdom: Oxford University Press.

Avgerou, C., & Walsham, G. (Eds.). (2000). *Information technology in context: Studies from the perspective of developing countries.* Aldershot, United Kingdom: Ashgate.

Bodavala, R. (2002). ICT applications in public healthcare systems in India: A review. *ASCI Journal of Management, 31*(1-2), 56-66.

Braa, J., Heywood, A., & Shung King, M. (1997). District level information systems: Two cases from South Africa. *Methods of Information in Medicine, 36*(2), 115-121.

Braa, J., Monteiro, E., & Sahay, S. (2004). Networks of action: Sustainable health information systems across developing countries. *MIS Quarterly, 28*(3), 337-362.

Braa, J., & Nermukh, C. (2000). Health information systems in Mongolia: A difficult process of change. In C. Avgerou & G. Walsham (Eds.), *Information technology in context: Studies from the perspective of developing countries* (pp. 113-133). Aldershot, United Kingdom: Ashgate.

Braa, J., Macome, E., Mavibe, J. C., Nhampossa, J. L., da Costa, J. L., Manave, A., et al. (2001). A study of the actual and potential usage of information and communication technology at district and provincial levels in Mozambique with a focus on the health sector. *Electronic Journal in Information Systems for Developing Countries, 5*(2), 1-29.

Chilundo, B. (2004). *Integrating information systems of disease-specific health programmes in low income countries: The case study of Mozambique.* Unpublished doctoral dissertation, University of Oslo, Faculty of Medicine, Oslo, Norway.

Coakes, E., Willis, D., & Lloyd-Jones, R. (2000). Graffiti on the long wall: A sociotechnical conversation. In E. Coakes, D. Willis, & R. Lloyd-Jones (Eds.), *The new sociotech: Graffiti on the long wall* (pp. 3-12). London: Springer-Verlag.

Gupta, D. M., & Chen, C. L. (1996). Introduction. In D. M. Gupta, C. L. Chen, & T. N. Krishnan (Eds.), *Health, poverty & development in India* (pp. 1-22). Delhi, India: Oxford University Press.

Hanseth, O., Ciborra, C., & Braa, K. (2001). The control devolution: ERP and the side effects of globalization. *The Data Base for Advances in Information Systems, 32*(4), 34-46.

Heeks, R., Mundy, D., & Salazar, A. (2000). Understanding success and failure of healthcare information systems. In A. Armoni (Ed.), *Healthcare information systems, challenges of the new millennium* (pp. 96-128). Hershey, PA: Idea Group.

Helfenbein, S., et al. (1987). *Technologies for management information systems in primary health care* (issue paper). Geneva, Switzerland: World Federation of Public Health Associations.

Jacucci, E., Shaw, V., & Braa, J. (2005). *Standardization of health information systems in South Africa: The challenge of local sustainability.* Proceedings of the Eighth International Working Conference of IFIP WG 9.4: Enhancing Human Resource Development through ICT, Abuja, Nigeria.

Jarvenpaa, S. L., & Leidner, D. E. (1998). An information company in Mexico: Extending the resource-based view of the firm to a developing country context. *Information Systems Research, 9*(4), 342-361.

Kling, R. (1987). Defining the boundaries of computing across complex organisation. In R. Boland & R. Hirschheim (Eds.), *Critical issues in information systems research* (pp. 307-362). New York: Wiley.

Kling, R., & Lamb, R. (2000). IT and organizational change in digital economies: A sociotechnical approach. In B. Kahin & E. Brynjolfsson (Eds.), *Understanding the digital economy: Data, tools and research* (pp. 295-324). Cambridge, MA: The MIT Press.

Kling, R., & Scacchi, W. (1982). The web of computing: Computer technology as social organisations. *Advances in Computing, 21,* 1-90.

Lippeveld, T., Sauerborn, R., & Bodart, C. (2000). *Design and implementation of health information systems.* Geneva, Switzerland: World Health Organisation.

Lippeveld, T. J., Foltz, A., & Mahouri, Y. M. (1992). *Transforming health facility-based reporting systems into management information systems: Lessons from the Chad experience* (Development Discussion Papers No. 430). Cambridge, MA: Harvard Institute of International Development.

Madon, S. (1993). Introducing administrative reform through the application of computer-based information systems: A case study in India. *Public Administration and Development, 13*(1), 37-48.

Madon, S., Sahay, S., & Sahay, J. (2004). Implementing property tax reforms in Bangalore: An actor-network perspective. *Information and Organization, 14,* 269-295.

Madon, S., Sahay, S., & Sudan, R. (2005). *E-governance and health care in Andhra Pradesh, India: Reflecting upon the mutual linkages between macro and micro.* Unpublished manuscript.

Mohanty, P. K., Jones, K., & Rao, S. J. (2004). *Good governance initiatives in Andhra Pradesh 2003.* Hyderabad, India: Centre for Good Governance.

Mosse, E., & Nielsen, P. (2004). Communication practices as functions, rituals and symbols: Challenges for computerization of paper-based information systems. *The Electronic Journal of Information Systems in Developing Countries, 18*(3), 1-17.

Mosse, E., & Sahay, S. (2003). Counter networks, communication and health information systems: A case study from Mozambique. In *Proceeding from IFIP TC8 & TC9/WG8.2 Working Conference on Information Systems Perspectives and Challenges in the Context of Globalisation,* pp. 35-51.

Nhampossa, J. L. (2004). Strategies to deal with legacy information systems: A case study from the Mozambican health sector. *Innovations through Information Technology: Proceedings of the 15th Information Resources Management Association International Conference.* Retrieved March 21, 2005, from http://folk.uio.no/leopoldo/Publications/Papers/IRMA_USA.pdf

Nhampossa, J. L., & Sahay, S. (2005). Social construction of software customisation: The case of health information systems from Mozambique and India. In *Proceedings of the Eighth International Working Conference of IFIP WG 9.4: Enhancing Human Resource Development through ICT, Abuja, Nigeri*a.

Office of the Commissioner of Family Welfare. (2003, May 13). *Various official circulars. Circular – I* (Rc No. FHIMS/9511/2003). Hyderabad, India: Author.

Opit, L. J. (1987). How should information on healthcare be generated and used? *World Health Forum, 8,* 409-438.

Piotti, B., Chilundo, B., & Sahay, S. (2005). *An institutional perspective on health sector reform and the process of reframing health information systems: Case studies from Mozambique* (Working Paper 9). Retrieved September 14, 2005, from http://www.ifi.uio.no/forskning/grupper/is/wp/092005.pdf

Quraishy, Z., & Gregory, J. (2005). Implications of (non) participation of users in implementation of the Health Information System Project (HISP) in Andhra Pradesh: Practical experiences. In *Proceedings of the Eighth International Working Conference of IFIP WG 9.4: Enhancing Human Resource Development through ICT, Abuja, Nigeria.*

Sahay, S. (1998). Implementing GIS technology in India: Some issues of time and space. *Accounting Management and Information Technologies, 8,* 147-188.

Sahay, S. (2000, May 24-26). *Information flows, local improvisations and work practices.* Paper presented at the IFIP WG 9.4 Conference, Cape Town.

Sahay, S. (2001). Introduction. *The Electronic Journal of Information Systems in Developing Countries, 5*, 1–6.

Sahay, S., & Walsham, G. (2005). *Scaling of health information systems in India: Challenges and approaches*. Proceedings of the Eighth International Working Conference of IFIP WG 9.4: Enhancing Human Resource Development through ICT, Abuja, Nigeria.

Sandiford, P., Annett, H., & Cibulski, R. (1992). What can information systems do for primary health care? An international perspective. *Social Studies and Medicine, 34*(10), 1077-1087.

Sauerborn, R., & Karam, M. (2000). Geographic information systems. In T. Lippeveld, R. Sauerborn, & C. Bodart (Eds.), *Design and implementation of health information systems* (pp. 213-224). Geneva, Switzerland: World Health Organisation.

Sauerborn, R., & Lippeveld, T. (2000). Introduction. In T. Lippeveld, R. Sauerborn, & C. Bodart (Eds.), *Design and implementation of health information systems*. Geneva, Switzerland: World Health Organisation.

Singh, M. (2005). *PM launches National Rural Health Mission*. Retrieved August 31, 2005, from *http://pmindia.nic.in/speech/content.asp?id=101*

Tomasi, E., Facchini, L. A., & Maia, M. F. S. (2004). Health information technology in primary health care in developing countries: A literature review. *Bulletin of the World Health Organization, 82*(11), 867- 869.

Walsham, G. (1993). *Interpreting information systems in organisations*. Cambridge: John Wiley & Sons.

Walsham, G. (2001). *Making a world of difference: IT in a global context*. Chichester, United Kingdom: John Wiley.

World Health Organisation (WHO). (1987). *Report of the interregional meeting on strengthening district health systems based on primary health care* (WHO/SHS/DHS/87.13). Unpublished document.

World Health Organisation (WHO). (2005). *Health and the millennium development goals*. Avenue Appia: Author.

Endnotes

[1]   A mandal is an administrative unit.

[2]   A habitation is a group of households in a village. It is also a unit of data for the census.

[3]   For more on HISP activities in India, see Sahay and Walsham (2005) and Braa, Monteiro, and Sahay (2004).

ANMs (auxiliary nurses and midwives) and MPHAs (multipurpose health assistants) are synonyms for health assistants.

The quotes that are presented here are not verbatim but with slight alterations to clarify language usage.

Glossary

AP: State of Andhra Pradesh, India

ANMs: Auxiliary Nurses and Midwives or health assistants

CFW: Commissioner of Family Welfare

DMHO: District Medical and Health Office

DHIS: District Health Information System

FHIMS: Family Health Information Management System

FWD: Family Welfare Department

GIS: Geographic Information System

HISP: Health Information System Programme

HIS: Health Information System

IHC: India Health Care Project

IHIMS: Integrated Health Information Management System

MPHS: Multipurpose Household Survey

PDA: Personal Digital Assistant

PHC: Primary Health Centre

SC: Subcentre

Chapter XII

An Explanatory Approach to the Political Uses of ICT Initiatives for Participation:
Institutions, Context, and Characteristics of the Actors

Rosa Borge, Open University of Catalonia, Spain

Abstract

Political actors use ICTs in a different manner and in different degrees when it comes to achieving a closer relationship between the public and politicians. Usually, political parties develop ICT strategies only for electoral campaigning and therefore restrain ICT usages to providing information and establishing a few channels of communication. By contrast, local governments make much more use of ICT tools for participatory and deliberative purposes. These differences in usages have not been well explained in the literature because of a lack of a comprehensive explanatory model. This chapter seeks to build the basis for this model, that is, to establish which factors affect and condition different political uses of ICTs and which principles underlie that behaviour. We consider that political actors are intentional and their behaviour is mediated by the political institutions and the socioeconomic context of the country. Also, though, the actor's own characteristics, such as the type and size of the organization or the model of e-democracy that the actor upholds, can have an influence in launching ICT initiatives for approaching the public.

Introduction

More than a decade has passed since the invention of the World Wide Web, based on the global development of the Internet, and, although it has spread very quickly throughout our personal lives, the marketplace, and civil society, it is not developing so fast in crucial areas of the political realm. Political actors, such as parties, or political institutions, such as parliaments or governments, are reluctant to use the Internet widely for connecting with or approaching citizens. Nevertheless, in public administration we can see a steady use of the Internet in order to provide services and information to the public and reduce the procedures that citizens must carry out. In addition, at the local level, at least in Europe,[1] public authorities are launching ICT initiatives much more than parties or parliaments for contacting their citizens and engaging them in the affairs of the municipality.

However, even public administrations and local governments are not using the Internet as extensively as the business sector, the organisations of the civil society, or individuals in their social and personal relationships. It seems that public authorities and political structures are lagging behind in the technological transformations that are affecting the private sector and relationships among individuals. So what are the reasons for this lesser use of ICTs among political actors and inside political institutions? Few studies have been carried out to answer this question. Some authors assert that there are a number of elements ranging from organisational to cultural elements that hinder the assimilation of new technologies by political actors and institutions in contrast to private companies. Political parties and representative institutions such as parliaments are more centralised, less flexible, older, and much less dependent on the "customer-citizen" than many companies in the private sector (Kippen & Jenkins, 2004; Prats, 2005), and all these trends greatly hinder a successful integration of new technologies. Society, business, and communications have changed, among other factors, because of a wider Internet usage, but the core institutions and actors of the political system are still using primarily old technological artifacts and do not appear to be very willing to transform their unidirectional relationship with the public.

Many more studies comparing the efficient integration of ICTs in business and society with the difficulties for their deployment in the representative political system are needed. Yet, it is also very important to discern why some political actors use the new ICTs much more frequently than others. This search for an explanation is not just of academic or scientific interest, but is also of interest to politicians, public-sector officials, or development professionals who need to understand what the constraints and factors favouring deployment of ICTs are. Technicians, politicians, or activists interested in developing ICT initiatives in a transformative way for democracy must be informed of the costs and benefits of that usage and of the incentives and hurdles that they may come across.

We suspect that similar factors to the ones considered above (organisational, cultural) are affecting differences in political uses. We also know, due to the large accumulation of knowledge in the analysis of collective behaviour, political institutions, and human agency, that the political actors' behaviour could be analysed as intentional and, at the same time, structured by political institutions and the social and cultural context.

To this effect, the main goal of the chapter will be to introduce the basic elements for the construction of a model that explains the differences in Internet usage by different political actors. These basic elements are a number of variables that must be taken into account when attempting to explain these differences in behaviour. We will not be drawing up a complete detailed model, but rather we will provide an outline of the variables that conform the structure for explanation. We leave the definition of the interactions inside the model and the very construction of the model itself for further studies. Our contributions are to bring out explanatory variables not before considered in ICT literature, to compare the variables already studied in the literature, and to think about the constraints, incentives, and opportunities that political actors face regarding ICT developments.

Internet usages vary within each country and from country to country, and they can change rapidly. In addition, the search for explanations is very difficult since contagion and diffusion of the political uses of ICT among countries and among political actors render the analysis without clear explanatory variables. In a time of rapid change and fast diffusion of technologies, and in an increasingly globalised world, it is difficult to determine who or what shapes the course of political action, precisely, toward the new technologies. Several analysts have found common patterns and stages in the adoption of ICT by public institutions such as public administrations,[2] but literature on explanations is still at the beginning, and results are sometimes partial and contradictory.[3]

Nevertheless, we believe that social sciences should strive to understand these new phenomena and to give insights and information to public authorities, politicians, and the public in general. Also, as we mentioned before, there are enough theories, models, and methods that can be applied to shed some light on this area and thereby increase our understanding of the issues involved.

Political uses of ICTs: The Ladder of Political Participation

Before we can begin to develop the outline of the explanatory model, we have to define what political ICT usages means. In other words, what do we mean when we refer to different uses of ICT by political actors? There are a wide range of ICT initiatives with very different characteristics undertaken by parties, parliaments, public administrations, and the many other kinds of political organisations. ICTs are being used for facilitating internal communication and processes inside the political organisations or institutions, but in our study, we will be analysing specifically the external initiatives addressed to the public. These are the initiatives that can contribute to revitalising one of the pillars of democracy: the relationship between citizens and their representatives. We must bear in mind that many citizens are dissatisfied[4] with the way the system of democratic representation works, and the Internet and other ICTs could be a useful tool for bringing the public and politicians closer. In this sense, the Internet is being used to provide information to the public through Web sites, to establish

Figure 1. Ladder of citizen participation

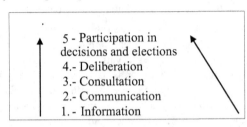

channels of communication, such as online forums, and to expand channels of participation by means of surveys, elections, and consultations online.

In an attempt to order the various ICT experiences in public engagement, several classification scales have been developed by various analysts (Arnstein, 1969; Coleman & Gøtze, 2001; Goss, 1999; Navarro, in press; Organization for Economic Cooperation and Development [OECD], 2001). All of them range from the lowest step, which is the information level, to the participation in decision making, which is situated at the highest level. The progression on the scale depends on the extent of citizens' power in determining political decisions. Taking as a starting point the participation scale proposed by Arnstein, we outline a ladder of participation with five degrees distributed as follows.

A large number of empirical studies and reports describing ICT usages by different political actors have been carried out.[5] These studies show that, generally speaking, political parties remain at the lower levels of participatory usage of ICT: information and less frequently, communication (Norris, 2001; Trechsel, Kies, Mendez, & Schmitter, 2003). In addition, government executives limit themselves to providing the public with information (and services) online through their Web sites (Chadwick & May, 2003). On the contrary, parliaments use ICTs more than parties and executives to develop bidirectional communication between the members of the parliament and their constituents (Coleman, Taylor, & van de Donk, 1999; Trechsel et al,2003.). It is becoming common to establish channels of communication and consultation on the parliamentary Web sites to allow citizens to have their say about law projects and amendments, in what is called "open parliament."[6]

More and more different areas of public administrations are moving toward the consultation level because they have an interest in knowing citizens' opinions and satisfaction about public administration services and procedures (Accenture, 2005). And, much more frequently than the other political actors and institutions, city councils achieve the highest level, which is the one of deliberation and participation in political decisions and binding votings, beyond those already established by the ordinary system of elections (Borge, 2005; Clift, 2004; Coleman & Gøtze, 2001).

Of course, there are variations from this general rule. In countries like the USA, party candidates use the Internet widely and in a very innovative way. For example, Howard Dean raised money and attracted numerous supporters with the help of already well-established Web tools, bloggers, and Internet-based communities. He used Web tools like Meetup.com to form a support and fundraising group, and also received the support of the majority of the members of MoveOn.org. His campaign for the Democratic party's presidential nomination was not centralized and led by a headquarters, but it was based instead on the Meetup.com site so that any supporter could coordinate meetings.[7] As a result, he came close to winning the Democratic nomination for presidential candidate in spite of the lack of the financial support of big firms and mainstream organizations.

In addition, breaking the general rule of the lack of participatory and deliberative aims within governments, some national and regional executives use the Internet to involve their citizens in important political issues such as constitutional reforms, controversial public policies, or the entry into international organizations. For instance, the British executive is the pioneer in using online solutions for participation in government decisions. Since 1997, it has developed a consultation policy on law proposals, government planning, and decisions, based on a combination of online tools such as forums, e-mails, live chats, and face-to-face meetings and panels.[8] Recently, the Catalan government has also deployed a participatory process in order to get the public involved in the reform of the Catalan Statute of Autonomy. This initiative combined a very wide array of off-line and online actions. The online actions were threefold. First, there was an e-mailbox called "The government listens to you," where citizens could send an e-mail with their proposals, opinions, and criticisms regarding the statutory reform. Citizens were answered by the government in 24 hours. This became the most successful medium, with 4,530 e-mails. Second, an online forum where the citizens could discuss the reform was available, and third, there was a mailing list to which the citizens could subscribe in order to receive information about the events, conferences, and workshops about the statute.[9]

In conclusion, we can summarise the state of ICT usage by political actors with the following three statements:

1. Organisations from civil society and the business sector use ICT much more for contacting citizens and customers than political actors and institutions.

2. Parties, parliaments, and executives launch ICT-based initiatives mainly for information and communication, but rarely for consultation, deliberation, or participation in the decision-making process or in binding elections. By contrast, public administrations, and especially city councils, tend to develop ICT-based strategies to engage citizens in public affairs through online channels for consultation, deliberation, or participation.

3. Notwithstanding the latter rule, in a few countries, some parties, parliaments, and government executives also use the Internet for consultation, deliberation, and participation.

Explanations of the Political Uses of ICTs; Methodological and Theoretical Approaches

In looking for explanations for the different behaviour, the first and second statements cited above lead us to consider the diverse goals, values, and characteristics among political actors. If political parties, parliaments, and governments, in no matter what country, act differently from municipalities and public administrations, it is because they differ in their intrinsic characteristics (i.e., type of organisation), objectives, or values (i.e., models of democracy adopted). Nevertheless, in a few countries, parties, parliaments, and governments go a little further on the ladder of participation, and, therefore, the explanations must lie in the specific characteristics of countries, such as their political institutions or other contextual variables. Consequently, we compare a wide array of factors that may possibly affect ICT usages by the different political actors and in different countries.

Furthermore, an enormous variety of different technologies is combined for achieving the objectives that political actors seek when approaching the public. For instance, a combination of mailing lists, newsgroups, and areas on Web sites with documents available is frequently used for providing information to citizens. Bidirectional communication is usually developed making use of e-mail and chat rooms located on the Web site. Deliberation online is achieved using, in the first place, all the media cited above, and then by developing online forums, conferences, or bulletin boards. There are also other technological elements for consultation, for example, Web-based forms of various kinds that are used for online petitions, surveys, and nonbinding referenda. Participation in the decision-making process, being the highest degree on the scale, is based on many of the technologies mentioned above that can be combined into different variants (deliberative e-polls, e-citizens' juries, e-citizens' panels, etc.[10]) with the objective of reaching a final decision that is binding for public authorities.

Therefore, the dependent variable (ICT usages by different political actors) and the independent variables (explanatory factors) are extremely varied. As regards the explanatory factors and in the case of collective political actors, the literature has concentrated mainly on the institutional factors (types of government, level of decentralisation, single-chamber or two-chamber systems, district magnitude, types of voting lists, etc.), the characteristics of the organisations (party size, ideology, longevity, whether the party is in power or in the opposition, etc.), and a large number of contextual variables (technological diffusion in the country, economic development, population, educational level, level of democratisation, etc.) that can affect ICT usages.

Given this variety, analysts trying to explain differences in behaviour between actors from different countries proceed by following two divergent methodologies. On the one hand, some authors select few cases and few explanatory variables in order to make the analysis more manageable and much more precisely addressed toward the confirmation of a specific hypothesis. Normally, they select cases on the independent variable; that is, cases are chosen for analysis taking into account which values on the independent variable could affect the dependent variable differently. This procedure assures no bias in case selection, but when the values of explanatory variables are very limited and no previous control variables are introduced, inferences will not be sufficiently sound for wide generalisation (King, Keohane, & Verba, 1994). Nevertheless, this kind of analysis can be very important in the first stages of the study of a new phenomenon because it serves to discover the possible explanatory variables when there is no empirical evidence. For example, following this procedure of selecting a few explanatory variables and few cases (although many observations), authors such as Zittel (2001) and Costafreda (2005) have discovered the significant role of political institutions, such as the type of government (parliamentary vs. presidential system) or some elements of the electoral system (district magnitude and types of voting lists). Notwithstanding the significant assets of this methodology, the fact of having only a few cases and few explanatory variables, usually without controlling spurious or participatory variables, restrains inferences and limits conclusions.

On the other hand, another methodology also used consists of testing various types of explanatory factors in many countries and making numerous observations. This is the methodology followed by research teams like the one led by A. Trechsel (Trechsel et al., 2003) and important authors like Pippa Norris (2001). In these studies, the selection of cases is not intentional but a random selection drawn from a large population (Norris); or, if it is of a manageable size, researchers can select the entire population (Trechsel et al.). This procedure guarantees an unbiased sample of cases and, in this sense, conclusions can be generalised and are more valid than when few cases and few explanatory variables are examined (King et al., 1994). Nevertheless, in my opinion, the flaw of this method is on the side of the explanatory factors because they are analysed one after the other without a hierarchical pattern that could put order and meaning among the numerous possible explanations. The consequence is that, although the same cases are analysed, results between studies are contradictory, and explanatory variables found to be significant in reliable studies like the ones carried out by Norris or by Zittel (2001) are found to be nonsignificant in Trechsel et al.'s work.[11]

The absence of an organised pattern of explanations is due to poorly developed theoretical models, in this case, models able to account for the behaviour of collective actors toward new technologies, or in other words, models dealing with political actors' actions while at the same time offering insights into the sociopolitical uses of technology.

In political science and in sociology, there are several approaches and models that aim to explain the behaviour of collective political actors, and which have proven to be very successful. For example, there is the Political Opportunity Structure (POS), which explains that social movements and interest groups achieve their objectives and a power share when the institutions of the political system are accessible, porous, and open to their demands and participation (Kitschelt, 1990; Kriesi, Koopmans, Duyvendak, & Giugni, 1995). Institutional structures promote or deter collective actors from action by means of the incentives and benefits they would provide. The significance of institutions is also acknowledged by New Institutionalism (March & Olsen, 1989), where institutions are no longer passive constraints or a determining factor, but rather play an active role in establishing the preferences and interests of collective actors (Hoff, 2000).

Furthermore, regarding technological usages, some authors (Hoff, 2000; Aibar & Urgell, 2003; Welp, Urgell, & Aibar, 2005) point out that the SCOT (Social Construction of Technology) theory as formulated by Bijker (1995) is currently the most promising theory for studying the interplay between structures (institutions, organisations), culture, and behaviour toward technologies. The social constructivist approach put forward by Bijker states that the group uses of technology are mediated by structures and culture and, therefore, they must be analysed within this context.

Basic Elements and Principles
for an Explanatory Model

In my opinion, a successful explanatory model would be a combination of the two theoretical approaches mentioned above: the one that recognises the relevance of institutions and the one that highlights that the usages of technology depend on the nature of organisations and the culture where technology is deployed. At this point, we will try to lay the basis for an explanatory model that combines three sets of elements:

1.   The political institutions within which the collective actors must play. The research literature pinpoints the district magnitude, the type of voting list, the type of government, and the level of decentralisation.

2.   The socioeconomic and technological context characterising the environment where the actors perform, that is, some aggregate characteristics of the country (for example, technological diffusion, socioeconomic development) or of the city or town (town size) where the actors act.

3.   The nature of the collective political actors, which refers to their different characteristics in terms of aims, organisation, and values.

Continuing with the theoretical approaches cited above, there is an interplay between the three groups of factors that can be described as follows.

Collective actors make use of ICTs when institutions and context promote and facilitate their use, but always depending on the characteristics of the actors. This means that institutions and context impinge upon the structure of costs and benefits of collective action, but actors' preferences depend on the objectives, culture, and organisation of the actors. We start from the assumption that collective actors are rational agents that use ICTs if they are useful for achieving their objectives and if there are enough institutional and contextual incentives for fulfilling their objectives better by means of ICTs. In contrast, collective actors will not make use of ICTs if they do not envisage their utility for achieving their objectives, and the surrounding institutions and context do not provide opportunities for meeting the actors' goals using ICTs.

The logic of the behaviour described above can be illustrated well by comparing two different actors that show opposing behaviour regarding the deployment of ICTs, as we have already mentioned in previous pages: political parties and city councils. In most countries, the former make very poor use of ICTs in order to reach out to the public (basically, providing information and establishing one-way channels of communication; Norris, 2001; Trechsel et al., 2003). The latter tend to use ICTs much more, in most countries, for involving citizens in participatory and deliberative processes (Chadwick & May, 2003, pp. 294-295; Clift, 2004; Coleman & Gøtze, 2001).

Taking into account the findings shown by the literature, we will detail the variables that could be the most influential within each of the three groups of elements for the case of parties and city councils.

Political Institutions

Regarding political institutions, and for the case of parties, the literature points to the district magnitude, the type of voting list (Costafreda, 2005), and the type of government (Zittel, 2001) as the most relevant variables. For local governments, we think that the most important variable could be the level of local decentralisation of the country and the consequential power share, budget, and attributions that city councils enjoy. In addition, legal enforcement and subsidies for developing ICT channels for participation are proving to be crucial.

If the district magnitude is very small (uninominal or binominal) and the type of voting list is unblocked or open, parties will design ICT media to reach the voters better because candidates depend much more directly on the voters than in the case of proportional systems with large districts and blocked voting lists in which nomination depends on the power struggles inside the party. This is one of the reasons why parties in Chile, the United Kingdom, and Germany design their Web sites not only for informational purposes, but also for communication and deliberation (Costafreda, 2005; Trechsel et al., 2003). The same reasoning could be applied to the type of government. In presidential systems, parties and their presidential candidates have more incentives to launch ICT initiatives in order to contact and convince possible voters than in parliamentarian systems in which the election of the head of the government is indirect through the members of the parliament. Also, the fact that a party or a party co-alition winning in the elections in parliamentary democracies possesses the power to make and break governments imposes a rigid discipline on parliamentary majorities and on the party itself, and pushes representatives and candidates to concentrate on internal bargaining (Zittel, 2001, p.19). On the contrary, in presidential systems, parties and representatives have much more room to establish a closer relationship with their constituents, followers, and voters (Zittel, 2001, p.20). Zittel defends that this institutional feature is one of the most important explanations for the greater communicative ICT usage by U.S. parties as compared with their European counterparts.

With respect to local governments, the most important variable is the level of decentralisa-tion of the country regarding the local level, as municipalities will tend to deploy ICT-based channels of communication and participation more frequently if they have the sufficient autonomy, legal competences, and financial resources to do so. We consider that not only political decentralisation could achieve power and resources for the city councils, but also deconcentration or functional autonomy, where the central state gives up the management of some important functions and services to the local government. This would be one of the reasons why local governments in the United Kingdom, the Netherlands, and Finland have undertaken so many ICT initiatives for engaging their citizens in local public decisions. In addition, decentralisation is becoming a key political aim of Latin American governments, and new participatory bodies, including different ICTs usages, are being set up at the local level in countries such as Bolivia, Colombia, Brazil, and Venezuela.

Other important conditions for undertaking ICT initiatives are the legal framework and the financial incentives provided by other levels of government. For example, several planning schemes in the United Kingdom and several laws in Spain and Catalonia[12] compel local governments to design participatory plans that include the launching of ICT initiatives. Also, in these countries, higher level governments award subsidies to the city councils that develop participatory projects, including the use of ICTs. This has contributed enormously to the emergence of ICT-based strategies for participation in Catalonia.[13]

Socioeconomic and Technological Context

With reference to the socioeconomic and technological context, the variables commonly studied in the case of political parties (Norris, 2001; Trechsel et al., 2003) are the technological diffusion inside the country, the socioeconomic development, the population size, and the level of democratisation. These variables are characteristics of the country and must be controlled in order to see the real influence of the institutional variables. Trechsel et al. (2003) demonstrated in their study of 25 European countries, the European Union, and 144 party Web sites that economic development (measured by per capita GNP [gross national product]) and population size of the country have no significant correlation with an extensive use by parties of ICTs for communicative or deliberative purposes. Nor does technological diffusion have an impact on developing party Web sites with communication and deliberation channels (Trechsel et al., 2003, p.27). Nevertheless, Norris arrived at different conclusions. Her study encompasses 179 countries and 1,371 party Web sites. She found that the strongest and most significant indicator of the presence of all parties online is technological diffusion, followed by levels of socioeconomic development.[14] Also, after controlling for socioeconomic and technological development, the level of democratisation[15] in a country proved unrelated to the information or communication functions of parties. Therefore, it seems that the opposite conclusions from the two studies could be due to the number and type of cases analysed, and also to the different indicators used for measuring the variables. Norris examines countries from the whole world, while Trechsel's team focused on European countries. Consequently, in Norris' cases, there is much greater variation, which makes socioeconomic and technological development significant for explaining the deployment of ICTs. In addition, the differences in measurement of socioeconomic development (much more complete in Norris) and technological diffusion (much more complete in Trechsel et al.) could have led to different conclusions.

Leaving aside political parties, studies on e-government have shown that a country's GDP (gross domestic product) or per capita income affect positively governmental response via ICTs to citizens' demands for information and services (Altman, 2002; La Porte, Demchak, & de Jong, 2002; United Nations [UN], 2005, pp.117-118). This phenomenon occurs in both OECD and non-OECD countries. Nevertheless, this relationship is not a perfect correlation because it can be mediated by each country's political institutions and culture, or each actor's aims and intentions. This is the case of Latin American countries, where D. Altman (2002) found that the more citizens are satisfied with democracy and have interpersonal trust, the lower the extent of e-government in each country. He argues that in Latin America, when there is a high satisfaction with the regime and interpersonal trust, politicians do not have enough incentives to promote e-government given the lack of economic resources and materialist perceptions in comparison to well-developed and post-materialist countries.

Regarding local governments, we can hypothesise that the socioeconomic development of the country or the city, and the technological diffusion in the country or city, or even the level of democratisation can affect the development of ICT strategies for communication, deliberation, and participation. Unfortunately, we do not have any information of this kind because the majority of studies on ICT usages by local governments are merely descriptive. Only municipality size has been analysed, although by means of simple cross-tabulations, that is, without considering relationships with other possible explanatory variables. The results show, for example, that in Catalonia, the majority of municipalities with under 20,000 citizens have not already deployed interactive spaces with their citizens on their Web sites, although in the last 2 years, these small municipalities have made a big effort to open up informative Web sites and provide access via broadband (Observatori de la Societat de la Informació [OBSI], 2004). Larger municipalities have more technical and monetary resources for implementing ICT strategies for communication with their citizens and for participation. Yet, management and politics are not so complicated in small local governments and therefore reforms toward participation or communication by means of ICTs could be more affordable and manageable once a minimum population threshold is surpassed (for example, in Catalonia, the threshold could be situated at 20,000 inhabitants). Also, the lack of resources could be overcome through digital platforms shared by several city councils, as is being done in Catalonia or in Emilia-Romagna (Italy).[16]

Characteristics of the Collective Actors

In relation to the characteristics of the collective actors, we considered three variables: actors' objectives, the models or discourses on e-democracy held by the actors, and the type of organisation. These three factors are intertwined since models or discourses on e-democracy depend on actors' aims (Hoff, 2000), and at the same time, the type of organisation could condition those aims (Strom, 1990). Nevertheless, in order to simplify our outline of an explanatory model, we will focus on how objectives, models, and organisation independently affect behaviour toward ICTs.

Objectives

The literature on party behaviour within the rational-choice approach has stated three models of party behaviour based on their objectives or aims: (a) vote seeking, (b) office seeking, and (c) policy seeking (Strom, 1990). These objectives or aims could also be shared by other political actors such as local governments. Therefore, the idea is that parties and local governments will launch different ICT initiatives depending on their objectives. Of course, having one of the objectives does not preclude the others. In addition, we have to take into account that parties' or local governments' aims are featured by institutional and organisational constraints (Strom, 1990). For example, vote-seeking behaviour will be more likely to be found in majority systems (small-district magnitudes, two-party systems, low-fragmentation policies) or when parties are expected to win a large share of the vote (close to 50% in multiparty systems) where strategic party interaction disappears and voting power leads directly to policy influence and office benefits (Strom, 1990, p. 592). Parties with these goals will develop attractive Web sites in order to "sell" the candidate and party, but will also use party Web sites and candidates' Web sites more extensively for mobilising their followers, engaging new and young voters, and contacting constituents, as is already happening in the United Kingdom and the USA.

We could hypothesise that local governments are more focused on carrying out their policy goals. Yet, they certainly want to stay in office and, therefore, they need to maintain their voters and gain more. Local governments, mostly driven by the aim of achieving votes and renewing incumbency, will not risk engaging in deliberative or participatory experiences based on ICT initiatives as the results of those experiences are uncertain in terms of gaining votes. By contrast, local governments that are mainly policy seekers will tend much more to engage citizens and networks of actors in the policy process (by means of ICTs or others) since involvement of the interested public and organised actors could guarantee an easier implementation of policies (Goss, 2001; Sabel & O'Donnell, 2000). However, just as in the case of parties, the preferences of city councils for one or the other objective depend on the incentives and constraints that local authorities will face in the institutional setting: for example, whether the central state, the regional government, or other institutions provide technical or financial support for developing participatory devices based on ICTs, or whether a legal obligation exists for city councils to deploy informative and participatory channels. As we saw before, these would be some of the incentives and constraints faced by, for example, Catalan or British municipalities.

Models of Democracy and Role of the ICTs

Very closely related to the actor's objectives are different models of democracy in which ICTs play or could play a role. These models are pursued or assimilated by the political actors, and are showed and expressed in the discourses, strategies, and actions of the actors. Parties or city councils defend or have assimilated, more or less explicitly, different models of democracy and the role of ICTs.

There are several important studies on e-democracy models (Bellamy, 2000; Hagen, 2000; Van Dijk, 2000). These models are necessary to evaluate how ICT developments could transform the political processes and are useful for making sense of the role of ICTs inside the democratic system. They are formed by a combination of different crucial features (norms, values, institutions) that characterise the political system and the use of ICTs. Among the different studies, Bellamy's, with Hoff, Horrocks, and Tops (2000), creation and explanation of the models stands out. The main features of the models are the view on citizenship, the dominant democratic value, the political nexus, the central form of political participation, the main political intermediary, the dominant procedural norm, and the typical ICT application. The models are the consumer, the demo-elitist (or neo-corporatist), the neo-republican, and the cyberdemocratic model (Hoff et al, 2000, p.7.). Applying these models to specific cases, Tops, Horrocks, and Hoff (2000) have determined that parties are closer to the consumer model (representative democracy where the citizen is a customer who has to be well informed and deserves good public services), while local governments defend more often a neo-corporatist (pluralist democracy based on welfare policies) or a neo-republican (participatory democracy based on a strong and autonomous civil society) model of democracy. Nevertheless, the cases studied by Tops et al. are only three countries (Denmark, Great Britain, and The Netherlands) and a few parties and ICT experiences (electronic citizen card, electronic public service delivery, closed-circuit television) taking place in those countries. Therefore, more case studies are needed in order to generalise with respect to the position of the actors.

Type of Organisation

Characteristics of their own organisation affect the behaviour of collective actors. In the case of parties, Strom (1990, p. 593) identifies several organisational properties that influence party behaviour. Among these, we have selected two that may possibly affect the deployment of ICTs by parties: organisational form (capital or labour intensive) and intraparty democracy.

Party organisations are very intensive in capital when they rely on advertising technology, marketing tools, and monetary resources for the electoral campaign, for gathering information about the electorate, or for implementation of party policy. They are also the parties that receive the largest amount of money from private donations. By contrast, labour-intensive parties rely more on activists to develop these functions and they get less money from private donations. Nevertheless, in recent years, even leftist parties are shifting toward greater reliance on capital and technology as it has become a more successful strategy for mobilising supporters and getting votes (Strom, 1990, p. 575). Therefore, we can hypothesise that capital-intensive parties use ICTs widely and Web sites mainly for campaigning, while labour-intensive parties do not use so many ICT resources but frequently include participatory channels on their Web sites. For example, in Spain, analysis of party Web sites shows that capital-intensive parties like the Partido Popular or Convergència i Unió have developed highly attractive Web sites from a marketing point of view and have used other technical devices for the campaign, such as mobile phones, videoconferences, instant messaging, and so forth. On the contrary, labour-intensive parties like Iniciativa per Catalunya or Izquierda Unida have displayed well-constructed interactive spaces and recruitment channels on their Web sites that larger parties have not developed (Borge & Alvaro, 2004).

The same reasoning could be applied to centralised parties vs. decentralised ones. The latter are internally more democratic and participatory, and therefore ICTs could be used for building deliberative and participatory channels. Decentralised parties transfer decisions on policy and programmes to party conferences, congresses, and committees, and the candidates for office are usually elected by means of primaries. This organisational profile could favour uses of ICTs for participatory and voting purposes. For example, in 1996, the Democratic Party in Arizona held primary elections using three channels: postal mail, the Internet, and ordinary voting. Forty-one percent of the votes were cast by Internet, and the level of participation increased sevenfold (Gibson, 2001).

Moreover, other organisational factors have been studied as possible influences on party usages of ICTs: party size and party ideology (Norris, 2001; Trechsel et al., 2003). Ideological orientation (left-right) does not have an impact on more Internet-based usages (Norris, 2001, p. 170; Trechsel et al., 2003, p.26). Only party size (major-minor) has a significant impact. Yet the difference is very small: Among the 179 countries analysed by Norris (2001, p. 156), about one third of all fringe electoral parties had developed a Web site compared with 47% of minor parties and over one half of all major parties. Trechsel et al (2003, p.26). also found that the difference in ICT introduction between major and minor parties is not important. Both authors believe that whatever political force—major or minor, left or right, incumbent or challenger—when an actor gains some initial advantage by innovating with ICT, in a short time its competitors will catch up. (Norris, 2001, p.170; Trechel et al.,2003, p.17)

The variables mentioned above are suited specifically for parties, but we think that there is one that can clearly affect ICT usages by city councils: local government size, that means, the resources and staff available. Municipality size has been analysed in previous pages and is closely related to local government size. As we stated before, larger municipalities have more technical and monetary resources and more personnel for implementing ICT-based strategies for communication and participation. But local politics in a small town could be more manageable and the lack of resources can be overcome through digital platforms and digital know-how shared by several city councils. Therefore, mayors from small or medium-size cities that are also policy seekers could choose and afford the implementation of ICT tools for connecting with the public or for engaging citizens in policy decisions.

Conclusion

In the preceding pages we have tried to put some order into an area of research that is changing rapidly and that has been analysed without a systematic explanatory approach: ICT usages by political actors for connecting and engaging the public. Political actors use ICT in a very different manner depending on the type of political actor (we have examined the contrast between parties and city councils) but also on the characteristics of the country. Therefore, taking into account the findings of the literature, which are only parts of the explanatory puzzle, we have developed the basis for an explanatory model of different behaviours.

We consider that collective political actors are intentional and their behaviour is affected by the political institutions and the context in which they act. The basic elements of the model are political institutions such as the type of government, the level of decentralisation, the district magnitude, and the type of voting list; the socioeconomic and technological context; the objectives and models of e-democracy that actors hold; and the type of organisation. Consequently, part of the explanation is rooted in the contextual level and the other pertains to the level of the actors. We consider that this is the necessary combination for understanding the different political behaviours in ICT development.

The background logic is that political actors will use ICTs for achieving their objectives if there are enough institutional incentives and a favourable context for doing so. Some political institutions (district magnitude, type of voting lists, type of government) favour ICT uses for communication and deliberation in the case of parties, but other institutional features (level of decentralization, legal enforcement and subsidies) affect much more municipalities when it comes to developing ICT initiatives for participation and deliberation. Also, there are contextual variables such as the size or dimension that seem to affect municipalities much more than parties. In any case, when institutions and context are controlled and equal, that is, when we compare actors from the same country, some characteristics of collective actors such as actors' objectives (vote seekers or policy seekers) or e-democracy models adopted arise as explanatory.

Specifically, as we have shown, political parties are encouraged to make use of ICT devices if the electoral system is a majoritarian one (especially with small district magnitudes and unblocked and open voting lists) or if the type of government is presidential. Local governments are more affected by the level of decentralization, the financial incentives, and the legal framework. A high level of decentralization and legal and financial measures in favour of participation are crucial for the city councils to use ICTs in participatory strategies. On the other hand, the variables characterising the socioeconomic and technological context have been analysed by several authors and public institutions, and the results are that technological diffusion in the country and socioeconomic development affect the assimilation of ICT media by parties, governments, and public administrations throughout the world. In the case of municipalities, their small size hinders the development of interactive Web sites, though this problem can be solved by creating digital platforms jointly. Regarding the nature and aims of political actors, we arrived at the conclusion that the parties and local governments that focus mainly on gaining or maintaining votes and that are defenders of a consumer model of e-democracy will not undertake ICT initiatives for deliberation or participation. On the contrary, city councils and parties mainly driven by policy achievement or a demo-elitist or neo-republican model will be more open to developing these techniques. Moreover, organisational properties such as organisational form (capital- or labour-intensive type of party), intraparty democracy, and party or local government dimensions can condition the deployment of ICTs for communicative and participatory purposes. Labour-intensive, decentralized, and internally democratic parties, as well as medium or large city councils will tend to develop these communication and participation techniques more than capital-intensive, centralised parties or small city councils.

In conclusion, professionals, officials, and politicians willing to deploy ICT tools for approaching the public must bear in mind the constraints and circumstances that they will face. In addition, they must be explicitly aware of their objectives and values in relation to the role of citizens in the political process. Therefore, the set of variables related throughout the chapter must be taken into account.

We leave for future research the building of a more defined and complete theoretical construct of explanations that can be applied to other political actors apart from parties and local governments. In fact, we have not fully specified the relationships between the explanatory variables and the implications of the conditions established, but we have outlined the crucial principles and elements that should structure an explanatory model of ICT usages by political actors.

Acknowledgment

I greatly appreciate the comments and revisions made by Ana Sofía Cardenal, Yanina Welp, and Joseph Hopkins from the Open University of Catalonia; Josep María Reniu from the University of Barcelona; plus those made by several anonymous reviewers.

References

Accenture. (2005). *Leadership in customer service: New expectations, new experiences.* Retrieved December 29, 2005, from http://www.accenture.com/Global/Research_and_Insights/By_Industry/Government/LeadershipExperiences.htm

Aibar, E., & Urgell, F. (2003). *La provisión de servicios en línea en el e-gobierno: Un estudio de caso sobre un proyecto de ventanilla única interadministrativa.* Paper presented at the Sixth Congress of the AECPA, Barcelona, Spain.

Altman, D. (2002). Prospects for e-government in Latin America: Satisfaction with democracy, social accountability, and direct democracy. *International Review of Public Administration, 7*(2), 5-20.

Arnstein, S. (1969). A ladder of citizen participation. *Journal of the American Institute of Planners, 1*, 216-224.

Bellamy, C. (2000). Modelling electronic democracy: Towards democratic discourses for an information age. In J. Hoff, I. Horrocks, & P. Tops (Eds.), *Democratic governance and new technology* (pp. 33-53). London: Routledge.

Bijker, W. E. (1995). *Of bicycles, bakelites and bulbs: Towards a theory of sociotechnical change.* Cambridge, MA: The MIT Press.

Borge, R. (2005). La participación electrónica: Estado de la cuestión y aproximación a su clasificación. *IDP Revista de Internet, Derecho y Política, 1*. Retrieved December 20, 2005, from *http://www.uoc.edu/idp/1/dt/esp/borge.pdf*

Borge, R., & Alvaro, A. (2004, February). *Partidos políticos e Internet en España: ¿Herramienta de democratización o arma electoral?* Paper presented at the Sixth Basque Congress of Sociology, Bilbao, Spain.

Brugué, J. (2005, September). *Participación y nuevo estatuto de autonomía para catalunya.* Paper presented at the Seventh Congress of the AECPA, Madrid, Spain.

Chadwick, A., & May, C. (2003). Interaction between states and citizens in the age of the Internet: "e-Government" in the United States, Britain, and the European Union. *Governance: An International Journal of Policy, Administration, and Institutions, 16*(2), 271-300.

Clift, S. (2004). *E-government and democracy: Representation and citizen engagement in the information age.* Retrieved December 29, 2005, from *http://www.publicus.net/articles/cliftegovdemocracy.pdf*

Coleman, S., & Gøtze, J. (2001). *Bowling together: Online public engagement in policy deliberation.* London: Hansard Society & BT. Retrieved December 20, 2005, from http://bowlingtogether.net/about.html

Coleman, S., Taylor, J., & van de Donk, W. (1999). *Parliament in the age of the Internet.* Oxford, United Kingdom: Oxford University Press.

Contini, F., & Fabri, M. (Eds.). (2001). *Justice and technology in Europe: How ICT is changing the judicial business.* Amsterdam: Kluwer.

Costafreda, A. (2005). *Determinismo institucional versus determinismo tecnológico: TICs y representación política en Chile y España.* Unpublished doctoral dissertation, Institut de Ciències Polítiques i Socials, Barcelona, Spain.

Dalton, R. J., & Watenberg, M. P. (Eds.). (2000). *Parties wPartisans: Political change in advanced industrial democracies.* New York: Oxford University Press.

Espuelas, J. M. (2005). Avaluació del funcionament del Web del nou estatut. *Papers sobre Democràcia Electrònica, 43*. Retrieved December 20, 2005, from http://www.democraciaweb.org/informeestatut.pdf

Gibson, R. (2001). Elections online: Assessing Internet voting in light of the Arizona democratic primary. *Political Science Quarterly, 116*(4), 561-583.

Goss, S. (1999). *Managing working with the public in local government.* London: Kogan Page.

Goss, S. (2001). *Making local governance work: Networks, relationship and the management of change.* Houndmills: Palgrave MacMillan.

Hagen, M. (2000). Digital democracy and political systems. In K. L. Hacker & J. Van Dijk (Eds.), *Digital democracy* (pp. 54-69). London: Sage.

Hoff, J. (2000). Technology and social change: The path between technological determinism, social constructivism and new institutionalism. In J. Hoff, I. Horrocks, & P. Tops (Eds.), *Democratic governance and new technology* (pp. 13-32). New York: Routledge.

Hoff, J., Horrocks, I., & Tops, P. (2000). Introduction: New technology and the crises of democracy. In J. Hoff, I. Horrocks, & P. Tops (Eds.), *Democratic governance and new technology* (pp. 1-10). New York: Routledge.

Kaase, M., & Newton, K. (1995). *Beliefs in government* (Vol. 5). New York: Oxford University Press.

King, G., Keohane, R. O., & Verba, S. (1994). *Designing social inquiry: Scientific inference in qualitative research.* Princeton: Princeton University Press.

Kippen, G., & Jenkins, G. (2004). The challenge of e-democracy for political parties. In P. M. Shane (Ed.), *Democracy online.* (pp.253-265). New York: Routledge.

Kitschelt, H. (1990). New social movements and the decline of party organization. In R. J. Dalton & M. Kuechler (Eds.), *Challenging the political order: New social and political movements in Western democracies.* (pp. 179-208) London: Polity Press.

Kriesi, H., Koopmans, R., Duyvendak, J. W., & Giugni, M. G. (1995). *New social movements in Western Europe: A comparative analysis.* London: UCL Press.

La Porte, T. M., Demchak, C. C., & de Jong, M. (2002). Democracy and bureaucracy in the age of the Web: Empirical findings and theoretical speculations. *Administration & Society, 34*(4), 411-446.

March, J., & Olsen, J. (1989). *Rediscovering institutions: The organizational basis of politics.* New York: Free Press.

Navarro, M. (in press). Defining and measuring e-democracy: A case study on Latin American local governments. In M. Gascó (Ed.), *Latin America online: Cases, successes and pitfalls.* Hershey, PA: IDEA Publishing Group.

Norris, P. (2001). *Digital divide: Civic engagement, information poverty and the Internet worldwide.* Cambridge, United Kingdom: Cambridge University Press.

Observatori de la Societat de la Informació (OBSI). (2004). *Enquesta sobre l'adopció de les tecnologies de la informació i la comunicació a la administració local de catalunya.* Retrieved September 20, 2006, from http://www10.gencat.net/dursi/pdf/si/observatori/Informe_TIC_ajuntaments_2003.pdf

Organization for Economic Cooperation and Development (OECD). (2001). *Citizens as partners: Information, consultation and public participation in policy-making.* Paris: PUMA, Author.

Prats, J. O. (2006). Nuevas tecnologías, democracia y eficacia de las instituciones políticas. *Papers, 78, 151-168.*

Putnam, R., Leonardi, R., & Nanetti, R. Y. (1994). *Making democracy work: Civic traditions in modern Italy.* Princeton: Princeton University Press.

Sabel, C. F., & O'Donnell, R. (2000). *Democratic experimentalism: What to do about wicked problems after Whitehall.* Paper presented at the OECD Conference on Devolution and Globalisation, Glasgow, Scotland. Retrieved September 20, 2006, from http://www2. law.columbia.edu/sabel/papers/glasPO.html

Strom, K. (1990). A behavioral theory of competitive political parties. *American Journal of Political Science, 34*(2), 565-598.

Tops, J., Harrocks, I., & Hoff, P. (2000). New technology and democratic renewal. In J. Hoff, I. Horrocks, & P. Tops (Eds.), *Democratic governance and new technology* (pp. 173-184). New York: Routledge.

Trechsel, A. H., Kies, R., Mendez, F., & Schmitter, P. C. (2003). *Evaluation of the use of new technologies in order to facilitate democracy in Europe* (Scientific and Technological Options Assessment Series, 116 EN Working Paper No. 10). Retrieved Septmeber 20, 2006, from *http://c2d.unige.ch/int/OverviewInstits/Main_Report_final%201.pdf*

United Nations (UN). (2005). *UN global e-government readiness report 2005: From e-government to e-inclusion* (UNPAN 2005/14). New York: Author. Retrieved September 20, 2006, from http://unpan1.un.org/intradoc/groups/public/documents/un/unpan021888. pdf

Van Dijk, J. (2000). Models of democracy and concepts of communication. In K. L. Hacker & J. Van Dijk (Eds.), *Digital democracy* (pp. 30-53). London: Sage.

Welp, Y., Urgell, F., & Aibar, E. (2005, September). *La e-gobernanza: Propuesta para el análisis.* Paper presented at the Seventh AECPA Congress, Madrid, Spain.

Wong, W., & Welch, E. (2004). Does e-government promote accountability? A comparative analysis of Websites openness and government accountability. *Governance: An International Journal of Policy, Administration, and Institutions, 17*(2), 275-297.

Zittel, T. (2001, April). *Electronic democracy and electronic parliaments.* Paper presented at the Joint Sessions of Workshops of the ECPR, Grenoble, France.

Endnotes

[1]   Contrary to what is occurring much more frequently in Europe, an analysis of 17 Latin American municipalities carried out by M. Navarro (in press) shows that these local governments have only deployed online channels for information.

[2]   Most public administrations have undergone three phases in the process of ICT assimilation: first, introduction of ICTs only for administrative routines and for facilitating internal communication and management; second, attempts to digitalise all the internal processes and to provide online all the information and services to the citizens; and third, the change of focus onto the demand side (the citizens' needs and interests) and toward digitalisation only if added value is achieved (Accenture, 2005; Chadwick & May, 2003; Contini & Fabri, 2001; Welp, Urgell, & Aibar, 2005).

[3]   Literature on explanations about different political uses of ICTs will be analysed in the following pages.

4   Since the 1970s, many indicators have shown that there is a certain degree of crisis in the representative democratic system, such as, the growing distrust toward main political institutions, politicians, and parties; the drop in membership of political parties and trade unions; the fall in electoral participation; the increased disaffection for political issues; and the steady rise of nonconventional participation (Dalton & Watenberg, 2000; Kaase & Newton, 1995; Putnam et al., 1994).

5   Most of them are case studies (Chadwick & May, 2003; Coleman, Taylor, & van de Donk, 1999; Costafreda, 2005; Hoff, Horrocks, & Tops, 2000; Zittel, 2001), although there are also comparative analyses of countries (Altman, 2002; La Porte, Demchak, & de Jong, 2002; Norris, 2001; Trechsel et al., 2003; Wong & Welch, 2004).

6   Examples of open parliaments are the Scottish (http://www.scottish.parliament.uk), the Catalan (http://www.parlament-cat.net and http://www.democraciaweb.org), and the Basque (http://www.parlamento.euskadi.net) Parliaments. The British Parliament (http://www.parliament.uk) cannot be considered an open parliament since it does not allow citizens' participation every time there is a law project or other parliamentarian initiatives, but it provides the e-mail addresses, Web sites, and blogs of members of parliament so citizens can contact them and participate in the channels established by each of them.

7   Today, the official site of Howard Dean, called "Democracy for America" (http://www.democracyforamerica.com), is dedicated to recruiting, promoting, and funding progressive candidates at all levels of government and to keeping alive the network of people that was set up for the campaign for the 2004 nomination. In that sense, local meetings are still organised through the Meetup.com.

8   The first initiative of this kind was the Web site "Have Your Say," in which citizens were encouraged to inform themselves and discuss about the government's Freedom of Information White Paper (http://www.foi.democracy.org.uk/html/about.html). Nowadays, the UK government has opened a consultation line for specific policies and laws through its own Web site http://www.direct.gov.uk/Dl1/Directories/Public-Consultations/fs/en.

9   This participatory process is already closed, but two large reports on that experience are located on the Web site of the Catalan government: http://www16.gencat.net/idi-gol/cat/documents.htm. In addition, more analysis about the results of this experience can be found in Espuelas (2005) and Brugué (2005).

10   For a good description of different technologies and methods for online communication, deliberation and participation see Coleman & Gøtze (2001) and Clift (2004).

11   For example, in Trechsel et al. (2003), the different types of government (presidential vs. parliamentary systems) does not have any effect on the online presence of legislatures in 35 European countries. However, as we stated before, Zittel (2001), following the most different-case approach, which included three countries, found that the legislatures in the presidential system use Internet technology more for communication purposes in contrast with the much more passive and unidirectional uses of the parliamentary systems.

12   In 2003, a new law was passed in Spain to modernize the local government (Law 57/2003). That law requires local governments to deploy channels and mechanisms for favouring the citizens' participation in local affairs.

[13]   In 2005, the Catalan government enacted, for the first time, an order for providing financial aid to local plans to increase public participation and for the development of ICT-based initiatives for consultation and participation at the local level (ORDRE REP/119/2005).

[14]   Technological diffusion is measured by the proportion of the population online and socioeconomic development is measured by the Human Development Index from the United Nations Development Program (Norris, 2001, p.166).

[15]   The level of democratisation refers to the indicator of Political Rights and Civil Liberties figured out by the Freedom House Annual Survey (Norris, 2001, p.166).

[16]   These digital platforms for electronic communication and participation can be consulted at http://www.e-consensus.org/consensus and http://www.regionedigitale.net. More information about the Catalan platform and the specific experiences carried out are available at Borge (2005).

About the Authors

Mila Gascó holds an MBA and a PhD in public-policy evaluation. She received the Award Enric Prat de la Riba, granted for the best PhD thesis on public management and administration, given by the Escola d'Administració Pública de Catalunya in Barcelona, Spain. She is a senior analyst at the International Institute on Governance of Catalonia and an associate professor at the Universitat Oberta de Catalunya (Open University of Catalonia). She has a wide teaching experience, having worked as a full professor in the Rovira i Virgili University in Tarragona, Spain, as well as a broad researching experience. She has taken part in numerous national and international seminars, has published both in Spanish and English, and has supervised a number of PhD theses. Dr. Gascó has also collaborated with several institutions such as the provincial government of Barcelona (Diputació de Barcelona), the World Bank Development Gateway, the United Nations Development Program (UNDP), the University of Hull in the United Kingdom, the Mayor's Office in Valencia (Venezuela), and the governments of Brazil and Dominican Republic. Her main interests are related to public policies that allow the transition of a society to the so-called knowledge era. In particular, she is interested in e-government and e-governance, and the use of ICTs for human development and public-policy evaluation.

Fran Equiza is the director of the International Cooperation of Intermón Oxfam, the largest Spanish nongovernmental organization (NGO) for development. He holds an MBA, a master's in applied economics analysis, a master's degree in information and knowledge society studies, and an advanced studies diploma in political science. At present, he is a PhD candidate in the International and Interdisciplinary PhD program in the Information and Knowledge Society (Open University of Catalonia). Mr. Equiza has wide experience in the development and cooperation of the development fields where he has worked for more than 10 years. He has been the vice president of the Society for International Development in Catalonia, the director of Educación sin Fronteras (Education without Borders), the director of the International Institute on Governance, the director of human resources in the Internal Organization of Intermón Oxfam, and the executive assistant to the general director of the latter. He has vast consulting, teaching, and writing experience on issues such as Sen's human-development concept, poverty and alleviation strategies, NGO management, ICTs for development (ICT4D), and institutional building.

Manuel Acevedo holds a master's degree in mechanical engineering and a master's information and knowledge society studies. Currently, he is a PhD candidate in the International and Interdisciplinary PhD Program in the Information and Knowledge Society (Open University of Catalonia), focusing on ICT mainstreaming in cooperation agencies. Mr. Acevedo has been involved in ICT for human development since 1994, when he joined the UNDP. At the Regional Bureau for Latin America and the Caribbean (1996-1997), he formed part of the UNDP Info XXI group, which promoted the integration of ICT into UNDP's culture and operations. In 2000, he set up a novel e-Volunteering unit at the UN volunteers' agency, launching both UNITeS (United Nations Information Technology Service) and the UN Online Volunteering Service. Mr. Acevedo served as cochair of the UN ICT Task Force's Capacity Building Committee (2002-2003), and he represented the UN volunteer program during the first phase of the World Summit on the Information Society (WSIS). Living in Madrid now, he is an independent consultant on ICT4D. He is also introducing ICT4D into the curricula of some university programs on international development, and is helping the Spanish government to integrate ICT into Spanish international cooperation policies and practices.

* * *

Alex Robinson is a graduate of the School of Oriental and African Studies (SOAS) of the University of London. He is currently conducting doctoral research at the University of Huddersfield on a studentship awarded by the Centre for Enterprise, Ethics, and the Environment. He is also a member of the ICT4D Collective at Royal Holloway of the University of London. His research interests include ICT for development with particular reference to poverty reduction, localized market networks in the least developed countries, the role of local political institutions in development, the concepts of participation and community-based development in development discourse and practice, and tourism in Indonesia. He has conducted academic research and development consultancy work in the United Kingdom and Indonesia.

Aman Bhandari is a PhD student in the Division of Health Policy and Management at UC Berkeley's School of Public Health. This past year, he worked at UCSF on pharmaceutical policy, outcomes, and technology. His research at UCSF ranged from reviewing ethical guidelines for conducting clinical trials in developing countries to looking at replicating innovative ways to reduce costs of prescription drugs for the low-income elderly. He received his MPH in epidemiology from the University of Minnesota. Previous to his studies at UC

Berkeley, he worked as a director for the Knowledge and Social Responsibility Program for the National Conference for Community and Justice, and also worked for a health economics research group at the Stanford Veterans Affairs Medical Center.

Bantu Morolong holds a PhD in international and intercultural educational policy studies from the University of Alberta (Canada) and an MA in sociology from Michigan State University. She is a lecturer at the University of Botswana. Dr. Morolong has taught, researched, published, and presented papers at regional and international meetings, covering the following areas of interest: rural development, literacy, sociology of adult education, gender, education and development, women and the law, the potential role of ICTs in poverty reduction, gender and the environment, and gender dynamics in the changing family with special reference to access to and control over resources.

Ben Bellows is a PhD student in epidemiology, assessing social and economic determinants of health outcomes and service utilization under comparative health financing policies for reproductive health and STD treatment services in East Africa. Ben graduated with a BA in economics and history from the University of Michigan in 1996. He served in the U.S. Peace Corps in Ecuador from 1997 to 2000. Following his service, he worked at the U.S. Centers for Disease Control and Prevention for several years to develop training programs in HIV counseling and testing with national government partners in Kenya, Uganda, Zambia, and Namibia. He graduated from the University of California (UC) Berkeley's MPH program in 2004. Ben's current doctoral work is with the German Development Bank (KfW), the Kenyan National Coordinating Agency on Population and Development (NCAPD), the Uganda Ministry of Health, and the Mbarara University of Science and Technology, Uganda. Ben also blogs periodically about politics and policy regarding HIV/AIDS.

Bobak Rezaian holds a PhD in mechanical engineering, with extensive research, teaching, and consulting experience in the design and implementation of information systems, computational science and technology, and knowledge sharing. He is a senior informatics specialist in the Africa region of the World Bank. He has been working on ICT-related initiatives in sub-Saharan Africa for more than a decade. He has worked on various ICT projects, including the design and implementation of local and wide area networks, data acquisition and control systems, health and education networks, public-sector management information systems, and distance learning networks.

Constantin Gaindric holds a PhD in computer science and a PhD in operations research. He is the president of the National Council of Accreditation and Attestation of Moldova Republic as well as the principal researcher at the Institute of Mathematics and Computer Science of the Academy of Sciences of Moldova. Dr. Gaindric is particularly interested in operations research, decision-support systems, mathematical modeling, and information-society technologies. He is author of two books and 93 articles, as well as the editor in chief of the computer-science journal of Moldova.

Edward Halpin holds a PhD in public policy. He is a reader in social informatics within the School of Information Management (Leeds Metropolitan University), director of the Praxis Centre (Centre for the Study of Information and Technology for Peace, Conflict Resolution, and Human Rights), and acting joint head of the School of Applied Global Ethics within the Leslie Silver International Faculty. Dr. Halpin has a background in politics, community development, and information application. Over the past 7 years, his research has focused on the use of information and communication technologies for human and child rights. He has also carried out research for the European Parliament's Scientific and Technical Options (STOA) Unit and was the recipient of funding from the UK Arts and Humanities Research Council. This work has involved him in working alongside colleagues from organizations such as Save the Children, the Child Rights Information Network (CRIN), and Amnesty International. He has published widely on these subjects including a book on human rights and the Internet.

Galina Magariu holds a PhD in computer science. She is a leading researcher at the Institute of Mathematics and Computer Science of the Academy of Sciences of Moldova. Dr. Magariu's main interests include formal languages and compiler construction, discrete simulation systems' design and application, and information-society technologies. She is the author of three books and 42 articles, as well as a member of the editorial board of the computer-science journal of Moldova.

Jaspal S. Sandhu is a PhD student in the College of Engineering at UC Berkeley. His research focuses on the design and evaluation methods for rural health technology, emphasizing ICT. He has experience working in India, and is now working on design projects in the California Central Valley (ICT for health promotion) and the Guatemalan highlands (wood-burning cookstoves). He is planning a project focusing on the design of ICT systems for the continuing education of rural health workers in Mongolia, beginning in late 2006. In industry, he has worked in manufacturing, mechanical design, product development, and software-engineering roles for several firms, including Intel and Nokia. He received his master's (2002) and bachelor's (1999) degrees from the Massachusetts Institute of Technology.

John Lannon lectures on information systems at the Kemmy Business School (University of Limerick), where he also works on an internationally coordinated curriculum-development program in intercultural communication. He holds a master's in peace and development studies (University of Limerick), and is a PhD candidate and associate staff member at the Praxis Centre (Centre for the Study of Information and Technology for Peace, Conflict Resolution and Human Rights) in the Leeds Metropolitan University. He is an active campaigner with Amnesty International, a director of Soweto Connection (an HIV/AIDS support organization), and has lived and worked in South Africa. He has also worked for many years in the private sector as a software designer and project manager, focusing mainly on telecommunications network management systems. He is currently working on the development of an online database for the human-rights and -development movements, using free and open-source software.

Liudmila Burtseva holds a PhD in computer science. She is a senior researcher at the Institute of Mathematics and Computer Science of the Academy of Sciences of Moldova. Her research is focused on discrete events simulation, general programming technologies, and information-society technologies. She is author of 17 articles.

Mahad Ibrahim is a PhD student in the School of Information at UC Berkeley. His current research focuses on developing better mechanisms to improve information access in developing regions, the design and evaluation of health technologies, and exploring issues of privacy in ubiquitous computing. He spent all of 2005 in Egypt researching the adoption and usage of ICT among marginalized populations as a Fulbright Scholar. Currently, he is teaching a course "ICT for Development: Context, Strategies and Impacts" that he codesigned in the School of Information at UC Berkeley. He also has experience working on health-related issues. Mahad worked in providing HIV/AIDS education to at-risk youth and for the District of Columbia's HIV/AIDS surveillance division. He has also worked on analyzing ubiquitous computing deployments in hospitals. Prior to attending UC Berkeley, Mahad worked in the IT industry for several years. He has his bachelor's (1999) in applied economics and management from Cornell University, and a master's (2002) in information management and systems from UC Berkeley.

Narima Amin migrated from Guyana to Canada in 1985. She studied economics and international development studies at the University of Toronto. Since graduating in 1992, she became involved in the field of microcredit and microfinance. She currently lives in Seattle with her husband Masud and daughter Iman.

Ranjini Raghavendra is a doctoral candidate at the Institute for Women's Studies, Lancaster University, United Kingdom. Her research interests are in the areas of ICTs in health and education, ICTs in rural development, and gender and development.

Rebecca Lekoko works in the Department of Adult Education at the University of Botswana. Her teaching, research, and publications focus on professional preparation, especially of extension workers. Dr. Lekoko's experience as a teacher and trainer has seen her working as a consultant in producing English literacy materials with writers from the Department of Non-Formal Education. She has published a Setswana grammar book and contributed a story in an anthology of short stories, both published by Heinemann, Botswana. She has cowritten a book on program planning for adult learners for the African Perspective Series. She is currently writing a reader and teacher's guide (books) for elementary school (Macmillan, South Africa). She has some published journals and book chapters.

Rosa Borge is a political science lecturer at the Open University of Catalonia (Barcelona, Spain). She holds a PhD in political science and sociology from the Deusto University (Bilbao, Spain). She is specialised in political behaviour and social sciences methodology. She is actually working on electronic democracy issues such as electronic political participation. Her last article classified and evaluated the electronic participation experiences in the world, specifically in Spain and in Catalonia ("Revista de Internet, Derecho y Política," UOC, 2005).

Also, she has taken part in a handbook on advanced research techniques in political science (*Técniques d'Investigació en Ciència Política II*, FUOC Publishers, Barcelona, 2005). She has been a visiting scholar at the Center for Political Studies at the University of Michigan and a researcher and teaching assistant at the Pompeu Fabra University (Barcelona, Spain).

Shafika Isaacs holds a master's in science and technology policy from the Science Policy Research Unit (SPRU) at the University of Sussex. She is the executive director of SchoolNet Africa (SNA), one of Africa's first African-led NGOs, which promotes learning and teaching through the use of ICTs in African schools. She also serves on the steering committee of the UN ICT Task Force's Global eSchools and Communities Initiative (GeSCI), on the board of directors of OneWorld Africa and Ungana Afrika, on the advisory board of the Southern African Network for Educational Technology and eLearning (SANTEC), on the advisory committees of the Global Teenager Project and the WSIS Youth Caucus, and on the advisory team of the Open Education Resources project of the Global Development Gateway. She is also a member of the Council of the Free and Open Source Software Foundation for Africa (FOSSFA) and a board member of SchoolNet South Africa.

Simone Cecchini is an economist with the Social Statistics Unit at the United Nations Economic Commission for Latin America and the Caribbean (ECLAC), based in Santiago (Chile). His research focuses on social indicators and on uses of ICT for poverty reduction in the developing world. Mr. Cecchini holds a degree in political science from the University of Florence (Italy), a master's in international trade and investment policy from the Elliott School of International Affairs in Washington, DC, and a master's in business administration from the Universidad Católica of Chile. Before joining the United Nations, Mr. Cecchini worked as a research analyst in the World Bank's poverty-reduction department.

Svetlana Cojocaru holds a PhD in computer science. She is a leading researcher at the Institute of Mathematics and Computer Science of the Academy of Sciences of Moldova. Dr. Cojocaru's main interests include formal and natural languages processing, computer algebra, and information-society technologies. She is the author of three books and 89 articles, as well as the executive editor of the computer-science journal of Moldova.

Sundeep Sahay is a professor at the Department of Informatics, University of Oslo, Norway. His research interests are in the broad domain of globalization, ICTs, and changes in work, with a particular focus on health care and developing countries.

Tatiana Verlan is a probationer scientific researcher at the Institute of Mathematics and Computer Science of the Academy of Sciences of Moldova. Her work is particularly focused on information-society technologies. She is the author of 13 articles as well as the technical editor of the computer-science journal of Moldova.

Index